ANNUAL EDITIONS

Human Sexualities

Thirty-First Edition

EDITOR

Bobby Hutchison
Modesto Junior College

Bobby Hutchison is a Professor of Psychology and Human Sexualities at Modesto Junior College in California. Professor Hutchison graduated from the University of California at Santa Barbara with degrees in psychology and sociology. He also has an academic background in the biological sciences and French language and literature, having completed the equivalent of a major in French. He focused on sex research and sex education during his graduate studies. He has published numerous articles, essays, and reviews in psychology, sociology, education, and history journals.

Professor Hutchison conducts trainings on adolescent psychosexual development, sexual risk-taking, lesbian/gay/bisexual/transgender youth, teen pregnancy, and sexually transmitted infections. His work with foster and adoptive families has been recognized by awards from the local county board of supervisors and child welfare agency. Through his work on campus, in the community, and with *Annual Editions,* Professor Hutchison is committed to promoting the application of academic theory and scientific research in everyday life.

D1502076

Mc Graw Hill **Higher Education**

Boston   Burr Ridge, IL   Dubuque, IA   New York   San Francisco   St. Louis
Bangkok   Bogotá   Caracas   Kuala Lumpur   Lisbon   London   Madrid   Mexico City
Milan   Montreal   New Delhi   Santiago   Seoul   Singapore   Sydney   Taipei   Toronto

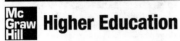

Higher Education

ANNUAL EDITIONS: HUMAN SEXUALITIES, THIRTY-FIRST EDITION

1 2 3 4 5 6 7 8 9 0 QPD/QPD 0 9

ISBN 978–0–07–351634–9
MHID 0–07–351634–1
ISSN 1091–9961

Managing Editor: *Larry Loeppke*
Senior Managing Editor: *Faye Schilling*
Developmental Editor: *Debra Henricks*
Editorial Coordinator: *Mary Foust*
Editorial Assistant: *Nancy Meissner*
Production Service Assistant: *Rita Hingtgen*
Permissions Coordinator: *Lenny J. Behnke*
Senior Marketing Manager: *Julie Keck*
Marketing Communications Specialist: *Mary Klein*
Marketing Coordinator: *Alice Link*
Project Manager: *Sandy Wille*
Design Specialist: *Tara McDermott*
Senior Production Supervisor: *Laura Fuller*
Cover Graphics: *Kristine Jubeck*

Compositor: Laserwords Private Limited
Cover Images: © Brand X Pictures/Jupiterimages/RF (inset); © Getty Images/RF (background abstract), © Think Stock/RF (top right montage), © Stockbyte/Getty Images/RF (bottom right montage), © Getty Images/RF (bottom left montage), © Getty Images/RF (top left montage)

Library in Congress Cataloging-in-Publication Data
Main entry under title: Annual Editions: Human Sexualities. 31/e.
 1. Sexual Behavior—Periodicals. 2. Sexual hygiene—Periodicals. 3. Sex education—Periodicals.
4. Human relations—Periodicals. I. Hutchison, Bobby, *comp*. II. Title: Human Sexualities.
658'.05

Editors/Advisory Board

Members of the Advisory Board are instrumental in the final selection of articles for each edition of ANNUAL EDITIONS. Their review of articles for content, level, currentness, and appropriateness provides critical direction to the editor and staff. We think that you will find their careful consideration well reflected in this volume.

Preface

"Sex lies at the root of life and we can never learn to reverence life until we know how to understand sex."

Many editions of this book have opened with the above quote from Havelock Ellis, a late nineteenth century sexologist. Sex researchers and educators today persist in our belief that an accurate understanding of sex and sexualities is essential to fully appreciate the human condition. It is one piece of a bigger puzzle. But it is an essential piece. This perspective, which is at the very heart of the book, is reflected as a continuing tradition. The original purpose and core values of this book have never changed. With the passage of time, however, some things have changed.

Perhaps, nowhere can we find more change and diversity than in the sexual landscape of the world today. Globalization and technology have brought in new possibilities for more complex human connections. In the more than three decades of this book's publication, vast changes have occurred in the study of human sexualities, and in society as a whole. Human sexuality has come into its own as an interdisciplinary field within academia. When this book was first published, there were few academic programs for students seriously interested in studying sex. Today, there are undergraduate majors and minors in human sexuality studies as well as dedicated graduate programs. Related areas of inquiry such as women's studies, lesbian/gay/bisexual/transgender studies, and ethnic studies have thrived. What was once an area of inquiry that drew suspicion among "serious" scholars is now a flourishing academic field with its own journals, conferences, and degree programs. Sex researchers from diverse academic perspectives, make rich and lasting contributions to their own disciplines such as biology, psychology, sociology, anthropology, education, nursing, public health, and medicine to name just a few.

The multidisciplinary nature of sex education and research is reflected throughout this book. The title of this book has been updated from the original (and singular) *Human Sexuality* to the plural *Human Sexualities.* This is a subtle change, but one that is important. The rich diversity in the field as well as the diverse lives of those we study are reflected in the new title *Human Sexualities.* We have a better understanding today of the incredible range of not only sexual behaviors but also identities, experiences, perspectives, voices, and social

worlds. There is also an ever increasing understanding of the importance of a range of biological processes on sexual development and behavior. What we once talked about in the singular (as if it were a unified, single, easily identified phenomenon) has often now become plural. Today, we speak of heterosexualities, homosexualities, and bisexualities. This reflects greater evidence that there are multiple developmental pathways to who we are. In sum, the new title of this book is reflective of the diversity of the world today and the people we study, as well as the richness and variety of perspectives in a multidisciplinary, dynamic area of inquiry.

The book's title isn't the only thing that has changed. Most of the articles that appear in this edition are new to the book. With few exceptions, selected articles are no more than three years old prior to going to publication. This new edition has also been reorganized and sections have been re-titled. *Annual Editions: Human Sexualities* is now organized into seven major units.

Social and Cultural Foundations explores a range of topics from historical, social, and cultural contexts. *Biological Foundations* examines both reproductive capacities as well as sexual pleasure and desire. *Sexualities and Development* considers a variety of issues that relate to different stages of our lives. The unit on *Intimacies and Relationships* includes articles on love, and different types of intimate relationships and experiences. *Gender and Sexual Diversity* provides insights into perspectives on gender as well as sexual orientations. *Sexual Health and Well-Being* looks at what can go wrong with our sexual health and what we can do about it. The last unit, *Sexualities and Social Issues,* explores topics that are frequently in the news or at the center of the "culture wars."

These many changes relate well to the current sexuality textbooks as well as to important trends in research and teaching today. The organization of this volume is intended to provide the reader the greatest flexibility possible, making this book the most useful, dynamic, ancillary text of human sexuality in the market.

The updated *Internet References* can be used to further explore the many topics presented in this book. These useful websites are cross-referenced by number in the *Topic Guide.* You may be surprised by what you will learn about human sexualities just from doing a little bit of browsing on some of these sites.

All articles included in this book have been carefully reviewed and selected for their quality, readability, currentness, interest and usefulness. They present a variety of viewpoints on human sexualities. Some of what you will read, you may personally relate to. Some of it, you may find hard to understand, or even upsetting. Some points of view you will agree with, some you will not. Whatever your experience with these articles, I hope you will learn from each of them.

Appreciation and thanks go to Larry Loeppke, Managing Editor and Debra Henricks, Developmental Editor at McGraw-Hill. They have been incredibly supportive of the changes in this edition. Debra has held my hand throughout the process, providing essential support and guidance. I have enjoyed our many discussions, emails, and working with both of them.

I want to thank the previous academic editors of *Annual Editions: Human Sexuality,* Ollie Pocs and Susan Bunting for their inspiring work. Susan Bunting foresaw some of the changes that would take place in this edition, when she wrote about the shift in language from sexuality to sexualities. When I was an undergraduate in my first human sexuality course, we were assigned *Annual Editions: Human Sexuality* edited by Ollie Pocs. I got hooked on studying sex, in part because of *Annual Editions.* I never could have guessed, as I held that book in my hands and read it, that I would one day take over the editing and writing responsibilities of that very book. There may be a student reading this, who will one day be at the helm of *Annual Editions: Human Sexualities.*

Much gratitude and thanks go to Janice and John Baldwin, my professors who inspired and taught me when I was an undergraduate at the University of California at Santa Barbara. Their courses and research continue to inspire and educate a large, dynamic student population as well as other sex educators and researchers.

I am most thankful to my amazing daughter, Anaïs, who is my biggest inspiration. Being a parent, I find that I care even more about each of the topics we cover in human sexuality. Everything in life, including this course, takes on so much more meaning than I ever thought possible.

Finally, many thanks to those who have submitted articles for this anthology or reviewed articles from previous editions. The many updates and changes in this new edition are a direct result of readers' input. Students and professors have told us what they think, and we have responded accordingly. Because of that feedback, this is one of the most useful and up-to-date books available today. Please tell us what you think by returning the postage-paid Article Rating Form located on the last page. Also, if you know of a recent article that you think should be included please let us know by giving the title, source, and publication information for that article at the very bottom of the rating form. We very much look forward to hearing from you and receiving your feedback.

Bobby Hutchison

Bobby Hutchison
Editor

v

Contents

UNIT 1
Social and Cultural Foundations

The concepts in bold italics are developed in the article. For further expansion, please refer to the Topic Guide.

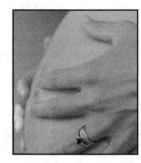

UNIT 2
Biological Foundations

UNIT 3
Sexualities and Development

The concepts in bold italics are developed in the article. For further expansion, please refer to the Topic Guide.

UNIT 4
Intimacies and Relationships

The concepts in bold italics are developed in the article. For further expansion, please refer to the Topic Guide.

UNIT 5
Gender and Sexual Diversity

The concepts in bold italics are developed in the article. For further expansion, please refer to the Topic Guide.

UNIT 6
Sexual Health and Well-Being

The concepts in bold italics are developed in the article. For further expansion, please refer to the Topic Guide.

UNIT 7
Sexualities and Social Issues

The concepts in bold italics are developed in the article. For further expansion, please refer to the Topic Guide.

The concepts in bold italics are developed in the article. For further expansion, please refer to the Topic Guide.

Correlation Guide

The *Annual Editions* series provides students with convenient, inexpensive access to current, carefully selected articles from the public press. **Annual Editions: Human Sexualities, 31/e** is an easy-to-use reader that presents articles on important topics such as *biology, gender, health,* and many more. For more information on *Annual Editions* and other *McGraw-Hill Contemporary Learning Series* titles, visit www.mhcls.com.

This convenient guide matches the units in **Annual Editions: Human Sexualities, 31/e** with the corresponding chapters in two of our best-selling McGraw-Hill Human Sexuality textbooks by Hyde/DeLamater and Kelly.

Annual Editions: Human Sexualities, 31/e	Understanding Human Sexuality, 10/e by Hyde/DeLamater	Sexuality Today, 9/e by Kelly
Unit 1: Social and Cultural Foundations	**Chapter 1:** Sexuality in Perspective	**Chapter 1:** Cultural, Historical, and Research Perspectives on Sexuality
Unit 2: Biological Foundations	**Chapter 5:** Sex Hormones, Sexual Differentiation, Puberty, and the Menstrual Cycle **Chapter 6:** Conception, Pregnancy, and Childbirth **Chapter 8:** Sexual Arousal	**Chapter 4:** Human Sexual Arousal and Response **Chapter 10:** Reproduction, Reproductive Technology, and Birthing **Chapter 11:** Decision Making about Pregnancy and Parenthood
Unit 3: Sexualities and Development	**Chapter 5:** Sex Hormones, Sexual Differentiation, Puberty, and the Menstrual Cycle **Chapter 9:** Sexuality and the Life Cycle: Childhood and Adolescence **Chapter 10:** Sexuality and the Life Cycle: Adulthood **Epilogue:** Looking to the Future: Sexuality Education	**Chapter 6:** Sexuality in Infancy, Childhood, and Adolescence **Chapter 7:** Adult Sexuality and Relationships
Unit 4: Intimacies and Relationships	**Chapter 10:** Sexuality and the Life Cycle: Adulthood **Chapter 11:** Attraction, Love, and Communication	**Chapter 9:** Sexuality, Communication, and Relationships
Unit 5: Gender and Sexual Diversity	**Chapter 5:** Sex Hormones, Sexual Differentiation, Puberty, and the Menstrual Cycle **Chapter 9:** Sexuality and the Life Cycle: Childhood and Adolescence **Chapter 12:** Gender and Sexuality **Chapter 13:** Sexual Orientation: Gay, Straight, or Bi?	**Chapter 5:** Developmental and Social Perspectives on Gender **Chapter 6:** Sexuality in Infancy, Childhood, and Adolescence **Chapter 13:** Sexual Orientation, Identity, and Behavior **Chapter 14:** The Spectrum of Human Sexual Behavior
Unit 6: Sexual Health and Well-Being	**Chapter 9:** Sexuality and the Life Cycle: Childhood and Adolescence **Chapter 17:** Sexual Disorders and Sex Therapy **Chapter 18:** Sexually Transmitted Infections	**Chapter 17:** Sexually Transmitted Diseases, HIV/AIDS, and Sexual Decisions **Chapter 18:** Sexual Dysfunctions and Their Treatment
Unit 7: Sexualities and Social Issues	**Chapter 6:** Conception, Pregnancy, and Childbirth **Chapter 7:** Contraception and Abortion **Chapter 14:** Variations in Sexual Behavior **Chapter 15:** Sexual Coercion **Chapter 16:** Sex for Sale **Chapter 19:** Ethics, Religion, and Sexuality **Chapter 20:** Sex and the Law	**Chapter 8:** Sexual Individuality and Sexual Values **Chapter 10:** Reproduction, Reproductive Technology, and Birthing **Chapter 15:** Sex, Art, the Media, and the Law **Chapter 16:** Sexual Consent, Coercion, Rape, and Abuse

Topic Guide

This topic guide suggests how the selections in this book relate to the subjects covered in your course. You may want to use the topics listed on these pages to search the Web more easily.

On the following pages a number of Web sites have been gathered specifically for this book. They are arranged to reflect the units of this Annual Editions reader. You can link to these sites by going to *http://www.mhcls.com*.

All the articles that relate to each topic are listed below the bold-faced term.

Abortion
42. Flower Grandma's Secret
43. You Can't Do That on Television
44. Sex, Politics, and Morality at the FDA: Reflections on the Plan B Decision

Abuse
25. Behind the Cloak of Polygamy
45. Guess Who's Watching Porn
47. The Sex Offender Next Door
48. Sexual Assault on Campus: What Colleges and Universities Are Doing about It
49. Human Rights, Sex Trafficking, and Prostitution

Adoption
18. Torn between Two *Mothers*
33. Children of Lesbian and Gay Parents

Adulthood, later
4. Everyone's Queer
11. A Man's Shelf Life
12. The Orgasmic Mind
13. Women's Sexual Desire: A Feminist Critique
18. Torn between Two *Mothers*
19. Staying up Late with Sue
20. Women's Sexuality as They Age: The More Things Change, the More They Stay the Same
21. Free as a Bird and Loving It
22. Happily Never Married
23. This Thing Called Love
24. Pillow Talk
25. Behind the Cloak of Polygamy
26. Love at the Margins: Extreme Relationships Demand Extreme Commitment
27. My Cheatin' Heart
31. (Rethinking) Gender
32. Finding the Switch
33. Children of Lesbian and Gay Parents
34. Broadcast News: The Insider Is Out
35. Sex, Health & Happiness
42. Flower Grandma's Secret

Adulthood, middle
4. Everyone's Queer
11. A Man's Shelf Life
12. The Orgasmic Mind
13. Women's Sexual Desire: A Feminist Critique
18. Torn between Two *Mothers*
19. Staying up Late with Sue
20. Women's Sexuality as They Age: The More Things Change, the More They Stay the Same
21. Free as a Bird and Loving It
22. Happily Never Married
23. This Thing Called Love
24. Pillow Talk
25. Behind the Cloak of Polygamy
26. Love at the Margins: Extreme Relationships Demand Extreme Commitment
27. My Cheatin' Heart

29. Learning and Gender
31. (Rethinking) Gender
32. Finding the Switch
33. Children of Lesbian and Gay Parents
34. Broadcast News: The Insider Is Out
35. Sex, Health & Happiness
42. Flower Grandma's Secret

Adulthood, young
4. Everyone's Queer
11. A Man's Shelf Life
12. The Orgasmic Mind
13. Women's Sexual Desire: A Feminist Critique
14. How to Talk about Sex
15. The Birds and the Bees and Curious Kids
16. What to Tell the Kids about Sex
17. Teenage Fatherhood and Involvement in Delinquent Behavior
18. Torn between Two *Mothers*
19. Staying up Late with Sue
20. Women's Sexuality as They Age: The More Things Change, the More They Stay the Same
21. Free as a Bird and Loving It
22. Happily Never Married
23. This Thing Called Love
24. Pillow Talk
25. Behind the Cloak of Polygamy
26. Love at the Margins: Extreme Relationships Demand Extreme Commitment
27. My Cheatin' Heart
29. Learning and Gender
30. Goodbye to Girlhood
31. (Rethinking) Gender
32. Finding the Switch
33. Children of Lesbian and Gay Parents
34. Broadcast News: The Insider Is Out
35. Sex, Health & Happiness
42. Flower Grandma's Secret
45. Guess Who's Watching Porn
48. Sexual Assault on Campus: What Colleges and Universities Are Doing about It

Anatomy, male and female
5. A Mind Dismembered: In Search of the Magical Penis Thieves
12. The Orgasmic Mind
20. Women's Sexuality as They Age: The More Things Change, the More They Stay the Same
31. (Rethinking) Gender
36. Fighting the Cancer a Mammo Can't Catch
37. When Sex Hurts

Biology
6. Afterbirths in the Afterlife: Cultural Meaning of Placental Disposal in a Hmong American Community
9. Starting the Good Life in the Womb
10. Success at Last
11. A Man's Shelf Life
12. The Orgasmic Mind
13. Women's Sexual Desire: A Feminist Critique

Internet References

The following Internet sites have been selected to support the articles found in this reader. These sites were available at the time of publication. However, because Web sites often change their structure and content, the information listed may no longer be available. We invite you to visit *http://www.mhcls.com* for easy access to these sites.

Annual Editions: Human Sexualities 31/e

General Sources

World Health Organization: Sexual Health
http://www.who.int/topics/sexual_health/en/

The World Health Organization (WHO) maintains this website to provide educational information on the organization's sexual health activities and programs. This is a great resource for facts, statistics, reports and educational materials on sexual health around the world.

National Institutes of Health (NIH)
http://www.nih.gov

Consult this site for links to extensive health information and scientific resources. The NIH is one of eight health agencies of the Public Health Service, which in turn is part of the U.S. Department of Health and Human Services.

SIECUS
http://www.siecus.org

Visit the Sexuality Information and Education Council of the United States (SIECUS) home page to learn about the organization, to find news of its educational programs and activities, and to access links to resources in sexuality education.

SexInfo
http://www.soc.ucsb.edu/sexinfo/

SexInfo is based out of the University of California at Santa Barbara. The site is run by advanced human sexuality students under the supervision of two UCSB sexuality professors. All aspects of sex and sexuality are covered on this website with great articles and Q&As.

The Kinsey Institute for Research in Sex, Gender, and Reproduction
http://www.indiana.edu/~kinsey/

This is the official website for Indiana University's Kinsey Institute. This website will be helpful to anyone interested in the scientific study of sex. Check out their latest news and events section as well as their resources. Find out about the history of this important research institute.

The Society for the Scientific Study of Sexuality
http://www.sexscience.org/

SSSS is a professional association of sex researchers from a many different scientific disciplines. According to their website, they are "[t]he oldest professional society dedicated to the advancement of knowledge about sexuality." Have a look at their ethics statement as well as the various kinds of publications they sponsor.

UNIT 1: Social and Cultural Foundations

Department of State: Human Rights
http://www.state.gov/g/drl/hr/

The U.S. State Department's Web page for human rights includes country reports, fact sheets, reports on discrimination

and violations of human rights, plus the latest news covering human rights issues from around the world.

SocioSite: Feminism and Women's Issues
http://www.sociosite.net/topics/women.php

Visit the University of Amsterdam "Social Science Information System" to gain insights into a number of issues that affect both men and women. It provides biographies of women in history, an international network for women in the workplace, links to family and children's issues, and much more.

Woman in Islam: Sex and Society
http://www.jamaat.org/islam/WomanSociety.html

This Web site is sponsored by the secretary general of Pakistan offering objective analysis and explanations regarding a woman's role in Islamic society. Topics include marriage, family matters, and sex within Islamic society.

Women's Human Rights Resources
http://www.law-lib.utoronto.ca/Diana/

This list of international women's human rights Web sites provides interesting resources on marriage and the family; rights of girls; sexual orientation; slavery, trafficking, and prostitution; and violence against women.

UNIT 2: Biological Foundations

Ask NOAH About Pregnancy: Fertility & Infertility
http://www.noah-health.org/en/search/health.html

New York Online Access to Health (NOAH) seeks to provide relevant, timely, and unbiased health information for consumers. You will find extensive links to a variety of resources about infertility treatments and issues at this interesting website.

Childbirth.Org
http://www.childbirth.org

This interactive site about childbirth options is from an organization that aims to educate consumers to know their options and provide themselves with the best possible care to ensure healthy pregnancies and deliveries. The site and its links address a myriad of topics, from episiotomy to water birth.

Planned Parenthood
http://www.plannedparenthood.org

Visit this well-known organization's home page for links to information on the various kinds of contraceptives and pregnancy prevention options (including outercourse and abstinence) as well as discussions of other topics related to sexuality and reproduction.

Infertility Resources
http://www.ihr.com/infertility/index.html

This site includes links to the Oregon Health Sciences University Fertility Program and the Center for Reproductive Growth in Nashville, Tennessee. Ethical, legal, financial, psychological, and social issues are discussed.

Internet References

UNIT 3: Sexualities and Development

World Association for Sexology
http://www.tc.umn.edu/nlhome/m201/colem001/was/wasindex.htm

The World Association for Sexology works to further the understanding and development of sexology throughout the world. Access this site to explore a number of issues and links related to sexuality throughout the lifespan.

SIECUS
http://www.siecus.org

Visit the Sexuality Information and Education Council of the United States (SIECUS) home page to learn about the organization, to find news of its educational programs and activities, and to access links to resources in sexuality education.

Teacher Talk
http://education.indiana.edu/cas/tt/tthmpg.html

This home page of the publication Teacher Talk from the Indiana University School of Education Center for Adolescent Studies will lead you to many interesting teacher comments, suggestions, and ideas regarding sexuality education and how to deal with sex issues in the classroom. The section of the website that is of the greatest interest to sexuality is Volume 1, Issue 3.

American Association of Retired Persons (AARP)
http://www.aarp.org

The AARP, a major advocacy group for older people, includes among its many resources suggested readings and Internet links to organizations that deal with the health and social issues that may affect one's sexuality as one ages.

National Institute on Aging (NIA)
http://www.nih.gov/nia/

The NIA, one of the institutes of the National Institutes of Health, presents this home page to lead you to a variety of resources on health and lifestyle issues that are of interest to people as they grow older.

UNIT 4: Intimacies and Relationships

American Psychological Association
http://www.apa.org/topics/homepage.html

By exploring the APA's resources you will be able to find links to an abundance of articles and other information related to interpersonal relationships throughout the life span.

SexInfo: Love and Relationships
http://www.soc.ucsb.edu/sexinfo/?article=A2J8

The Love and Relationships section of the SexInfo website provides students and the general public with an excellent overview of relationship issues, including communication and building effective relationships.

Bonobos Sex and Society
http://songweaver.com/info/bonobos.html

This site, accessed through Carnegie Mellon University, includes an article explaining how a primate's behavior challenges traditional assumptions about male supremacy in human evolution.

Go Ask Alice
http://www.goaskalice.columbia.edu

This interactive site provided by Healthwise, a division of Columbia University Health Services, includes discussion and insight into a number of personal issues of interest to college-age people—and those younger and older. Many questions about physical and emotional health and well-being in the modern world are answered.

UNIT 5: Gender and Sexual Diversity

SocioSite: Feminism and Women's Issues
http://www.sociosite.net/topics/women.php

Visit the University of Amsterdam "Social Science Information System" to gain insights into a number of issues that affect both men and women. It provides biographies of women in history, an international network for women in the workplace, links to family and children's issues, and much more.

Woman in Islam: Sex and Society
http://www.jamaat.org/islam/WomanSociety.html

This Web site is sponsored by the secretary general of Pakistan offering objective analysis and explanations regarding a woman's role in Islamic society. Topics include marriage, family matters, and sex within Islamic society.

Women's Human Rights Resources
http://www.law-lib.utoronto.ca/Diana/

This list of international women's human rights Web sites provides interesting resources on marriage and the family; rights of girls; sexual orientation; slavery, trafficking, and prostitution; and violence against women.

The Intersex Society of North America (ISNA)
http://www.isna.org/

ISNA maintains this resource for anyone interested in the issue of intersex conditions. Physicians, therapists, parents, intersexed individuals and many others will want to learn more about the problems caused by stigma and lack of knowledge for people who are born intersexed.

Parents, Families, and Friends of Lesbians and Gays
http://www.pflag.org

This is the site of PFLAG: Parents, Families and Friends of Lesbians and Gays. Information and downloadable pamphlets with information and support on a variety of topics including "coming out" can be found here.

The Gay, Lesbian & Straight Education Network
http://www.glsen.org/cgi-bin/iowa/all/home/index.html

The Gay, Lesbian & Straight Education Network (GLSEN) provides resources for teachers, parents and students. They promote safe school environments for all students regardless of sexual orientation.

UNIT 6: Sexual Health and Well-Being

World Health Organization: Sexual Health
http://www.who.int/topics/sexual_health/en/

The World Health Organization (WHO) maintains this website to provide educational information on the organization's sexual health activities and programs. This is a great resource for facts, statistics, reports and educational materials on sexual health around the world.

National Cancer Institute: Breast Cancer
http://www.cancer.gov/cancertopics/types/breast

The National Institutes of Health (NIH) National Cancer Institute runs this Breast Cancer website. Find out more about breast cancer and treatment options here. This site includes information on both male and female breast cancer.

Internet References

National Cancer Institute: Ovarian Cancer
http://www.cancer.gov/cancertopics/types/ovarian

The National Institutes of Health (NIH) National Cancer Institute runs this Ovarian Cancer website. Find out more about ovarian cancer and treatment options here. This site includes a wide range of information on ovarian cancer.

National Cancer Institute: Testicular Cancer
http://www.cancer.gov/cancertopics/types/testicular/

The National Institutes of Health (NIH) National Cancer Institute runs this Testicular Cancer website. Find out more about testicular cancer and treatment options here. This site includes a wide range of information on testicular cancer.

SexInfo: Sexually Transmitted Infections
http://www.soc.ucsb.edu/sexinfo/?article=VN5j

The Sexually Transmitted Infections section of the SexInfo website provides students and the general public with essential information on various kinds of STIs. There is also an excellent discussion of STIs and communication issues, including sharing sexual histories with a new partner. This is not to be missed!

The Johns Hopkins University HIV Guide Q&A
http://www.hopkins-hivguide.org/q_a/index.html?categoryId= 9352&siteId=7151#patient_forum

This is a Q&A forum for patients and clinicians run by Johns Hopkins University's Professor Joel Gallant, an internationally recognized expert on HIV disease and Editor in Chief of the *HIV Guide*.

The Body: The Complete HIV/AIDS Resource
http://www.thebody.com/index.html

On this site you can find essential basics about HIV disease, learn about treatments, exchange information in forums, and gain insight from experts.

UNIT 7: Sexualities and Social Issues

Planned Parenthood
http://www.plannedparenthood.org

Planned Parenthood has an "Abortion Issues" section to provide information on reproductive rights.

Rape, Abuse and Incest National Network (RAINN)
http://www.rainn.org/

RAINN is committed to providing "anti-sexual assault" information and education. Learn about rape, incest and other kinds of sexual victimization as well as what you can do to make a difference. There are a variety of resources, including *RAINN's 2008 Back-To-School Tips for Students*.

The Child Rights Information Network (CRIN)
http://www.crin.org

The Child Rights Information Network (CRIN) is a global network that disseminates information about the Convention on the Rights of the Child and child rights among nongovernmental organizations (NGOs), United Nations agencies, intergovernmental organizations (IGOs), educational institutions, and other child rights experts.

Child Exploitation and Obscenity Section (CEOS)/U.S. Department of Justice
http://www.usdoj.gov/criminal/ceos/trafficking.html

This site introduces the reader to essential information about trafficking and sex tourism. There are links to sex trafficking of minors and child prostitution FAQs in addition to other resources at this site.

UNIT 1

Social and Cultural Foundations

Unit Selections

Key Points to Consider

- From the selected readings, what kinds of variations related to sexualities have you noted across cultures and times? Are the differences significant? Why? Why not?

- Were you surprised by any of the cultural or historical differences you read about? If so, what surprised you the most?

- Have you ever spoken to someone your age (in person or online) from another culture/country about sexuality-related ideas, norms, education, or behaviors? If so, what did you learn? What did you think about what they shared with you?

- Is our culture too permissive or too rigid with respect to sexual norms, expectations, and laws? What is the basis of the beliefs you expressed?

- Do we talk too much or too little about sex in our culture? Explain.

- Does either of the genders have a wider range of acceptable behaviors? If so, which? Why?

- What do you think can and should be done about HIV disease?

Student Web Site
www.mhcls.com

Internet References

Department of State: Human Rights
http://www.state.gov/g/drl/hr/

SocioSite: Feminism and Women's Issues
http://www.sociosite.net/topics/women.php

Woman in Islam: Sex and Society
http://www.jamaat.org/islam/WomanSociety.html

Women's Human Rights Resources
http://www.law-lib.utoronto.ca/Diana/

Human sexuality is a dynamic and complex force that involves psychological, sociocultural, and physiological facets. Our sexualities include our biological, psychological and social selves. However strong the influence of biology, we learn what it means to be sexual, and to behave sexually within the structure and parameters of the era in which we live, through our families, social groups, the media, and the society as a whole. By studying different cultures and times, we see more clearly the interplay between the biological, psychological and sociocultural factors influencing sexualities. With a strong sociocultural foundation, we are better equipped to understand the individual within the broader generational and societal contexts.

Anthropological and historical evidence indicate that there is remarkable variation in human sexualities across cultures and times. Indeed, people of different civilizations during various historical periods have engaged in an amazing variety of sexual behaviors. What is common here and now wasn't always so. There seems to be a strong temptation to think that how we do things in our culture is simply the "natural" way to do things. Cross-cultural and historical studies call that assumption about what we consider "natural" very much into question.

For several centuries, Western civilization, especially Western European and, in turn, American cultures, has been characterized by an "antisex ethic." Antisex belief systems include a variety of negative views and expectations about sex and sexualities, including denial, fear, restriction, and the detachment of sexual feelings and behavior from the wholeness of personhood or humanity. Indeed, it has only been in the last 50 years that the antisex proscriptions against knowing or learning about sex have lost their stranglehold. More and more people can find accurate information about their sexual health, sexual functioning, and birth control without fear of social disproval or even eternal damnation. For sex educators, this is a cause for celebration. As with many things, there's also another side to the coin. Access to accurate information about sex is not available uniformly around the world. While we may live in a global economy, where technology and travel have created new opportunities and challenges, there is still incredible repression and suppression of human (often female) sexualities in the world. In some societies today, women and sexual minorities sometimes pay with their lives for expressing who they are. It would be hard to overstate the magnitude of the unspeakable human rights violations occurring right this very minute around the world. Sexuality is often a focus for some of the most extreme forms of social control.

Societies can and do change. Political, economic, and scientific/technological changes have created new possibilities for the expression of human sexualities. The industrial revolution provided new opportunities for people to move away from home-based modes of production and economies. Some people were freed from the social and family constraints that were

© The McGraw-Hill Companies, Inc./Christopher Kerrigan, photographer

necessary for survival. Moving to large population centers, selling one's labor, and living independently became increasingly possible. Within our society, there have been important shifts in the past few decades that have impacted sexualities and relationships. The liberation of women from the kitchen and their participation in the workforce meant that women were no longer required to stay in abusive or unfulfilling relationships. Changes in the legality and availability of birth control and abortion, the reconsideration of democratic values of individual freedom and the pursuit of happiness, demographic shifts in age groups, the growth of the mass media, and the ushering in of the computer age have all influenced the expression of human sexualities in very complex ways.

Some changes in the sexual landscape have simply been unintended and unanticipated by-products of technological and/or historical shifts. Some changes have been hard fought and won by social groups. In the United States, these groups include the earliest feminists, the suffragettes, civil rights organizers, and lesbian/gay/bisexual and transgender activists. So-called sodomy laws suffered a serious defeat with a 2003 ruling by the U.S. Supreme Court. Same-sex marriage is now legal in all of Canada, European countries such as Spain and Norway, and in California and Massachusetts. At the time this book went to press, the situation in California remained uncertain, due to a proposition initiative on the ballot. In addition to same-sex marriage, civil/legal partnerships (with varying benefits) for same-sex couples are now found in numerous U.S. States and in many countries around the world.

Many interest groups continue to work for social change in various areas related to our study of human sexualities. Intersexed people have organized, and are pushing for greater understanding and rights for intersexed children. Their goal is to educate parents and doctors in order to protect intersexed children's bodies from irreversible surgeries before they are able to consent. Others have organized to protest routine circumcision of boys. International groups have formed in order to fight against female circumcision and genital infibulation. These are just a few examples. But they illustrate the range of issues, from the past to the present, that can help us better understand the social and cultural contexts of human sexualities.

This unit overviews historical, cross-cultural, and current issues in order to show the incredible variations and interesting connections in our values, practices, and experiences of human sexualities. In doing so, readers are challenged to adopt a very broad perspective through which their examination of today's sexualities, and their experiences of their own sexualities, can be more meaningful. By examining various social, cultural and historical influences, we are better equipped to avoid a return to a reliance on a fear-based "antisex ethic," while striving to evaluate the impact and value of the social changes that have so profoundly affected sexualities today.

Vox Populi: Sex, Lies, and Blood Sport

Gossip in the glory days of Rome was just like ours—but written in stone.

HEATHER PRINGLE

P liny the Elder, the Roman savant who compiled the eclectic 37-book encyclopedia *Historia Naturalis* nearly 2,000 years ago, was obsessed with the written word. He pored over countless Greek and Latin texts, instructing his personal secretary to read aloud to him even while he was dining or soaking in the bath. And when he traveled the streets of Rome, he insisted upon being carried everywhere by slaves so he could continue reading. To Pliny, books were the ultimate repository of knowledge. "Our civilization—or at any rate our written records—depends especially on the use of paper," he wrote in *Historia Naturalis.*

Pliny was largely blind, however, to another vast treasury of knowledge, much of it literally written in stone by ordinary Romans. Employing sharp styli generally reserved for writing on wax tablets, some Romans scratched graffiti into the plastered walls of private residences. Others hired professional stonecutters to engrave their ramblings on tombs and city walls. Collectively, they left behind an astonishing trove of pop culture—advertisements, gambling forms, official proclamations, birth announcements, magical spells, declarations of love, dedications to gods, obituaries, playbills, complaints, and epigrams. "Oh, wall," noted one citizen of Pompeii, "I am surprised that you have not collapsed and fallen, seeing that you support the loathsome scribblings of so many writers."

More than 180,000 of these inscriptions are now cataloged in the *Corpus Inscriptionum Latinarum,* a mammoth scientific database maintained by the Berlin-Brandenburg Academy of Sciences and Humanities. The *Corpus* throws open a large window on Roman society and reveals the ragged edges of ordinary life—from the grief of parents over the loss of a child to the prices prostitutes charged clients. Moreover, the inscriptions span the length and breadth of the empire, from the Atlantic coast of Spain to the desert towns of Iraq, from the garrisons of Britain to the temples of Egypt. "It would be impossible to do most of Roman history without them," says Michael Crawford, a classicist at University College London.

The *Corpus* was conceived in 1853 by Theodor Mommsen, a German historian who dispatched a small army of epigraphists

to peruse Roman ruins, inspect museum collections, and ferret out inscribed slabs of marble or limestone wherever they had been recycled, including the tops of medieval bell towers and the undersides of toilet seats. Working largely in obscurity, Mommsen's legions and their successors measured, sketched, and squeezed wet paper into crevices. Currently, *Corpus* researchers add as many as 500 inscriptions each year to the collection, mostly from Spain and other popular tourist destinations in the Mediterranean where excavations for hotel and restaurant foundations reveal new epigraphic treasures.

Packed with surprising details, the *Corpus* offers scholars a remarkable picture of everyday life: the tumult of the teeming streets in Rome, the clamor of commerce in the provinces, and the hopes and dreams of thousands of ordinary Romans—innkeepers, ointment sellers, pastrycooks, prostitutes, weavers, and wine sellers. The world revealed is at once tantalizingly, achingly familiar, yet strangely alien, a society that both closely parallels our own in its heedless pursuit of pleasure and yet remains starkly at odds with our cherished values of human rights and dignity.

The Gift of Bacchus

To most Romans, civilization was simply untenable without the pleasures of the grape. Inscriptions confirm that wine was quaffed by everyone from the wealthy patrician in his painted villa to soldiers and sailors in the roughest provincial inns. And although overconsumption no doubt took a toll, wine was far safer than water: The acid and alcohol in wine curbed the growth of dangerous pathogens.

Epicures took particular delight in a costly white wine known as Falernian, produced from Aminean grapes grown on mountain slopes south of modern-day Naples. To improve the flavor, Roman vintners aged the wine in large clay amphorae for at least a decade until it turned a delicate amber. Premium vintages—some as much as 160 years old—were reserved for the emperor and were served in fine crystal goblets. Roman oenophiles, however, could purchase younger vintages of

Falernian, and they clearly delighted in bragging of its expense. "In the grave I lie," notes the tombstone of one wine lover, "who was once well known as Primus. I lived on Lucrine oysters, often drank Falernian wine. The pleasures of bathing, wine, and love aged with me over the years."

Estate owners coveted their own vineyards and inscribed heartfelt praises for "nectar-sweet juices" and "the gift of Bacchus" on their winepresses. Innkeepers marked their walls with wine lists and prices. Most Romans preferred their wine diluted with water, perhaps because they drank so much of it, but they complained bitterly when servers tried to give them less than they bargained for. "May cheating like this trip you up, bartender," noted the graffito of one disgruntled customer. "You sell water and yourself drink undiluted wine."

So steeped was Roman culture in wine that its citizens often rated its pleasures above nearly all else. In the fashionable resort town of Tibur, just outside Rome, the tomb inscription of one bon vivant counseled others to follow his own example. "Flavius Agricola [was] my name. . . . Friends who read this listen to my advice: Mix wine, tie the garlands around your head, drink deep. And do not deny pretty girls the sweets of love."

Pleasures of Venus

Literary scholars such as C. S. Lewis (who wrote, among many other things, *The Chronicles of Narnia*) have often suggested that romantic love is a relatively recent invention, first surfacing in the poems of wandering French and Italian troubadours in the 11th and 12th centuries. Before then, goes the argument, couples did not know or express to one another a passionate attachment, and therefore left no oral or written record of such relationships. Surviving inscriptions from the Roman Empire paint a very different portrait, revealing just how much Romans delighted in matters of the heart and how tolerant they were of the love struck. As one nameless writer observed, "Lovers, like bees, lead a honeyed life."

Many of the infatuated sound remarkably like their counterparts today. "Girl," reads an inscription found in a Pompeian bedroom, "you're beautiful! I've been sent to you by one who is yours." Other graffiti are infused with yearning that transcends time and place. "Vibius Restitutus slept here alone, longing for his Urbana," wrote a traveler in a Roman inn. Some capture impatience. "Driver," confides one, "if you could only feel the fires of love, you would hurry more to enjoy the pleasures of Venus. I love a young charmer, please spur on the horses, let's get on."

Often, men boasted publicly about their amorous adventures. In bathhouses and other public buildings, they carved frank descriptions of their encounters, sometimes scrawling them near the very spot where the acts took place. The language is graphic and bawdy, and the messages brim with detail about Roman sexual attitudes and practices. Many authors, for example, name both themselves and their partners. In Rome, men who preferred other men instead of women felt no pressure to hide it.

A large and lucrative sex trade flourished in Roman cities, and prostitutes often advertised their services in short inscriptions. One of the stranger aspects of Roman life is that many wealthy families rented out small rooms in their homes as miniature brothels, known as *cellae meretriciae*. Such businesses subsidized the lavish lifestyles of the owners. At the other end of the sex trade were elegant Roman courtesans. In Nuceria, near present-day Naples, at least two inscriptions describe Novelli Primigenia, who lived and worked in the "Venus Quarter." So besotted was one of her clients that he carved: "Greetings to you, Primigenia of Nuceria. Would that I were the gemstone (of the signet ring I gave you), if only for one single hour, so that, when you moisten it with your lips to seal a letter, I can give you all the kisses that I have pressed on it."

Most Roman citizens married, and some clearly enjoyed remarkably happy unions. One inscription unearthed just outside Rome records an epitaph for a particularly impressive woman, composed by her adoring husband. Classicists have fervently debated the identity of this matron, for the epitaph recalls the story of Turia, who helped her husband escape execution during civil unrest in the first century B.C. The inscription has crumbled into fragments, however, and the section containing the name of the woman has been lost, but it is clear her cleverness and audacity saved the day for her spouse. "You furnished most ample means for my escape," reads the inscription, elegantly carved by a stonecutter. "With your jewels you aided me when you took off all the gold and pearls from your person, and handed them over to me, and promptly, with slaves, money, and provisions, having cleverly deceived the enemies' guards, you enriched my absence."

Little Darlings

A prominent French historian, Philippe Ariès, has theorized that it was not until the beginning of industrialization—which boosted the standard of living in Europe during the 18th and 19th centuries—that parents began bonding deeply with their babies. In earlier times, infant mortality rates were staggering, leading parents to distance themselves emotionally from babies who might perish from malnutrition or infection before learning to walk.

Intriguingly, studies of Roman tomb inscriptions lend credence to Ariès's idea. The British classicist Keith Hopkins has estimated, based on comparative demographic data, that 28 percent of all Roman children died before reaching 12 months of age. Yet epigraphists have found relatively few inscribed tombs for Roman infants in Italy: Just 1.3 percent of all funerary stones mark such burials. The statistical discrepancy suggests to many classicists that parents in ancient Rome refrained from raising an expensive marble monument for a child, unwilling to mourn publicly or privately.

Some Romans, however, could not and did not repress the love they felt for their infants. As many graffiti reveal, they celebrated a baby's birth in an openly sentimental manner recognizable to parents today. "Cornelius Sabinus has been born," announced a family in a message carved in a residential entranceway, a spot where neighbors and passersby could easily see it. Others went further, jubilantly inscribing the equivalent of baby pictures. "Iuvenilla is born on Saturday the 2nd of August, in the second hour of the evening," reads one such announcement; nearby, someone sketched in charcoal a picture of a newborn.

The epitaphs composed for infant tombs also disclose a great deal about the intense grief some parents suffered. One inscription describes a baby whose brief life consisted of just "nine sighs," as if the parents had tenderly counted each breath their newborn had taken. Another funerary inscription describes in poignant detail a father's grief. "My baby Acerva," he wrote, "was snatched away to live in Hades before she had her fill of the sweet light of life. She was beautiful and charming, a little darling as if from heaven. Her father weeps for her and, because he is her father, asks that the earth may rest lightly on her forever."

Other carved messages supply details about schooling. As children learned to write, local walls served as giant exercise books where they could practice their alphabets. On one, a young student scrawled what seems to be a language arts drill, interlacing the opening letters of the Roman alphabet with its final ones—A X B V C T. In another inscription, a Roman couple marveled at the eloquence of their 11-year-old son, who had entered a major adult competition for Greek poetry. The boy took his place, they noted, "among 52 Greek poets in the third lustrum of the contest, [and] by his talent brought to admiration the sympathy that he had roused because of his tender age, and he came away with honor." The young poet died shortly after his performance.

The Sporting Life

The Romans loved to be entertained, and few things riveted them more than the spectacle of gladiatorial combat. Sports fans fervently tracked the career records of the most skilled gladiators and laid wagers on their survival, while well-to-do female admirers stole into gladiator barracks by night, prompting one combatant, Celadus, to boast in an inscription that he was "the girls' desire." That most gladiators were slaves forced to fight to the death for an afternoon's entertainment of the public did not trouble most Romans: They believed that a demonstration of bravery in the arena brought nobility to even the lowliest slave and that the price—death—was worth it.

So ingrained were gladiatorial games in Roman culture that senior government officials dug into their own pockets and emptied public purses to stage them. To pack an arena, the sponsor often advertised the games with an *edicta munerum,* an inscription painted by teams of professional artists on walls near the local amphitheater. One surviving poster describes how Decimus Lucretius Satrius Valeris, a priest of Nero, and another prominent Roman sponsored a major event in Pompeii spanning five consecutive days before the ides of April. The expensive attractions included 20 pairs of gladiators, the "customary [wild] beast hunt," and "awnings" to shade spectators against the summer sun.

The gladiators steeled themselves for the battle ahead, practicing their deadly swordplay. The devout among them prayed to gods for a victory. In a North African barrack, Manuetus the Provocator, a gladiator who fought with a short, straight sword, made a last vow, promising to "bring Venus the gift of a shield if victorious." Outside the gladiators' barracks, scribes painted walls with announcements and programs for the upcoming event, listing the combatants' names and career records.

On the day of the games, raucous and bloodthirsty crowds flooded the arena. At Rome's Colosseum, each spectator held a tessera, a ticket corresponding to a number inscribed on one of the building's 80 arcades. Each arcade then led ticket holders to a staircase and a specific section of seating. As spectators waited for the bloody combat matches to begin, they snacked on bread or cakes purchased from stalls outside the arena. Local chefs baked breads especially for the games, employing molds bearing designs of dueling gladiators and the name of the baker.

At the end of each fatal match, stretcher bearers hustled out on the floor of the arena to collect the fallen gladiator and carry his body to a nearby morgue, or *spoliarium.* There officials slit the man's throat to ensure that he was truly dead: Roman bettors despised fixed matches. Friends and family members then claimed the body and, if they possessed sufficient funds, raised a tomb in his memory. "To the reverend spirits of the Dead," inscribed one grieving widow. "Glauca was born at Mutina, fought seven times, died in the eighth. He lived 23 years, 5 days. Aurelia set this up to her well-deserving husband, together with those who loved him. My advice to you is to find your own star. Don't trust Nemesis [patroness of gladiators]; that is how I was deceived. Hail and Farewell."

As studies of epitaphs show, skilled gladiators rarely survived more than 10 matches, dying on average at the age of 27.

Ancient Pipe Dreams

Some of the humblest inscriptions shed surprising light on one of the glories of Roman technology, revealing just how close ancient metalworkers came to a major coup—the invention of printing. In the Roman waterworks, messages were raised in relief on the lead pipes that fed fountains, baths, and private homes. As a rule, these short texts recorded the name of the emperor or the municipal official who had ordered and paid for the expansion of the water system.

To form these inscriptions, workers first created small individual molds for each letter in the Latin alphabet. They then spelled out the name of the emperor or official by selecting the appropriate letter molds, placing them into a carved slot in a stone slab. Ensuring that the molds lay flush with the surface of the stone, they locked the type into place and laid the stone slab on a large flat tray. Then they poured molten lead across slab and tray, forming a large metal sheet. Once cooled, the sheet could be rolled into a cylinder and soldered at the seam. On the pipe's contour, the emperor's name appeared in elevated letters.

The pipemakers' ingenuity in using movable type to form a line of text is eerily similar to the method used by Johannes Gutenberg and other European printers more than 1,000 years later. As Canadian classicist A. Trevor Hodge has noted, this overlooked Roman technology "tempts one into speculating how close the ancient world was to making the full-scale breakthrough into printing." But the Romans failed to capitalize on this remarkable invention.

Perhaps they were simply too immersed in the culture of carved and painted words to see the future of print—the real writing on the wall.

From *Discover,* June 2006, pp. 63–66. Copyright © 2006 by Discover Syndication. Reprinted by permission.

The Baby Deficit

As fertility rates decline across the developed world, governments are offering big incentives for childbearing. Experts don't expect them to have much effect.

MICHAEL BALTER

Last month, from the podium of the Kremlin's grandiose Marble Hall, Russian President Vladimir Putin expounded on subjects vital to his nation's future—economic growth, technological modernization, and world trade—then he turned to the "most important" matter. "What I want to talk about," Putin said in his annual speech before the Federal Assembly, "is love, women, children. I want to talk about the family, about the most acute problem facing our country today—the demographic problem." Reminding the deputies that Russia's 143-million-strong population was declining by almost 700,000 people each year, Putin proposed a fistful of incentives to boost the country's flagging birthrate. They include raising the childcare benefit of 700 rubles ($26) per month to 1500 rubles for a first child and 3000 rubles for a second child, and paying 18 months of maternity leave equal to at least 40% of a mother's previous wages.

Putin is not the only politician talking about babies these days. Earlier this year, Poland's Parliament approved a one-time payment of 1000 zlotys ($328) for each child born, and this month, German Chancellor Angela Merkel proposed a 1-year paid leave for women who have children. When Australia introduced its own generous "baby bonus" in 2004, the country's treasurer Peter Costello exhorted parents to have "one for Mum, one for Dad, and one for the country." On 1 July, Australia's bonus will jump from $2250 to $3002 per child (in U.S. dollars) and will reach $3762 by 2008. Meanwhile, pro-family inducements have been in place for many years in France, Sweden, and other European countries.

"The popularity of baby-bonus schemes among governments is difficult to understand."

—Anne Gauthier, University of Calgary

Political leaders and economists see plenty of justification for spending all this money. In the European Union (E.U.),

for example, low birthrates have already begun to shrink the population, and demographers project that the E.U. will lose between 24 million and 40 million people during each coming decade unless fertility is markedly raised (*Science,* 28 March 2003, p. 1991). Population losses could bring a raft of negative economic consequences in the industrialized world, as well as greater stresses on social security and health care systems as the proportion of older citizens increases. "The changes projected for the United States are not as dramatic as those projected for other areas—particularly Europe and Japan—but they nonetheless present substantial challenges," then-Federal Reserve Board chair Alan Greenspan told a 2004 symposium on population aging in Jackson Hole, Wyoming.

Although these trends are most pronounced in the developed world, fertility declines are now also being detected even in less affluent areas of Latin America and Asia. Roughly half of the world's nations, with more than 40% of the human population, now have birthrates below replacement levels, and fertility rates are falling steadily in most developing countries as well. To be sure, demographers predict that the world's population will continue to increase for decades to come, rising from its current 6.5 billion to somewhere between 8 billion and 11 billion by 2050 (see sidebar, p. 177). But nearly all of this increase will be in developing countries.

Population researchers nevertheless are currently engaged in a lively debate over just what, if anything, developed countries can do to increase family size. Some believe very low fertility rates are here to stay. "The popularity of baby-bonus schemes among governments is difficult to understand," says Anne Gauthier, a sociologist at the University of Calgary in Canada. "While the additional financial support is bound to be welcomed by parents, the overall effect on fertility is likely to be small."

Others argue that even modest boosts in the birthrate can make a difference. "We can only expect relatively small effects of policy on fertility, but relatively small effects are important when fertility is low," says demographer Peter McDonald of the Australian National University (ANU) in Canberra, whose advocacy of pro-family policies helped bring about Australia's baby bonus. Yet both sides agree that falling fertility rates might be irreversible once they drop below a certain level—what some demographers have begun to call the "low-fertility trap."

The Demographic Transition

Predicting population trends is a tricky business, fraught with assumptions about what humans are likely to do in the future. Most demographers rely on a complex parameter called the total fertility rate (TFR). For any particular country and year, the TFR is a hypothetical measure of the average number of children that nation's women would bear during their lifetimes if, at each stage of their lives, they behaved exactly like women in each age group did during that year. By comparing TFRs from one year to another, demographers can track fertility trends. Leaving aside the effects of immigration and emigration, if a population is to remain the same size, both parents must replace themselves. For industrialized countries, demographers define a replacement-level TFR as 2.1—slightly more than a flat rate, to account for the small fraction of children who die before reaching reproductive age.

Yet nearly all of the world's industrialized nations have TFRs well below this magic number. Russia's current TFR is only 1.28 (which ties it with Italy and Spain), Poland's is 1.25, Germany's is 1.39, and Australia's is 1.76, which helps explain the alarm expressed by political leaders in those countries. Even the E.U. nations with the highest birthrates, France and Ireland, are falling short of replacement, with TFRs of 1.84 and 1.86, respectively. Nor is the baby shortage restricted to Europe: South Korea's TFR is 1.27 and Japan's is 1.25. Only the United States, exceptional in the developed world, hits the replacement mark, with a TFR of 2.09.

Today's low TFRs are an unexpected consequence of a so-called demographic transition to lower fertility rates that began in Europe in about 1800 and is still taking place in much of the world. As advances in health and hygiene increased the likelihood of a child surviving to reproduce, both death and birthrates started to fall, especially in industrialized countries. Although TFRs remain high in some of the world's poorest countries—Niger has the highest TFR, 7.46—the demographic transition is either under way or completed in most nations. The process has taken place even in relatively poor countries such as Mexico, where TFR dropped from 6.5 to 2.5 between 1975 and 2005, and the Philippines, which saw a decline from 6.0 to 3.2 during the same period. However, demographers had assumed that the decline would stop when replacement-level TFRs were reached. "During the early 1970s, everyone talked about the magic floor of replacement," says David Reher, a population historian at the Complutense University of Madrid, Spain. "Nobody thought it would go below 2.1."

Yet by 1975, several European countries, as well as the United States and Canada, had already dipped below this floor. (Although the United States has now come back up to replacement level, Canada's TFR has continued to plummet and now stands at 1.61.) This trend, which many demographers and economists call the "second demographic transition," has its roots in the social changes that swept much of the Western world during the 1960s and 1970s. As women entered the labor force in increasing numbers and obtained easier access to effective

Total Fertility Rates
- 1.1–1.9
- 2.0–2.9
- 3.0–3.9
- 4.0–5.9
- 6.0–8.1
- N A

Source: U.N. Population Prospects

contraception and as conflicts between work and childbearing intensified, parents began to delay the timing of their first child, which inevitably led to a reduction in the total number of offspring. These shifts were accompanied by a constellation of new attitudes toward family, career, and personal autonomy that are not easily quantified, researchers say. "Human reproductive behavior is profoundly social," says Jennifer Johnson-Hanks, a demographer and anthropologist at the University of California, Berkeley. "It is structured by social categories, value systems, and power relations." John Bongaarts, a demographer at the Population Council in New York City, adds that personal choice has come to play a much bigger role in reproductive decisions. In earlier days, Bongaarts says, "people tended to do what society expected of them. Over time, individual agency has become more important."

Social factors also explain the United States' anomalously high fertility rate, population experts say. Although relatively higher birthrates among some ethnic groups and more recently arrived immigrants, including Hispanics, explain part of the difference, the TFR for non-Hispanic whites is still about 1.85, equivalent to the highest rates seen in Europe. "There are several factors that make the TFR in the U.S. higher than in many European countries," Bongaarts says, including a higher rate of unwanted pregnancies due to restrictions on birth-control information, a lower unemployment rate, and a greater tendency for women to have children earlier in life than in Europe. Gauthier adds that a stronger emphasis on religion and "traditional values" in the United States also tends to favor larger families.

Aged and Dependent

The key reason that economists and other experts are worried about low fertility rates is that they accelerate an overall "aging" of a population, in which the proportion of elderly adults relative to the active labor force increases. The consequences of an increase in this so-called dependency ratio are hard to predict, says demographer James Trussell of Princeton University. "The economic burden of the elderly will depend on their health, on employment opportunities, and on the social institutions that support their care," Trussell says. "But it is clear that it will be a challenge." One way that many developed countries meet the challenge now is through immigration, which tends to increase the number of younger workers. Yet few demographers see immigration as the answer.

"As a short-term solution, it is necessary, and it is happening," says Reher. "But there are very serious doubts about whether it is a long-term solution. Migrant fertility starts higher than that of the native population but very quickly descends towards local fertility levels." Trussell agrees: "To have an appreciable effect on the aging of a population, you would need massive immigration, which is not politically acceptable in either Europe or the U.S."

That leaves raising birthrates as the only solution, assuming that a solution to low fertility rates is possible—and desired. Some demographers take heart in an apparent gap between how many children parents would ideally like to have if they felt they could manage it and how many they actually do have. In

The Bomb That Wasn't

When Stanford University entomologist Paul Ehrlich published *The Population Bomb* in 1968, the world's human population was about 3.5 billion. Yet the worst of Ehrlich's widely publicized predictions, including the starvation of hundreds of millions of people in mass famines, have not come true. Still, the world's population is expected to continue to grow until at least 2050, according to estimates by the United Nations Population Division (esa .un.org/unpp). Just how much it will increase depends on future fertility, which is very difficult to predict. U.N. population experts have examined three hypothetical fertility trends, which they term medium, low, and high. Under the medium scenario, population would reach 9.1 billion by 2050, but the low and high scenarios project as few as 7.6 billion people and as many as 10.6 billion.

Nearly all of this growth will be in developing countries, with major contributions from nations such as India, Pakistan, Nigeria, Bangladesh, and China. (Even the United States, with its relatively youthful population, will add significant numbers.) Fueled by very high fertility rates, between now and 2050, population is expected to at least triple in some nations, such as Afghanistan, Burundi, Chad, Democratic Republic of Congo, Mali, and Uganda—despite high HIV infection rates in many African countries. Yet over the long term, fertility is expected to drop dramatically in even the poorest countries, from an average of five children per woman now to about 2.6 in 2050; and under the U.N.'s medium scenario, average worldwide fertility will decline to 2.05 by 2050, and to just over 1.5 in the low scenario, well below the replacement level.

"Virtually all countries are headed towards replacement-level fertility or below," says Ronald Lee, a demographer at the University of California, Berkeley. "But there may be pauses and reversals along the way, sometimes lasting decades." If so, the population bomb may ultimately fizzle out—that is, assuming an already stressed planet can survive the onslaught of 9 billion human beings.

this gap, some see wiggle room for fertility-enhancing policies. Thus, public-opinion surveys carried out by the E.U. as part of its Eurobarometer program have suggested that this gap amounts to an average of about 0.5 children per woman. Indeed, baby bonuses and other pro-family measures are in part designed to make it easier financially for families to fulfill this ideal. But Gauthier questions whether the gap is actually that large. In a study in press at the journal *Population Research and Policy Review,* she concludes that the "window of opportunity" for family policies might actually be as little as 0.1 to 0.2 children per woman.

Gauthier and other researchers agree nevertheless that pro-family policies have had some positive effect on fertility rates in countries such as France, whose TFR of 1.84 is the second highest in the E.U. after Ireland. "There are no fewer than 38 measures in favor of families with children," says demographer Laurent Toulemon of the National Institute of Demographic Studies in Paris. For example, mothers receive 16 weeks of maternity leave at more than 80% of their normal pay, which is extended to 26 weeks beginning with a third child. Parents also receive numerous direct allowances to help provide for young children, and the number of publicly funded nursery schools has expanded in recent years to the extent that nearly every child is guaranteed a place. In fact, there are so many pro-family policies, says Toulemon, "that it is almost impossible to evaluate the impact of each one" on fertility.

Despite these generous allotments, however, France's relatively high fertility rate in European terms is still below replacement. The same is true of Sweden, where government officials credit bountiful policies designed to make life easier for working parents with recent gains in TFR from about 1.6 to 1.8. Yet Gigi Santow, formerly of Stockholm University and now an independent demographer in Sydney, Australia, says that this fertility jump was not due to baby bonuses or other direct attempts to create a baby boom. "Swedish fertility rates may well have responded to the government's integrated web of cradle-to-grave social policies," Santow says. She adds that fertility plummeted during the economic recession that hit Sweden during the 1990s, despite the policies then in place.

Proving that financial incentives can actually raise fertility rates is very difficult—and demographers do not always agree. "We cannot carry out an experiment," says Gauthier. "We can only look historically at what has happened and rely on cross-national differences in policies." Earlier this month, for example, Australia's news media were abuzz with reports of the latest birth figures from the Australian Bureau of Statistics, showing that 261,404 babies were born in 2005, 2.4% more than the previous year and the highest number since 1992. Treasurer Costello was quick to credit the baby bonus: The daily newspaper *The Australian* quoted Costello as "delighted that at least some families have been taking up the challenge."

ANU's McDonald says that although it is too early to carry out "rigorous research" on the reasons for the increase, most of the additional births are to women in the middle to late part of their childbearing years. This suggests that the message may have been heard: "If you want to have children, it is risky to delay too long," McDonald says. And although McDonald concedes that "most of the 261,000 women who gave birth in 2005 would have had the baby without" the baby bonus, the extra money "can make a difference" to middle income families who make "close calculations" about the impact of parenting. McDonald estimates that Australia's TFR for 2005, when published in November, should rise from about 1.76 to 1.82.

But Robert Birrell, director of the Center for Population and Urban Research at Monash University in Clayton, Australia, says that a number of other factors may have weighed much more heavily, especially "the impact of the current economic boom in Australia, which has seen an increase in the rate of employment for men and particularly women in recent years." Santow agrees: "I would not leap immediately to the conclusion that Peter Costello should be given the credit."

Low-Fertility Spiral

The uncertain response to incentives suggests to some demographers that governments need to do even more to make child rearing attractive. "Many things that we've tried aren't big enough," says Bongaarts. "To move behavior, you need real incentives; you need thousands of dollars. . . . You have to pull all the levers you have, and maybe you will get halfway there." But pulling those levers might end up being too costly, Trussell says. "Policies that would work would be so expensive that they will never be implemented."

And some researchers have begun to think that it might actually be too late to reverse the trend in countries with the lowest fertility levels. At several recent population meetings, for example, McDonald has warned that once a nation's TFR falls below

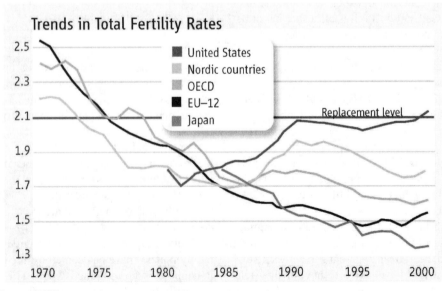

Trends in Total Fertility Rates

Legend:
- United States
- Nordic countries
- OECD
- EU–12
- Japan

Replacement level

Source: OECD

1.5, a downward demographic spiral sets in that makes it much more difficult to recover. "This is the safety zone," McDonald says. "Countries should try hard to avoid falling below it."

A team led by Wolfgang Lutz, a demographer at the International Institute for Applied Systems Analysis (IIASA) in Laxenburg, Austria, has taken McDonald's observation further and argued that countries with a TFR of 1.5 or lower may have crossed into permanent negative population growth. Lutz calls this hypothesis, which he presented most recently at this spring's annual meeting of the Population Association of America in Los Angeles, California, the "low-fertility trap." Lutz and other colleagues at IIASA and the Vienna Institute of Demography argue that the new social norms created by low fertility rates create a self-reinforcing negative feedback loop. It is locked in place by a reduction in ideal family size, aging of the population, and other effects on the labor market that make having fewer and fewer children inevitable. As evidence, Lutz and his colleagues cite data from the Eurobarometer survey showing that in Germany and Austria—nations with TFRs of 1.39 and 1.36, respectively—young adults now consider their ideal family sizes to be as low as 1.7 children on average.

"Germany is the extreme example of this phenomenon, with around 30% of young people not intending to have children," says McDonald. On the other hand, McDonald does not agree that there is no turning back for countries whose TFRs fall this low: "This does make Germany a tougher nut to crack, but I would never declare the game as over."

Yet Reher sees little reason for optimism. "When fertility is drastically below replacement, it doesn't go up, no matter how many policies and how much money is thrown at it," he says. "We are in the midst of a cascading fertility decline. Even a TFR of 1.7 is not safe; it is a disaster if you look a couple of generations down the line."

Indeed, Reher, at the July 2005 annual meeting of the International Union for the Scientific Study of Population in Tours, France, presented a paper suggesting an even more dismal picture. Reher argued that low fertility rates were now entrenched in the social structure of developed countries and a growing number of developing countries as well. Although the momentum of past high fertility rates would continue to fuel an increase in the entire world's population for some decades to come, this would eventually stop. Rather, Reher maintained, much of the world is now on the cusp of a prolonged period of population decline. The resulting population aging would lead to labor shortages even in developing countries. The result could be an economic disaster, Reher warned. "Urban areas in regions like Europe could well be filled with empty buildings and crumbling infrastructures as population and tax revenues decline," he prognosticated, adding that "it is not difficult to imagine enclaves of rich, fiercely guarded pockets of well-being surrounded by large areas which look more like what we might see in some science-fiction movies."

Most population researchers agree that there is plenty to worry about in current worldwide demographic trends. Yet few are ready to accept the direst parts of Reher's doomsday scenario—at least not yet. "I wouldn't be surprised" if population shrinkage "happens in a lot of places in the world," says Gauthier, although she adds that "it is much harder to believe in Africa," where the population is expected to at least double by 2050. And Santow comments that although Reher's predictions "may well be sensible," she sees "nothing terrifying about a drop in the size of Europe's population. Any decline will take time, and economies will adjust. Governments should not expend energy to maintain the status quo. Governments should plan for the future, not try to reintroduce the past."

Three 'Rules' That Don't Apply

A historian upends conventional wisdom.

STEPHANIE COONTZ

Marriage has changed more in the last 30 years than in the previous 300. People today have unprecedented freedom about whether, when and whom to marry, and they are making those decisions free from the huge social and economic pressures that once had them marching in lockstep.

In such periods of massive change and diversification, it is useless to see averages as descriptions of the typical experience. They are simply the artificial addition of the experiences of many different subgroups, each of which may be going in a different direction, divided by the total number of people. That is why so many old assumptions and predictions have turned out to be wrong.

When I look at the 1986 *NEWSWEEK* story, I see three old "rules" of marriage that are particularly bad guides for modern relationships. Two have already been overturned. And the third is in the process of being overturned.

The first is that women who delay marriage are condemning themselves to lifelong singlehood. This had some truth in the 1950s and early 1960s, when the economic and social pressures to marry early were enormous. One psychiatrist wrote in 1953 that "a girl who hasn't a man in sight by the time she is 20 is not altogether wrong in fearing that she may never get married." So women made sure to set their sights on a potential husband early. The average age of first marriage was 20, with the greatest single number of women marrying at 18. Very few women married for the first time after 24. It was easy to assume that a woman who hadn't married by the end of her 20s would never marry.

That turned out to be wrong. As more women went to school and worked for a longer period of time, the average age of marriage rose. But perhaps more important, the breakdown of the rigid, cookie-cutter life course of the 1950s created more variation in when people left home, went to work and got married, so there was a wider range of dispersal from the average.

This is a different world than the 1950s. The average age at first marriage for women is now almost 26. For women with a B.A. it is more than 27, and for women with master's or professional degrees it is 30. And there is huge variation within each average, so that more women now marry for the first time in their 40s, 50s and even 60s than ever before in history.

The second "rule" is that women who remain single to pursue higher education or a successful career are less likely to marry. That was true for hundreds of years, and remained true for women born up to 1960, those who reached marriageable age in the 1980s. So as late as 1986 it seemed a safe prediction. But even then it was already being overturned. For women born since 1960, this rule has ceased to apply. Today, although the average college grad marries almost two years later than the average woman—and the average woman who gets an advanced degree marries almost five years later—they are *more* likely to marry than women with low levels of education.

This "rule" has recently been recycled as women's graduation rates have outstripped men's. Many people claim men aren't willing to marry educated, independent women. But that's no longer true. Men are now much more likely to marry women who are their educational and economic peers. Also, the pool of men available to older women has grown because women are now more willing to marry younger men, and younger men are now more willing to marry them.

The third "rule" is that people who marry earlier and later than average have a higher risk of divorce. On average, that's still true. But those averages are derived from a world that no longer describes the lives of most educated women who postpone marriage, and I believe this rule may be on its way out, too. The people who married late used to be those who were least competitive in the marriage market. But today, with educated and professional women having a much better chance of marrying late than women with low education or earnings, my educated guess is that this old rule will also cease to apply.

The divorce rate has gone down for college-educated women in the last two decades, while it has gone up for those without college. And it is college-educated women who have the best chance of marrying late. Women with education and earnings have more ability to leave a bad marriage, but they also have more ability to change the terms of marriage to make them more satisfying for both partners. And they are the ones most likely to choose husbands who support equality.

So the bottom line is, chart your own course. Don't rush into marriage because some so-called expert waves depressing averages at you. Don't avoid it because you fear divorce. Marriage is more work today than it was at a time when gender roles were nonnegotiable, when men had the legal right to the final say in many family arguments and when women had to stick it out because they couldn't afford to leave. But the payoffs of a good marriage are also higher than in the past. And many of the older marriages being contracted now are between people who have the skills to construct those good marriages—more egalitarian men, more savvy women and lovers who have deeper friendships.

STEPHANIE COONTZ is the author of *"Marriage, a History: How Love Conquered Marriage" (Viking)*. She is director of research at the Council on Contemporary Families.

Everyone's Queer

LEILA J. RUPP

When I was growing up, one of my Quaker mother's favorite expressions was "Everyone's queer except thee and me, and sometimes I think thee is a little queer, too." Even as a child, I loved both the sentiment and the language, and then later I got a special kick out of the possibilities of the word "queer." But until I sat down to write this piece, I had never thought about how appropriate the saying is to a consideration of the history of sexuality. For the most striking thing about the literature is that the vast majority of what we know about sexuality in the past is about what is "queer," in the sense of non-normative. We assume that "normative" describes most of what happened sexually in the past, but we know very little about that. Except what the history of nonnormative sexuality—same-sex, commercial, non- or extra-marital, or in some other way deemed inappropriate—can tell us. And that, it turns out, is quite a lot.

Like motherhood or childhood, sexuality, we once assumed, had no history. Now we know better.

Like motherhood or childhood, sexuality, we once assumed, had no history. Now we know better. Sexuality, consisting of, among other elements, sexual desires, sexual acts, love, sexual identities, and sexual communities, has not been fixed over time and differs from place to place. That is, whether and how people act on their desires, what kinds of acts they engage in and with whom, what kinds of meanings they attribute to those desires and acts, whether they think love can be sexual, whether they think of sexuality as having meaning for identities, whether they form communities with people with like desires—all of this is shaped by the societies in which people live. On the streets of New York at the turn of the nineteenth century, men engaged in sexual acts with other men without any bearing on their identity as heterosexual, as long as they took what they thought of as the "male part." Women embraced their women friends, pledged their undying love, and slept with each other without necessarily interfering with their married lives. Knowing these patterns, it begins to make more sense that Jonathan Katz wrote a wonderfully titled book. *The Invention of Heterosexuality* (1995). for it was only when certain acts and feelings came to be identified as the characteristics of a new type of person, "the homosexual,"

that people began to think of "heterosexuals".[1] And what defined a heterosexual? Someone who did not, under any (or almost any) circumstances, engage in same-sex love or intimacy or sex. That this never became a hard and fast rule throughout U.S. society is suggested by the recent attention to life on "the down low," the practice of some black men who secretly engage in sex with other men but live in heterosexual relationships, or to patterns of sexuality among Latino men.[2] But the important point here is that normative heterosexuality—what scholars sometimes call "heteronormativity—can only be defined in contrast to what it is not. Which is why the history of nonnormative sexuality and the concept of "queer" is so important.

So how did people come to think of themselves as homosexual or bisexual or heterosexual or transsexual? That is one of the interesting questions that historians have explored. We now know a great deal about the development of the concepts by the sexologists, scientists, and social scientists who studied sexual behavior, but we also are learning more about the complex relationship between scientific definitions (and, in the case of transsexuality, medical techniques) and the desires and identities of individuals.[3] For example, Lisa Duggan, in her book *Sapphic Slashers* (2000), details the ways that publicity about a notorious lesbian murder in Memphis in the late nineteenth century both fed on and fed into such diverse genres as scientific case studies and French novels.[4] In his work on New York, George Chauncey opens the curtains on an early twentieth-century world in which men were not homosexual or heterosexual, despite the categorizations of the sexologists, but instead fairies or pansies, wolves or husbands, queers or "normal" men depending on their class position, ethnicity, and sexual role (the part one plays in a sexual act—generally penetrator or encloser).[5] And Joanne Meyerowitz, in *How Sex Changed* (2002), reveals that even before the publicity about Christine Jorgensen's sex-change surgery hit American newsstands, individual men and women wrote of their longings to change sex and bombarded physicians with questions and demands.[6] That is, we do not have the doctors and scientists to thank for our identities; their definitions sometimes enabled people to come to an understanding of their feelings and actions, sometimes to reject the definitions. But it was observation of individuals and communities that led the sexologists to their thinking about categories in the first place. We, as homosexuals and heterosexuals and bisexuals, were not created out of thin air.

Identities—and by identities I mean not just homosexual or gay or lesbian, but all their elaborate manifestations such as fairy, faggot, pogue, lamb, bulldagger, ladylover, butch, stud, fem—have a complex relationship to behavior, as the contemporary case of life on the down low makes clear. Over time, the sexologists came to define homosexuality not as gender inversion—effeminacy in men and masculinity in women—but as desire for someone of the same sex. By extension, heterosexuals felt no such desire. But how to explain men who identified as heterosexual but had (appropriately masculine-defined—that is, insertive rather than receptive) sex with other men? Or, in the case of women who came to be known as "political lesbians" in 1970s lesbian feminist communities, women who identified as lesbians but didn't have sex with women?[7] Identity and behavior are not always a neat fit, as the revelations of widespread same-sex sexual interactions in the famous Kinsey studies of male and female sexuality made clear to a stunned American public in the postwar decades. In response to his findings, based on interviews with individuals about their sexual behavior, Kinsey developed a scale to position people in terms of their behavior on a spectrum from exclusively heterosexual to exclusively homosexual.[8]

Another aspect of the relationship of identity to behavior is suggested by some of the labels people claimed for themselves, for many of them referred to a preference for specific kinds of sexual acts, sexual roles, or sexual partners. George Chauncey's research on the Naval investigation into "perversion" in Newport, Rhode Island, in the second decade of the twentieth century revealed the very specific terms used for those who preferred particular acts and roles.[9] In his study of the Pacific Northwest, Peter Boag describes a preference for anal or interfemoral intercourse in the intergenerational relationships between "wolves" and "punks" among transient laborers.[10] Liz Kennedy and Madeleine Davis's study of the working-class lesbian bar community in Buffalo, New York, in the 1940s and 1950s makes clear how central sexual roles were, at least in theory, to the making of butches and fems.[11] One identity, that of "stone butch," was defined by what a woman did not do, in this case desire and/or allow her lover to make love to her.

One of the things that historians' uncovering of the sexual acts that took place between people of the same sex reveals is how these changed over time. Sharon Ullman's research shows that oral sex between men was considered something new in the early twentieth century. When the police in Long Beach, California, broke up a "society of queers," they were confounded to discover that they were having oral rather than anal sex and concluded that that didn't really count as homosexual sex. The men themselves dubbed oral sex "the twentieth-century way".[12] Likewise, Kennedy and Davis found that butches and fems in Buffalo did not engage in oral sex. We know, or should know, that cultures in different times and places foster different kinds of sexual acts. Kissing, for example, is a relatively recent Western innovation as something erotic. But on the whole, as Heather Miller has pointed out, historians of sexuality have paid very little attention to the actual sexual acts in which people—and especially heterosexual people—engage.[13] One of the things that nonnormative sexuality can tell us about heteronormativity is what kinds of sexual acts are acceptable. We know, for example,

that heterosexual oral sex was something confined to prostitution—at least in theory—until the early twentieth century. What prostitutes, both male and female, were willing to do, especially for increased fees, tells us something about what "respectable" women were probably not.

In addition to interest in desire, love, sexual acts, and identities—and the complex relationships among them—historians of sexuality have concentrated on the building of communities and on struggles to make the world a better place. Martin Meeker, in his book *Contacts Desired* (2006), uncovers the communications networks that made same-sex sexuality visible and both resulted from and contributed to the building of communities and the homophile movement in the post-Second World War decades.[14] His concentration on a wide variety of media adds to incredibly rich research on different communities. In addition to Chauncey on New York, Kennedy and Davis on Buffalo, and Boag on Portland, there's Esther Newton on Cherry Grove, telling the story of the creation of a gay resort.[15] In the same vein, Karen Krahulik has detailed the ways that Provincetown became "Cape Queer".[16] Marc Stein, in *City of Sisterly and Brotherly Loves* (2000), uses the history of Philadelphia to detail, among other things, the relationship between lesbian and gay worlds in the city and in the movement.[17] Nan Alamilla Boyd, in her study of San Francisco, shows not only how the city by the Bay became a gay mecca (something Meeker addresses as well from a different perspective), but also how queer culture and the homophile movement had a more symbiotic relationship than we had thought.[18] A collection of articles on different communities, *Creating a Place for Ourselves* (1997), provides even more geographical diversity, as does John Howard's work on the vibrant networks gay men fashioned in the rural South.[19]

> We know that, without the concept of homosexuality, there would be no heterosexuality. Without knowing which sexual desires and acts are deemed deviant, we would not know which ones passed muster. Knowing how identities are created, institutions established, communities built, and movements mobilized, we learn from the margins what the center looks like.

What these studies collectively reveal is the way economic, political, and social forces, especially in the years since the Second World War, enhanced the possibilities for individuals with same-sex desires to find others like themselves, to build institutions and communities, to elaborate identities, and to organize in order to win basic rights: to gather, work, play, and live. This despite the crackdown following the war, which David Johnson argues in *The Lavender Scare* (2004) was more intense and long lasting than the effort to root Communists out of government.[20] These works on diverse communities have also fleshed out the

story John D'Emilio tells of the rise of the homophile movement in his classic *Sexual Politics, Sexual Communities* (1983)
and responded to the question of how the war shaped the experiences of gay men and women first told by Allan Bérubé in his
1990 book *Coming Out Under fire.*[21]

Increasingly, research on same-sex sexuality and other forms
of nonnormative sexuality has attended to the relationship of
sexual desires and identities to gender, class, race, and ethnicity.
Lisa Duggan's *Sapphic Slashers,* for example, tells the story of
white middle-class Alice Mitchell's murder of her lover Freda
Ward intertwined with the Memphis lynching that drove Ida B.
Wells from her hometown and into her anti-lynching crusade.
Judy Wu and Nayan Shah attend to how ethnicity shaped sexuality in the Chinese American community.[22] John D'Emilio's
biography of Bayard Rustin makes his identity as a black gay
man inseparable from considering his role in the civil rights
movement.[23] George Chauncey and Peter Boag detail different
ways that class distinctions emerged in forms of male same-sex
sexuality on opposite sides of the continent. Karen Krahulik
makes ethnicity and class central to the story of the coexistence,
sometimes peaceful and sometimes not, of gay and lesbian pioneers and Portuguese fishermen in Provincetown. And Kevin
Mumford, in *Interzones* (1997), argues for the centrality of the
areas of New York and Chicago in which racial mixing and all
sorts of nonnormative sexuality took place for the shaping of
both mainstream and gay culture.[24]

Which brings us back to the notion of the queerness of us
all. We know that, without the concept of homosexuality, there
would be no heterosexuality. Without knowing which sexual
desires and acts are deemed deviant, we would not know which
ones passed muster. Knowing how identities are created, institutions established, communities built, and movements mobilized,
we learn from the margins what the center looks like.

What we do know more directly about normative sexuality tends to be about prescription, and we know that directives
about how to act are not necessary if everyone is behaving
properly. So Marilyn Hegarty has shown how the forces of
government, the military, and medicine cooperated and competed both to mobilize and contain women's sexuality in the
interests of victory during the Second World War.[25] Carolyn
Lewis's forthcoming work on the premarital pelvic exam in the
1950s reveals the cold war anxieties that lay behind the initiative to teach women how to enjoy and reach orgasm through
heterosexual vaginal intercourse.[26] To take another example, in
her forthcoming book, Susan Freeman explores sex education
directed at girls in the 1950s and 1960s, revealing, among other
things, the ways that girls pushed to learn what they needed to
know.[27] These contributions—examples from my own students
or former students—add to what we know about heteronormativity from scholars such as Sharon Ullman, Beth Bailey, David
Allyn, and Jeffrey Moran.[28]

So my mother was right, except she didn't go far enough. As
Dennis Altman pointed out in arguing for the "homosexualization of America," and as my own work with Verta Taylor on
drag queens and the responses they evoke in audience members
reveals, in a wide variety of ways, from what we desire to how
we love to how we make love to how we play, we are all a little
queer.[29] And we have a lot to learn from the history of nonnormative sexualities.

Endnotes

1. Jonathan Ned Katz, *The Invention of Heterosexuality*
   (New York: Dutton, 1995).

2. See, for example, J. L. King, On *the Down Low: A Journey Into
   the Lives of "Straight" Black Men Who Sleep with Men*
   (New York: Broadway Books, 2004); Tomás Almaguer,
   "Chicano Men: A Cartography of Homosexual Identity and
   Behavior," *differences: A Journal of Feminist Cultural Studies*
   3 (Summer 1991): 75–100; Don Kulick, *Travesti: Sex, Gender,
   and Culture among Brazilian Transgendered Prostitutes*
   (Chicago: University of Chicago Press, 1998); Annick Prieur,
   *Mema's House, Mexico City. On Transvestites, Queens,
   and Machos* (Chicago: University of Chicago Press, 1998);
   Claibome Smith, "Gay Caballeros: Inside the Secret World of
   Dallas' *Mayates,*" *Dallas Observer* (January 13, 2005).

3. On sexology, see Jennifer Terry, *An American Obsession:
   Science, Medicine, and Homosexuality in Modern Society*
   (Chicago: University of Chicago Press, 1999).

4. Lisa Duggan, *Sapphic Slashers: Sex, Violence, and American
   Modernity* (Durham, NC: Duke University Press, 2000).

5. George Chauncey, *Gay New York: Gender, Urban Culture,
   and the Making of the Gay Male World,* 1590–1940 (New York:
   Basic Books, 1994),

6. Joanne Meyerowitz, *How Sex Changed: A History of
   Transsexuality in the United States* (Cambridge, MA: Harvard
   University Press, 2002).

7. See Arlene Stein, *Sex and Sensibility: Stories of a Lesbian
   Generation* (Berkeley: University of California Press, 1997).

8. Alfred Kinsey et al., *Sexual Behavior in the Human Male*
   (Philadelphia: W.B. Saunders Col, 1948); Kinsey et al., *Sexual
   Behavior in the Human Female* (Philadelphia: W.B. Sanders
   Co., 1953).

9. George Chauncey Jr., "Christian Brotherhood or Sexual
   Perversion? Homosexual Identities and the Construction of
   Sexual Boundaries in the World War I Era," *Journal of Social
   History* 19 (1985): 189–212.

10. Peter Boag, *Same-Sex Affairs: Constructing and Controlling
    Homosexuality in the Pacific Northwest* (Berkeley: University
    of California Press. 2003).

11. Elizabeth Lapovsky Kennedy and Madeline D. Davis, *Boots of
    Leather, Slippers of Gold: The History of a Lesbian Community*
    (New York: Routledge, 1993).

12. Sharon Ullman, " 'The Twentieth Century Way:' Female
    Impersonation and Sexual Practice in Turn-of-the-Century
    America," *Journal of the History of Sexuality* 5 (1995): 573–600.

13. Heather Lee Miller, "The Teeming Brothel: Sex Acts, Desires,
    and Sexual Identities in the United States, 1870–1940" (Ph.D.
    diss., Ohio State University, 2002).

14. Martin Meeker, *Contacts Desired: Gay and Lesbian
    Communications and Community,* 1940s–1970s (Chicago:
    University of Chicago Press, 2006).

15. Esther Newton, *Cherry Grove, Fire Island: Sixty Years in
    America's First Gay and Lesbian Town* (Boston: Beacon Press,
    1993).

16. Karen Christel Krahulik, *Provincetown: From Pilgrim Landing to Gay Resort* (New York: New York University Press, 2005).

17. Marc Stein, *City of Sisterly and Brotherly Loves: Lesbian and Gay Philadelphia, 1945–1972* (Chicago: University of Chicago Press, 2000).

18. Nan Alamilla Boyd, *Wide Open Town: A History of Queer San Francisco to 1965* (Berkeley: University of California Press, 2003).

19. Brett Beemyn, ed., *Creating a Place for Ourselves: Lesbian, Gay, and Bisexual Community Histories* (New York: Routledge, 1997); John Howard, ed., *Carryin' on in the Lesbian and Gay South* (New York: New York University Press, 1997); and Howard, *Men Like That: A Southern Queer History (Chicago:* University of Chicago Press, 1999).

20. David K. Johnson, *The Lavender Scare: The Cold War Persecution of Gays and Lesbians in the Federal Government* (Chicago: University of Chicago Press, 2004).

21. John D'Emilio, *Sexual Politics, Sexual Communities: The Making of a Homosexual Minority in the United States, 1940–1970* (Chicago: University of Chicago Press, 1983); Allan Bérubé, *Coming Out Under Fire: The History of Gay Men and Women in World War II* (New York: Free Press, 1990).

22. Judy Tzu-Chun Wu, *Doctor Mom Chung of the Fair-Haired Bastards: The Life of a Wartime Celebrity* (Berkeley: University of California Press, 2005); Nayan Shah, *Contagious Divides: Epidemics and Race in San Francisco's Chinatown* (Berkeley: University of California Press, 2001).

23. John D'Emilio, *Lost Prophet: The Life and Times of Bayard Rustin* (New York: Free Press, 2003).

24. Kevin J. Mumford, *Interzones: Black/White Sex Districts in Chicago and New York in the Early Twentieth Century* (New York: Columbia University Press, 1997).

25. Marilyn Elizabeth Hegarty, "Patriots, Prostitutes, Patriotutes: The Mobilization and Control of Female Sexuality in the United States during World War II" (Ph.D. diss., Ohio State University, 1998). Revised version forthcoming from the University of California Press.

26. Carolyn Herbst Lewis, "Waking Sleeping Beauty: The Pelvic Exam, Heterosexuality and National Security in the Cold War," *Journal of Women's History* 17 (2005): 86–110.

27. Susan Kathleen Freeman, "Making Sense of Sex: Adolescent Girls and Sex Education in the United States, 1940–1960" (Ph. D, diss., Ohio State University, 2002). Revised version to be published by the University of Illinois Press.

28. Sharon R. Ullman, *Sex Seen: The Emergence of Modern Sexuality in America* (Berkeley; University of California Press, 1997); Beth Bailey, *Sex in the Heartland,* 1st paperback ed. (Cambridge, MA: Harvard University Press, 2002); David Allyn, *Make Love, Not War. The Sexual Revolution, An Unfettered History,* 1st paperback ed. (New York: Routledge, 2001); Jeffrey P. Moran, *Teaching Sex: The Shaping of Adolescence in the 20th Century* (Cambridge, MA: Harvard University Press, 2000).

29. Dennis Altman, *The Homosexualization of America* (New York: St. Martin's Press, 1982); Leila J. Rupp and Verta Taylor, *Drag Queens at the 801 Cabaret* (Chicago: University of Chicago Press, 2003).

LEILA J. RUPP is Professor and Chair of Women's Studies at the University of California, Santa Barbara. She is the author of *A Desired Past: A Short History of Same-Sex Love in America* (1999) and coauthor, with Verta Taylor, of *Drag Queens at the 801 Cabaret* (2003). She is currently working on a book called "Sapphistries."

A Mind Dismembered
In Search of the Magical Penis Thieves

FRANK BURES

No one is entirely sure when magical penis loss first came to Africa. One early incident was recounted by Dr. Sunday Ilechukwu, a psychiatrist, in a letter some years ago to the *Transcultural Psychiatric Review*. In 1975, while posted in Kaduna, in the north of Nigeria, Dr. Ilechukwu was sitting in his office when a policeman escorted in two men and asked for a medical assessment. One of the men had accused the other of making his penis disappear. This had caused a major disturbance in the street. As Ilechukwu tells it, the victim stared straight ahead during the examination, after which the doctor pronounced him normal. "Exclaiming," Ilechukwu wrote, "the patient looked down at his groin for the first time, suggesting that the genitals had just reappeared."

According to Ilechukwu, an epidemic of penis theft swept Nigeria between 1975 and 1977. Then there seemed to be a lull until 1990, when the stealing resurged. "Men could be seen in the streets of Lagos holding on to their genitalia either openly or discreetly with their hand in their pockets," Ilechukwu wrote. "Women were also seen holding on to their breasts directly or discreetly, by crossing the hands across the chest. . . . Vigilance and anticipatory aggression were thought to be good prophy-laxes. This led to further breakdown of law and order." In a typi-cal incident, someone would suddenly yell: *Thief! My genitals are gone!* Then a culprit would be identified, apprehended, and, often, killed.

During the past decade and a half, the thievery seems not to have abated. In April 2001, mobs in Nigeria lynched at least twelve suspected penis thieves. In November of that same year, there were at least five similar deaths in neighboring Benin. One survey counted fifty-six "separate cases of genital shrinking, disappearance, and snatching" in West Africa between 1997 and 2003, with at least thirty-six suspected penis thieves killed at the hands of angry mobs during that period. These incidents have been reported in local newspapers but are little known outside the region.

For years, I followed this trend from afar. I had lived in East Africa, in Italy, in Thailand, and other places too, absorbing their languages, their histories, their minutiae. I had tried to piece together what it might be like not just to live in those places but really to *be* in them, to jump in and sink all the way to the bottom of the pool. But through these sporadic news stories, I was forced to contemplate a land more foreign than any I had ever seen, a place where one's penis could be magically blinked away. I wanted to see for myself, but no magazine would send me. It was too much money, too far, and too strange. Finally, when my wife became pregnant, I realized that it might be my one last reckless chance to go, and so I shouldered the expenses myself and went.

On my first morning in the Mainland Hotel, a run-down place with falling ceiling tiles and broken locks, I awoke to a din, and I realized that it was simply the city: the clatter of the 17 million people of Lagos. It was louder than any metropolis I had ever heard. My windows were closed, but it sounded as if they were wide open. For the next few days, I wandered around the city not quite sure where to begin. I went to bookstores and took motorcycle taxis and asked people I met, friends of friends, but without much insight or luck.

Eventually I found my way to Jankara Market, a collection of cramped stands under a patchwork of corrugated-tin sheets that protect the proffered branches, leaves, seeds, shells, skins, bones, skulls, and dead lizards and toads from the elements. All these items are held to contain properties that heal, help, or harm, depending on what one needs them to do. The market is better known for the even darker things one can buy. At Jankara, one can buy *juju:* magic. On my first trip to Jankara, to look around, I met a woman who loved me, she said, and wanted to, marry me. When I told her I was already married, she threatened to bind me to her magically with two wooden figures so that I would not sleep at night until I saw her. But she said it with a glint in her eye, so I didn't worry.

A few days later, I returned to Jankara to ask her some ques-tions. As soon as I walked into the dark, covered grounds of the market, she saw me.

"Ah," she said. "You have come back!"

"Yes," I said.

"Sit here," she said, and pointed to a bench. She sat down across from me. "What did you bring me?"

I showed her some fruit I had brought.

"Ah, very nice," she said and started to eat, even though it was daytime in the middle of Ramadan and she was Muslim. "How is your wife?"

"She is good."

"And what about your other wife?"

"Who is that?' "

"'Who is that?' she said in mock surprise. "I think you know who that is. That is me."

"That is nice," I said. "But in America it's not possible."

A man came up to her and handed her a crumpled piece of paper with a list of ingredients on it. She peered at the list, then got up and went around collecting sticks and leaves and seeds and plants. She chopped them all up and put them in a bag. While she was doing this, the man sat next to me on a bench.

"Is that for you?" I asked.

"Yes," he said. "It makes you very strong."

Then another man came up and put in his order. It was something for the appendix, he said. When he was gone, the woman sat down next to me.

"I have a question," I said.

"Yes."

"In my country, we don't have *juju*."

"Yes."

"But I was reading in the paper about penis snatchers—"

"Ah," she interrupted me. "Don't listen to them. That is not true. If I touch your thing like this"—and here she touched my leg—"is your penis gone?"

"No," I said, uneasily. "But what if I come to you and ask you for protection? Can you do it?"

"Yes, I can."

"How much?"

"One thousand naira. Two thousand. Even up from there." This was a large sum by Nigerian standards—more than $15.

"Do you have many people come and ask for this?"

"Yes," she said in a low voice. She looked around."Many."

Nigeria was not the first site of mysterious genital disappearance. As with so many other things, its invention can be claimed by the Chinese. The first known reports of "genital retraction" date to around 300 B.C., when the mortal dangers of *suo-yang*, or "shrinking penis," were briefly sketched in the *Nei Ching*, the *Yellow Emperor's Classic Text of Internal Medicine*. Also in China, the first full description of the condition was recorded in 1835, in Pao Siaw-Ow's collection of medical remedies, which describes *suo-yang* as a "ying type of fever" (meaning it arises from too much cold) and recommends that the patient get a little "heaty" yang for balance.

Fears of magical penis loss were not limited to the Orient. The *Malleus Maleficarum*, medieval Europeans' primary guidebook to witches and their ways, warned that witches could cause one's *membrum virile* to vanish, and indeed several chapters were dedicated to this topic. Likewise the *Compendium Maleficarum* warned that witches had many ways to affect one's potency, the seventh of which included "a retraction, hiding or actual removal of the male genitals." (This could be either a temporary or a permanent condition.)

Even in the 1960s, there were reports of Italian migrant workers in Switzerland panicking over a loss of virility caused by witchcraft.

These fears, however, seem to have been largely isolated; mass panics over genital retraction were not recorded until 1874. This was the year that, on the island of Sulawesi, a certain Benjamin Matthes was compiling a dictionary of Buginese when he came across a strange term, *lasa koro*, which meant "shrinking of the penis," a disease that Matthes said was not uncommon among the locals and "must be very dangerous." Sporadic reports of *koro*, as it came to be known, recurred over the years, and during the late twentieth century the panics proliferated. In 1967, an epidemic of *koro* raced through Singapore, affecting some five hundred men. In 1976, in northern Thailand, at least two thousand people were afflicted with *rokjoo*, in which men *and* women complained that their genitals were being sucked into their bodies. In 1982, there were major *koro* epidemics in India and again in Thailand, while in 1984 and 1985, some five thousand Chinese villagers in Guangdong province tried desperately to keep their penises outside their bodies using whatever they had handy: string, chopsticks, relatives' assistance, jewelers' clamps, and safety pins. But the phenomenon was given little notice by Western scientists, who considered such strange mental conditions to be "ethnic hysterias" or "exotic psychoses."

This way of thinking has changed, thanks largely to the work of a Hong Kong–based psychiatrist named Pow Meng Yap. In the early 1950s, Yap noticed a strange thing: a trickle of young men coming into his office, complaining that their penises were disappearing into their bodies and that when this happened they would die. After seeing nineteen such cases, Yap published a paper in the *British Journal of Psychiatry* entitled: "*Koro*—A Culture-Bound Depersonalization Syndrome." For years, Yap had been interested in the interplay among culture, mind, and disease. In an earlier paper, "Mental Diseases Peculiar to Certain Cultures," Yap had discussed other similar conditions: *latah*, a trance/fright neurosis in which the victim obeys commands from anyone nearby; *amok*, unrestrained outbursts of violence (as in "running amok"); and *thanatomania*, or self-induced "magical" death. *Koro* fit quite well among these other exotic maladies. In fact, it was perhaps the best example of a phenomenon that can arise only in a specific culture, a condition that occurs in a sense *because* of that culture. Yap saw that these ailments had this one feature in common, grouped them together, and gave them a name that, in spite of all the controversy to follow, would stick. They were "culture-bound syndromes."

Under this rubric, *koro* and the other culture-bound syndromes are now treated with more respect, if not total acceptance. Science is, after all, the quest for universality. In psychiatry, this means all minds are treated the same and all conditions should exist equally across the world. Some thought that calling *koro* "culture-bound" was an end-run around the need for universality, a relativistic cop-out. Were these syndromes really caused by different cultures? Or were they just alternate names for afflictions that plagued, or could plague, every culture? This was precisely what I had come to Nigeria to find out, though so far with little success.

few days after I arrived in Lagos, an article appeared in the newspaper. The headline read: COURT REMANDS MAN OVER FALSE ALARM ON GENITAL ORGAN DISAPPEARANCE. According to the paper, a young man named Wasiu Karimu was on a bus when he "was said to have let out a strident cry, claiming that his genital organ had disappeared. He immediately grabbed [Funmi] Bello, who was seated next to him, and shouted that the woman should restore his 'stolen' organ." They got off the bus, and a crowd of "miscreants" swarmed around the woman, ready to kill her. But a passing police patrol intervened, stopped her from being lynched, and escorted them both to the police station, where Karimu told the commissioner "his organ was returning gradually." The paper gave the exact address where Wasiu Karimu lived, so I decided to try and find out what exactly had transpired in his pants.

The day was already hot when a friend of a friend named Akeem and I rolled into Alagbado, the dusty, run-down town on the far edge of Lagos where Wasiu Karimu lived. We drove past clapboard shacks and little restaurants, through huge muddy pools, past people watching us from doorways, until we came to the address given in the paper. Chickens and goats scattered in front of our car, which we had borrowed from a journalist and which said press on the windshield. The house was an ample two-story affair with a little shop next to it. We got out and asked a girl if Wasiu lived there.

"Yes," she said, "but he is not around."

Akeem went into the yard in front of Wasiu Karimu's house, and a woman jumped in front of him. She said she was Wasiu's mother and began yelling at him to get out of the yard. Akeem retreated to the car, and we stood there in the middle of the road, in the sun. Wasiu Karimu was nowhere to be found, so we decided to wait for him to show up. But after about twenty minutes, several men came around the corner and took up posts around Wasiu's house. A couple of them were holding long sticks.

Akeem turned to me and said, "Local Area Boys."

In Lagos, the Area Boys are thugs—a law unto themselves. They have multiplied since the military dictatorship fell in 1998, seeding a new kind of terror throughout the city. These young men had an ugly swagger, and they looked as if they had run to get there. I could see sweat start to drip down Akeem's head.

"Let us go," he said.

"Wait a minute," I said. We had come a long way—in fact, I had come all the way from America for this and did not know how many chances I would get to speak to someone whose penis had actually been stolen. So I made us wait. I don't know why. I suppose I figured we weren't doing any harm. I only wanted to ask a few questions. I walked to the shop next to Wasiu Karimu's house and bought something to drink.

The young girl at the shop said, "Sir, are you looking for someone?"

"Yes," I said. "Wasiu Karimu."

"Sir," she said, "maybe you should just go now, before there are problems. It will be easier for everyone."

I walked back to the car. "Okay," I said to Akeem. Now I had a sick feeling. My own back was drenched with sweat. "Let's go."

Akeem shook his head and looked down the road. It had been cut off with two large wooden blocks and a car. There was no way out.

One of the local Area Boys looked particularly eager to deliver some punishment. He ran into the street with his cane and whacked it on the ground. "We will *beat* the press," he yelled. "We will *beat* the press."

The young men huddled together in front of Wasiu Karimu's house. After a long delay, they called Akeem over. He talked to them for a little bit. Then they called me over. They wanted to see the article about Wasiu. I pulled the wrinkled photocopy out of my pocket and handed it over.

A quiet man in a 50 Cent T-shirt was clearly the leader. He took the article, unfolded it, and read through it.

"Let us see your I.D.," he said. I hadn't brought my passport, for exactly this reason, and my driver's license had disappeared from my hotel room. All I had with me was an expired YMCA membership card, which I handed over.

The leader, whose name was Ade, took it and turned it over. He handed it to a lanky man with crooked teeth, who looked at it briefly, then handed it back.

"Do you know who we are?" asked Ade.

I did not.

"We are O.P.C. You know O.P.C.?"

The O.P.C. was the O'odua People's Congress, a quasi-political organization that was halfway between the Area Boys and a militia. They were violent and arbitrary. Recently, they had killed several policemen in Lagos, and in some parts of the city they were being hunted by the government.

"We have to make sure," Ade said, "you are not coming here to do some harm. Maybe you were sent here by that woman." The woman, he meant, who stole Wasiu Karimu's penis.

There was a crash, as a glass bottle exploded against one of the tires on our car. Both Akeem and I jumped.

"No," I said trying to be calm. "I just want to ask some questions. Is he around?"

"He is not around."

They talked among themselves in Yoruba, then Ade's henchman with the bad teeth told the story. Unbeknownst to me at the time, Wasiu Karimu himself was apparently there, listening from a distance. Akeem told me later he was sure he had seen him—a little guy standing at the back, young and nervous.

Wasiu, Bad Teeth told me, had gotten on the bus and sat down next to this woman. He didn't have a watch, so he asked her what time it was. She didn't know. Then the conductor came around and asked her for her fare. She didn't have that either. As she stood up to get out of the bus, she bumped into Wasiu.

"Then," he said, "Wasiu Karimu felt something happen in his body. Something not right. And he checked and his thing was gone."

"Was it gone," I asked, "or was it shrinking?"

"Shrinking! Shrinking! It was getting smaller."

And as he felt his penis shrink, Wasiu Karimu screamed and demanded the woman put his penis back. The conductor told them both to get off the bus, and a crowd closed in on the accused, not doubting for an instant that the woman could do such a thing. But as soon as she saw trouble coming, Bad Teeth said, she replaced Wasiu's manhood, so when the police took him down to the station, they thought he was lying and arrested him instead.

"What did she want the penis for?" I asked Bad Teeth.

"For *juju*," he said, "or maybe to make some money."

Behind us, from the corner of my eye, I could see that the roadblocks had been removed.

"Do you have anything else you want to ask?"

"No," I said. "I don't think so."

"Okay," he said. "You are free to go."

"Thank you."

I nodded to Akeem. We got in the car and drove away.

T he debate over the term "culture-bound syndrome" seems to have simmered down as our understanding of "culture" has evolved. These days the terms "culture-bound" and, more often, "culture-related" have been grudgingly accepted; after all, how is Western medicine supposed to categorize such ailments as *hikikomori*, in which Japanese children refuse to leave their rooms for years on end, or *dhat*, in which Indians and Sri Lankans become ill with anxiety over semen loss, or *zar*, in which some Middle Easterners and North Africans are possessed by a spirit, or *hwa-byung*, the "fire illness" of Korean women in which anger is said to be manifesting itself in physical symptoms including "palpitations" and "a feeling of mass in the epigastrium"? How can we fit these, and a dozen other ailments, neatly into the pages of the *DSM-IV*, the *Diagnostic and Statistical Manual of Mental Disorders*, the Western bible of maladies of the mind? The fact is that there was no good place until Pow Meng Yap created one—ill-fitting as it may be—for these unruly members of the family of mental conditions whose causes cannot be found just in one mind but instead must be sought in the social. These conditions are not purely psychogenic, as psychiatry's universalists once held all things must be. They are also sociogenic, or emerging from the social fabric.

This debate has mirrored a larger debate that took place in the twentieth century over whether culture was something pure, something existing independently of the people who lived in it—something with an almost supernatural ability to shape those people into fundamentally different beings—or merely accumulated wisdom, the chance collection of the behavior of a group of individuals. Was culture a quasi-independent superorganism that shaped people? Or was it just a collection of human organisms? Did it produce us, or did we produce it?

Lately, a more nuanced conception of culture has emerged, as evolutionary psychology begins to shed some light on what exactly culture is. It is neither nature nor nurture. It is both at the same time, a positive feedback loop of tendencies and behaviors and knowledge and beliefs. It is, as the science writer Matt Ridley has called it, nature via nurture, or as primatologist Frans de Waal put it in his book *The Ape and the Sushi Master,* "an extremely powerful modifier—affecting everything we do and are, penetrating to the core of human existence."

In 1998, Charles Hughes, co-editor of *Culture-Bound Syndromes: Folk Illnesses of Psychiatric and Anthropological Interest,* one of the few books on the phenomenon, wrote a scathing critique of the *DSM-IV*'s treatment of culture-bound syndromes, which had been gathered together in the back of the book in an appendix as if they were still under glass, a museum of exotica where nothing had changed since these ills were considered "ethnic psychoses" that affected primitive people but not us. Hughes argued that the borders around culture-bound syndromes are inherently fuzzy and that to rope them off at the back of the *DSM-IV* is a farce. He lamented the lack of a "short course in sophisticated cultural awareness" for psychiatrists and said that "[t]o use the class-designated term 'culture-bound [psychiatric] syndromes' is comparable to using the terms 'culture-bound religion,' 'culture-bound language,' or 'culture-bound technology,' for each of these institutional areas is shaped by, and in its specific details is unique to, its cultural setting."

In other words, everything else in the *DSM-IV,* and in life, is culture-bound, too. While *koro* and its culture-bound kin languish at the back, other conditions such as multiple personality disorder, bulimia nervosa, type A personality, muscle dysmorphia, belief in government-implanted computer chips, and pet hoarding are given universal status because Western psychiatrists cannot see beyond their own cultural horizons.

S tarrys Obazi sat across the table from me at Mr. Bigg's, a cheap fast-food place on the north side of Lagos where we had agreed to meet. Around us, other Nigerians walked past with their trays and sat down to eat their burgers and watch rap videos on the television behind us. Starrys dug into his chicken. A wiry little man with a nasal voice, he had been an editor for fourteen years at *FAME,* a Nigerian celebrity tabloid, until the publisher mysteriously stopped paying him. Jobs, even low-paying editorial jobs, were tough to come by in Lagos, and it had been several years since Starrys had held one.

Here, in the flesh, finally, was a man whose penis had been stolen. It happened one day in 1990, when Starrys was a reporter at the *Evening Times.* While he was waiting for a bus to take him to work, a man approached him and held out a piece of paper with a street name on it.

"Do you know where this is?" the man asked, without saying the name. Starrys did not know the street, and he thought this was strange. He didn't believe the street existed. Then another man behind Starrys, without seeing the paper, said where the street was. This was even stranger.

The two men walked away, and Starrys started to feel something he had never felt before.

"At that moment," Starrys told me, leaning forward, "I felt something depart my body. I began to feel empty inside. I put my hand into my pants, and touched my thing. It was unusually small—smaller than the normal size. And the scrotum was flat. I put my fingers into the sockets, and they were not there. The testes were gone. And I was just feeling empty!" His voice strained as he recalled the panic of that day.

Starrys ran after the men and confronted them. "Something happened to my penis!" he told the man who had asked for directions. The man said he had no idea what Starrys was talking about.

"Something told me inside not to shout," he said. "Because as soon as I shouted, he would have been lynched. And if he was lynched, how could I get my penis back?"

I watched as Starrys finished his chicken and wiped his hands. "*It was one quarter of its normal size,*" he said emphatically, as if, even now, even he could not believe it had happened. But Starrys, a journalist and a worldly man, did believe it. And as I listened to him tell his story, I almost believed it, too. I could feel the intensity, the fear. It made a kind of sense, even if it didn't make sense at all. I could start to see the world that his fear came from. I could see what it was built on, and for a few minutes I could imagine standing there with Starrys on a street corner, alone in the world, helpless and missing my most cherished possession. I let go of my doubts and gave in to the panic in Starrys's voice, and it was real, utterly. And I was afraid. This was how *koro* could be caught.

Starrys continued with his story. Despite the men's denials, one of them agreed to accompany Starrys to a nearby hospital to document the theft. But just as they arrived at the hospital, the man grabbed Starrys and bellowed, "LET'S GO IIIIN!" And at that moment something happened.

"When he grabbed me," Starrys said, "I felt calm again. I felt an inner calm. I checked my testes, and they were there." He checked his penis as well, and the missing three quarters had returned. The doctor examined Starrys and pronounced him fine. On hearing Starrys's story, though, the doctor admonished the penis thief to quit causing trouble on the street.

I thought about Starrys. He had been a skeptic before his encounter; but on that day, his inner world shifted, and he became afraid. He stopped giving directions. He stopped trusting strangers. He *knew* that magical penis loss was a real and terrifying possibility. He had, in a sense, been drawn into the culture, into its beliefs, so far that he had caught this culture-bound syndrome.

We all go through a similar process of being formed by the culture around us. It is something described well in Bruce Wexler's book *Brain and Culture: Neuroscience, Ideology and Social Change,* in which Wexler argues that much of human conflict arises from our efforts to reconcile the world as we believe it to exist (our internal structures) with the world we live in. According to Wexler, we develop an inner world, a neuropsychological framework of values, cause and effect, expectations, and a general understanding of how things work. This inner world, which underpins our culture, forms through early adulthood, after which we strive to ensure it exists, or continues to exist, in the world outside. Those inner structures can change in adulthood, but it is more difficult given our decreased brain plasticity.

That different internal structures exert different pressures on the mind (and body) should not be surprising. Every culture has its own logic, its own beliefs, its own stresses. Once one buys into its assumptions, one becomes a prisoner to the logic. For some people, that means a march toward its more tragic conclusions.

Not long ago, medical researchers noticed a strange phenomenon: Turks in Germany, Vietnamese in England, and Mexicans in America all registered better health than native residents. This phenomenon has come to be called the "healthy migrant effect." Although most of the research has focused on physical indicators (cancer, heart disease, diabetes, etc.), recent studies have started to look at the mental health of immigrants, which seems to show a similar pattern. In 2000, one study concluded that first-generation Mexican immigrants have better mental health than their children born in the United States, despite the latter group's significant socioeconomic advantages—a finding, it noted, that was "inconsistent with traditional tenets on the relationship among immigration, acculturation, and psychopathology." The stress of immigration is assumed to have major mental-health costs, but here the opposite seemed to be true: the longer immigrants remained in a developed country, the worse their mental health became.

For this reason, the healthy-migrant effect is also called the "acculturation paradox": the more acculturated one is, the less healthy one becomes. One study of Turkish immigrants to Germany showed the effect to last for at least a generation. A subsequent 2004 study of Mexican immigrants to the United States showed that "[w]ith few exceptions, foreign-born Mexican Americans and foreign-born non-Hispanic whites were at significantly lower risk of *DSM-IV* substance-use and mood-anxiety disorders compared with their US-born counterparts." These included alcohol and drug abuse, major depression, dysthymia, mania, hypomania, panic disorder, social and specific phobia, and generalized anxiety disorder. The longer they lived in the United States, the more they showed the particular damage to the mind that our particular culture wreaks. People who come to America eventually find themselves subject to our own culture-related syndromes, which the *DSM-IV* can easily recognize and categorize, as acculturation forces their internal worlds to conform to the external world, i.e., the American culture that the *DSM-IV* knows best.

I could feel something similar happening to me in Nigeria. I could feel plates shifting. I did not try to hold them back. As I listened to the tales of friends of friends, as I read the horror stories in newspapers, as I watched the angry crowds on television, as I saw the fear and hatred in the eyes of the young O.P.C. men, and as I sat across from Starrys Obazi and heard the panic in his voice, I could feel my own mind opening to this world where such things were possible. I could see the logic. I could feel the edge of belief. Something was starting to make sense. Now and then I would catch myself feeling strangely vulnerable between my legs.

I was almost there, and it was time to see if I could get in just a little further.

The winding streets of Lagos were packed with people. Tens of thousands, coming and going, moving along sidewalks, jamming the streets so thickly that cars had to push through them at a crawl, blaring their horns and parting crowds like a snowplow.

I was far from Jankara Market when I started out and headed southwest toward Idumota, to walk through some of the most crowded streets in the world, where I hoped to brush up against the boundary of this culture. I wanted to look back and see someone checking if his manhood was still in place.

I climbed some stairs near a bank and stopped to watch the city flow by. I walked back down the stairs and jumped into the onrush. I moved with it. Together we were packed tightly, but we rarely touched. The winding streams of people ran easily along, next to one another. I moved farther into the city, and as I did, I watched the people pass within inches of me, then feint, slip by, barely brushing me. At first I tried to nudge a few people with my shoulder, but most were too fast, too alert, too leery.

Walking along, I caught one man on the shoulder with mine. But when I looked back, it seemed like he hadn't even noticed.

Then I clipped another man a little harder, but when I looked back, it was like I wasn't even there. I bumped a few more people lightly, until finally I caught one man enough that I'm sure he knew it was purposeful.

But the magic failed. He didn't reach down and grab himself, didn't point to me, didn't accuse. He didn't even give me a dirty look. I was swimming in the water, but I could not get all the way in, no matter how deep I dove. And so I let go, walked on, and allowed the current to carry me wherever it would.

FRANK BURES writes frequently about Africa. He lives in Madison, Wisconsin.

Afterbirths in the Afterlife
Cultural Meaning of Placental Disposal in a Hmong American Community

Interviews were conducted with 94 Hmong Americans in California's Central Valley to explore attitudes regarding placental disposition and the cultural values that affect those attitudes. Research indicated a persistence of the traditional belief that placentas should be buried at home. The placenta is perceived to be essential for travel by the soul of the deceased into the spirit world to rejoin ancestors. Older respondents (older than age 35) and those who self-identified as animists were most likely to believe in the importance of home placental burial. Comments by respondents indicated some reluctance on the part of Hmong patients to ask health care providers for permission to take placentas home. Incorporating non-Western patients' traditional health care practices into Western health care delivery may be facilitated by an awareness of the reluctance of some patients to verbalize their wishes.

DEBORAH G. HELSEL, PHD, RN AND MARILYN MOCHEL, RN

The Hmong people were part of the second wave of Southeast Asian refugees who fled to the United States in the wake of the Vietnam War. Whereas the first wave was composed of the more educated, affluent, and Westernized urban Vietnamese, the second wave, which included the Lao Hmong, arrived with far fewer material and vocational resources. Before the war came and forever changed their lives and culture, the Hmong were a preliterate, agrarian, animistic people living in a "cultural deep-freeze" behind a mountainous barrier in the highlands of Southeast Asia as swidden farmers, using slash-and-burn techniques (Garrett, 1974, p. 82). Hmong birth rates in Southeast Asia were quite high (Kunstadter, 1983). Babies were born at home without birth attendants other than the husband. Shortly after the delivery, the new father buried his child's placenta in the family's home, ensuring that the child's soul would eventually be able to rejoin ancestors in the spirit world (Fadiman, 1997).

Hmong alliance with pro-Western forces ultimately meant communist retribution and subsequent forced emigration from their homeland following the war. Although initially resettled throughout the nation, the Hmong secondarily migrated in large numbers into California's Central Valley for family reunification, farmland, and the availability of generous and accessible state-run assistance programs (Strand & Jones, 1985; Viviano, 1986). California soon became home to more than half of all U.S. Hmong, and more than two thirds of the Hmong people in California settled in the Central Valley, clustered in Fresno and Merced Counties (Olney, 1986;

Strand & Jones, 1985). Recently, there have been a growing number of Hmong Americans emigrating from California to other areas of the country, including Minnesota, Wisconsin, and North Carolina, in search of jobs, but California remains home to more Hmong than any other state (Clemings, 2001; Saechao, 2001).

Hmong Americans have faced many challenges, conflicts, and misunderstandings as they struggle to adjust to life in the United States. Many of these clashes concerned health care. Specifically, traditional Hmong practices and beliefs, coupled with high fertility rates, have produced frustrations within both the Hmong American community and the U.S. health care community in finding ways to provide culturally appropriate reproductive health care (Helsel, Petitti, & Kunstadter, 1992; Rumbaut & Weeks, 1986). Virtually every aspect of reproductive health, from contraceptive methods and child spacing to prenatal care and route of delivery, has produced conflict and noncompliance; the Hmong solution often has been to employ a union of Western health care, animistic ceremonies, and herbal remedies (McMahon, 1988; Moua, 1991). Although some of the misunderstandings and conflicts may have been ameliorated with two decades of Hmong residence in the United States as well as the presence of a generation of Hmong Americans born and/or socialized here, other issues remain unresolved.

The purpose of this research was to explore Hmong Americans' attitudes regarding placental disposition, the cultural values that affect those attitudes, and perceptions of the willingness of Western health care providers to accommodate Hmong patients' wishes regarding placental disposal. Attitude is generally understood to convey the subjective impressions, perspectives, or the inner state of actors (Geertz, 1973). Traditional Hmong attitudes and the associated cultural values regarding the placenta appeared to be at odds with the Western health care providers' concept of the placenta as medical waste. As Birdsong (1998) noted, "the human placenta has little cultural value in contemporary western biomedicine" (p. 190), which has generally discarded it immediately after childbirth. By contrast, the Hmong believe that the placenta is the infant's first "clothing"; the soul of the deceased must return to the place his or her placenta was buried to retrieve this afterlife "garment." Only by wearing his or her placental "jacket" can the soul find safe passage to the spirit world and be reunited with ancestors. If the spirit of the deceased cannot find his or her placenta, he or she will spend eternity wandering (Fadiman, 1997).

Methods
Population and Sample
Data were collected at a multicultural health community center in Merced County, California. The center provides services and programs designed to improve access to culturally sensitive health care and provide health education and support services to an ethnically diverse county population that includes Lao Hmong. The center is also the site of several social and cultural programs for the Hmong, including after-school tutoring programs, Hmong music and dance lessons, and women's group meetings.

At three separate cultural events held at the community center in the fall of 1999, every adult and adolescent attendee (a total of 105) was approached and asked to participate in this research. The content and purpose of the research was explained to each potential respondent. Anonymity and confidentiality were assured; respondents were not asked to give their names. Of those asked, 94 (89.5%) agreed to participate.

Data Collection and Instrument
Interviews were conducted by four bilingual Hmong employees of the community center in either Hmong or English according to the request of the respondent. Interviewers were trained by the authors in the interview process and participated in the design of the instrument. Each question on the instrument was translated by each of the interviewers and translations were compared to ensure validity. English instruments were used for all subjects and the interviewer interpreted and translated into Hmong.

A descriptive design, integrating both quantitative and qualitative analytic techniques, was used for this study. Information gathered included the sex, age, religion, and length of residence in United States; respondents were then asked a brief series of questions on their beliefs about placentas! Do you believe in burying the placenta? Do you believe burying the placenta is a good thing to do for the soul? And do you believe that if the placenta is not buried this will cause problems for the soul? Finally, respondents were questioned about past experiences with placental disposition. The instrument concluded with an open-ended question in which respondents were asked to comment on their beliefs, observations, or concerns regarding placental disposition.

Data Analysis
Using SPSS, quantitative analysis consisted of descriptive and inferential statistics, including chi square. Qualitative analysis in the form of grounded theory was utilized to analyze response to open-ended questions. Grounded theory enables an understanding of the perceptions of the respondents themselves through a careful analysis of the concepts and categories that emerge from the interview text (Strauss & Corbin, 1990).

Results
The group of respondents consisted of slightly more women (51.1%) than men (45.7%). About half the group was 35 years or younger (53.2%) and half was 36 and older (46.8%); 74% had been in the country for at least 10 years and 43.6% had been here 16 years or more. Of the respondents, 73.4% self-described as animist, whereas 10.6% reported that they were Christian. A few described themselves as "believing in shamans" or as being both animist and Christian.

The most significant predictors of belief in placental burying were age ($p = .001$) and religion ($p = .001$). In the 36 to 50 age group, 93.8% reported that they "believed in burying the placenta at home," as did 92.9% of the 51 to 65 age group and 100% of those older than 65. This relationship between age and traditional belief in placental disposition was confirmed by answers to a later question, "Do you believe that not burying the placenta will cause problems for the soul?" ($p = .014$); 86.7% of those age 36 to 50, 87.5% of those age 51 to 65, and 88.9% of those older than 65 answered affirmatively. Whereas 72.7% of those in the younger than age 20 group and 48% of those in the 20 to 35 age group reported that they believed in burying the placenta at home, only 37.5% of those younger than 20 and 56% of those age 20 to 35 believed it would cause problems for the soul if it was not buried. These results are summarized in Table 1.

Religion also was significant; 87.5% of those who self-described as "animist" reported that they believed in burying the placenta. Again, these results were confirmed by a subsequent question, "Do you believe that burying the placenta is a good thing to do for the soul?" ($p = .000$); 91.2% of the "animists" and 66.6% of the "Christians" answered affirmatively. These results are summarized in Table 2. Neither gender nor length of residence in United States proved to be significant predictors of belief in placental burying.

Table 1 Effect of Age on Belief in Placental Burying

| Age | Belief in Burying Placenta | | |
	Yes	No	Total
Younger than 20	8 (72.7)	3 (27.3)	11
20–35	12 (48)	13 (52)	25
36–50	15 (93.8)	1 (6.3)	16
51–65	13 (92.9)	1 (7.1)	14
66 and older	9 (100)	0 (0)	9
Missing/don't know/declined			19

Pearson chi-square	
Value	18.597
df	4
p	.001

Note. Numbers in parentheses are percentages.

Table 2 Effect of Religion on Belief in Placental Burial

| Religion | Belief in Burying Placenta | | |
	Yes	No	Total
Animist	49 (87.5)	7 (12.5)	56
Christian	5 (71.4)	2 (28.6)	7
Buddhist	0 (0)	2 (100)	2
Other	5 (45.5)	6 (54.5)	11
Animist and Christian	0 (0)	1 (100)	1
Missing/don't know/declined			17

Pearson chi-square	
Value	19.603
df	4
p	.001

Note. Numbers in parentheses are percentages.

Of the 42 respondents, 38 (90%) who had babies born at home in Southeast Asia reported that they had buried their placentas. Of the 77 respondents who reported experience with U.S. hospital births (personal or familial), only 11 (11.7%) "asked a doctor or nurse for the placenta." Of that number, 5 were given the placenta. One of the 5 who were allowed to take the placenta home reported that she had some convincing to do; when questioned as to why she wanted the placenta, she explained that "I had seven girls; I wanted a son." Another female respondent reported she was offered the placenta but that she had declined to take it home since "there wasn't any place to bury it." She did, however, tell the doctor to "tie a knot in the placenta [cord] so she could have a boy next time."

Respondents evidenced an obvious reluctance to ask for permission to take their placentas home. Comments included, "I knew the doctor would never give it to me"; "We knew that many people have asked and could not get it so we did not even

ask"; and "The doctor will not let us because he does not understand our religion." A few respondents expressed their wishes that their beliefs about the need for placental burying could be accommodated. One noted, "The hospital should allow us to take our placentas home. How will [our children's] souls know where to go otherwise?" Another said, "Young people born in this country may have many more problems when they die, I think." Several described other, less spiritual reasons for taking home their placentas: dried placentas of first-born sons have medicinal value; if placentas are buried level, babies will not spit up; if one ties a knot in the cord of a girl's placenta before burial, the next child will be a son.

Several who had been denied the opportunity to bury their infants' placentas suggested a possible remedy: The aid of a shaman could be enlisted to help find the placentas of their U.S.-born children in the spirit world.

Some of the youngest (younger than 20 years old) respondents noted that they had been unaware of the custom of or reasons for placental burial but expressed a desire to follow Hmong tradition when they had children of their own; one young woman noted, "I believe that if your family believes the placenta should be buried then you should have it buried; I believe strongly in the Hmong culture."

Discussion

Many cultures, ancient and modern, have rituals and beliefs surrounding placental disposal (Davidson, 1985). Birdsong (1998) suggests that "in all cultures, pregnancy is an anxiety-provoking event" (p. 180). That anxiety, however, resolves at different times: with the safe delivery of the infant in most Western cultures but not until after the proper disposal of the placenta in many non-Western cultures such as the Hmong. Not only does proper placental burial mark the end of the risky process of childbirth but such rituals also allow a "sense of control or mastery" over a frightening time of liminality, a sort of in-between time of transition from one state of being to another (unborn-to-human; pregnant woman-to-mother) (Birdsong, 1998, p. 190). Placental rituals become "anxiety-releasing mechanisms that provide a means of control over the future health and welfare of child, mother and community" (Davidson, 1985, p. 75).

The location in which placentas are traditionally buried also reveals much about anticipated gender roles within the Hmong community. Placentas must be buried at one's home in specific locations. Boys' placentas are buried near the center post of the house (a place of honor) because sons will remain with the family (even after he marries, he will bring his wife home to live with his family), whereas girls' placentas will be buried near a door or her parents' bed because girls will, inevitably, leave their birth families when they marry (Birdsong, 1998; Fadiman, 1997).

This research indicates the persistence of traditional Hmong beliefs about placental burying. This appears to support Yinger's (1981) theory of assimilation. He suggested that acculturation does not necessarily imply the shedding of one's traditional culture and subsequent replacement with the cultures of one's new homeland but that "acculturation is additive as well as substitutive". He described a process whereby the acculturating individual adds elements, including religious elements, to his or her existent cultural repertoire instead of merely replacing the old with the new. Assimilation proceeds to greater and lesser extent depending on the ethnic group as well as the individual. Yinger indicates that the persistence of traditional cultural elements even as new cultural elements are added can "reduce anomiec and the sense of alienation . . . in a complex and confusing world".

Certainly, the Hmong have made a quantum leap in time and place within the last two decades. The persistence of age-old beliefs and practices may lend cohesion to a community in transition. Although it could be argued that because they were attending social functions specifically for Hmong families at the community center, the group of respondents we interviewed were somewhat more likely to be traditionally Hmong in their beliefs. It appeared that despite the fact that most of the Hmong with whom we spoke had lived in the United States for at least a decade, traditional Hmong beliefs in placental burying clearly persisted. This was particularly evident in the older members of this community and those who self-described as "animist," but these beliefs also are apparently being transmitted across generations. As Hmong American youngsters experience the birth of siblings to their families and as they approach childbearing age themselves, they may be instructed by older family members on the meaning of placental burial. Those in the 20- to 35-year-old group of respondents seem torn between what they feel they must accept in practice and what they believe may result from those practices, noting the hope that certain shamanic ceremonies could remedy the consequences for their infants' souls of not burying their placentas. Some responses implied that given the constraints of urban living, there is simply nowhere for them to bury placentas even if they were allowed to take them home.

The assumption that the placenta is medical waste and should be treated as such may be culturally inappropriate for some groups of patients, including the Hmong. *The California State Department of Health Services Revision of Policy Regarding Treatment of Waste Placentas* (1997) has made provisions for religious, ethnic, or cultural exemptions to the policy of managing placentas as medical waste (treated by incineration), stating, "when, by virtue of the fact that a placenta has intrinsic value to a patient, it is not a waste, it therefore in those cases cannot be classified as medical waste" (p. 2). As a result of cultural beliefs, the placenta is not considered to be medical waste and it need not be treated as such.

Reluctance by health care providers to allow patients to take their placentas home may not, of course, be entirely based on legal or public health concerns. Fadiman (1997)

has noted that some health care personnel may simply find the idea distasteful. Implications for future research include an exploration of health care providers' beliefs and attitudes on traditional Hmong placental disposal requests. This may facilitate incorporating and accommodating those beliefs into health care practices. Awareness by health care providers of patients' beliefs coupled with an awareness that they may be reluctant to verbalize their wishes is essential in view of our increasingly diverse patient population. Asking Hmong American patients, for example, if they would prefer to take their placentas home could not only serve to accommodate placental disposal preferences but also could help to assure the patients and their families that their health care providers are committed to cultural competency in patient care.

References

Birdsong, W. (1998). The placenta and cultural values. *Western Journal of Medicine, 168*(3), 190–193.

California State Department of Health Services Revision of Policy Regarding Treatment of Waste Placentas. (1997). Sacramento, CA: Health and Welfare Agency.

Clemings, R. (2001, September 10). Fresno's Hmong leave for new lives. *Fresno Bee,* pp. A1, A12.

Davidson, J. (1985). The shadow of life: Psychosocial explanations for placenta rituals. *Culture, Medicine and Psychiatry, 9*(1), 75–92.

Fadiman, A. (1997). *The spirit catches you and you fall down: A Hmong child, her American doctors, and the collision of two cultures.* New York: Farrar, Straus, and Giroux.

Garrett, W. (1974). No place to run. *National Geographic, 145*(1), 77–112.

Geertz, C. (1973). *The interpretation of cultures.* New York: Basic Books.

Helsel, D., Petird, D., & Kunstadter, P. (1992). Pregnancy among the Hmong: Birthweight, age and parity. *American Journal of Public Health, 82*(10), 1361–1364.

Kunstadter, P. (1983). Highland populations in northern Thailand. In J. McKinnon & W. Bhruksassi (Eds.), *Highlanders of Thailand* (pp. 15–45). Kuala Lumpur, Malaysia: Oxford University Press.

McMahon, J. (1988, July 29). Hmong sharman: A blend of religion, medicine. *Merced Sun-Star,* pp. 9–10.

Moun, J. (1991). *Herbal and heating treatments vs. Western medical treatment among Southeast Asian refugee communities in the United States.* Unpublished manuscript. California State University, Stanislans, Sociology Department, Turlock, California.

Olney, D. (1986). Population trends. In G. Hendricks, B. Downing, & A. Deinard (Eds.), *The Hmong in transition* (pp. 179–184). New York: Center for Migration Studies.

Rumbaut, R., & Weeks, J. (1986). Fertility and adaptation: Indo-Chinese refugees in the United States. *International Migration Review, 20*(2), 428–461.

Saechao, P. (2001, December 15). Hmong exodus seen in Merced. *Merced Sun-Star,* pp. A1, A8.

Strand, P., & Jones, W. (1985). *Indo-Chinese refugees in America: Problems of adaptation and assimilation.* Durham, NC: Duke University Press.

Strauss, A., & Corbin, J. (1990). *Basics of qualitative research.* Newbury Park, CA: Sage.

Viviano, P. (1986, August 31). Strangers in the promised land [Image]. *San Francisco Chronicle,* pp. 15–21, 38.

Yinger, J. (1981). Toward a theory of assimilation and dissimilation. *Ethnic and Racial Studies, 4*(3), 249–264.

DEBORAH G. HELSEL, PhD, RN, is an assistant professor in the Department of Sociology at California State University, Fresno. She received her PhD in medical sociology from the University of California, San Francisco. Her research interests include medical sociology and culture competency in health care. MARILYN MOCHEL, RN, is a program manager and certified diabetes educator at Healthy House and California Health Collaborative. She received her associate of arts degree in nursing from Hartnell Community College at Salinas, California. She presently lives and works in a county with a large proportion of Hmong immigrants.

Gender Is Powerful
The Long Reach of Feminism

NANCY MACLEAN

Of all the movements of the Sixties, those involving gender, enlisted the largest number of participants and produced the deepest transformation in American society. Emboldened by the wider activism of the era, especially the black freedom movement, and spurred by seismic changes in the economy and family life, feminists attracted a growing following after 1966 as they set out to end the reign of gender inequality in American institutions and culture. Within a few years, lesbians and gay men too showed new daring in laying claim to the nation's core promises of freedom and equality. Public debate has since raged between supporters and opponents of these movements over a host of specific issues: the Equal Rights Amendment, abortion, affirmative action, gay school teachers, and more. Yet underlying the specific conflicts were profound alterations in political economy and culture that made gender issues matter as never before to activists on all sides—and to millions of ordinary citizens.

As is common with new social movements, early scholarship on second wave feminism took its cue from journalism and its inspiration from personal experience. Authors of the formative studies of the women's movement such as Jo Freeman and Sara Evans had themselves participated in the struggle, and so had intimate knowledge of their subjects. They showed, in the words of Evans' subtitle, "the roots of women's liberation in the civil rights movement and the New Left." Evans, in particular, focused on young women activists' recognition that "the personal is political" and showed how they used consciousness-raising discussion sessions to deepen understanding of the social roots of seemingly personal problems and develop innovative practices to address them, such as rape crisis centers[1]. Yet, rich as these works were, closeness to the events led to greater interest in immediate concerns than in the deep structure of change.

Most textbooks today follow early participants and journalists in taking a short view of the movement. The texts lead students to think that organizing for gender equality stopped after women won the vote in 1920 and suddenly "reawakened," the oft-used word, in the 1960s. Certainly there is some truth to this view: in the late Sixties, the ranks of women activists surged, their supporters multiplied many times over, and the pace of reform accelerated. Within just a few years, women won protection from employment discrimination, inclusion in affirmative action, abortion law

reform, greater representation in media, equal access to athletics, congressional passage of an Equal Rights Amendment, and much more[2]. Yet students are ill-served by the notion that such a powerful force came out of nowhere, or even that its main cause was the youthled movements of the "Sixties."

Forty years have passed since some activists coined the phrase "women's liberation" and others formed the National Organization for Women (NOW), In that time a wealth of new scholarship has revealed the far deeper roots of these movements, both in social changes over generations and in political history reaching back to the early twentieth century. What made some kind of change in the gender order feel necessary to so many was, most immediately, the demise of the family wage system: the male breadwinner/female homemaker model that shaped government policy and employer practices, even though it never described the reality of millions of American households. Just as important, however, were profound demographic changes sweeping every industrial society; infant mortality and birth rates declined, life expectancy surged, and women entered the paid labor force in massive numbers. In this context, popular understanding of marriage and the very meaning of life changed: no longer expecting to die soon after their last child left home, women came to want more from men, marriage, education, and themselves. That is why even countries that had no equivalent upheaval in the 1960s nevertheless generated their own variants of feminism as they sought to cope with these massive changes using the tools of the democratic process, above all, new public policies suited to changing family forms and individual life cycles[3].

While one track of recent history reveals how a seemingly new movement accomplished so much so quickly, another provides a deep context for why so many welcomed feminism. The feminist movement, in other words, was not new at all. The ranks of self-described "feminism" dwindled after 1920, to be sure, as the elite, white National Women's Party made that label anathema to women working for wider social justice thanks to its leaders' single-minded quest for an Equal Rights Amendment, a gender-blind approach that threatened hard-won, gender-conscious reforms like protective legislation[4]. But tens of thousands of others continued to try to improve the lives of women between 1920 and 1965 through their work in the labor movement and in such organizations as the National Consumers League, the National Council of Negro Women, and the YWCA[5].

This grassroots base made possible an ambitious organizing effort after World War II, a broad-based left-led coalition called the Congress of American Women. It joined women's equality to peace and wider social reforms, such as full employment, government sponsored child care facilities, and an end to racial segregation. CAW anticipated all of the agenda of second wave feminism save its sexual politics, and had more black women in leadership positions than any other feminist movement in U.S. history[6]. Such broad advocacy was enabled by changes in the infrastructure of American politics that began in the Progressive Era and expanded in the New Deal and war years. Feminism's goals and accomplishments depended on prior national commitment to a federal regulatory state to advance social citizenship, and on the mass membership organizations that ensured continued government commitment to a welfare state in the face of opposition from northern corporate Republicans and southern white supremacist Democrats.

One reason the Rip van Winkle account of feminism seemed plausible for so long was that the postwar Red Scare hurt organizing among women as it did labor and civil rights activism. CAW was a broad coalition, but communist women had played a key role in bringing it together. Under the harsh glare of investigation by the House Un-American Activities Committee and a demand by the attorney general that the organization must register as a "foreign agent," membership plummeted from a claimed high of 250,000 to just 3,000. Gerda Lerner, who later became a pioneer historian of women and president of the OAH, was then a rank-and-file CAW activist, a Jewish refugee from Nazism, and a Communist Party member herself. She burned all her records in terror of what the Right's new power portended. Most other groups doing innovative work for gender equality in 1940s and 1950s were affected in some way, and individual leaders became much more cautious. But many continued working, forming a human bridge between eras more propitious to activism as they labored quietly but steadily in arenas ranging from the American Civil Liberties Union to the United Auto Workers Women's Commission[7].

This existing infrastructure helps explain how feminists were able to make such stunning headway after the formation of NOW and the take off of women's liberation. The wide array of leaders from earlier groups came together in the President's Commission on the Status of Women, which in turn spurred state-level women's commissions that became organizing centers. In 1963, the PCSW issued its major report calling for wide-ranging reform to end sex discrimination. Textbooks thus get it wrong when they credit Betty Friedan's bestselling 1963 book, *The Feminine Mystique,* for the rise of second wave feminism. What the book did, rather, was name what so many women were already feeling and invigorate those already acting. Friedan developed her expert aim, moreover, in the Popular Front of the 1940s as a labor-left journalist. Her book thus built on far more than her experience as a suburban wife and mother[8].

Similarly, some of feminism's greatest policy victories in the 1960s and 1970s came as a result of using tools won by other movements. By far the most important was the employment section of the Civil Rights Act of 1964, Title VII, won by the black freedom movement to end occupational segregation. Women used it not only to enter good jobs of all kinds long closed to them but also to end pregnancy discrimination and fight sexual harassment. Indeed they raised foundational questions about gender and power with reverberations in every area of American life. Title VII also encouraged new coalitions between feminists and labor and civil rights groups of all kinds that expanded the constituency pushing for gender equity. Without a Title VII, NOW and small women's liberation never would have achieved so many successes so quickly, if they achieved them at all[9].

Part of what made feminism so successful is the way that, almost from the outset, women in different situations developed their own variants and organized for the goals most important to them. As historian Nancy Cott wrote of the first wave, "feminism was an impulse that was impossible to translate into a program without centrifugal results"[10]. The trite caricature of a white middle-class movement obscures this far more interesting history. From the beginning, black women inside and outside the movement put forth their own visions of gender justice, often with a particular focus on how the combined impact of racism and sexism hurt black families and harmed men as well as women. Latina feminists soon advanced a critique of *machismo* and of the constraining role of the Catholic Church in their communities. And so it went: Native American women, working-class women in trade unions, Jewish women. Catholic women, sex workers, older women, and women with disabilities all described what gender equality would mean from their vantage points and worked to achieve it[11]. Initial friction notwithstanding, over time these differences enriched the very definition of feminism while enlisting the commitment of a vast spectrum of Americans[12].

Seen in the light of this older and broader story, the lesbian and gay quest for equality seems almost inevitable. It too responded to changes in family life and gender as it emphasized mutual love as the basis for domestic partnership, regardless of the sex of each partner. Like feminism, this movement built on foundations laid during the New Deal and World War II newly accepted ideas about the rights of citizens and the role of government, newly powerful grassroots movements of labor and the left, massive same-sex armed forces, and a new capacity to enforce rights made possible by an expanded administrative state. It was no accident that the first gay rights group, the Mattachine Society, was founded in the wake of World War II by left-wing activists such as Harry Hay, or that it identified gay rights *with* "our fellow minorities . . . the Negro, Mexican, and Jewish Peoples"[13].

The cold war had subdued this organizing, too, as it encouraged a "lavender scare" that cost more government workers their jobs than did the Red Scare itself. The State Department alone boasted in 1950 that it was firing one suspected homosexual a day[14]. But as in the case of women's equality, the social and cultural changes driving this movement were too powerful for repression to succeed over the long term. Thanks to being held back artificially in the 1950s, the gay liberation movement, like the women's movement, exploded with greater force in the 1960s—most dramatically in the four-night-long Stonewall riot in New York City in 1969. And the gay movement too generated a panoply of different organizations, the division of labor among which enabled the movement to work on various fronts—from creating its own media to changing municipal law, medical knowledge, and the practices of police and employers[15].

For movement opponents, however, open homosexuality dramatized the separation of sexuality and reproduction that traditionalists already feared. It also showed how pliable gender was: its very existence implied there was no "natural" way for men or women to behave and so raised unprecedented questions about gender hierarchy and the meaning of family. Further, what would it mean to grant equal rights for lesbians and gay men? That would require acknowledging the legitimacy of rights enforcement for others, too, beginning with blacks, something that conservatives in the North and South had long resisted. In short, on virtually every front that mattered to the right, this new movement seemed a particular challenge[16].

With a focus on the deeper roots and larger stakes of these movements, it is easier to make sense of the phenomenon of mass antifeminism among women. Mobilized in 1972 by the veteran conservative activist Phyllis Schlafly in a group called STOP ERA, female antifeminism proved powerful enough to defeat the Equal Rights Amendment, which had sailed through both houses of Congress in 1972 after the surge of pro-equality activism. In my experience the paradox of women who fought gender equality is a great hook for teaching; it is hard to imagine, for example, African Americans organizing to fight passage the Civil Rights Act. On the face of it, it is so odd that students who yawn at feminism itself sit up to figure this out.

Solving the puzzle of why some women fought against equal treatment for their sex requires looking at how the family wage system and its breakdown drove gender-conscious politics of all kinds. Different groups of women came up with different answers to the decline of the family wage and the deep alterations in marriage and family because they stood in very different relation to these developments. Women who feel that they have benefited from the changes of recent years often become feminists, who try to further dismantle the old male dominated system in the name of equality and fairness. Yet many women who feel they have lost or will lose from the changes have rallied to the old system's defense[17]. Both reactions are understandable in a society that provides less of a social safety net than any other comparably developed nation. In western Europe, by contrast, which has more public policy supports for family well being and a stronger ethic of social solidarity, antifeminism is far weaker and there is no mass-based or influential analogue to America's religious right[18].

Analysis of the deep structure of gender politics also helps to make sense of the prominent place of issues of masculinity, femininity, family, and sexuality in other movements of the era not ostensibly concerned with gender. For example, historians have recently used gender analysis to reveal new dimensions of civil rights and black nationalism, the Chicano youth movement, and the conflict over the war in Vietnam. Their studies reveal how heated gender rhetoric signaled underlying concerns that influenced conduct once beyond the purview of women's history[19].

This call for a new framework based on "the long women's movement" promises both challenges and opportunities for teachers of the U.S. survey[20]. It demands more of teachers, who will have to supply storyline, analysis, and documents that current textbooks do not. Most texts say little or nothing about women's organizing between 1920 and 1966, and almost none mentions the decisive role of the labor movement and broader progressive organizations, not explicitly feminist, in helping to advance women's equality. Taking the long view may also require sacrificing some of the attention-getting drama that dominates journalistic accounts. Time spent on media magnets like the demonstration at the 1969 Atlantic City Miss America Pageant may have to make room for how older women in the 1940s and 1950s worked for measures that would reduce the burden of the "double day" on working women, when few young people were paying attention. Given the widespread concern among today's students about how they will manage to combine employment and family commitments, that seems a fair trade[21].

Indeed, the concept of a long women's movement offers pedagogical benefits that more than offset its start-up costs. Incorporating the best new scholarship, it introduces students to a cast of activists far more diverse than they meet in the worn-out stereotype of a "reawakened" white, middle-class movement based in the Northeast. The actors in these broader struggles look more like today's student bodies in class, race, religion, and region, if not in age, and therefore are more likely to hold their interest. Perhaps the most enticing advantage of "the long women's movement" framework for teachers, however, is that it reinforces earlier lessons by deepening student understanding of the present-day ramifications of the Progressive Era, the New Deal, the cold war, the civil rights movement, and the rise of political conservatism. It offers, that is, an opportunity for the ever-elusive synthesis. Not least, in a time of rapid worldwide economic restructuring and political disorientation, it provides students a better understanding of how momentous democratic change has really come about in the past.

Notes

1. Sara M. Evans, *Personal Politics: The Roots of Women's Liberation in the Civil Rights Movement and the New Left* (New York: Knopf, 1979); Jo Freeman, *The Politics of Women's Liberation: A Case Study of an Emerging Social Movement and Its Relation to the Policy Process* (New York: David McKay, 1975); also Alice Echols, *Daring to Be Bad: Radical Feminism in America, 1967–1975* (Minneapolis: University of Minnesota Press, 1989); Ruth Rosen, *The World Split Open: How the Modern Women's Movement Changed America* (New York: Viking, 2000).

2. For an overview, see Winifred D. Wandersee, *On the Move: American Women in the 1970s* (Boston: Twayne, 1988); Susan M. Hartmann, *From Margin to Mainstream: American Women and Politics since 1960* (New York: Alfred A. Knopf, 1989).

3. Barbara Ehrenreich, *The Hearts of Men: American Dreams and the Flight From Commitment* (New York: Anchor Books, 1983); Nancy MacLean, "Postwar Women's History: From the 'Second Wave' to the End of the Family Wage?" in *A Companion to Post-1945 America,* ed. Roy Rosenzweig and Jean-Christophe Agnew (London: Blackwell, 2002); Stephanie Coontz, *Marriage, a History. From Obedience to Intimacy, or How Lave Conquered Marriage* (New York: Viking, 2005); Estelle Freedman, *No Turning Back: The History of Feminism and the Future of Women* (New York: Ballantine, 2003).

4. Nancy F. Cott, *The Grounding of Modern Feminism* (New Haven: Yale University Press, 1987); Leila Rupp and Verta Taylor, *Survival in the Doldrums: The American Women's Rights Movement, 1945 to the 1960s* (New York: Oxford University Press, 1987).

5. Vicki L. Ruiz, *Cannery Women, Cannery Lives: Mexican Women, Unionization, and the California Food Processing Industry, 1930–1950* (Albuquerque: University of New Mexico, 1987); Nancy F. Gabin, *Feminism in the Labor Movement: Women and the United Auto Workers, 1935–1975* (Ithaca: Cornell University Press, 1990); Deborah Gray White, *Too Heavy a Load: Black Women in Defense of Themselves, 1894–1994* (New York: W. W. Norton, 1998); Landon R.Y. Storrs, *Civilizing Capitalism: The National Consumers' League, Women's Activism, and Labor Standards in the New Deal Era* (Chapel Hill: University of North Carolina Press, 2000); Bruce Fehn, *Striking Women: Gender, Race and Class in the United Packinghouse Workers of America* (Iowa City: University of Iowa Press, 2003); Dorothy Sue Cobble, *The Other Women's Movement: Workplace justice and Social Rights in Modem America* (Princeton: Princeton University Press, 2005), An excellent documentary that makes this case, is *Step by Step: Building a Feminist Movement* (Videocassette, Wisconsin Public Television, 1998; distributed by Women Make Movies).

6. Amy Swerdlow, "The Congress of American Women: Left-Feminist Peace Politics in the Cold War" in *U.S. History as Women's History: New Feminist Essays,* ed. Linda K. Kerber, Alice Kessler-Harris, and Kathryn Kish Sklar (Chapel Hill: University of North Carolina Press, 1995).

7. Gerda Lerner, *Fireweed: A Political Autobiography* (Philadelphia: Temple University Press, 2002); also Landon R.Y. Storrs, "Red Scare Politics and the Suppression of Popular Front Feminism: The Loyalty Investigation of Mary Dublin Keyserling," *Journal of American History* 90 (Sept. 2003): 491–524; Susan Lynn, *Progressive Women in Conservative Times: Racial Justice, Peace, and Feminism, 1945 to the 1960s* (New Brunswick: Rutgers University Press, 1992); Joanne Meyerowitz, *Not June Cleaver. Women and Gender in Postwar America* (Philadelphia: Temple University Press, 1994); Susan M. Hartmann, *The Other Feminists: Activists in the liberal Establishment* (New Haven: Yale University Press, 1998).

8. Cynthia Harrison, *On Account of Sex: The Politics of Women's Issues, 1945–1968* (Berkeley: University of California Press, 1988); Daniel Horowitz, *Betty Friedan and the Making of "The Feminine Mystique": The American Left, the Cold War, and Modern Feminism* (Amherst: University of Massachusetts Press, 1998).

9. Hartmann, *The Other Feminists;* Nancy MacLean, *Freedom Is Not Enough: The Opening of the American Workplace* (Cambridge: Harvard University Press and the Russell Sage Foundation, 2006); also Cobble, *The Other Women's Movement.*

10. Cott, *Grounding of Modem Feminism,* 282.

11. For a sample, see Nancy Seifer, *"Nobody Speaks for Me!": Self-Portraits of American Working Class Women* (New York: Simon and Schuster, 1976); Asian Women United of California, *Making Waves: An Anthology of Writings By and About Asian American Women* (Boston: Beacon Press, 1989); Beverly Guy-Sheftall, ed. *Words on Fire: An Anthology of African-American Feminist Thought* (New York: The New Press, 1995); Alma M. Garcia, *Chicana Feminist Thought: The Basic Historical Writings* (New York: Routledge, 1997).

12. Freedman, *No Turning Back;* Sara M. Evans, *Tidal Wave: How Women Changed America at Century's End* (New York: Free Press, 2003); Benita Roth, *Separate Roads to Feminism: Black, Chicana, and White Feminist Movements in America's Second Wave* (New York: Cambridge University Press, 2004); Kimberly Springer, *Living for the Revolution: Black Feminist Organizations, 1968–1980* (Durham: Duke University Press, 2005).

13. Quote from "Statement of Purpose" in Van Gosse, *The Movements of the New Left, 1950–1975: A Brief History with Documents* (Boston: Bedford Books, 2005), 40; Allan Berube, *Coming out under Fire: The History of Gay Men and Women in World War Two* (New York: Free Press, 1990); Leisa D. Meyer, *Creating GI Jane: Sexuality and Power in the Woman's Army Corps during World War II* (New York: Columbia University Press, 1996); John D' Emilio, *Sexual Politics, Sexual Communities: The Making of a Homosexual Minority in the United States, 1940–1970,* 2nd ed, (Chicago: University of Chicago Press, 1998); Martin Meeker, "Behind the Mask of Respectability: Reconsidering the Mattachine Society and Male Homophile Practice, 1950s and 1960s," *Journal of the History of Sexuality* 10 (Jan. 2001): 78–116.

14. David K. Johnson, *The Lavender Scare: The Cold War Persecution of Gays and Lesbians in the Federal Government* (Chicago: University of Chicago Press, 2004).

15. John D'Emilio, "After Stonewall," in his *Making Trouble: Essays on Gay History, Politics, and the University* (New York: Routledge, 1992), 234–74; *Creating Change: Sexuality, Public Policy, and Civil Rights,* ed. John D'Emilio, William B. Turner, Urvashi Vaid (New York: St. Martin's Press, 2000).

16. On the import of the separation of sexuality and reproduction, see John D'Emilio and Estelle B. Freedman, *Intimate Matters: A History of Sexuality in America* (New York: Harper & Row, 1988): on conservatives and civil rights, see MacLean. *Freedom Is Not Enough,* esp. chaps, 2, 7, and 9.

17. Kristin Luker, *Abortion and the Politics of Motherhood* (Berkeley: University of California Press, 1984); Jane J. Mansbridge, *Why We Lost the ERA* (Chicago: University of Chicago Press, 1986): MacLean, "Postwar Women's History."

18. The best source of up-to-date information is the Institute for Women's Policy Research: <http://wvvw.iwpr.org/>. For U.S. distinctiveness and its roots, see Barry D. Adam, "The Defense of Marriage Act and American Exceptionalism: The 'Gay Marriage' Panic in the United States," *Journal of the History of Sexuality* 12 (April 2003): 259–76, esp. 265–66.

19. Vicki L Crawford, et al, eds., *Women in the Civil Rights Movement: Trailblazers and Torchbearers, 1941–1965* (Bloomington: Indiana University Press, 1990); Scot Brown, *Fighting for US: Maulana Karenga, the US Organization, and Black Cultural Nationalism* (New York: New York University Press, 2003); Ramon A. Cutierrez, "Community, Patriarchy and Individualism: The Politics of Chicano History and the Dream of Equality." *American Quarterly* 45 (March 1993): 44–72; Joshua B. Freeman, "Hardhats: Construction Workers, Manliness, and the 1970 Pro-War Demonstrations," *Journal of Social History* (Summer 1993): 725–44; Robert D. Dean, *Imperial Brotherhood: Gender and the Making of Cold War Foreign Policy* (Amherst: University of Massachusetts Press, 2001): Justin David Suran, "Coming out against the War. Antimilitarism and the Politicization of Homosexuality in the Era of Vietnam," *American Quarterly* 53 (Sept., 2001): 452–488.

20. On "the long civil rights movement," see Jacquelyn Dowd Hall, "The Long Civil Rights Movement and the Political Uses of the Past," *Journal of American History* (March 2005): 1233–63; also *Time Longer than Rope: A Century of African American Activism, 1850–1950,* ed. Charles M. Payne and Adam Green (New York: New York University Press, 2003).

21. For a model from the civil rights movement of how much is gained by changing the vantage point in this way, see Charles Payne, *I've Got the Light of Freedom: The Organizing Tradition and the Mississippi Freedom Struggle* (Berkeley: University of California Press, 1995).

NANCY MACLEAN professor of history and African American studies and chair of the history department at Northwestern University. She is author of *Freedom Is Not Enough: The Opening of the American work place* (Harvard University Press, 2006) and *The Modern Women's Movement: A Brief History with Documents* (Bedford Books, forthcoming , 2007)

From *OAH Magazine of History,* October 2006, pp. 19–23. Copyright © 2006 by Organization of American Historians. Reprinted by permission via the Copyright Clearance Center.

How AIDS Changed America

The plague years: It brought out the worst in us at first, but ultimately it brought out the best, and transformed the nation. The story of a disease that left an indelible mark on our history, our culture and our souls.

DAVID JEFFERSON

Jeanne White-Ginder sits at home, assembling a scrapbook about her son, Ryan. She pastes in newspaper stories about his fight to return to the Indiana middle school that barred him in 1985 for having AIDS. She sorts through photos of Ryan with Elton John, Greg Louganis and others who championed his cause. She organizes mementos from his PBS special, "I Have AIDS: A Teenager's Story." "I just got done with his funeral. Eight pages. That was very hard," says White-Ginder, who buried her 18-year-old son in 1991, seven years after he was diagnosed with the disease, which he contracted through a blood product used to treat hemophiliacs. The scrapbook, along with Ryan's bedroom, the way his mother left it when he died, will be part of an exhibit at the Children's Museum of Indianapolis on three children who changed history: Anne Frank. Ruby Bridges. And Ryan White. "He put a face to the epidemic, so people could care about people with AIDS," his mother says.

At a time when the mere threat of avian flu or SARS can set off a coast-to-coast panic—and prompt the federal government to draw up contingency plans and stockpile medicines—it's hard to imagine that the national response to the emergence of AIDS ranged from indifference to hostility. But that's exactly what happened when gay men in 1981 began dying of a strange array of opportunistic infections. President Ronald Reagan didn't discuss AIDS in a public forum until a press conference four years into the epidemic, by which time more than 12,000 Americans had already died. (He didn't publicly utter the term "AIDS" until 1987.) People with the disease were routinely evicted from their homes, fired from jobs and denied health insurance. Gays were demonized by the extreme right wing: Reagan adviser Pat Buchanan editorialized in 1983, "The poor homosexuals—they have declared war against nature, and now nature is exacting an awful retribution." In much of the rest of the culture, AIDS was simply treated as the punch line to a tasteless joke: "I just heard the Statue of Liberty has AIDS," Bob Hope quipped during the rededication ceremony of the statue in 1986. "Nobody knows if she got it from the mouth of the Hudson or the Staten Island Fairy." Across the river in Manhattan, a generation of young adults was attending more funerals than weddings.

In 1995, Americans regarded HIV/AIDS as the nation's most urgent health problem. Today, only 17% rank it as the top concern.

All poll results are from the Kaiser family foundation's 2006 "Survey of Americans on HIV/AIDS," conducted among 2,517 Americans nationwide.

As AIDS made its death march across the nation, killing more Americans than every conflict from World War II through Iraq, it left an indelible mark on our history and culture. It changed so many things in so many ways, from how the media portray homosexuality to how cancer patients deal with their disease. At the same time, AIDS itself changed, from a disease that killed gay men and drug addicts to a global scourge that has decimated the African continent, cut a large swath through black America and infected almost as many women as men worldwide. The death toll to date: 25 million and counting. Through the crucible of AIDS, America was forced to face its fears and prejudices—fears that denied Ryan White a seat in school for a year and a half, prejudices that had customers boycotting restaurants with gay chefs. "At first, a ton of people said that whoever gets AIDS deserves to have AIDS, deserves to literally suffer all the physical pain that the virus carries with it," says Tom Hanks, who won an Oscar for playing a gay lawyer dying of the disease in 1993's "Philadelphia." "But that didn't hold." Watching a generation of gay men wither and die, the nation came to acknowledge the humanity of a community it had mostly ignored and reviled. "AIDS was the great unifier," says Craig Thompson, executive director of AIDS Project Los Angeles and HIV-positive for 25 years.

Without AIDS, and the activism and consciousness-raising that accompanied it, would gay marriage even be up for debate today? Would we be welcoming "Will & Grace" into our living rooms or weeping over "Brokeback Mountain"? Without red ribbons, first worn in 1991 to promote AIDS awareness, would we be donning rubber yellow bracelets to show our support for cancer research? And without the experience of battling AIDS, would scientists have the strategies and technologies to develop the antiviral drugs we'll need to battle microbial killers yet to emerge?

AIDS, of course, did happen. "Don't you dare tell me there's any good news in this," says Larry Kramer, who has been raging against the disease—and those who let it spread unchecked—since it was first identified in 1981. "We should be having a national day of mourning!" True. But as we try to comprehend the carnage, it's impossible not to acknowledge the displays of strength, compassion and, yes, love, that were a direct result of all that pain and loss. Without AIDS, we wouldn't have the degree of patient activism we see today among people with breast cancer, lymphoma, ALS and other life-threatening diseases. It was Kramer, after all, who organized 10,000 frustrated AIDS patients into ACT UP, a street army chanting "Silence equals death" that marched on the White House and shut down Wall Street, demanding more government funding for research and quicker access to drugs that might save lives. "The only thing that makes people fight is fear. That's what we discovered about AIDS activism," Kramer says.

Fear can mobilize, but it can also paralyze—which is what AIDS did when it first appeared. And no one—not the government, not the media, not the gay community itself—reacted fast enough to head off disaster. In the fiscally and socially conservative climate of Reagan's America, politicians were loath to fund research into a new pathogen that was killing mostly gay men and intravenous drug users. "In the first years of AIDS, I imagine we felt like the folks on the rooftops during Katrina, waiting for help," says Dr. Michael Gottlieb, the Los Angeles immunologist credited as the first doctor to recognize the looming epidemic. When epidemiologist Donald Francis of the federal Centers for Disease Control in Atlanta tried to get $30 million in funding for an AIDS-prevention campaign, "it went up to Washington and they said f—off," says Francis, who quit the CDC soon after, defeated.

"Gay Cancer," as it was referred to at the time, wasn't a story the press wanted to cover—especially since it required a discussion of gay sex. While the media had a field day with Legionnaire's disease, toxic shock syndrome and the Tylenol scare, few outlets paid much attention to the new syndrome, even after scores of people had died. The New York Times ran fewer than a dozen stories about the new killer in 1981 and 1982, almost all of them buried inside the paper. (NEWSWEEK, for that matter, didn't run its first cover story on what "may be the public-health threat of the century" until April 1983.) The Wall Street Journal first reported on the disease only after it had spread to heterosexuals: NEW, OFTEN-FATAL ILLNESS IN HOMOSEXUALS TURNS UP IN WOMEN, HETEROSEXUAL MALES, read the February 1982 headline. Even the gay press missed the story at first: afraid of alarming the community and inflaming antigay forces, editors at the New York Native slapped the headline DISEASE RUMORS LARGELY UNFOUNDED atop the very first press report about the syndrome, which ran May 18, 1981. There were a few notable exceptions, particularly the work of the late Randy Shilts, an openly gay journalist who

convinced his editors at the San Francisco Chronicle to let him cover AIDS as a full-time beat: that reporting led to the landmark 1987 book "And the Band Played On," a detailed account of how the nation's failure to take AIDS seriously allowed the disease to spread exponentially in the early '80s.

Many gay men were slow to recognize the time bomb in their midst, even as people around them were being hospitalized with strange, purplish skin cancers and life-threatening pneumonia. Kramer and his friends tried to raise money for research during the 1981 Labor Day weekend in The Pines, a popular gay vacation spot on New York's Fire Island. "When we opened the collection boxes, we could not believe how truly awful the results were," says Kramer. The total? $769.55. "People thought we were a bunch of creeps with our GIVE TO GAY CANCER signs, raining on the parade of Pines' holiday festivities." The denial in some corners of the gay community would continue for years. Many were reluctant to give up the sexual liberation they believed they'd earned: as late as 1984, the community was bitterly debating whether to close San Francisco's gay bathhouses, where men were having unprotected sex with any number of partners in a single night.

With death a constant companion, the gay community sobered up from the party that was the '70s and rose to meet the unprecedented challenge of AIDS. There was no other choice, really: they had been abandoned by the nation, left to fend for themselves. "It's important to remember that there was a time when people did not want to use the same bathroom as a person with AIDS, when cabdrivers didn't want to pick up patients who had the disease, when hospitals put signs on patients' doors that said WARNING. DO NOT ENTER," recalls Marjorie Hill, executive director of Gay Men's Health Crisis in New York. Organizations like GMHC sprang up around the country to provide HIV patients with everything from medical care to counseling to food and housing. "Out of whole cloth, and without experience, we built a healthcare system that was affordable, effective and humane," says Darrel Cummings, chief of staff of the Los Angeles Gay & Lesbian Center. "I can't believe our community did what it did while so many people were dying." Patients took a hands-on approach to managing their disease, learning the intricacies of T-cell counts and grilling their doctors about treatment options. And they shared what they learned with one another. "There's something that a person with a disease can only get from another person with that disease. It's support and information and inspiration," says Sean Strub, who founded the magazine Poz for HIV-positive readers.

It took a movie star to get the rest of the nation's attention. In the summer of 1985, the world learned that Rock Hudson—the romantic leading man who'd been a symbol of American virility—was not only gay, but had full-blown AIDS. "It was a bombshell event," says Gottlieb, who remembers standing on the helipad at UCLA Medical Center, waiting for his celebrity patient to arrive, as news helicopters circled overhead. "For many Americans, it was their first awareness at all of AIDS. This prominent man had been diagnosed, and the image of him looking as sick as he did really stuck." Six years later, basketball legend Magic Johnson announced he was HIV-positive, and the shock waves were even bigger. A straight, healthy-looking superstar athlete had contracted the "gay" disease. "It can happen to anybody, even me, Magic Johnson," the 32-year-old announced to a stunned nation, as he urged Americans to practice safe sex.

Given the tremendous stigma, most well-known public figures with AIDS tried to keep their condition a secret. Actor Brad Davis, the star of "Midnight Express," kept his diagnosis hidden for six years, until he died in 1991. "He assumed, and I think rightly so, that he wouldn't be able to find work," says his widow, Susan Bluestein, a Hollywood casting director. After Davis died, rumors flew that he must have been secretly gay. "That part of the gossip mill was the most hurtful to me and my daughter," says Bluestein, who acknowledges in her book "After Midnight" that her husband was a drug addict and unfaithful—but not gay.

With the disease afflicting so many of their own, celebrities were quick to lend support and raise money. Elizabeth Taylor was among the first, taking her friend Rock Hudson's hand in public, before the TV cameras and the world, to dispel the notion that AIDS was something you could catch through casual contact. Her gesture seems quaint today, but in 1985—when the tabloids were awash with speculation that Hudson could have infected actress Linda Evans by simply kissing her during a love scene in "Dynasty"—Taylor's gesture was revolutionary. She became the celebrity face of the American Foundation for AIDS Research. "I've lost so many friends," Taylor says. "I have so many friends who are HIV-positive and you just wonder how long it's going to be. And it breaks your heart."

Behind the scenes, Hollywood wasn't nearly as progressive as it likes to appear. John Erman recalls the uphill battle getting the 1985 AIDS drama, "An Early Frost," on TV. "The meetings we had with NBC's Standards and Practices [the network's censors] were absolutely medieval," says Erman. One of the censors' demands: that the boyfriend of the main character be portrayed as "a bad guy" for infecting him: "They did not want to show a positive gay relationship," Erman recalls. Ultimately, with the support of the late NBC Entertainment president Brandon Tartikoff, Erman got to make the picture he wanted—though major advertisers refused to buy commercial time during the broadcast. Within a decade, AIDS had changed the face of television. In 1991, "thirtysomething" featured a gay character who'd contracted the disease. And in 1994, on MTV's "The Real World," 23-year-old Pedro Zamora, who died later that same year, taught a generation of young people what it meant to be HIV-positive.

If TV was slow to deal with AIDS, cinema was downright glacial. "Longtime Companion," the first feature film about the disease, didn't make it to the screen until 1990, nine years into the epidemic. "There was a lot of talk before the movie came out about how this was going to hurt my career, the same way there was talk about Heath Ledger in 'Brokeback Mountain'," says Bruce Davison, who received an Oscar nomination for his role. As for "Philadelphia," Hanks is the first to admit "it was late to the game."

Broadway was the major exception when it came to taking on AIDS as subject matter—in part because so many early casualties came from the world of theater. "I remember in 1982 sitting in a restaurant with seven friends of mine. All were gay men either working or looking to work in the theater, and we were talking about AIDS," recalls Tom Viola, executive director of Broadway Cares/Equity Fights AIDS. "Of those eight guys, four are dead, and two, including myself, are HIV-positive." By the time Tony Kushner's Pulitzer Prize-winning "Angels in America" made its Broadway debut in 1993, some 60 plays about the disease had opened in New York. Producer Jeffrey Seller remembers how he was told he "could never do a show on Broadway that's about, quote unquote, AIDS, homosexuality and drug addiction." He's talking about "Rent," which a decade later still draws capacity crowds.

The world of "Rent" is something of an artifact now. Just before it hit Broadway in 1996, scientists introduced the anti-retroviral drug cocktails that have gone on to extend the lives of millions of patients with HIV. Since then, the urgency that once surrounded the AIDS fight in the United States has ebbed, as HIV has come to be seen as a chronic, rather than fatal, condition. But the drugs aren't a panacea—despite the fact that many people too young to remember the funerals of the '80s think the new medications have made it safe to be unsafe. "Everywhere I go, I'm meeting young people who've just found out they've been infected, many with drug-resistant strains of the virus," says Cleve Jones, who two decades ago decided to start stitching a quilt to honor a friend who had died of AIDS. That quilt grew to become an iconic patchwork of more than 40,000 panels, each one the size of a grave, handmade by loved ones to honor their dead. Ever-expanding, it was displayed several times in Washington, transforming the National Mall into what Jones had always intended: a colorful cemetery that would force the country to acknowledge the toll of AIDS. "If I'd have known 20 years ago that in 2006 I'd be watching a whole new generation facing this tragedy, I don't think I would have had the strength to continue," says Jones, whose own HIV infection has grown resistant to treatment.

Inner strength is what has allowed people living with HIV to persevere. "They think I'm gonna die. You know what, they better not hold their breath," Ryan White once told his mother. Though given six months to live when he was diagnosed with HIV, Ryan lived five and a half years, long enough to prod a nation into joining the fight against AIDS. When he died in 1990 at the age of 18, Congress named a new comprehensive AIDS funding act after him. But the real tribute to Ryan has been the ongoing efforts of his mother. "I think the hostility around the epidemic is still there. And because of religious and moral issues, it's been really hard to educate people about this disease and be explicit," says White-Ginder, who continues to give speeches about watching her son live and die of AIDS. "We should not still be facing this disease." Sadly, we are.

UNIT 2
Biological Foundations

Unit Selections

Key Points to Consider

- How does biology influence your sexuality? In other words, how important is the role that biology plays in determining your experience of desire, pleasure, sexual functioning, reproduction, etc?

- How much do you know about your sexual anatomy and sexual functioning?

- What are the benefits of learning about sexual anatomy and sexual functioning?

- What assumptions do we make about male and female reproductive capacities?

- How important is the quality of the prenatal environment for the developing fetus?

- What happens in the brain when an individual experiences an orgasm?

- Are men and women more similar or dissimilar when it comes to sexual desire?

- What do the predominant models of sexual desire tell us about our assumptions about male and female sexualities?

Student Web Site
www.mhcls.com

Internet References
Ask NOAH About Pregnancy: Fertility & Infertility
   http://www.noah-health.org/en/search/health.html
Childbirth.Org
   http://www.childbirth.org
Planned Parenthood
   http://www.plannedparenthood.org
Infertility Resources
   http://www.ihr.com/infertility/index.html

Whereas *Unit 1* focused on *Social and Cultural Foundations,* this unit explores the biological influences on our sexual development and functioning. As we have learned, knowledge of social and cultural processes that impact sexualities provide us with part of the picture in our attempt to understand sexualities. Another essential part of the picture, explored here in this unit, is biology.

We are biological beings with the capacity for a range of sexual behaviors, as well as for reproduction. Even though most people have the capacity for sexual reproduction, infertility issues are common in today's society. There are far too many aspects of sexual biology that many people simply do not know enough about. Most of us have an incomplete understanding of how our bodies work. This is especially true of our bodily responses and functioning during sexual activity. Efforts to develop a healthy sexual awareness may be severely hindered by misconceptions and the lack of quality information about anatomy and physiology.

Part A of this unit explores *Reproductive Capacities.* This section directs attention to the development of a clearer understanding and appreciation of the workings of biological processes in relation to human reproduction. While human reproduction is as old as humanity, many things are changing in today's society at an amazing pace. New technologies have had a major impact on reproductive capacities. Women in their 60s, and even 70s, have given birth recently. Major news media outlets reported the summer before this book went to press that a 70 year old woman had given birth to twins. Reporters noted that she was old enough to be her children's great grandmother. At the same time, other women struggle with the pain and stress of infertility with few options, if any, available to them. Still others remain "childless by choice."

Lesbian, gay, and transgender people are becoming parents in larger numbers than ever before. Many gay people have had biological children through heterosexual marriages, before "coming out." Some gay men and lesbians opt for pregnancy through artificial insemination, co-parenting as friends or as (nonsexual) gay family units. Lesbians can opt to have biological children using known or anonymous sperm donors. Gay men are increasingly having biological children through traditional or gestational surrogates. Recently, a transgender man was able to give birth to a biological child because he had chosen to keep his uterus. Lesbian, gay, and transgender people adopt children through private adoption agencies, some specializing in gay families, as well as from public agencies through the foster care system. Choices abound, and the world is getting more and more diverse.

New technologies and reproductive options have affected "the how" of reproduction, but personal, social, and cultural forces have also affected "the who," "the when," and the "when not." Unplanned pregnancies and parenthood in the United States and worldwide continue to present significant, sometimes devastating problems for parents, children, families, and society.

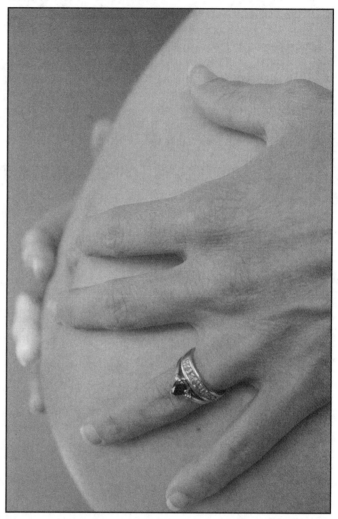

© Getty Images

Topics explored here, in *Unit 2,* link to topics such as parenthood, contraception, and abortion in the units that follow.

Given that reproduction is such an important theme in our look at biology, it should come as no surprise that in this unit we consider the impact of the prenatal environment on the developing fetus. It is important to understand how choices that are made during pregnancy can have a lasting impact on the child. Today, child protective services struggle with the impact of amphetamines, heroin, and cocaine among other nonprescription drugs on substance exposed newborns. Should taking "meth" during pregnancy be considered abuse and neglect of the fetus? Should the child be removed and placed into protective custody? What are the lifelong consequences for behavior and learning for someone who was substance exposed in utero? These are a few of the issues that confront us as a society today. Matters of biology can quickly become social issues of urgent importance. As you read through the articles in this section, you will be able to see more clearly that matters of sexual biology and behavior go well beyond the biological realm. The articles included hint at some of the psychological, social, and cultural origins and consequences of sexual behaviors as well.

Part B of this unit is dedicated to *Pleasure and Desire*. Sexual desire and pleasure involve many complex processes, some of which are biological in origin. Cognitions, emotions and biology can all influence our experiences with sexual desire and sexual pleasure. Central to these experiences—whether they be cognitive, emotional, or biological—is the most important sex organ of all: the brain. We know various things about the brain and the many roles it plays in the experience of sex. There are numerous brain structures that are of interest, including the cerebrum, the pituitary gland, and the hypothalamus, among others. We can also look at "systems" such as the limbic system, which is the seat of emotion. The limbic system includes such structures as: the amygdala, the anterior thalamic nuclei, the hippocampus, and the limbic cortex. Various structures and systems of the brain as well as the peripheral nervous system function together and communicate in highly complex ways to coordinate the feelings of sexual pleasure. You will see from the articles in this section that we have come a long way since the days of Sigmund Freud, in our understanding of the brain and its importance to sex.

However important biological processes are, there are some criticisms of the models of sexual desire that have been constructed. This section also entertains some alternative perspectives and explanations of sexual desire. Although you will learn much from this unit, you will quickly come to understand that there are still many unanswered questions. I hope that the articles in *Unit 2* stimulate your interest in what should become a lifelong search for answers.

Starting the Good Life in the Womb

Pregnant women who eat right, watch their weight and stay active can actually improve their unborn babies' chances of growing into healthy adults.

W. ALLAN WALKER, MD AND COURTNEY HUMPHRIES

Most pregnant women know they can hurt their babies by smoking, drinking alcohol and taking drugs that can cause birth defects. But they also may be able to "program" the baby in the womb to be a healthier adult. New research suggests that mothers-to-be can reduce the risk of their babies developing obesity, high blood pressure, heart disease and diabetes by monitoring their own diet, exercise and weight.

The science behind this is relatively new and still somewhat controversial. In the late 1980s, a British physician and epidemiologist named David Barker noticed that a group of Englishmen who were born small had a higher incidence of heart disease. Studies showed that rates of obesity, high blood pressure and diabetes—illnesses that often are associated with heart disease—are higher in men born small. Barker proposed that poor nutrition in the womb may have "programmed" the men to develop illness 50 years or more later.

The "Barker Hypothesis" is still hotly debated, but it is gaining acceptance as the evidence builds. Because organs develop at different times, it appears that the effects of too little food during pregnancy vary by trimester. One example comes from study of the Dutch Hunger Winter, a brief but severe famine that occurred during World War II. Pregnant women who didn't get enough to eat in their first trimester had babies who were more likely to develop heart disease. If they were in their second trimester, their babies were at risk for kidney disease. A poor diet in the last three months led to babies who had problems with insulin regulation, a precursor of diabetes.

More-recent research has focused on the negative effects of too much food during pregnancy. Women who gain excessive weight during pregnancy are more likely to have babies who are born large for their age and who become overweight in childhood. A recent study from the National Birth Defect Prevention Study found that obesity in pregnancy also increases a baby's risk for birth defects, including those of the spinal cord, heart and limbs.

A mother's nutrition and exercise patterns during pregnancy influence the long-term health of the baby by shaping her baby's metabolism. "Metabolism" includes everything that allows your body to turn food into energy—from the organ systems that process food and waste to the energy-producing chemical reactions that take place inside every cell. It is the collective engine that keeps you alive.

A mother's body may influence her baby's metabolism on many levels: the way organs develop, how appetite signals get released in the brain, how genes are activated, even the metabolic chemistry inside the baby's cells. Research now shows that the environment of the womb helps determine how a baby's metabolism is put together, or "programs" it for later health. The science of fetal programming is still new; it will be a long time before we have all the answers, since these health effects emerge over a lifetime. But several principles already are clear for a pregnant woman.

The first is to get healthy before pregnancy. Weighing too little or too much not only hampers fertility but can set the stage for metabolic problems in pregnancy. Doctors used to think of body fat as nothing more than inert insulation, but they know now that fat is an active tissue that releases hormones and plays a key role in keeping the metabolism running. Women should also eat a balanced diet and take prenatal vitamins before pregnancy to ensure that their bodies provide a good environment from the beginning.

The amount of weight gain is also critical. Women who gain too little weight during pregnancy are more likely to give birth to small babies, while women who gain too much weight are likely to have large babies. Paradoxically, both situations can predispose a child to metabolic disease. The weight gain should come slowly at first—about two to eight pounds in the first trimester, and one pound per week after that for normal-weight women. Obese women (with a body-mass index, or BMI, higher than 29) should gain no more than 15 pounds.

Pregnancy Pounds

Putting on too much or too little weight during pregnancy can predispose the baby to metabolic disorders. The right amount to gain:

Body-mass index (BMI) before pregnancy	Recommended weight gain
Less than 19.8 (underweight)	28–40 lb.
19.8–25 (normal weight)	25–35
26–29 (overweight)	15–25
Greater than 29 (obese)	No more than 15

Source: "Programming Your Baby for a Healthy Life" by W. Allan Walker, M.D., and Courtney Humphries

During pregnancy, women are already more susceptible to metabolic problems such as gestational diabetes and preeclampsia (high blood pressure), so choosing foods that help your metabolism run smoothly is important. Eating whole grains and foods rich in protein and fiber while avoiding foods high in sugar can help even out rises and falls in blood sugar. Pregnant women should eat about 300 extra calories per day while they're pregnant. But, as always, the quality of the calories matters even more. It's important to eat a diet rich in nutrients, since a lack of specific nutrients in the womb can hamper a baby's long-term health. A clear example is folic acid, without which the brain and spinal cord do not develop properly. But new research is uncovering other nutrients that may have subtler but long-lasting effects on health.

Studies suggest that women could benefit from taking omega-3 fatty-acid supplements, particularly those containing docosahexaenoic acid (DHA, for short), a type of fat that has been shown to help prevent prematurity and contribute to healthy brain development. A recent study found that women with more vitamin D in their bodies have children with stronger bones; adequate vitamin D is also needed for organ development.

Women may have different nutrient needs because of genetic differences, but to be safe every woman should take a daily prenatal vitamin before and during pregnancy. But supplements, whether in the form of a pill, a fortified shake or energy bar, don't replace the nutrients found in fruits, vegetables, low-fat meats, whole grains and other foods.

The energy you expend is as important as what you take in. Regular activity helps keep a woman's metabolism running smoothly and offsets problems of pregnancy like varicose veins, leg cramps and lower back pain. Pregnant women should avoid high-impact activities, especially late in their pregnancies.

All this may sound daunting, but most of the changes are simple ones that will improve a mother's long-term health as well as her children's.

W. ALLAN WALKER MD, the Conrad Taff Professor of Pediatrics at Harvard Medical School, and COURTNEY HUMPHRIES, a science writer, have written "The Harvard Medical School Guide to Healthy Eating During Pregnancy." For more information, go to health.harvard.edu/newsweek.

Success at Last

Couples fighting infertility might have more control than they think.

Deborah Kotz

Tracy Ryan had given up hope of having a second child. Two years of trying to conceive, including three failed artificial inseminations, had finally culminated in a successful in vitro fertilization—and 2-year-old Christopher. But further attempts at in vitro had left Ryan, 35, disappointed and exhausted. Desperate to feel better, the stay-at-home mom from Fair Haven, N.J., decided to try acupuncture, kick her six-can-a-day Diet Pepsi habit, and eat more fish, fruits, and vegetables. Eight weeks later and slimmer by 7 pounds, Ryan was shocked to discover that she was pregnant. "I was literally shaking when I saw the pregnancy test," she says. "My husband made me buy a different brand to verify it."

Ryan can't know whether to thank coincidence or her lifestyle changes for 9-month-old Brendan. But a growing body of evidence suggests that controllable factors (and not just a delay in childbearing) may be a reason 1 in 8 couples can't conceive. Success depends on the delicately timed release of four reproductive hormones, and all sorts of factors—too little iron in the blood, too much or too little body fat, too much exercise—can throw the sequence out of whack. "We're finding that everything matters—and moderation in terms of stress, body weight, diet, and physical activity is what's important," says Joel Evans, assistant clinical professor of obstetrics, gynecology, and women's health at the Albert Einstein College of Medicine and author of *The Whole Pregnancy Handbook.*

No one is talking about magic bullets. Some women will do everything right and still get the maddening diagnosis of "unexplained infertility." But institutions as well regarded as Duke University and Beth Israel Medical Center in New York are so convinced of the possibilities that they've recently opened "holistic fertility care" centers that offer women trying to conceive acupuncture, nutrition counseling, and relaxation classes. And a growing number of IVF clinics now host on-site yoga classes. At the very least, making healthful changes in the hope of improving your odds of a baby is bound to pay off in other ways.

Get Ready

Sometimes, the body's refusal to get pregnant can be a sign of its wisdom, says Tracy Gaudet, an obstetrician-gynecologist and executive director of Duke Integrative Medicine. Being overweight, for instance, puts a woman at risk of such pregnancy complications as high blood pressure, diabetes, and an abnormally large baby. So it may be no accident that excess estrogen produced by body fat interferes with ovulation. The body also may be saying "whoa" when a woman carries too little fat to sustain a growing baby: In underweight women, the pituitary gland releases less of the ovulation hormones FSH and LH.

Research from Harvard Medical School suggests that being at either end of the weight spectrum accounts for nearly 40 percent of failures to ovulate. Gaudet advises aiming for a body fat percentage in the range of 20 to 25 percent and a body mass index—a measure relating weight to height—of 20 to 25. That would equal about 117 to 145 pounds for someone 5 feet, 4 inches tall.

It's smart to quit smoking well before trying to get pregnant, too. A number of studies have shown that tobacco use can stretch the time it takes to conceive by a year or more, possibly because toxins in cigarette smoke accelerate the aging of a woman's eggs and damage the fallopian tubes. In fact, a 2006 study by Columbia University researchers found that women who smoked 14 cigarettes a day entered menopause an average of three years earlier than those who never smoked.

Why Dad's Habits Matter, Too

Two thirds of the time, the man is a contributing—if not the sole—explanation for a couple's infertility, according to the American Society of Reproductive Medicine. After a man hits 35, the amount and quality of his sperm decrease, which can lead to both difficulty in conceiving and a higher risk of miscarriage. There's no turning back the clock, but men, like women, can take steps to slow it down:

- **Get to a fighting weight.** A study published last year found that moderately overweight men who have a body mass index of 26 to 28 (the equivalent of carrying about 175 to 205 pounds on a 5-foot, 9-inch frame) were 50 percent more apt to be infertile than men at a healthy weight. Obese men had an even greater risk. Excess fat may increase the temperature of the scrotum, reducing sperm quality, and also raise levels of estrogen, lowering sperm counts. Being underweight creates a shortage of testosterone, which affects sperm production as well. Aim for a BMI of 19 to 25 (or about 130 to 170 pounds if you're 5 foot 9).
- **Check your diet.** You may want to temporarily limit your soy intake to once or twice a week. Tofu, soybeans, miso soup, and soy milk contain estrogenlike chemicals that in some animal studies seemed to lower sperm counts. Watch out, too, for fish with high levels of fertility-inhibiting mercury, advises Columbia University male fertility expert Harry Fisch.
- **Turn down the heat.** Since excessive heat can lower sperm counts, men planning to conceive should stay away from the sauna and hot tub. And they should take the laptop off their laps; the heat given off can be damaging, too, according to a 2005 study in the *Journal of Urology*. Boxers instead of briefs? The verdict is out, but some experts worry that wearing spandex during a workout can trap heat and reduce sperm counts. (A common cause of male infertility, a heat-trapping bundle of engorged veins in the scrotum called a varicocele, is treatable with minor surgery.)
- **Stay clean.** Performance-enhancing pills that contain DHEA, THG, andro, or other steroidlike substances can interfere with sperm production; and smoking, recreational drugs, and alcohol can damage sperm. So you're better off saying no.

—D.K.

If you haven't ditched trans fats for other reasons already, this is a good time. A recent finding from the Harvard Nurses Health Study suggests that eating as little as 4.5 grams per day—the amount in one glazed Krispy Kreme cruller—could disrupt ovulation. Study author Jorge Chavarro, a research fellow in the department of nutrition at Harvard School of Public Health, notes that the results need to be replicated before firm conclusions can be drawn but speculates that trans fats could indirectly lead to a rise in testosterone, which suppresses the function of the ovaries. "Check for the trans fat content on food labels, and avoid any foods with partially hydrogenated oils in the ingredients list," he advises. His research group also found a link between low levels of dietary iron and a failure to ovulate, possibly because iron is important for the maturation of the egg.

There isn't one ideal preconception diet, but emphasizing nonprocessed foods like whole grains, fruits, and vegetables will steer you away from trans fats. It's also wise to limit your intake of large fish such as tuna and swordfish, since the mercury they contain has been shown in animal studies to affect fertility. In terms of alcohol consumption, the consensus is that a glass of wine on occasion is probably fine. But how much alcohol is safe isn't known.

Many factors—too much or too little body fat, too much exercise—can throw key hormones out of whack.

On the flip side, it's possible to be too fit. Women who work out intensely can have trouble getting pregnant, possibly because reproductive hormones are suppressed when the body interprets excessive calorie burning or physical stress as danger. A study published last fall in the journal *Obstetrics & Gynecology* found that those who regularly exercised four or more hours per week were 40 percent less likely to conceive after their first IVF treatment than sedentary women. "Walking is fine, but spinning classes are out," says Alice Domar, an assistant professor of obstetrics, gynecology, and reproductive biology at Harvard Medical School and author of *Conquering Infertility.* "I generally recommend that my patients keep their heart rate below 110."

Couples who are actively trying to conceive need to understand some biology: Several hours before ovulation, the pituitary gland normally sends out a surge of LH, which causes the ovary's follicle to release an egg. But say you have a fender bender before the surge happens or suddenly discover you need a $10,000 roof repair. Such stresses can signal the pituitary gland that the body is in trouble, which slows the release of LH. If you have perfectionist tendencies, a single tear-your-hair-out day could be enough to disrupt ovulation that month, says infertility researcher Sarah Berga, a professor of obstetrics and gynecology at Emory University School of Medicine. Even if ovulation occurs, a shortage of LH could mean a shortage of progesterone, which is necessary to nourish and sustain a fertilized egg.

Skipping meals or taking a long run when you're feeling frantic might make matters worse. In a study of monkeys published last month, Berga and her colleagues created mild stress for one group by moving the monkeys to a new cage and found that 12 percent developed abnormal menstrual cycles. In the second group, which was moved plus given less food and a daily one-hour session on a treadmill, 70 percent experienced irregular menstruation.

Overcoming the level of stress associated with chronic infertility may require more formal interventions. On their first visit, about 40 percent of women seeking infertility treatments exhibit the same range and severity of symptoms—irritability, difficulty concentrating, sleep disturbances—as people diagnosed with an anxiety disorder, says Harvard's Domar. She developed a 10-week workshop for infertile women now in use around the country that includes group therapy, nutrition counseling, and relaxation techniques such as deep breathing, meditation, and yoga. In two studies, Domar and her colleagues found that 55 percent of women who took the workshop while getting fertility treatment wound up giving birth to a healthy baby compared with 20 percent of women who had treatment alone. "The women who took the class were also less anxious and depressed and had a much easier time coping with the medical procedures," Domar says.

Heidi Fallon, 36, of Ayer, Mass., found this to be true when she took Domar's workshop at Boston IVF 15 months ago after going through three unsuccessful rounds of treatment and a miscarriage. The class taught Fallon focused breathing techniques that she used while stuck in rush-hour traffic and provided comforting connections with other infertile women. "They knew exactly what I was going through—how hard it was when a friend or relative got pregnant," she says. An IVF cycle during the 10-week session produced Fallon's 9-month-old triplets.

In one study, women who exercised four or more hours a week were 40 percent less likely to succeed at IVF.

For some infertile couples, a phone call to a travel agent seems to do the job. "My friends raise their eyebrows whenever I take a vacation," says Meredith Collins, 35, of Portsmouth, R.I. After three failed tries at artificial insemination, Collins took a much-needed break from her busy paint-your-own-pottery store and infertility treatments and headed to a beach in the Dominican Republic, where she promptly became pregnant with her now 19-month-old son. Her 6-month-old son was also conceived naturally on a 2006 family getaway to a quiet bed-and-breakfast.

Since the point is a healthy baby, success at getting pregnant doesn't mean it's OK to relax back into old habits. About 10 to 15 percent of pregnancies end in miscarriage, and lifestyle factors linked to infertility are probably responsible for some of them. In a study published last year, Danish researchers found that smokers had a higher risk of miscarrying during the first few weeks of pregnancy than nonsmokers. Stress, caffeine, and alcohol might also be associated with miscarriages, though the data have been conflicting.

Longer term, evidence is mounting that a pregnant woman's lifestyle and diet can affect her baby well into adulthood. Children born to mothers battling depression or anxiety during pregnancy appear to be smaller and to weigh less as they grow, for example. The American College of Obstetricians and Gynecologists now recommends that clinically depressed women consider staying on their antidepressant medication while pregnant (with the exception of Paxil, which has been tied to birth defects). One recent study suggested that expectant mothers who eat more than three servings of fish a week deliver babies with higher IQs, while gaining too much weight during pregnancy seems to raise a child's risk of developing obesity or diabetes as an adult.

And too little vitamin D puts babies at risk of asthma, type 1 diabetes, and bone deformities, says Lisa Bodnar, an assistant professor of epidemiology at the University of Pittsburgh whose research shows that, even with prenatal vitamins, most pregnant women aren't getting enough. She recommends at least 1,000 international units of vitamin D a day; most prenatal supplements contain 400 IUs. Clearly, there's good reason to make choices that go beyond standard practice. But most are common sense.

A Man's Shelf Life

As men age, their fertility decreases and the health risks to their unborn offspring skyrocket. But men who attend to their health can slow down the reproductive clock.

MARK TEICH

Women have long understood that general fitness and age are both critical to conceiving a healthy child. But their partners often feel absolved of such concerns; men tend to think they can drink, carouse, smoke like coal trains, and conceive whenever they want, with no impact on fertility or their future offspring. Would that it were so.

"Everybody was familiar with the concept of women's biological clock, but when we introduced 'male' to the equation, the reaction was 'What are you talking about? Men can have children at *any* age,'" recalls urologist Harry Fisch, director of the Male Reproductive Center at Columbia Presbyterian Hospital in New York City and author of *The Male Biological Clock.* "It became a social issue. Men do not like to be told they have a problem"

Nonetheless, a virtual tidal wave of recent research has made it irrefutable: Not only does male fertility decrease decade by decade, especially after age 35, but aging sperm can be a significant and sometimes the *only* cause of severe health and developmental problems in offspring, including autism, schizophrenia, and cancer. The older the father, the higher the risk. But what's truly noteworthy is not that infertility increases with age—to some degree, we've known that all along—but rather that older men who can still conceive may have such damaged sperm that they put their offspring at risk for many types of disorders and disabilities.

"Men thought they were getting off scot free, and they weren't. The birth defects caused by male aging are significant conditions that can cause a burden to families and society," says Ethylin Wang Jabs, professor of pediatric genetics at Johns Hopkins University and leader of a recent study showing the link between aging paternity and certain facial deformities in offspring. "We now know that men and women alike could be increasing the risk of infertility or birth defects by waiting too long to have children." In other words, by looking for perfection in your life before you conceive, there's a very real chance you'll have less perfect kids."

By looking for perfection in your life before you conceive, there's a very real chance you'll have less perfect kids.

In the past several years, studies worldwide have found that with each passing decade of their lives and with each insult they inflict on their bodies, men's fertility decreases, while genetic risk to offspring slowly mounts. The range of findings is staggering: Several studies have shown that the older the man, the more fragmented the DNA in his ejaculated sperm, resulting in greater risk for infertility, miscarriage or birth defects. Investigations out of Israel, Europe, and the United States have shown that non-verbal (performance) intelligence may decline *exclusively* due to greater paternal age; that up to a third of all cases of schizophrenia are linked to increasing paternal age; and that men 40 and older are nearly six times more likely to have offspring with autism than men under age 30. Other research shows that the risk of breast and prostate cancer in offspring increases with paternal age.

Fisch has found that when both parents are over 35, paternal aging may be responsible for as many as half of all cases of Down syndrome, formerly thought to be inherited from the mother. And recent studies show that half a dozen or more rare but serious birth defects appear to be inherited exclusively from the father, including Apert syndrome, Crouzon syndrome, and Pfeiffer syndrome (all characterized by facial abnormalities and the premature fusion of skull bones) as well as achondroplasia (the most common form of dwarfism).

Male versus Female Mutations

Scientists have long known that advanced paternal age (like increased maternal age) played *some* role in fertility problems and birth defects. Yet because the reports mainly involved children who died before birth or who had extremely rare disorders,

45

no one really rang the alarm. Now, with new studies linking the father's age to relatively frequent, serious conditions like autism, schizophrenia, and Down syndrome, the landscape is shifting.

If you want to father a child after age 40, get in the best shape of your life.

Women have unfairly borne the brunt of the blame for birth defects. When the conditions were familial, passed on through chromosomal lineage, women were somehow widely believed culpable, even though such defects can be traced to either partner. "But what we're finding now is that in humans as well as in other mammals, when there's a *new* genetic change—called 'de novo or sporadic point mutation'—it almost always happens in the male parent," says Dolores Malaspina, chair of psychiatry at New York University Medical Center. And these de novo mutations increase in frequency with the age of the male parent.

These mutations could reflect the differences in male and female reproduction, notes Jabs. By the time females reach their teen years, their eggs have already been formed—just one new egg matures each month. Men, on the other hand, produce millions of sperm cells every time they ejaculate. After each ejaculation, they must literally *replicate* those cells, and each replication multiplies the chance for a DNA "copy error"—a genetic chink in the sperm DNA. The more ejaculations a man produces, the greater the chance for chinks to arise, leading to increased point mutation and thus increased infertility and birth defects. While a woman's reproductive capacity halts more or less abruptly after all her eggs have been used up somewhere in their forties or fifties, men experience a longer, more gradual winnowing and disintegration. "We believe that something in men's DNA replication machinery keeps becoming less efficient and less accurate with age, and the problems accumulate," says Jabs.

A Chilling Finding

The biggest news—the father's role in brain disorders—has come to light largely because of research from Israel, where birth records routinely include the age of the male parent. The first unsettling finding linked paternal age and schizophrenia.

"In our first study, looking at every pregnancy in Jerusalem from 1964 to 1976, we found that increased age in the father predicted increased cases of schizophrenia in the children," explains Malaspina, who was on the team doing the work. "In our second study we found that when the cases arose from new mutations—not familial inheritance—it almost always could be traced to the genetics of the father. Somewhere between a quarter and a third of the cases could be explained *only* by the age of the father—a threefold risk linked to fathers older than 50 compared with those in their 20s." Studies in Sweden and California produced almost identical results.

Male Health: The Long Shot

From puberty on, reproductive health and the viability of sperm continue to evolve.

Teens

Until age 13 or 14, sperm is not fully formed, increasing the risk of infertility or birth defects. Sperm may be extremely healthy in older teens, who are famous for their potency. But risky teen behavior may put sperm at risk.

20s

These are prime years for male reproduction. Men have the maximum amount of mature sperm cells and the least DNA damage. The risk of producing birth defects or causing other problems in offspring is as low as it ever will be.

30s

Testosterone levels start to decline at age 30, bringing a decrease in potency. By 32–34, fertility begins to fall. Men who are 35 or older are twice as likely to be infertile as men under age 25. The mid-thirties also bring a significant increase in sperm DNA damage and thus an increased risk of producing birth defects. One in 99 fathers ages 30–35 sire children with schizophrenia versus one in 141 for fathers under age 25.

40s

Type 2 diabetes and metabolic syndrome, involving pre-diabetes symptoms and cardiovascular risk factors, start to occur more often in men. Both disorders are strongly associated with below normal levels of testosterone, lowering potency. Erectile dysfunction (ED) starts to be a problem in a number of men. The risk of schizophrenia doubles in children of fathers in their late forties compared with children of fathers under age 25. Men 40 and older are nearly six times more likely to have offspring with autism than men younger than 30.

50s

Erectile dysfunction increases for many men. By age 50, the DNA cells that create sperm have gone through more than 800 rounds of division and replication, vastly decreasing the quality of sperm and increasing the chances of mutation and birth defects. The risk of schizophrenia almost triples for children of fathers 50 and older; one in 47 fathers sires a child with the condition.

60s

At the age of 60, 85 percent of sperm is clinically abnormal, something researchers attribute to normal aging.

The autism findings are even more disturbing: Men 40 and older in the Israeli study were almost six times as likely to have offspring with autism than men under 30. Some researchers believe that older fathers may hold a clue to the vast upsurge in autism cases in the past decade. "With older and older couples having children—in the past two years, for the first time, more babies are being born to women over age 30 than under age 30, and on average, male partners tend to be older than female partners—it's very feasible that paternal age is a major predictor of autism," asserts Fisch.

Minor Damage Is the Worst Kind

Perhaps the creepiest aspect of the new findings is that a little genetic damage in men's sperm may actually be worse than a lot of damage. "When we started doing the research, our first concern was fertility, and these new studies do show that fertility maybe compromised by DNA damage. But that's not the most important thing" declares Charles Muller, lab director of the Male Fertility Clinic at the University of Washington in Seattle.

The greater threat to offspring is the less flagrant DNA damage that gets passed on. Experts like Muller believe that a substantial amount of the damage is caused by free radicals—the destructive, highly reactive particles produced by our body's energy factories, the mitochondria, as we metabolize oxygen. "One of the scariest things we're finding is that sperm DNA is damaged by even *low* levels of free radicals. Whereas high levels of damage lead to infertility, miscarriages, or spontaneous abortions, low levels chew up the DNA but the sperm can still fertilize," Muller states.

Complicating matters, sperm is incapable of repairing itself; Muller and his colleague Narendra P. Singh find that as men age, natural processes such as apoptosis—in which damaged cells naturally commit suicide to protect the body—become increasingly less efficient and less able to eliminate damaged DNA. Resulting defects may not show up until offspring are adults and it's too late to trace the cause. Damage may then be passed from one generation to the next.

"In short, the biggest genetic threat to society may not be infertility but fertile old men," says University of Wisconsin in Madison geneticist James F. Crow.

The Playing Field Levels

The new findings have profound implications for any potential parent. Women may increasingly feel they share the onus of potential infertility and birth defects with men. Older women, focused though they are on their own reproductive timetable, may increasingly view their partner's age with a wary eye. When both parents are aging, the risks to offspring multiply. "If women are under age 35, the father's age may not matter that much, but if the mother is over 35, advanced male age can be a real problem," says Jabs.

For men, the findings maybe, above all, a clarion call to take better care of themselves. "This should make men reconsider their role and responsibility in childbearing," says Barbara Willet, of the Best Start childhood resource center in Ontario, Canada. "Aging in men is an important issue, but *health* is the key issue. It's as if we're suddenly aware that men who want to be fathers need to be healthy, too."

One key is testosterone, necessary for the maturation of sperm. "If you have less testosterone, you have worse sperm."

Protecting the Family Jewels

Anything that hurts a man's health hurts his sperm. The good news: preserving your reproductive potential will also keep you healthy.

- **Protect Your Heart**—"What's bad for your heart is bad for your penis," says Columbia's Harry Fisch. Erections depend on arterial flow from the heart, and when that's reduced or blockage occurs, erectile dysfunction (ED) is often close behind. Get an annual physical including heart checkup and cholesterol test once you reach your 30s. If your cholesterol is high, cholesterol-lowering medicine may help.
- **Stay Active**—"If you're trying to have a child in your 30s, 40s, or 50s, getting into the best shape of your life will give you the highest testosterone level possible," says Fisch.
- **Watch Your Weight**—Potbellies and excessive waist size are often telltale signs of heart disease. They also generate heat that can reach the testicles, decreasing the testosterone in sperm. In general, the bigger the belly, the lower the testosterone. Eat a balanced, low-fat diet, and reduce your calorie intake.
- **Take Antioxidants**—such as vitamin C or E, since they may help battle free radicals that play a part in breakdown of sperm DNA.
- **Don't Smoke, Drink to Excess, or Abuse Drugs**—All of these behaviors accelerate DNA breakdown in sperm and put the heart and other organs at risk.
- **Avoid Hot Baths, Jacuzzis, and Hot Tubs**—All can reduce sperm counts for three to six months.
- **Keep Laptops on the Desk**—Balancing laptops on the lap raises the scrotum's temperature, say SUNY Stony Brook urologists.
- **See a Urologist**—if you are over 40, have toxic exposure, or have tried to conceive for a year. Sperm content and testosterone levels can both be evaluated. ED can be treated. You can also ask your doctor to refer you to a lab that tests DNA fragmentation in sperm.
- **Have Varicoceles Removed**—The urologist should always look for engorgements of the veins in scrotums, which can begin as early as adolescence. Almost 40 percent of infertile men have them. By trapping the blood flow in the scrotum, they can cook and choke the sperm, leading to risk of infertility. This is easily reversible.

Testosterone naturally starts to decline in the 30s, but also varies based on factors from weight to heart health. "Fat cells in a potbelly overheat the testes and break testosterone down; clogged arteries break it down. Whatever hurts your heart, hurts your penis," Fisch states.

Men typically don't think about their health, and we need to get them to. If you're drinking or smoking, if you're working in toxic environments with pesticides, X-rays, solvents, or ionizing radiation, these things affect you as well as women, and will ultimately affect the children you conceive.

Alarming though the findings may be to some, researchers have a clear directive: "Don't panic." "The research is still fresh" says Crow, "and more needs to be done before we start making sweeping recommendations like urging people to have children younger, or telling men to freeze their sperm after their 20s. I don't advocate asking the general public to change at this point, because while some of these mutations cause very severe effects, in the totality of things that can go wrong, this is not that large a part of the picture."

Freezing sperm may sometimes be the way to go. While frozen sperm may not be quite as potent as when it is fresh, it is not a proven problem. Since the turn of the last century, sperm of domestic animals has been frozen safely for as long as 75 years, says Muller. And frozen sperm is used routinely in humans for artificial insemination. Pregnancy rates and childbirth are right up there with regularly conceived birth, and there is no substantial DNA breakdown. If you're going to get a vasectomy, join the Army, or go through cancer therapy, "I'd advise you to freeze your sperm beforehand," Muller says.

Some men don't have to worry. Their sperm is fine in their 70s.

Most men can steer a gentler course just by watching their health. "Despite the new research, there's still a big difference between the female and the male biological clock," says Muller. "When the female's alarm goes off at the end, that's it. For men, the battery slowly winds down. Yes, chances of problems increase as the years pass, but some men have significant DNA damage at 35, while others go on forever—their sperm is fine in their 70s."

Men can't rewind their biological clocks, but they can slow them down, Fisch agrees. Just remember, once you're in your 40s, you're past your maintenance-free years—you have to take care of yourself. "If you want children from then on," he advises, "get into the best shape of your life."

MARK TEICH is a health writer based in Connecticut.

The Orgasmic Mind

Achieving sexual climax requires a complex conspiracy of sensory and psychological signals—and the eventual silencing of critical brain areas.

MARTIN PORTNER

She did not often have such strong emotions. But she suddenly felt powerless against her passion and the desire to throw herself into the arms of the cousin whom she saw at a family funeral. "It can only be because of that patch," said Marianne, a participant in a multinational trial of a testosterone patch designed to treat hypoactive sexual desire disorder, in which a woman is devoid of libido. Testosterone, a hormone ordinarily produced by the ovaries, is linked to female sexual function, and the women in this 2005 study had undergone operations to remove their ovaries.

After 12 weeks of the trial, Marianne had felt her sexual desire return. Touching herself unleashed erotic sensations and vivid sexual fantasies. Eventually she could make love to her husband again and experienced an orgasm for the first time in almost three years. But that improvement was not because of testosterone, it turned out. Marianne was among the half of the women who had received a placebo patch—with no testosterone in it at all.

Marianne's experience underlines the complexity of sexual arousal. Far from being a simple issue of hormones, sexual desire and orgasm are subject to various influences on the brain and nervous system, which controls the sex glands and genitals. And many of those influences are environmental. Recent research, for example, shows that visual stimuli spur sexual stirrings in women, as they do in men. Marianne's desire may have been invigorated by conversations or thoughts about sex she had as a result of taking part in the trial. Such stimuli may help relieve inhibitions or simply what a person's appetite for sex.

Achieving orgasm, brain-imaging studies show, involves more than heightened arousal. It requires a release of inhibitions and control in which the brain's center of vigilance shuts down in males; in females, various areas of the brain involved in controlling thoughts and emotions become silent. The brain's pleasure centers tend to light up brightly in the brain scans of both sexes, especially in those of males. The reward system creates an incentive to seek more sexual encounters, with clear benefits for the survival of the species. When the drive for sex dissipates, as it did with Marianne, people can reignite the spark with tactics that target the mind.

Fast Facts
Principles of Pleasure

1. Sexual desire and orgasm are subject to various influences on the brain and nervous system, which controls the sex glands and genitals.
2. The ingredients of desire may differ for men and women, but researchers have revealed some surprising similarities. For example, visual stimuli spur sexual stirrings in women, as they do in men.
3. Achieving orgasm, brain imaging studies show, involves more than heightened arousal. It requires a release of inhibitions engineered by shutdown of the brain's center of vigilance in both sexes and a widespread neural power failure in females.

Sex in Circles

Biologists identified sex hormones such as estrogen and testosterone in the 1920s and 1930s, and the first studies of human sexuality appeared in the 1940s. In 1948 biologist Alfred Kinsey of Indiana University introduced his first report on human sexual practices, *Sexual Behavior in the Human Male,* which was followed, in 1953, by *Sexual Behavior in the Human Female.* These highly controversial books opened up a new dialogue about human sexuality. They not only broached topics—such as masturbation, homosexuality and orgasm—that many people considered taboo but also revealed the surprising frequency with which people were coupling and engaging in sexual relations of countless varieties.

Kinsey thus debuted sex as a science, paving the way for others to dig below statistics into the realm of biology. In 1966 gynecologist William Masters and psychologist Virginia Johnson—who originally hailed from Washington University before founding their own research institute in St. Louis—described for the first time the sexual response cycle (how the body responds to sexual stimulation), based on observations of

382 women and 312 men undergoing some 10,000 such cycles. The cycle begins with excitation, as blood rushes to the penis in men, and as the clitoris, vulva and vagina enlarge and grow moist in women. Gradually, people reach a plateau, in which they are fully aroused but not yet at orgasm. After reaching orgasm, they enter the resolution phase, in which the tissues return to the preexcitation stage.

In the 1970s psychiatrist Helen Singer Kaplan of the Human Sexuality Program at Weill Medical College of Cornell University added a critical element to this cycle—desire—based on her experience as a sex therapist. In her three-stage model, desire precedes sexual excitation, which is then followed by orgasm. Because desire is mainly psychological, Kaplan emphasized the importance of the mind in the sexual experience and the destructive forces of anxiety, defensiveness and failure of communication.

In the late 1980s gynecologist Rosemary Basson of the University of British Columbia proposed a more circular sexual cycle, which, despite the term, had been described as a largely linear progression in previous work. Basson suggested that desire might both lead to genital stimulation and be invigorated by it. Countering the idea that orgasm is the pinnacle of the experience, she placed it as a mere spot on the circle, asserting that a person could feel sexually satisfied at any of the stages leading up to an orgasm, which thus does not have to be the ultimate goal of sexual activity.

Dissecting Desire

Given the importance of desire in this cycle, researchers have long wanted to identify its key ingredients. Conventional wisdom casts the male triggers in simplistic sensory terms, with tactile and visual stimuli being particularly enticing. Men are drawn to visual erotica, explaining the lure of magazines such as *Playboy*. Meanwhile female desire is supposedly fueled by a richer cognitive and emotional texture. "Women experience desire as a result of the context in which they are inserted—whether they feel comfortable with themselves and the partner, feel safe and perceive a true bond with the partner," opines urologist Jennifer Berman of the Female Sexual Medicine Center at the University of California, Los Angeles.

Yet sexual imagery devoid of emotional connections can arouse women just as it can men, a 2007 study shows. Psychologist Meredith Chivers of the Center for Addiction and Mental Health in Toronto and her colleagues gauged the degree of sexual arousal in about 100 women and men, both homosexual and heterosexual, while they watched erotic film clips. The clips depicted same-sex intercourse, solitary masturbation or nude exercise—performed by men and women—as well as male-female intercourse and mating between bonobos (close ape relatives of the chimpanzee).

The researchers found that although nude exercise genitally aroused all the onlookers the least and intercourse excited them the most, the type of actor was more important for the men than for the women. Heterosexual women's level of arousal increased along with the intensity of the sexual activity largely irrespective of who or what was engaged in it. In fact, these women were genitally excited by male and female actors equally and also responded physically to bonobo copulation. (Gay women, however, were more particular; they did not react sexually to men masturbating or exercising naked.)

The men, by contrast, were physically titillated mainly by their preferred category of sexual partner—that is, females for straight men and males for gay men—and were not excited by bonobo copulation. The results, the researchers say, suggest that women are not only aroused by a variety of types of sexual imagery but are more flexible than men in their sexual interests and preferences.

When it comes to orgasm, simple sensations as well as higher-level mental processes probably also play a role in both sexes. Although Kinsey characterized orgasm in purely physical terms, psychologist Barry R. Komisaruk of Rutgers University has defined the experience as more multifaceted. In their book *The Science of Orgasm* (Johns Hopkins University Press, 2006), Komisaruk, endocrinologist Carlos Beyer-Flores of the Tlaxcala Laboratory in Mexico and Rutgers sexologist Beverly Whipple describe orgasm as maximal excitation generated by a gradual summing of responses from the body's sensory receptors, combined with complex cognitive and emotional forces. Similarly, psychologist Kent Berridge of the University of Michigan at Ann Arbor has described sexual pleasure as a kind of "gloss" that the brain's emotional hub, the limbic system, applies over the primary sensations.

The relative weights of sensory and emotional influences on orgasm may differ between the sexes, perhaps because of its diverging evolutionary origins. Orgasm in men is directly tied to reproduction through ejaculation, whereas female orgasm has a less obvious evolutionary role. Orgasm in a woman might physically aid in the retention of sperm, or it may play a subtler social function, such as facilitating bonding with her mate. If female orgasm evolved primarily for social reasons, it might elicit more complex thoughts and feelings in women than it does in men.

Simple sensations and more complex mental processes probably contribute to orgasm in both sexes.

Forgetting Fear

But does it? Researchers are trying to crack this riddle by probing changes in brain activity during orgasm in both men and women. Neuroscientist Gert Holstege of the University of Groningen in the Netherlands and his colleagues attempted to solve the male side of the equation by asking the female partners of 11 men to stimulate their partner's penis until he ejaculated while they scanned his brain using positron-emission tomography (PET). During ejaculation, the researchers saw extraordinary activation of the ventral tegmental area (VTA), a major hub of the brain's reward circuitry; the intensity of this response is comparable to that induced by heroin. "Because ejaculation introduces sperm into the female reproductive tract, it would be critical for reproduction of the species to favor ejaculation as a most rewarding behavior," the researchers wrote in 2003 in *The Journal of Neuroscience.*

The scientists also saw heightened activity in brain regions involved in memory-related imagery and in vision itself, perhaps because the volunteers used visual imagery to hasten orgasm. The anterior part of the cerebellum also switched into high gear. The cerebellum has long been labeled the coordinator of motor behaviors but has more recently revealed its role in emotional processing. Thus, the cerebellum could be the seat of the emotional components of orgasm in men, perhaps helping to coordinate those emotions with planned behaviors. The amygdala, the brain's center of vigilance and sometimes fear, showed a decline in activity at ejaculation, a probable sign of decreasing vigilance during sexual performance.

To find out whether orgasm looks similar in the female brain, Holstege's team asked the male partners of 12 women to stimulate their partner's clitoris—the site whose excitation most easily leads to orgasm—until she climaxed, again inside a PET scanner. Not surprisingly, the team reported in 2006, clitoral stimulation by itself led to activation in areas of the brain involved in receiving and perceiving sensory signals from that part of the body and in describing a body sensation—for instance, labeling it "sexual."

When a woman reached orgasm, something unexpected happened: much of her brain went silent.

But when a woman reached orgasm, something unexpected happened: much of her brain went silent. Some of the most muted neurons sat in the left lateral orbitofrontal cortex, which may govern self-control over basic desires such as sex. Decreased activity there, the researchers suggest, might correspond to a release of tension and inhibition. The scientists also saw a dip in excitation in the dorsomedial prefrontal cortex, which has an apparent role in moral reasoning and social judgment—a change that may be tied to a suspension of judgment and reflection.

Brain activity fell in the amygdala, too, suggesting a depression of vigilance similar to that seen in men, who generally showed far less deactivation in their brain during orgasm than their female counterparts did. "Fear and anxiety need to be avoided at all costs if a woman wishes to have an orgasm; we knew that, but now we can see it happening in the depths of the brain," Holstege says. He went so far as to declare at the 2005 meeting of the European Society for Human Reproduction and Development: "At the moment of orgasm, women do not have any emotional feelings."

But that lack of emotion may not apply to all orgasms in women. Komisaruk, Whipple and their colleagues studied the patterns of brain activation that occur during orgasm in five

---

Domestic Bliss

Is the pursuit of sexual gratification vital to the health of an established relationship? In her book *Mating in Captivity* (HarperCollins, 2006), New York–based psychotherapist Esther Perel emphasizes the importance of eroticism and orgasm in a marriage. She chronicles the typical dissolution of a couple's sex life when the love bond becomes politically correct and excessively domesticated. To avoid sexual staleness, Perel advocates unusual strategies such as cultivating separateness—developing different interests and groups of friends from those of your partner, for example—instead of closeness, as a way of making your partner more mysterious and exciting. She also suggests looking for creative ways to let fantasy and even a little craziness thrive within the confines of a long-term relationship.

Other psychologists, however, advise against placing too much emphasis on orgasm in a mature relationship. In her book *Peace Between the Sheets* (Frog Books, 2003), couples therapist Marnia Robinson suggests that the journey to orgasm renders us prisoners to dopamine, a neurotransmitter secreted in the brain's reward centers. After all, dopamine underlies other addictive behaviors, from gambling to drug abuse. In Robinson's view, partners should mutually unite in pleasure, without the sexual relationship necessarily having to be crowned by orgasm.

—M.P.

---

women with spinal cord injuries that left them without sensation in their lower extremities. These women were able to achieve a "deep," or nonclitoral, orgasm through mechanical stimulation (using a laboratory device) of the vagina and cervix. But contrary to Holstege's results, Komisaruk's team found that orgasm was accompanied by a general activation of the limbic system, the brain's seat of emotion.

Among the activated limbic regions were the amygdala and the hypothalamus, which produces oxytocin, the putative love and bonding hormone whose levels jump fourfold at orgasm. The researchers also found heightened activity in the nucleus accumbens, a critical part of the brain's reward circuitry that may mediate orgasmic pleasure in women. In addition, they saw unusual activity in the anterior cingulate cortex and the insula, two brain areas that Rutgers anthropologist Helen Fisher has found come to life during the later stages of love relationships. Such activity may connect a female's sexual pleasure with the emotional bond she feels with her partner.

Pleasure Pill?

Disentangling the connections between orgasm, reproduction and love may someday yield better medications and psychotherapies for sexual problems. As Marianne's case illustrates, the answer is usually not as simple as a hormone boost. Instead her improvement was probably the result of the activation or inactivation of relevant parts of her brain by social triggers she encountered while participating in an experiment whose purpose centered on female sexual arousal. Indeed, many sex therapies revolve around opening the mind to new ways of thinking about sex or about your sexual partner [*see box on next page*].

Companies are also working on medications that act on the nervous system to stimulate desire. One such experimental compound is a peptide called bremelanotide, which is under development by Palatin Technologies in Cranbury, N.J. It blocks certain receptors in the brain that are involved in regulating basic drives such as eating and sex. In human studies bremelanotide has prompted spontaneous erections in men and boosted sexual arousal and desire in women, but the U.S. Food and Drug Administration has held up its progress out of concern over side effects such as rising blood pressure.

Continued scientific dissection of the experience of orgasm may lead to new pharmaceutical and psychological avenues for enhancing the experience. Yet overanalyzing this moment of intense pleasure might also put a damper on the fun. That is what the science tells us anyway.

Further Readings

Brain Activation during Human Male Ejaculation. Gert Holstege et al. in *Journal of Neuroscience,* Vol. 23, No. 27, pages 9185–9193; October 8, 2003.

Brain Activation during Vaginocervical Self-Stimulation and Orgasm in Women with Complete Spinal Cord Injury: FMRI Evidence of Mediation by the Vagus Nerves. Barry R. Komisaruk et al. in *Brain Research,* Vol. 1024, Nos. 1–2, pages 77–88; October 2004.

Testosterone Patch Increases Sexual Activity and Desire in Surgically Menopausal Women with Hypoactive Sexual Desire. James Simon et al. in *Journal of Clinical Endocrinology & Metabolism,* Vol. 90, No. 9, pages 5226–5233; September 2005.

Regional Cerebral Blood Flow Changes Associated with Clitorally Induced Orgasm in Healthy Women. Janniko R. Georgiadis et al. in *European Journal of Neuroscience,* Vol. 24, No. 11, pages 3305–3316; December 2006.

MARTIN PORTNER is a neurologist living in Brazil. He is author of *Inteligência Sexual* (*Sexual Intelligence,* Editora Gente, 1999). He lectures and leads workshops on the brain and creativity.

Women's Sexual Desire: A Feminist Critique

Jill M. Wood, Patricia Barthalow Koch, and Phyllis Kernoff Mansfield

Sexual desire is a key component of the current popular conceptualizations of sexual identity, sexual orientation, and sexual functioning and dysfunctioning. Some sexologists contend that no scholarly or scientific discussion of sexuality can occur without reference to it (Leiblum & Rosen, 2000; Levine, 2002). Even though sexual desire has been the topic of much recent research, there is a great deal of ambiguity and variation regarding the conceptualization, definition, operationalization, and application (in research and practice) of the term "sexual desire" as it relates to women (e.g., 'Basson, 2002b; Kaschak & Tiefer, 2002; Tiefer, 1995). This variation is profoundly related to the theoretical framework from which sexual desire is viewed. Most often sexual desire has been studied from a biomedical paradigm, as noted by Basson (2002a; 2002b), Rosen and Lieblum (1995), and Winton (2001). This paradigm posits sexuality as intrinsic, natural, and universal (Tiefer, 1988).

In contrast, feminist scholars and researchers have called for a critical analysis of the biomedical paradigm in favor of more woman-centered models of sexuality (e.g., Daniluk, 1998; McCormick, 1994; Tiefer, 1991, 1995, 2000). Feminism is not a monolithic ideology, but instead is defined and practiced in various ways by different people and groups (e.g., radical and liberal; McCormick). In its broadest interpretation, feminism represents advocacy for women's interests. In a stricter definition, it is the "theory of the political, social, and economic equality of the sexes" (LeGates, 1995, p. 494). Feminist sexology is the scholarly study of sexuality that is of, by, and for women's interests (Koch, 2004). Using diverse epistemologies, methods, and sources of data, feminist scholars examine women's sexual experiences and the cultural frame that constructs sexuality (Vance & Pollis, 1990). To this end, Pollis (1988) has proposed the following principles to overcome the deficits in understanding women's experiences, gender and gender asymmetry, and sexuality:

1. acknowledgement of the pervasive influence of gender in all aspects of social life, including the practice of science;
2. conceptualization of gender as a social category, constructed and maintained through the gender-attribution process;
3. emphasis on the heterogeneity of experience and the central importance of language, community, culture, and historical context in creating the individual; and
4. commitment to engage in research that is based on women's experience and is likely to empower them to eliminate sexism and contribute to societal change.

This article offers a critical feminist analysis of the biomedical conceptualization of women's sexual desire. We examine and critique five major features of the biomedical model of female sexual desire: (a) use of the male model as the standard, (b) use of a linear model of sexual response, (c) biological reductionism, (d) depoliticalization, and (e) medicalization of variation. We offer a "New View," an alternative to the biomedical model, for reconceptualizing women's sexual problems, and conclude with recommendations for feminist-based biopsychosocial research.

Use of the Male Model as the Standard for Sexual Desire

Traditionally, researchers and scholars have conceptualized sexuality as men's sexuality (Irvine, 1990). The field of sexuality has long focused on studies of men's sexual response and behavior that have established men's sexuality as the

ANNUAL EDITIONS

norm. This practice continues more than 100 years after the initial pioneering research in the field (Ussher, 1993). Tiefer (2000, p. 102) explained,

> ... too often in the sexological model of sexuality the normative standard has been man's sexual experience.... The idea that heterosexual impulses are the norm, that sexuality exists in individuals, that biological factors are the prime source of desire, that the best way to see sex is as a material series of physical changes in specific activities—assumptions in the sexological model—seem more in accordance with men's experience (or maybe we should say with the phallocentric experience).

This same pattern is found in the study of sexual desire. Sexual desire has traditionally been viewed, and mostly measured, as spontaneous sexual thoughts and fantasies and biological urges creating a need to self-stimulate or initiate sexual activities with a partner (Basson, 2002b; Leiblum, 2002). Throughout the history of sexology, this conceptualization of sexual desire became embodied in various terms, including sexual drive, appetite, interest, cravings, motivation, and libido. This type of spontaneous, active, and physically-driven sexual response is the one depicted in the traditional human sexual response model developed by Masters and Johnson (1966), although no specific desire phase was included in this four-stage model of excitement, plateau, orgasm, and resolution. Kaplan (1979) specifically identified sexual desire as the first stage in her triphasic model of sexual response, the other stages being excitement and orgasm. She stated (p. 10),

> Sexual desire or libido is experienced as specific sensations which move the individual to seek out, or become receptive to, sexual experience. These sensations are produced by the physical activation of a specific neural system in the brain. When (his system is active, a person is 'horny,' he may feel genital sensations, or he may feel vaguely sexy, interested in sex, open to sex, or even just restless. These sensations cease after sexual gratification, i.e., orgasm. When this system is inactive or under the influence of inhibitory forces, a person has no interest in erotic matters; he 'loses his appetite' for sex and becomes 'asexual.'

In fact, the *Diagnostic and Statistical Manual of Mental Disorders,* considered the "bible" of sexual classification of disorders and dysfunctions, continues to be based on Kaplan's model (Leiblum, 2001).

Irvine (1990) observed that many sex therapists have adopted these traditional views of sexual desire and view it as "a surging energy that can be switched on or off (p. 213). In summarizing the ambiguity in defining sexual desire, Tolman and Diamond (2001) opined that "according to the default view, sexual desires are discrete, easily identifiable experiences of lust (i.e., you know them when you feel them)" (p. 35).

The behaviors motivated by this type of spontaneous, active, and physically-driven response (e.g., sexual thoughts, fantasies, masturbation, initiation of partnered sex) are more common, on average, in men than women (Baumeister, Catanese, & Vohs, 2001; Beck, Bozman, & Qualtrough, 1991; Byers & Heinlien, 1989; Laumann, Gagnon, Michael, & Michaels, 1994; Leitenberg & Henning, 1995; O'Sullivan & Byers, 1992; Wallen, 2000). Many professionals and even the lay public have taken this as proof that men have more sexual desire than women, which appears true when using male standards. Yet such standards ignore the gendered division of social power so that gender differences are controlled for, posited as natural, or appear to be non-existent (Tiefer, 2000). As Tiefer (2000) argued, we should not assume that "women's sexual experience would be better, more normal, or more fulfilling, if it more closely paralleled men's" (pp. 84–85). Further, Leiblum (2002) conjectured, "If sexual drive [desire] was defined less in terms of amount of genital contact and more in terms of sexuality, women would be perceived as being more sensual than men" (p. 61).

To understand women's sexual desire from a perspective free of such male-centered bias, we must root its conceptualization in women's lived experience. For example, a grounded theory study of the experience and meaning of postmenopausal women's sexual desire illustrated differences in women's experiences as compared to the male standard of sexual desire (Wood, Mansfield, & Koch, under review). Through semi-structured telephone interviews, women (n = 22, ages 58-65, mean age = 62.4) conceptualized sexual desire as a whole-body feeling, including both emotional and physical aspects, for an interest in sexual activity, either with a partner or alone. They described their sexual desire in various ways, including willingness to participate in sex, energy that built within them, state of being, and interest in sex. Some women explained that it takes them a long time to "warm up" and feel sexual desire in their bodies. For these women, sexual desire was a willingness to participate in sex as opposed to a feeling of being "turned on." They commonly associated sexual desire with emotional feelings, including feeling closeness to a partner or wanting to experience intimacy with a partner through sex. Some of the women discussed physical indicators of sexual desire, most of which were non-genital, such as an increased heartbeat, feeling "butterflies," perspiring, or tingling sensations in their breasts. Other women had no awareness of their sexual desire in a bodily sense. When specifically asked, these participants distinguished between sexual desire and arousal, explaining that desire was an interest in sexual activity and arousal was being physically ready for sexual activity.

Use of a Linear Model of Sexual Desire

Besides their use of male sexuality as the standard, another feature of the traditional human sexual response models (e.g., Masters & Johnson, 1966, and Kaplan, 1979) is their linearity (Sugrue & Whipple, 2001). Each phase acts as a distinct precursor to the next phase (e.g., desire preceding arousal). This creates the assumption that there is only one "correct" way to move throughout the model to experience sexual response. However, Basson (2001b; 2002b) questioned the validity of these traditional linear sexual response models for women. Based on her clinical experience, she found that sexual desire is not always a precursor to sexual arousal (excitement) in women (Basson, 2001 a, 2001b). In addition, sexual desire is often motivated more by a desire for emotional intimacy than by a spontaneous urge. In Basson's circular model, sexual desire often does not occur until after the woman is involved in the sexual activity or may not occur at all. As Basson (2001 b) described sexual desire in this model:

> When a woman senses a potential opportunity to be sexual with her partner, although she may not 'need' to experience arousal and resolution for her own sexual well-being, she is nevertheless motivated to deliberately do whatever is necessary to facilitate a sexual interaction as she expects potential benefits that, though not strictly sexual, are very important. The increased emotional closeness, bonding, commitment, tolerance of each other's imperfections, and expectation of increased well-being of the partner all serve as highly valid motivational factors that activate the cycle (pp. 396–397).

To validate this circular model of sexual response, Basson interviewed 47 women who had been referred to a clinic with a diagnosis of "low sexual desire" (Basson, 2001b). About half of these women considered insufficient emotional intimacy an important factor contributing to their lack of sexual desire. They saw sexual desire as a continuation of nonsexual intimacy:

> ... the most common needs expressed were those outside of the bedroom—an appropriate atmosphere, partner's consideration, respect, and warmth, and physical affection ... In the area of sexual activity itself, leisurely, nongenital pleasuring was a common need as was genital but nonintercourse pleasuring (p. 400).

Other women reported a lack of desire due to remembered dyspareunia and the experience of pain, mental discomfort with sexual arousal (usually due to a history of childhood sexual abuse or current undesirable, even abusive, relationships), or striving for perfection, resulting in a tendency

to self-monitor their sexual experiences and their ability to please their partners sexually. Other researchers have also found that there are many reasons that women have sex that do not require sexual desire, including sex motivated by security, money, coercion, or fear (Heiman, 2001).

A nonlinear interaction between sexual desire and arousal was also described in focus group research exploring 80 women's (mean age = 34.3 years, range 18–84) experiences (Graham, Sanders, Milhausen, & McBride, 2004). During the discussions, the researchers found that women defined sexual desire as "sexual interest." They tended to consider sexual interest "more thoughtful" and sexual arousal "more physical," yet many women said that they did not clearly differentiate them. These women sometimes perceived sexual interest as preceding arousal and sometimes following it.

Biological Reductionism of Sexual Desire

Most sexologists and laypeople have historically viewed sexual desire as an innate, fixed, biologically-determined drive (Tolman & Diamond, 2001). Although research indicates that biological factors do influence women's sexual desire (Alexander & Sherwin, 1993; Sarrel, Dobay, & Witta, 1998; Wallen, 1995), the degree to which such factors determine women's sexual expression is a topic of considerable debate (for a review, see Sherwin, 1991). Researchers disagree as to the precise role that hormones play in determining or influencing women's sexual desire. The majority of the research focuses on androgens, primarily testosterone (Basson, 2003). Some research indicates that there is a relationship between women's amount of free testosterone, sexual desire, and sexual behavior (e.g., Riley & Riley, 2000). This research is typically based on correlations between measured testosterone and self-reported sexual desire. These studies often conclude that some women have an absence of sexual desire due to low levels of free testosterone. However, since most studies use correlations as statistical tests, a causative link between testosterone and sexual desire can not be inferred. Moreover, some researchers question the validity and reliability of hormonal assays used to determine women's free testosterone levels, since typically only one hormonal sample is used and the concentrations of hormones vary at different times across the day and from one day to the next (e.g., Voda, 1997).

Despite decades of research on the role of estrogen (e.g., Benedek & Rubenstein, 1939), the physiological effects of estrogen on sexual desire are not completely understood (Regan, 1999). In general, the estrogen research suggests that the relationship between sexual desire and estradiol in women is not a direct one (e.g., Kaplan, 1992; Leiblum, Bachmann, Kemmann, Colburn, & Schwartzman, 1983).

A good example of the indirect relationship between estrogen-related physiology and women's sexual desire is vaginal lubrication. Women who consistently experience concerns with lack of vaginal lubrication may avoid sexual interactions for fear of experiencing pain during intercourse (dyspareunia; Bachmann, 1990; McCoy, 1992). Thus, estrogen's effect on vaginal lubrication may facilitate a woman's sexual desire but does not cause it. Another way that estradiol may operate to influence sexual desire is through binding to neurotransmitters in the brain that affect the neurological components of mood (Bancroft, 1988).

Understanding the biological influences on sexual desire is important, and such study does not necessarily constitute a biomedical paradigm. However, when the biological determinants of desire are given undue influence and psychosocial factors are ignored or minimized, a biomedical paradigm emerges. Feminist sex researchers note that the assertion that hormones are the "cause" or even the primary determinants of women's sexual desire is an example of biological reductionism (e.g., Daniluk, 1998; McCormick, 1994; Tiefer, 1991, 1995, 2000). As Leiblum (2002) described, "While [hormones] fuel the flames of desire, psychological factors determine the intensity and direction of the flame. Inferring that hormones, in general, are the primary motivators of sexual activity in humans is a gross oversimplification" (p. 65).

In opposition to biological reductionism, research findings point to interpersonal and sociocultural contributors to the experience of sexual desire. As Basson (2001a) emphasized, sexual intimacy is the primary contributor to sexual desire for women, and this can be diminished through the lack of tenderness, mutuality, respect, communication, or pleasure from sexual touching; undue focus on the performance of vaginal-penile intercourse; or physical or emotional discomfort from any cause. Among the reasons that women give for being sexual, issues of enhanced emotional closeness and commitment, heightened sense of attraction and attractiveness, and physical pleasure that promotes sharing between the couple are very important (Basson, 2002b). Leiblum also emphasized the importance of relationship factors in determining sexual desire. Women lose sexual desire when they feel disrespected, devalued, or degraded and when their partners use poor sexual techniques or have sexual problems of their own (Leiblum, 2002; Leiblum & Rosen, 1988). In surveys of midlife women, poor body image, wanting more equality in one's sexual relationship, and wanting more passion from one's partner were significantly related to a decrease in a woman's sexual desire as they aged (Koch & Mansfield, 2001/2002; Koch, Mansfield, Thureau, & Carey, 2005; Mansfield, Koch, & Voda, 1998).

Feminist scholarship has produced an entire literature refuting the notion that human sexuality is a natural, intrinsic, and universal phenomenon by documenting sexual differences among individuals based on gender, class, race and ethnicity, history, culture, sexual identity and orientation, environmental factors, and even HIV status (e.g., Gagnon & Simon, 1973; McCormick, 1994; White, Bondurant, & Travis, 2000). Plummer (1995) asserted that each person's sexuality is a context- and culture-specific story that she or he lives while assuming that it is totally "natural" (biologically determined).

Depoliticizing Sexual Desire

Feminists emphasize that locating sexuality solely within the individual (e.g., biological reductionism described above) serves to depoliticize the nature of sexuality by ignoring the sociocultural, political, and relational factors that affect women's lives (Daniluk, 1998). Foucault (1980) argued that histo-socio-cultural factors work at a very basic level to construct sexual experiences, not simply by enhancing or restricting biology. As interpreted by Tolman and Diamond (2001),

> Foucault argued that conceptualizations of sexual desire as repressed 'essences' are *themselves* strategic social discourses that are crafted and deployed by those with social authority and power in the service of particular political and ideological ends. Importantly, such discourses are usually not visible as such; rather, they reflect what *appears* to be natural, factual, or objectively real (p. 38).

Subsequent feminist scholarship has uncovered numerous ways that majority men have been privileged in experiencing and acting on sexual desire, whereas women are restricted from such sexual agency (Duggan, 1990; Ramazanoglu & Holland, 1993). Fine (1988) provided an analysis of how the politicalization of sexuality education, as it was taught in New York City classrooms, resulted in a missing discourse of desire for adolescent females. She described the sexuality curriculum as focusing on young women saying "no" to a question that they had no power in framing. The adolescent's sexuality was negotiated by, for, and despite the young woman herself. For her, desire became entwined with danger, buttressing the concept of woman-as-victim. Rather than protecting young women from victimization, teenage pregnancy, and sexually transmitted diseases, as professed in the curriculum, the denial of their sexual desire and agency left them disempowered, conflicted, and confused about their sexuality.

This initial silencing of their sexual desire is difficult for women to overcome as they age. Institutional sexism again surfaced as a theme in the grounded theory study of postmenopausal women's experience of sexual desire (Wood, 2004). In reflecting back over their lives, these older women identified numerous negative messages that they had received regarding sexual desire from their families, schools, communities, religion, partners, and the media. The sexist messages they received included the sexual double standard (e.g., it was fine for men to be sexual actors but not for women), sex as dichotomized (e.g., women should only have sex for love), sexual silence (e.g., women should not express interest in sex), sex as reproduction (e.g., pleasure was not expected), and women's bodies as objects of desire (e.g. high expectations of attractiveness leading to body image concerns). One woman described how this institutional sexism affected her sexual desire in this way:

> The only way I can explain it, this feeling that my sexual desire is out there somewhere away from myself, is that there are all of these other forces dictating when a woman, at least in my generation, should and could have sex. And the rules or standards about women feeling turned on or interested in sex were even more confusing. You know: 'Have sex for your husband, get excited for him, but not too excited because you want him to feel like he can please you and satisfy you. Don't be turned on by other men who aren't your husband, that's wrong.' It's like someone else has dictated with who, where, and when I should have sex and how excited I should be about it. I just {pause}, it's like I just stopped trying to have it be mine. I gave up trying to understand and sort out all of those rules and mixed messages. . . . I rarely feel sexual desire anymore at all (p. 169).

Medicalization of Female Sexual Desire

Medicalization is a social process in which behaviors, conditions, or habits are considered matters of health and disease using the biomedical model (Tiefer, 2005). As Tiefer (2001b, p. 65) observed, "The medicalization of sexuality prescribes and demarcates sexual interests and activities, defining normality and deviance in the language of sexual health and illness" (Giami, 2000; Rubin, 1984; Tiefer, 1996). The biomedical view of sexual desire promotes concern over what constitutes "normal" versus "abnormal" and "high" versus "low" levels of desire. Such labeling presupposes that all women experience sexual desire similarly throughout differing times in their lives and in different relationships in a one-size-fits-all model. For example, Sugrue and Whipple (2001) argued that using the *DSM*, based on the triphasic model of sexual functioning, to classify women's sexual experiences "inaccurately pathologizes what seems normal and natural for many women" (p. 222).

Ussher (1993) emphasized that the process through which women's sexual desire is labeled and professionally defined has real-life implications: "Women clearly internalize these definitions of 'normal' sexual functioning and

as a result refer themselves for help, thus reinforcing the notion of pathology and of the need for expert intervention" (p. 19). This is evidenced by the fact that lack of sexual interest is currently the most common reason given by women for seeking sex therapy (Everaerd, Laan, Both, & van der Velde, 2000). Further, many community studies demonstrate that American women, especially during midlife, are concerned with their levels of sexual desire (Ellison, 2000).

Feminists emphasize that such biological reductionism spawns a disease-oriented approach to variation in desire (Leiblum, 2001). This disease-oriented approach posits women's bodies as "deficient," thus creating the need for medical and pharmacological intervention, typically via hormone (replacement) therapy (Boston Women's Health Book Collective, 2005; Shaw, 2001; Tiefer, 2001a). For example, research grounded in the biomedical paradigm tends to explain aging women's sexual desire in terms of "deteriorating" function and "deficient" levels of reproductive hormones related to the menopausal transition, as illustrated in this description of sexual functioning of post-menopausal women:

> Changes in sexual function occur in the majority of women during the premenopausal and immediate postmenopausal years. These changes include modification of the physiology of sex response, the development of sexual dysfunctions, and change in levels of sexual desire. Because these changes occur coincident with decreases in ovarian hormone production and with biological evidence of the effects of hormone *deficiency* (e.g., pelvic *atrophy*), there is reason to believe that altered sexual function is at least in part due to hormone *deficiency*. To this end, hormone replacement therapy (HRT) has the potential for restoring previous levels of sexual function and desire (Sarrel, 2000, p. 25, italics added).

Since sexual desire is an aspect of sexual response thought to be highly influenced by hormonal factors, it is seen as "treatable" with hormones, especially among menopausal women (e.g., Koster & Garde, 1993; Riley & Riley, 2000). Specifically, increasing women's level of sexual desire is often considered as the way to treat "female sexual dysfunction" (FSD; Galyer, Congaglen, Hare, & Conaglen, 1999; Basson, 2001b). This has resulted in an emphasis by the pharmaceutical industry to develop "Viagra-type" drugs to enhance women's sexual responding in hopes that they would be a financial boon, as Viagra has been (Moynihan, 2003). Since sildenafil (Viagra) "sprang" onto the market in 1998, more than 17 million men have gotten prescriptions to treat their erectile dysfunction, resulting in sales of $1.5 billion for Pfizer in 2001 (Moynihan). The new competitors (Lilly-ICOS's tadalfil and Buyer's vardenafil) are expected to have yearly sales of $1 billion each.

Thus, it is no coincidence that in October of 1998, an international consensus development conference, sponsored by educational grants by nine pharmaceutical companies, was convened by the Sexual Function Health Council of the American Foundation for Urologic Disease. Nineteen specialists in particular aspects of female sexuality (e.g., sex researchers, therapists, gynecologists, and urologists), most of whom had a professional relationship with the pharmaceutical companies, were invited to participate. The stated purpose was to address the shortcomings and problems associated with the previous classifications of "female sexual dysfunction" (Basson et al., 2000). The panel identified their primary goal as developing a consensus-based definition and classification scheme for FSD that would include psychogenic and organically-based disorders. They noted that previous diagnostic systems were ambiguous, inconsistent, or too limited based on the state of current knowledge. They agreed that "it may be useful to develop a classification system for female dysfunction that would parallel the clinical and basic science developments for men" (Basson et al., 2000, p. 889). Their other stated objectives included the development of guidelines for clinical evaluation, including identification of endpoints for treatment of FSD and the setting of priorities for future research.

As a result of this conference, participants recommended continuing the overall classification system used in the *DSM-IV: Diagnostic and Statistical Manual of Mental Disorders 4th Edition* (American Psychiatric Association, 2000). Although many disorders were redefined, the system endorsed by the participants included sexual desire disorders, sexual arousal disorder, orgasmic disorder, and sexual pain disorders. Although a debate ensued over a new classification for sexual satisfaction disorder, it was not adopted. Specifically, hypoactive sexual desire disorder was defined as "the persistent or recurrent deficiency (or absence) of sexual fantasies/thoughts, and/or desire for or receptivity to sexual activity, which causes personal distress" (Basson et al., 2000, p. 890). Many panelists lauded this definition as superior to the previous one since it added receptivity to the repertoire of initiation of sexual activity, yet receptivity went undefined. In addition, participants explained that adding the criterion of personal distress eliminated the discrepancy of classifying someone as "dysfunctional" when she did not feel concerned with her level of sexual desire.

The report and new classification system for FSD that resulted from the consensus conference was criticized on numerous fronts (see the *Journal of Sex & Marital Therapy*, 2001, vol. 27). For example, Everaerd and Both (2001) criticized the panel's devotion to empiricism through the emphasis of quantifiable measures and endpoints without showing "much awareness of their roles of social constructionists" (p. 137). Some sexologists called into question the proprietary nature of the conference (Fagan & Strand,

2001; Shaw, 2001). Some argued that the agenda of the consensus conference, sponsored primarily by pharmaceutical companies, was in actuality to define "female sexual dysfunction" in order to create a need and demand for drug treatment (Bancroft, Graham, & McCord, 2001; Hall, 2001; Tiefer, 2001a). As Tiefer (2002) conjectured:

> This consensus report . . . will be used by commercial interests to justify drug trial research designs that will exclude most of women's sexual issues . . . Federally approved, expensive, prescription drugs will then be advertised directly to women who have no other sources of information or help (p. 135).

Concerned with issues of power, feminists noted that the medical profession reaps power from the biomedical conceptualization of women's sexual desire (Shaw, 2001). Further, they observed that experts had defined normal sexual desire and classified desire disorders to facilitate treatment of a problem that they had, in essence, constructed (Moynihan, 2003; Tiefer, 1995, 2000, 2001a).

The Food and Drug Administration's Center for Drug Evaluation and Research released guidelines for drug trials on female sexual dysfunction shortly following the publication of the consensus report (FDA, 2002). The first drug trials tested the effects of sildenafil on women who were diagnosed with "female sexual arousal disorder" (Berman et al., 2001; Caruso, Intelesiano, Lupo, & Agnello, 2001). The results indicated that facilitating sexual arousal in women was not as simple as prescribing a pill. As Berman explained, "There is clearly a role for medical therapies, but not in isolation from emotional and relationship issues, which are equally if not more important with women" (Moynihan, 2003, p. 47). In February 2004, Pfizer announced that it was ending its research into the use of sildenafil with women due to poor results in the clinical trials.

The search for a drug to improve women's sexuality has shifted to increasing sexual desire through testosterone therapy. Proctor and Gamble was the first company to seek FDA approval for a testosterone patch, called "Instrinsa," to treat "hypoactive sexual desire disorder." The clinical trials for this drug were conducted with surgically menopausal women who were also using estrogen therapy. However, it was touted in the media that, if approved, this patch would probably be prescribed off-label for any woman, especially if she was reaching menopause. The results of the clinical trials showed that the placebo treatment (couples' counseling and support) increased the "endpoints" from women reporting two "satisfactory sexual episodes" to three a month (Tiefer, 2004). In comparison, the use of the testosterone patch added another sexual episode per month above that of the placebo group. However, at its December 2004 meeting, the FDA advisory committee did not find enough evidence of the effectiveness and (long-term) safety of Intrinsa to recommend approval of the drug to the FDA. Further, it recommended that more studies be conducted with naturally menopausal women, peri- and premenopausal women, and women with real-life stresses and health issues. Thus, Proctor and Gamble withdrew its application for approval of Intrinsa from the FDA.

A "New View" of Women's Sexual Problems

To contest the biomedical model that was beginning to dominate research on women's sexuality and treatment of women's sexual concerns, a group of twelve feminist scholars, therapists, and researchers organized their own Working Group in 2000 (Tiefer, 2001a). This Working Group produced a volume of commentary and research articles disputing the biomedical conceptualization of women's sexuality used to construct the *DSM* classification scheme for female sexual dysfunction (Kaschak & Tiefer, 2002). They identified what they considered the three most serious distortions of women's sexuality produced by the biomedical model, which "reduces sexual problems to disorders of physiological function, comparable to breathing or digestive disorders" (Kaschak & Tiefer, p. 3).

First was the false notion of sexual equivalency between women and men endorsed by traditional models of sexual response and an identical classification system of sexual disorders and dysfunctions, even though women's responses and concerns are not always similar to those of men. (Refer to the previous section, Use of the Male Model as the Standard). Second was the erasure of the relational context of sexuality from the classification of sexual problems by assuming "that one can measure and treat genital and physical difficulties without regard to the relationship in which the sex occurs" (Ibid., p. 3). (Refer to the previous section, Biological Reductionism). The final distortion was the leveling of differences among women (a combination of biological reductionism and depoliticalization—see previous sections). This leveling was explained in this way:

All women are not the same, and their sexual needs, satisfactions, and problems do not fit neatly into categories of desire, arousal, orgasm, or pain. Women differ in their values, approaches to sexuality, social and cultural backgrounds, and current situations, and these differences cannot be smoothed over into an identical notion of 'dysfunction'—or an identical, one-size-fits-all treatment (Ibid., p. 3).

The Working Group of "The New View of Women's Sexual Problems" recommended a different classification system for sexual concerns based on women's real-life experiences (Kaschak & Tiefer, 2002). To avoid the total medicalization of women's sexuality, they preferred the term "sexual problems" to "sexual dysfunction." Sexual problems were defined as "discontent or dissatisfaction with any emotional, physical, or relational aspect of sexual experience" (Ibid., p. 5). Women's sexual problems are "notoriously multifactorial in etiology" (Davis, 2001, p. 131). Thus, four comprehensive and interrelated areas were identified as the major contributors to women's sexual problems (Working Group, 2002, pp. 5-7). The first major contributor was sociocultural, political, or economic factors, including ignorance and anxiety due to inadequate sex education, lack of access to health services, or other social constraints. Clashes between cultural norms were also acknowledged as inhibiting sexual expression. Another feature of most women's lives—lack of interest, fatigue, or lack of time due to family and work obligations—was also targeted in this category.

Partner and relationship issues were identified as the second major contributor to women's sexual problems, including discrepancies or conflicts over specific sexual issues (e.g., preferences for sexual activity) or more generalized relationship or life issues, like financial or health problems. Negative partner characteristics (e.g., domineering) or behavior (e.g., abuse) were also emphasized in this category. The third category highlighted psychological factors contributing to sexual problems, including general personality problems, depression, or anxiety. The role of past or current negative experiences and their consequences in creating sexual aversion and inhibition was also emphasized. Finally, medical factors were also recognized as important, including numerous local or systemic medical conditions; pregnancy, sexually transmitted diseases, or other sex-related conditions; side effects of drugs, medications, or medical treatments; and iatrogenic conditions.

Although there is always more to learn, much multidisciplinary research and scholarship has been conducted on women's sexuality, including their sexual desire. Bancroft and colleagues (2001) have emphasized that sexual desire problems present clinicians with a vast, heterogeneous group of etiologies, but that it seems that the approach has become, "If we concentrate hard enough on the women's pelvis, these other issues will disappear" (p. 102). It should be noted that each of the factors described by the "New View" has been identified through clinical practice and/or research as specifically impacting women's sexual desire (e.g., Bancroft et al, 2001; Basson, 2001a, 2001b, 2002b; Duggan, 1990; Fine, 1988; Gabbard, 2001; Heiman, 2001; Kameya, 2001; Koch & Mansfield, 2001/2002; Koch et al., 2005; Leiblum, 2001, 2002; Leiblum & Rosen, 1988; Mansfield et al., 1998; Ramazanoglu & Holland, 1993; Surgrue & Whipple, 2001; Wood, 2004; Wood et al., in press).

Through numerous publications, presentations, and advocacy activities, the "New View" of women's sexual problems has gained recognition and made some inroads on sexual education, therapy, and public policy (see Kaschak & Tiefer, 2002; FSD Alert Campaign, 2006).

Recommendations for Future Research

It is clear that conceptualizations and experiences of sexual desire are complex and holistic for women. We make the following recommendations for exploring, in more valid and beneficial ways, the answers to the following questions (Levine, 2002; Tolman & Diamond, 2001):

1. What is sexual desire for women?
2. How does it operate in women's lives?
3. How might the range of differing sociocultural, political, economic, relational, psychological, and biological processes interact to shape different forms of sexual desire in different contexts over the lifespan?

First, researchers need to be more mindful of the limitations and biases inherent in the paradigms they are using. Terms like "deficient," "disorder," and "dysfunction" have epistemological implications which both illustrate and influence notions about the nature of women's sexual desire. Failing to address bias inherent in a research paradigm not only affects the validity of a study, but also limits the explanatory power of the researchers' conclusions.

Second, the real-world implications of research findings on the general population need to be considered. To date, a majority of the research on women's sexual desire has encouraged (if not created) a culture in which women's sexual lives are labeled as "normal" or "dysfunctional." Increasing numbers of women are finding their level of sexual desire categorized as "disordered" or "deficient," yet women have had little power in defining their experiences for themselves (or to researchers). To this end, women are, in essence, socialized to seek out the advice of "experts" for "treatment" (e.g., a drug) to remedy a "disorder" that may or may not be problematic for them (Bancroft, Loftus, & Long, 2003). Women's own conceptualizations of sexual desire and sexual problems should supplant those purported by the strictly biomedical model.

Finally, future research needs to employ paradigms that acknowledge multiple influences on women's sexual desire. More qualitative research designed to increase the understanding of women's sexual desire (and sexuality) is sorely needed. In addition, biopsychosocial models should be utilized to account for contextual factors that may directly or indirectly affect a woman's sexuality, in addition to the biological factors. In this approach, women's sexuality is conceptualized as the interaction of several factors, as opposed to being solely biologically or socioculturally determined (e.g., Tiefer, 1995; McCormick, 1994). As Tolman & Diamond (2001) have observed, "sexual desire represents, in many ways, an ideal 'laboratory' for interactions between biological and sociocultural aspects of sexuality" (p. 36). In women's lives, this "laboratory" is constantly processing the myriad of sociocultural, political, economic, relational, psychological, and biological factors, from the mundane to the traumatic, that holistically result in the (lack of) experience of sexual desire.

References

Alexander, G. M., & Sherwin, B. B. (1993). Sex steroids, sexual behavior, and attention for erotic stimuli in women using oral contraceptives. *New England Journal of Medicine, 299,* 1,145–1,150.

American Psychiatric Association. (2000). *Diagnostic and statistical manual of mental disorders.* (DSM-IV-TR, 4th edition, text revision). Washington, DC: author.

Bachmann, G. (1990). The ideals of optimal care for women at mid-life. In M. Flint, F. Kronenberg, & W. Utian (Eds.), *Multidisciplinary perspectives on menopause* (pp. 253–256). New York: New York Academy of Sciences.

Bancroft, J. (1988). Sexual desires and the brain. *Sexual and Marital Therapy, 3,* 11–27.

Bancroft, J., Graham, C. A., & McCord, C. (2001). Conceptualizing women's sexual problems. *Journal of Sex & Marital Therapy, 27*(2), 95–104.

Bancroft, J., Loftus, J., & Long, J. S. (2003). Distress about sex: A national survey of women in heterosexual relationships. *Archives of Sexual Behavior, 32*(1), 193–209.

Basson, R. (2001a). Human sex-response cycles. *Journal of Sex & Marital Therapy, 27,* 33–43.

Basson, R. (2001b). Using a different model for female sexual response to address women's problematic low sexual desire. *Journal of Sex & Marital Therapy, 27,* 395–403.

Basson, R. (2002a). A model of women's sexual arousal. *Journal of Sex & Marital Therapy, 28,* 1–10.

Basson, R. (2002b). Women's sexual desire—Disordered or misunderstood? *Journal of Sex & Marital Therapy, 28*(S), 17–28.

Basson, R. (2003). Commentary on "In the mood for sex—The values of androgens." *Journal of Sex & Marital Therapy, 29,* 177–179.

Basson, R., Berman, J., Burnett, A., Derogatis, L., Ferguson D., Fourcroy, J., et al. (2000). Report of the international consensus development conference on female sexual dysfunction: Definitions and Classifications. *The Journal of Urology, 163,* 888–893.

Baumeister, R., Catanese, K., & Vohs, K. (2001). Is there a gender difference in strength of sex drive? Theoretical views, conceptual distinctions, and a review of relevant evidence. *Personality and Social Psychology Review, 5*(3), 242–273.

Beck, J. G., Bozman, A. W., & Qualtrough, T. (1991). The experience of sexual desire: Psychological correlates in a college sample. *The Journal of Sex Research, 28,* 443–456.

Benedek, T., & Rubenstein, B. B. (1939). The correlations between ovarian activity and psychodynamic processes: 1. The ovulation phase. *Psychosomatic Medicine, 1,* 461–85.

Berman, J., Berman, L., Lin, H., Flaherty, E., Lahey, N., Goldstein, I., et al. (2001). Effect of sildenafil on subjective and physiologic parameters of the female sexual response in women with sexual arousal disorder. *Journal of Sex & Marital Therapy, 27,* 411–420.

Boston Women's Health Book Collective. (2005). *Our bodies, ourselves: A new edition for a new era.* New York: Peter Smith Publishing, Inc.

Brumberg, J. J. (1997). *The body project: An intimate history of American girls.* New York: Random House.

Byers, E. S., & Heinlein, L. (1989). Predicting initiations and refusals of sexual activities in married and cohabiting heterosexual couples. *The Journal of Sex Research, 26,* 210–231.

Caruso, S., Intelisano, G., Lupo, L., & Agnello, C. (2001). Premenopausal women affected by sexual arousal disorder treated with sildenafil: A double-blind, cross-over, placebo-controlled study. *British Journal of Obstetrics and Gynaecology. 108(6),* 623–8.

Daniluk, J. C. (1998). *Women's sexuality across the lifespan: Challenging myths, creating meanings.* New York: Guilford Press.

Davis, S. R. (2001). An external perspective on the report of the international consensus development conference on female sexual dysfunction. *Journal of Sex & Marital Therapy, 27(2),* 131–134.

Duggan, L. (1990). From instincts to politics: Writing the history of sexuality in the U.S. *The Journal of Sex Research, 27(1),* 95–110.

Ellison, C. R. (2000). *Women's sexualities: Generations of women share intimate secrets of sexual self-acceptance.* Oakland, California: New Harbinger Publications.

Everaerd, W., & Both, S. (2001). Ideal female sexual function. *Journal of Sex & Marital Therapy, 27(2),* 137–140.

Fveraerd, W., Laan, E., Both, S., & van der Velde, J. (2000). Female sexuality. In L. T. Szuchman, & F. Muscarella (Eds.), *Psychological Perspectives on Human Sexuality* (pp. 101–146). New York: John Wiley & Sons, Inc.

Fagan, P. J., & Strand, J. G. (2001). A call for non-proprietary peer-reviewed research. *Journal of Sex & Marital Therapy, 27(2),* 141–144.

Fine, M. (1988). Sexuality, schooling, and adolescent females: The missing discourse of desire. *Harvard Educational Review, 58(1),* 54–63.

Food and Drug Administration, Center for Drug Evaluation and Research. (2002). Available www.fda.gov/cder/guidance/index/htm.

Foucault, M. (1980). *The history of sexuality* (Vol. 1). New York: Vintage.

FSD Alert Campaign. (2006). Available www.fsd-alert.org.

Gabbard, G. O. (2001). Musings on the report of the international consensus development conference of female sexual dysfunction: Definitions and classifications. *Journal of Sex & Marital Therapy, 27(2),* 145–148.

Gagnon, J. H., & Simon, W. (1973). *Sexual conduct: The social sources of human sexuality.* Chicago: Aldine.

Gayler, K. T., Congaglen, H. M., Hare, A., & Congaglen, J. V. (1999). The effect of gynecological surgery on sexual desire. *Journal of Sex & Marital Therapy, 25,* 81–8.

Giami, A. (2000). Changing relations between medicine, psychology, and sexuality: The case of male impotence. *Journal of Social Medicine, 4,* 263–272.

Graham, C. A., Sanders, S. A., Milhausen, R. R., & McBride, K. R. (2004). Turning on and turning off; A focus group study of the factors that affect women's sexual arousal. *Archives of Sexual Behavior, 33(6):* 527–38.

Hall, M. (2001). Small print and conspicuous omissions: Commentary on the "FSD" classification report. *Journal of Sex & Marital Therapy, 27(2),* 149–150.

Harris, G. (2004, February 28). Pfizer gives up testing Viagra on women. *The New York Times,* Late Edition—Final, Section C. Page 1. Column 5.

Heiman, J. R. (2001), Sexual desire in human relationships. In W. Everaerd, E. Laan, & S. Both (Eds.), *Sexual appetite, desire and motivation: Energetics of the sexual system* (pp. 117–132). Amsterdam, Netherlands: Koninklijke Nederlandse Akademie van Wetenschappen.

Irvine, J. (1990). *Disorders of desire: Sex and gender in modern American sexology.* Philadelphia, PA: Temple University Press.

Kameya, Y. (2001). How Japanese culture affects the sexual functions of normal females. *Journal of Sex & Marital Therapy, 27(2),* 151–152.

Kaplan, H. S. (1979). *Disorders of sexual desire.* New York: Brunner/Mazel.

Kaplan, H. S. (1992). A neglected issue: The sexual side effects of current treatments for breast cancer. *Journal of Sex & Marital Therapy, 18,* 3–19.

Kaschak, E., & Tiefer, L. (Eds.). (2002). *A new view of women's sexual problems.* New York: Haworth Press.

Kingsberg, S. (2000). The psychological impact of aging on sexuality and relationships. *Journal of Women's Health & Gender-Based Medicine, 9(1),* S33–38.

Koch, P. B. (2004). Feminism and sexuality in the United States. In R. T. Francoeur & R. Noonan (Eds.). *The international encyclopedia of sexuality.* New York: Continuum.

Koch, P. B., & Mansfield, P. K. (2001/2002). Women's sexuality as they age: The more things change, the more they stay the same. *SIECUS Report, 30(2),* 10–16.

Koch, P. B., Mansfield, P. K., Thureau, D., & Carey, M. (2005). "Feeling frumpy": The relationships between body image and sexual response changes in midlife women. *The Journal of Sex Research, 42(3),* 1–9.

Koster, A., & Garde, K. (1993). Sexual desire and menopausal development: A prospective study of Danish women born in 1936. *Maturitas, 16(1),* 49–60.

Laumann, E. O., Gangnon, J. H., Michael, R. T, & Michaels, S. (1994). *The social organization of sexuality: Sexual practices in the United Slates.* Chicago: University of Chicago Press.

LeGates, M. (1995). Feminists before feminism: Origins and varieties of women's protests in Europe and North America before the twentieth century. In J. Freeman (Ed.), *Women: A feminist perspective.* Mountain View, CA: Mayfield.

Leiblum, S. R. (2001). Critical overview of the new consensus-based definitions and classification of female sexual dysfunction. *Journal of Sex & Marital Therapy, 27(2),* 159–168.

Leiblum, S. R. (2002). Reconsidering gender differences in sexual desire: An update. *Sexual and Relationship Therapy, 17(1),* 57–68.

Leiblum, S. R., Bachmann, G., Kemmann, E., Colburn, D., & Schwartzman, L. (1983). Vaginal atrophy in the postmenopausal woman: The importance of sexual activity and hormones. *Journal of the American Medical Association. 249*(16), 2,195–2,198.

Leiblum, S. R., & Rosen, R. C. (1988). Changing perspectives on sexual desire. In S. Leiblum & R. Rosen (Eds.), *Sexual desire disorders* (pp. 1–20). New York: Guilford Press.

Leiblum, S. R., & Rosen, R. C. (2000). *Principles and practice of sex therapy* (3 rd ed.). New York: Guilford Press.

Leitenberg, H., & Henning, K. (1995). Sexual fantasy. *Psychological Bulletin, 117,* 469–496.

Levine, S. B. (2002). Reexploring the concept of sexual desire. *Journal of Sex & Marital Therapy, 28,* 39–51.

Mansfield, P. K., Koch, P. B., & Voda, A. (1998). Qualities midlife women desire in their sexual relationships and their changing sexual response. *Psychology of Women Quarterly, 22,* 285–303.

Masters, W., & Johnson, V. (1966). *Human sexual response.* Boston: Little Brown.

McConnick, N. (1994). *Sexual salvation: Affirming women's sexual rights and pleasures.* Westport, CT: Praeger.

McCoy, N. L. (1992). The menopause and sexuality. In R. Sitruik-Ware & W. H. Utian (Eds.). *The menopause and hormonal replacement therapy* (pp. 73–100). New York: Marcel Dekker.

Moynihan, R. (2003). The making of a disease: Female sexual dysfunction. *British Medical Journal, 326,* 45–47.

Nusbaum, M., Gamble, G., Skinner, B., & Heiman, J. (2000). The high prevalence of sexual concerns among women seeking routine gynecological care. *Journey of Family Practice, 49*(3), 229–232.

O'Sullivan, L., & Byers, E. S. (1992). College students' incorporation of initiator and restrictor roles in sexual dating interactions. *The Journal of Sex Research, 29,* 435–446.

Plummer, K. (1995). *Telling sexual stories.* New York: Routledge.

Pollis, C. A. (1988). An assessment of the impacts of feminism on sexual science. *The Journal of Sex Research, 25,* 85–105.

Ramazanoglu, C., & Holland, J. (1993). Women's sexuality and men's appropriation of desire. In C. Ramazanoglu (Ed.). *Up against Foucault* (pp. 239–264). New York: Routledge.

Regan, P. C. (1999). Hormonal correlates and causes of sexual desire: A review. *The Canadian Journal of Human Sexuality, 8*(1), 1–16.

Riley, A., & Riley, E. (2000). Controlled studies on women presenting with sexual drive disorder: Endocrine status. *Journal of Sex and Marital Therapy, 26,* 269–83.

Rosen, R. C., & Leiblum, S. R. (1995). Treatment of sexual disorders in the 1990s: An integrated approach. *Journal of Consulting and Clinical Psychology, 63*(6), 877–890.

Rubin, G. (1984). Thinking sex: Notes for a radical theory of the politics of sexuality. In C. S. Vance (Ed.), *Pleasure and danger: Exploring female sexuality* (pp. 267–319). Boston: Routledge & Kegan Paul.

Sarrell, P. M. (2000), Effects of hormone replacement therapy on sexual psychophysiology and behavior in postmenopause. *Journal of Women's Health & Gender-Based Medicine, 9(S),* 25–32.

Sarrel, P., Dobay, B., & Witta, B. (1998). Estrogen and estrogen-androgen replacement for post-menopausal women dissatisfied with estrogen-only therapy: Sexual behavior and neuro-endocrine responses. *Journal of Reproductive Medicine, 43,* 847–856.

Shaw, J. (2001). Another Procrustean bed for female sexual functioning. *Journal of Sex & Marital Therapy, 27*(2), 211–214.

Sherwin, B. (1991). The psychoendocrinology of aging and female sexuality. *The Annual Review of Sex Research, 2,* 181–198.

Sugrue, D. P., & Whipple, B. (2001). The consensus-based classification of female sexual dysfunction: Barriers to universal acceptance. *Journal of Sex & Marital Therapy, 27*(2), 221–226.

Tiefer, L. (1988). A feminist perspective on sexology and sexuality. In M. Gergen (Ed.). *Feminist thought and the structure of knowledge* (pp. 16–26). New York: New York University Press.

Tiefer, L. (1991). Historical, scientific, clinical, and feminist criticisms of the "Human Sexual Response Cycle" model. *Annual Review of Sex Research, 2,* 1–23.

Tiefer, L. (1995). *Sex is not a natural act and other essays.* Boulder, CO: Westview Press.

Tiefer, L. (1996). The medicalization of sexuality: Conceptual, normative, and professional issues. *Annual Review of Sex Research, 7,* 252–282.

Tiefer, L. (2000). The social construction and social effects of sex research: The sexological model of sexuality. In C. B. Travis & J. W. White (Eds.), *Sexuality, society, and feminism* (pp. 79–109). Washington, DC: American Psychological Association.

Tiefer, L. (2001a). The "consensus" conference on female sexual dysfunction: Conflicts of interest and hidden agendas. *Journal of Sex & Marital Therapy, 27*(2), 227–236.

Tiefer, L. (2001b). The selling of "female sexual dysfunction." *Journal of Sex and Martial Therapy, 27*(5): 652–658.

Tiefer, L. (2002). Beyond the medical model of women's sexual problems: A campaign to resist the promotion of "female sexual dysfunction." *Sexual and Relationship Therapy, 17*(2), 127–135.

Tiefer, L. (2004). Showdown in Gaithersburg: The New View Report on the FDA Advisory Committee Hearing on Procter & Gamble's Testosterone Patch, "Intrinsa." Available www.fsd-alert.org.

Tiefer, L. (2005). Procter & Gamble's testosterone patch for women: A case study in the medicalization of sexuality. Plenary presentation at the World Association of Sexology, Montreal, Canada.

Tolman, D., & Diamond, L. (2001). Desegregating sexuality research: Cultural and biological perspectives on gender and desire. *Annual Review of Sex Research, 12,* 33–74.

Ussher, J. M. (1993). The construction of female sexual problems: Regulating sex, regulating women. In J. Ussher & C. Baker (Eds.), *Psychological perspectives on sexual problems.* London: Routledge.

Vance, C. S., & Pollis, C. A. (1990). Introduction: A special issue on feminist perspectives on sexuality. *The Journal of Sex Research, 27,* 1–5.

Voda, A. M. (1997). *Menopause, me, and you.* New York: Harrington Park Press.

Wallen, K. (1995). The evolution of female sexual desire. In P. R. Abramson & S. D. Pinkerton (Eds.), *Sexual nature/sexual culture* (pp. 57–79). Chicago: University of Chicago Press.

Wallen, K. (2000). Risky business: Social context and hormonal modulation of primate sexual desire. In K. Wallen & J. E. Schneider (Eds.), *Reproduction in context* (pp. 289–323). Cambridge, MA: Bradford Books, MIT Press.

White, J. W., Bondurant, B., & Travis, C. B. (2000). Social constructions of sexuality: Unpacking hidden meanings. In C. B. Travis & J. W. White (Eds.), *Sexuality, society, & feminism* (pp 11–34). Washington, DC: American Psychological Association.

Winton, M. A. (2001), Gender, sexual dysfunctions, and the Journal of Sex & Marital Therapy. *Journal of Sex & Marital Therapy, 27,* 333–337.

Wood, J. M. (2004). The experience and meaning of postmenopausal women's sexual desire: A grounded theory study. Unpublished doctoral dissertation. The Pennsylvania State University.

Wood, J. M., Mansfield, P. K., & Koch, P. B. (in press). Negotiating sexual agency: Postmenopausal women's meaning and experience of sexual desire. *Journal of Qualitative Health Research.*

Working Group on a "New View of Women's Sexual Problems." (2002). In E. Kaschak & L. Tiefer (Eds.), *A new view of women's sexual problems.* New York: Haworth Press.

UNIT 3

Sexualities and Development

Unit Selections

Key Points to Consider

- Do you remember having questions about your body, sex, or similar topics as a young child? Were you able to ask your parents? How did you get answers to your questions, and from whom?

- Do you remember any misinformation you had about the human body and/or sex when you were younger? Where did this misinformation come from? How was it corrected? Could any harm have come from this misinformation?

- If you are not a parent, imagine that you are. What kinds of questions from children about sex and sexuality do you think would be the most difficult for you to answer? If you are already a parent, have you faced any challenging questions from them? What concerns do you have about answering your child's questions? What do you think your greatest strengths are (or will be), as a parent helping your child to learn about sex and sexualities?

- How do you view sex and sexualities at your age? In what ways are your views different from those that you had when you were younger? How do you perceive the changes, and to what do you attribute them?

- Imagine a couple in the middle of a sexual encounter. Think about this for a moment. When you are finished, consider these questions: How old were they? If they were younger than middle age, can you replay your vision with middle-aged or older people? Why or why not?

- How does this relate to your expectations regarding your own romantic and/or sexual life a few decades from now?

- Do you ever think about your parents as sexual people? Your grandparents? Was considering these two questions upsetting for you? Embarrassing? Explain your answers as best you can.

Student Web Site
www.mhcls.com

Internet References

World Association for Sexology
   http://www.tc.umn.edu/nlhome/m201/colem001/was/wasindex.htm

Sexuality Information and Education Council of the United States
   http://www.siecus.org/

Teacher Talk
   http://education.indiana.edu/cas/tt/tthmpg.html

American Association of Retired Persons (AARP)
   http://www.aarp.org

National Institute on Aging (NIA)
   http://www.nih.gov/nia/

© Ryan McVay/Getty Images

Individual sexual development is a lifelong process that begins before we are born and continues until the day we die. Contrary to once popular ideas about this process, there are no latent periods in childhood or old age during which the individual is not a sexual being. Research into cognitive, social, and emotional development, however, reveals real differences through various life stages. This section devotes attention to different stages of life in relation to our close relationships, our identities, and our sexualities.

As children gain self-awareness, they naturally explore their own bodies, masturbate, display curiosity about the bodies of others, and show interest in the bodies of the people closest to them, such as their parents. Exploration and curiosity are important and healthy aspects of human development, yet adults sometimes make their children feel ashamed of being sexual, or for showing interest in the human body. When adults impose their own personal feelings upon a child's innocuous explorations into sexuality, fail to communicate with children about this essential aspect of human life, or behave toward children in sexually inappropriate ways, long-term damage can occur. This can hinder full acceptance and enjoyment of one's sexuality later in life. The harm that has been done to someone as child can further impact others—intimate partners, and one's own children. The damage can go far beyond that of the hurt child.

Adolescence, the social stage accompanying puberty, and the transition to adulthood, proves to be a very stressful period of life for many individuals, as they attempt to develop an adult identity and forge relationships with others. This is especially true for far too many lesbian, gay, bisexual and transgender adolescents. Extreme self-awareness, especially at this age, is not at all uncommon. During this period, young people of all sexual orientations may feel as though they are living in a fishbowl, as if everyone around them is examining their every action and reaction.

Partly because of the physical capacity of adolescents for reproduction, sexuality tends to be heavily censured by parents and society at this stage of life. Young people are living in increasingly complicated worlds. Prevailing societal messages are powerful, conflicting, and highly confusing. How do young people even start to make sense of the simultaneous messages of "Just Say No" and "Just Do It" to which they are constantly exposed? Mixed messages come from so many sources, including ads portraying adolescent bodies provocatively, and partially undressed images in "romance" novels, television shows, music videos, movies, and increasingly sexualized teenage "boy" and "girl" singers and actors. The Internet, with an endless supply of chat rooms and social networking websites, is another potential source of influence.

The media both influence and provide a reflection of individual and societal attitudes that place tremendous emphasis on sexual attractiveness (especially for females) and sexual competency (especially for males). The physical, emotional, and cultural pressures described in the preceding paragraphs combine to create confusion and anxiety in young adults about whether they are "normal." Information through education and assurances from adults can alleviate these stresses and facilitate positive and responsible sexuality. This is especially possible where there is trust and willingness to communicate across generations.

Sexuality finally becomes socially validated in adulthood, at least within heterosexual marriage. Whether we are young or old, gay or straight, bisexual, intersexed or transsexual, we have a lot more in common than many people realize. Regardless of our age, we all need accurate information about sex. Even as adults, we make social comparisons of various kinds, continuing to try to figure out where and how we fit into the world around us. We rely on the feedback we get from others and information on how others perceive us to actually tell us about ourselves. Peers provide some of that information. Some of it we get from our families. Perhaps much more of that information than we realize comes from the media.

Adult sexualities can be a source of joy, pain, validation, confusion, and so many other things both positive and negative. Many people seek fulfillment through their relationships. Keeping a relationship strong requires hard work and the commitment of both partners. Routine, boredom, stress, financial pressures, work, parenting responsibilities, and lack of effective communication can exact heavy tolls on the quantity and quality of sexual interactions. Sexual misinformation, myths, and unanswered questions—especially about changes in sexual arousal, response and functioning—can also undermine or hinder intimacy and sexual fulfillment in the middle years.

Sexuality in late adulthood has been misunderstood (and underestimated) because of the prevailing misconception that only the young and attractive people are sexual. Such an attitude has contributed significantly to the apparent decline in sexual interest and activity as one grows older. However, as population demographics have shifted and the baby boomer generation has aged, these beliefs and attitudes have begun to change. Physiological changes in the aging process are not, in and of themselves, detrimental to sexual expression. A life history of experiences, good health, and growth can make sexual expression in the later years one of the most rewarding and fulfilling experience. Today's aging population is becoming more vocal in letting their children and grandchildren know that as we age we don't grow out of sex; and that, in fact, it can get better with age.

How to Talk about Sex

Whether you have minor problems in bed or a love life dusty with disuse, here's the secret to connecting.

HEIDI RAYKEIL

Ten years ago, before kids and mortgages and All That, my husband and I were experts in the language of love. If sex is a form of communication, well, back then we were on the unlimited calling plan. We may not have always verbally expressed ourselves, but we always conveyed what we meant, physically or emotionally.

Then we had a baby.

Suddenly, I was not only uninterested in sex, I was also strangely confused about how to tell my husband. So while in some ways our daughter's birth brought us closer than ever, in other ways we started to grow apart.

I just didn't know how to explain to J.B. how tired I was, how my body hurt from being pinched and pulled by our baby, and how by the end of the day I couldn't imagine sharing it with anyone else. We both became prickly and defensive: I was sure that when J.B. wrapped his leg over mine at night it meant he was coming on to me (again); when I turned my back and pretended to be asleep, he assumed I no longer found him attractive. Bye-bye, language of love.

Whether it's right after the birth of a baby or a few years down the line, it seems like lots of happily married couples hit the sexual skids when they become parents. And most of them have heard sex therapists on TV and read articles and books, and know they should talk it out.

But there's the rub. Sex is a socially charged and highly personal issue that remains a bit taboo despite our seeming openness. And talking about not having sex? Chances are, the subject comes up when one of you wants it and the other doesn't. Bad time to talk. And who wants to crack open that can of worms later on when it's over? Besides, isn't sex supposed to be fun and spontaneous—like it used to be? Won't talking about it spoil the magic?

"Where's the magic if you're not having sex?" says Valerie Raskin, M.D., author of *Great Sex for Moms: Ten Steps to Nurturing Passion While Raising Kids.* But how do you start talking? What do you say? And how do you say it so you don't end up bruising egos or booting one of you to the couch? My husband and I started by paying attention to the distinction between how we talked about sex and the details of what we were talking about. To begin:

How to Talk
Just Leap In

Nichole Cook, of Pittsburgh, mom of Eleanor, 8, Odessa, 7, and Izabelle, 6, was embarrassed into silence not long after Eleanor was born: One time during sex she squirted breast milk all over her husband. "I was mortified. I thought it was gross—and totally not normal." Rather than telling him how she felt, though, Cook simply avoided sex altogether for the next couple of weeks.

While talking about sex can be awkward, no one yet has actually died of embarrassment. Dr. Raskin suggests breaking the ice simply by acknowledging how hard it is.

That's what Cook did, a few weeks later. "I was really nervous, but I finally just said, 'That was really embarrassing for me.' " As it turned out, her husband hadn't even noticed and didn't think it was a big deal anyway. "After that, we just made sure we had a towel handy. Now it's something we laugh about."

Rather than letting things build up, talking about it now makes room for more openness later.

Choose the Right Place and Tone

One of the worst fights J.B. and I had about sex was right after a failed attempt at it. I really wanted to be in the mood—even though I wasn't at all—so we got partway into the act before I admitted that things weren't working. We lay in bed trying to "talk" about what had happened. But we were so upset that we ended up blaming, and J.B. stormed angrily out of the room.

Thus, we discovered the importance of environment for having a fruitful discussion of our sex life. Choose a night when nothing else is planned and wait until the kids are asleep. Turn off the TV and the phone. This isn't an inquisition. It's an opportunity to reconnect with each other, to steal an intimate moment in a chaotic life. It's about how you show and share love, about something that should be fun and pleasurable.

What Is the Biggest Problem in Your Sex Life Right Now?

- 43% He wants sex more often than I do
- 34% We're both too tired and busy to be in the mood
- 12% Nothing
- 11% A lot about our sex life has changed and we're having trouble adjusting

—Parenting's MomConnection poll

J.B. and I have had some of our best talks late at night on our front stoop. We turn off the porch light, pour some wine, and sit side by side. There's something about not looking directly at each other (and the wine, maybe) that lets things flow. It may cut awkwardness to merge your heart-to-heart with an activity—try talking while hiking, or walking, or sorting through your penny jar.

Acknowledge the Problem

This is not the same as agreeing on the cause of the problem. It's just a way to get the conversation rolling. Dr. Raskin calls this "outing the secret—even though it's not really a secret." Begin by stating the obvious: "I know things aren't like they used to be," or "I know we haven't been having sex very much lately." Often, acknowledging this reality, without judgment, can bring a couple closer.

After that big fight, I realized that my husband and I had let things go far too long. While Ramona was napping the next day, I simply said: "I'm having a hard time with sex these days. I hate the way it's come between us, and it must really suck for you, too." The fact that I wasn't trying to deny or make excuses helped J.B. feel comfortable.

After listening to J.B., I realized he wasn't as angry about the situation as I'd thought. It annoyed him that I'd initiated sex when I didn't really want it, but he'd needed to leave the room to cool down because he simply couldn't change gears and talk rationally while he was still aroused. This not only helped me understand why he became so agitated but also made it easier for me to talk about what I was experiencing physically.

Asking and listening without getting defensive is an important part of this process. Repeat what your partner's saying and ask if you're understanding correctly. Ask, "is there more you want me to know?"

Look Forward, Not Back

Agree to make a fresh start. Don't pull out old fights; avoid generalizing or labeling. Saying things like "You never want sex" or "You're a sex fiend!" is just talking negatively about the past. We all say dumb things; don't waste time fighting about whether they're true.

It's also a bad idea to compare yourself to other couples. What's right for them isn't necessarily what's right for you. When Holly Wing's husband saw a poll in a magazine that claimed most of its readers had sex a lot more often than they

did each month, he kept referring to it—comparing their own not-nearly-so-much stats. Wing, a Berkeley mom of 2-year-old Clio, then started to counter with her own statistics, and before long they were locked in battle. "Instead of solving any problems, we were just getting really good at fighting!"

So stick to what you're feeling ("I feel sad that we're having trouble finding the time to make love") rather than accusations about how you measure up to others.

Stay Positive

"I don't want to talk about sex we haven't had anymore," Wing told her husband after another fight. "If you want to have sex seventeen times a month, well, then, let's go for it!" she said, naming his wildly optimistic ideal. Of course they didn't meet the goal, but the effort did help. Wing felt that her husband realized how hard it is to make time for (and want) frequent sex rather than just complaining about it. And he appreciated her willingness to give it a try.

Shooting for high numbers may not be your solution, but the attitude is admirable. Remind each other that you'll get through this and that you both want to work it out. Instead of saying, "You never woo me anymore," try "Remember that poem you wrote me on our honeymoon? That got me hot!" And if your conversation falls apart and you revert to blaming—stop. Don't try to win. Just end it and try again later when you've both cooled down.

What to Talk About
That There's Love behind Your Lovemaking

If you state explicitly, right up front, that you love and respect each other, and that in talking about this you're only talking about the way you show your love, you're both likely to feel more comfortable expressing your feelings. And keep reminding each other of your love and your mutual desire for each other's happiness—that should be the backdrop to your conversation.

The Meaning of Sex

You can't figure out how to fix your love life if you don't know what you want it to be. So discuss what physical intimacy represents to yourselves and in your relationship.

Women, for instance, often misunderstand the ways in which sex is important for many men. It's not just a matter of stereotypical gotta-have-it male urges but can be a critical form of emotional expression. For whatever combination of reasons, many men feel and express love physically, so they may experience a lack of sex as rejecting not only them but their offering of love as well.

The Definition of Sex

It's a good idea to talk openly about what actually constitutes "sex" to each of you. Is it only intercourse, or does it include other kinds of touching? A husband whose sex drive is at low ebb may be delighted to find that his wife will think him no less a man if he gives her a massage—with or without "extras"—instead of a more "demanding" service.

For Cook and her husband, sharing an understanding that she no longer felt sexual about her breasts was a breakthrough. "I felt like they were just for my kids, not him," she says. With that off the table, they were able to talk about what did still work for both of them.

That It's Not Him. Or You

Many factors mess with parents' love life, only rarely sexual skills or prowess. The list includes exhaustion, a light-sleeping child, hormones, embarrassment about weight gain, lack of time, difficulty shifting gears from parent to lover.

When Heidi Johnecheck, of Petosky, Michigan, mother of Max, 4, and Jaxon, 2, found a magazine article that listed ten reasons it's physically hard for moms to have sex—everything from vaginal dryness to sheer exhaustion—she tore it out and gave it to her husband. "As much as I'd tried to tell him, he just couldn't comprehend what 'I don't feel like it' meant," she says, and he took it personally. "But the article showed that it wasn't just me or just him."

Specific Ways to Make Things Better

Johnecheck and her husband decided to tackle one simple problem head-on: They made a kid-free visit to a local sex shop to buy some lubricants. "We actually made a date together," Johnecheck says, "and decided to just be silly and have fun with it."

Brainstorming about what might help you get back in the swing of things is a great way to move things forward. At the top of the list for most couples? "More private time," says Dr. Raskin. And while scheduling "date night" can help, think about it broadly. If nights out are expensive and infrequent, what about finding time in the mornings (when women's testosterone levels are highest, resulting in higher libido)? What about Saturday-afternoon naptime (when you'll both be less tired than at night)?

What's the Hardest Thing to Talk About, Sexually?

- 35% Our different levels of interest in sex
- 33% Something specific I'd like him to do differently or improve
- 18% How often we should have sex
- 14% Other

—*Parenting*'s MomConnection poll

Technique

This is not the time to be shy or coy. Be specific about yourself ("I'm finding that it takes me a lot longer to get excited lately"). If you want more mood setting than "Okay, the baby's asleep. Let's do this," ask for it: "First I'd like you to sit through a chick flick with me and hold my hand."

Your body and your life have changed since you had a child. Maybe there's something in particular that you do want that you never did before. Just say it: harder, softer, faster, slower, touch me here. And if you say what you do want your husband to do instead of just what you don't, he'll likely be turned on, too.

For me and J.B., when I finally could say "Not tonight" without worrying it would turn into a fight, a funny thing happened. It became easier for me to say yes. Because once I knew he understood my feelings, we started to address some of the underlying issues: I needed more time for myself, more romance, and more help with our daughter.

Those first years after the birth of Ramona were tough. But four years later I now see talking about sex as just another opportunity for expanding our intimacy—in and out of the bedroom.

HEIDI RAYKEIL's book about her and her husband's romantic life as parents, *Confessions of a Naughty Mommy: How I Found My Lost Libido*, was just published by Seal Press.

The Birds and the Bees and Curious Kids

Questions about sex come up when you least expect them—and sooner than you think. Here, the answers you need.

MARGARET RENKL

I once believed the birds and the bees weren't my problem. My husband would expertly field all the tough questions about sex our three sons threw our way: All I'd have to do is stand beside him and nod.

No such luck. When the topic finally came up, Dad was out for the evening. I was loading the dishwasher, and the boys were in the family room watching a nature show. From my post in the kitchen, I heard this serious PBS voice say, "Sex between sharks can get quite rough." A second later our oldest, 8-year-old Sam, appeared in the doorway with a funny look on his face.

I considered distracting him—"Ready for dessert, sweetie?"—long enough for his father to get home. But we'd always tried to be open about body parts and functions in our house, and I didn't want to freeze up just when straight talk was needed most.

I told him we'd talk at bedtime, and kept my promise. After our usual songs and stories, I took a deep breath and plunged into those shark-infested waters. "So, that show made you have some questions," I said. "Want me to answer them?" I told him the whole story—about how males and females make babies together, with the male depositing his sperm in the female. My son was appalled and disgusted—but also intrigued.

Variations on "the talk" don't always come up at convenient times or in predictable ways. So be prepared: below, the best strategies for handling the kinds of scenarios that catch parents most off guard.

Your 3-year-old is fascinated by her baby brother's diaper changes. "What's that?" she asks, pointing at his penis. How to respond: You may be tempted to change the subject quickly, and fasten that diaper even faster, but it's best to be matter-of-fact. "Some parents teach their children the names of every body part except the genitals, skipping them as if they don't exist," says Mark Schuster, M.D., a pediatrician and coauthor of *Everything You Never Wanted Your Kids to Know About Sex (But Were Afraid They'd Ask)*. That can give kids the idea that talking about your private parts is taboo. So

instead say, "That's how you can tell the difference between a girl and a boy. It's called a penis. You have a vagina."

Of course, just because you use the correct term doesn't mean she'll get it right on the first try. Nashville mom Laura Hileman once heard her 3-year-old son explaining to his brother, "Boys have penises, and girls have china." And don't be surprised if the question comes up again and again while your little one sorts it all out.

Hoping to demystify the potty for your toddler, you let her watch you pee. Soon she asks, "Why do you have hair down there?" How to respond: "Young children ask simple questions and don't need more than simple, partial answers," says Virginia Shiller, Ph.D., a licensed clinical psychologist in private practice in New Haven, Connecticut, and author of *Rewards for Kids!* Just say that it's natural for grown-ups to have hair in places that children don't, especially under their arms, between their legs, and, for men, on their faces. Birmingham, Alabama, mom Joan Watkins explained to her daughter Lora, 4, that when Lora gets to be a big girl like her mother and her aunts, she'll have hair covering her private parts, too.

Toddlers are big on imitation, and they're fascinated by the potty, so it's natural for them to wonder what you're up to in there. Letting your child join you in the bathroom from time to time is a good way to teach her there's nothing wrong or dirty about the human body.

Your child tells you her classmate has two mommies. "How can that be?" she asks. How to respond: Homosexuality may seem like a confusing subject—especially for kids who haven't even gotten the concept of heterosexuality down yet. But your explanation doesn't have to be complicated: "In Ginny's family, her two mommies love each other the way that Daddy and I do. So they live together, and both take care of Ginny."

The topic may also come up after your child hears a homosexual slur. Christi Cole's daughter Caitlyn, 6, said a boy at school had been telling kids in her class, "You're gay"—so of course she wanted to know what that meant. The Augusta, Georgia, mom explained that sometimes boys fall in love with boys and girls fall in love with girls, but that the boy at Caitlyn's school probably didn't really understand what he was talking about. Then she reminded her daughter that calling people names isn't nice and might hurt someone's feelings.

You're in line at the grocery store when your preschooler looks up and asks, "Why is my penis getting hard?" How to respond: If a question arises at an inopportune moment, it's okay to give an incomplete answer, along with a promise to fill in the rest later on. In this case, you can say quietly, "Oh, that happens sometimes. It will get soft again soon."

Joan Watkins says that when her two kids ask questions in an inappropriate place, she replies, "That's a really great question. We can talk more about it in the car, if you want." But it's important to come back to the question once you do get in the car: "Remember what you asked when we were at the store? Do you still want to talk about it?"

You've explained that when a mommy's egg and a daddy's sperm combine, a baby begins to grow. Now your 6-year-old asks, "How does the sperm get to the egg anyway?" How to respond: Explaining intercourse doesn't have to be a big deal. You might start by saying, "Daddies have to be close enough to mommies so the sperm can come out of their body and get into the mommy. The sperm comes out of the daddy's penis and goes right into the vagina, a special place in mommy's body made for keeping the sperm safe and helping it get to the egg." If your child asks additional questions, offer a slightly more detailed explanation: "A penis is made to fit into a vagina sort of like an arm fits into a sleeve."

Some parents use this talk as an opportunity to introduce a moral framework for sexuality. When her older child first asked the question, Watkins said, "God had a great plan for mommies and daddies to make babies. He designed them differently so they fit together like a puzzle. The sperm comes out of a daddy's penis and swims inside the mommy's body till it reaches the egg."

Your preschooler has been content so far with vague sex information like "Babies grow inside mommies." But now she wants to know what happens next: "How does the baby get out of there?" How to respond: Again, accurate but uncomplicated answers are best. Try, "Most babies come out through the mommy's vagina." If your child asks a follow-up question, you can add, "The vagina is like a tube inside the mommy. It stretches really wide so the baby can get outside."

If that doesn't satisfy your child, there may be another question behind the first, one she's too shy to ask. At 4, Loree Bowen's daughter, Kendall, repeatedly asked how her new baby brother or sister would get out, even after learning about the vagina. Finally, the Yorba Linda, California, mom realized her child was wondering whether her new little brother or sister would emerge covered with poop or pee. "So I told her there was a special opening just for babies, and we were done," she says.

Your grade-schooler's friend tells him how to get to an x-rated website. You walk into the family room later and find him staring at a naked woman on the screen. How to respond: First, try not to get angry. Your son's interest is only natural. Still, you need to make it clear that such material isn't appropriate for kids. Find a way to condemn the pornography nonjudgmentally without condemning him for his curiosity. Tell him calmly, "That's a website for adults; you need to stick to sites for kids." Then bookmark the sites you've approved—and be sure to download some parental controls for the family computer.

Contributing editor **MARGARET RENKL** lives in Nashville with her husband and three kids.

What to Tell the Kids about Sex

KAY S. HYMOWITZ

Sex education has been the Middle East of the culture wars and one of the longest-running, most rancorous battlegrounds of American social policy. For nearly 40 years, conservatives—many of them, though by no means all, observant Catholics and fundamentalist Christians—have been battling the increasing presence in the public schools of a permissive strain of sex education that came to be known as "comprehensive sexuality education." Unlike sex-ed programs from the first half of the twentieth century that had frowned on teen sex, comprehensive sexuality education affected a morally neutral or even positive stance toward adolescent sexual activity, supporting what was usually described as teenagers' "autonomous decision making," and promoting their use of contraception.

The spread of comprehensive sexuality education in the schools coincided with a steep rise in teen sexual activity. The number of teen girls who had had sex went from 29 percent in 1970 to 55 percent in 1990. Fourteen percent of sexually active teens had had four or more partners in 1971; by 1988, that number had increased to 34 percent. But though sex educators had sought to encourage teens to practice what they called "responsible decision making," their efforts did not seem to be paying off. Throughout the 1970s and 1980s American teenagers were not just having more sex; they were getting pregnant—and at rates that far surpassed those in other industrialized countries. Between 1972 and 1990, there was a 23 percent increase in the rate of teen pregnancy, and there was a similar increase between 1975 and 1990 in births to teen mothers.

The Culture War

Thus it is hardly surprising that the new sex ed became a rallying point for the populist uprising that eventually gave rise to Reagan Democrats, the school-choice movement, and other grassroots groups chafing at the social upheavals of the sixties. Traditionalist parents opposed to sex education were often the working- and middle-class mothers of school-aged children. Sex educators, on the other hand, had influential friends in Washington and New York, including Planned Parenthood, the Sexuality Information and Education Council of the United States (SIECUS), and leading professional groups like the American Medical Association. While the federal government never directly funded comprehensive sexuality-education programs, over the years it did provide numerous funding streams, such as that from the Centers for Disease Control's (CDC) Division of Adolescent and School Health (DASH), that were often used to support them.

True, in the early years of the Reagan administration, traditionalists had one notable success in Washington when Congress passed the Adolescent Family Life Act (AFLA), earmarking $11 million for programs to "promote chastity and self-discipline." But "the chastity bill," as it came to be called, became bogged down in the courts when opponents charged that it violated the separation of church and state, and it remained a marginal cause and the subject of much eye-rolling among health professionals. At any rate, by the time AFLA was passed, 94 percent of school districts saw "informed decision making" as the major goal of sex education according to a 1981 study by the Alan Guttmacher Institute, and for years after that, comprehensive sex education, though often sanitized for middle-class communities, was the national norm.

Today, the reign of comprehensive sex ed appears to be faltering. This is largely due to Title V, a junior provision of the Personal Responsibility and Work Opportunity Reconciliation Act (PRWORA), the landmark 1996 welfare-reform bill. Title V put substantial money behind what is now known as "abstinence education"—that is, teaching children to abstain from sexual intercourse. States could receive $50 million a year for five years in the form of a block grant as long as they matched three dollars for every four from the federal government. In 2000, Congress added another abstinence initiative called Special Projects of Regional and National Significance (SPRANS). Today, the federal government earmarks over $100 million annually for abstinence education.

But despite close analysis by researchers and journalists on the legislation and its impact on welfare mothers and their children, in the seven years since Congress passed welfare reform, Title V's rationale and legacy remain somewhat clouded.

A Broad Coalition

Critics and supporters of Title V can agree on one thing: At the time it was passed, it was a profoundly radical initiative. The architects of Title V believed that they were challenging not just the sex-ed establishment but American society overall. In a paper written for the American Enterprise Institute, Ron Haskins and Carol Statuto Bevan, congressional aides closely involved in writing Title V, conceded that "both the practices and standards in many communities across the country clash with the standard required by the law." And this, they wrote, "is precisely the point. . . . [T]he explicit goal of abstinence education programs is to change both behavior and community standards for the good of the country." Determined to avoid the fate of AFLA, whose language had been broad enough to sneak through some programs that were all but indistinguishable from those run by sexuality educators, the authors of Title V introduced a strict eight-point definition of abstinence education. These were "education or motivational programs" that had as their "exclusive purpose teaching the social, psychological and health gains from abstaining from sexual activity." Abstinence from sexual activity outside marriage, the definition also required, is "the expected standard for all school-age children." The bill allowed some flexibility—funded projects could not be inconsistent with any part of the definition but they didn't have to emphasize each part equally—but Title V was unusually specific, as well as unusually radical.

Yet much as abstinence education was promoted by social and religious conservatives determined to overthrow the liberal, nonjudgmental approach to sex ed, it also benefited from the reluctant backing of moderates frustrated with the status quo and the policies supporting it. Many Title V supporters saw a direct connection between welfare reform and sex-education reform; both could contribute to the battle against out-of-wedlock births tied to government dependency. PRWORA allows states to use a number of strategies intended to discourage out-of-wedlock births, such as a family cap and an end of direct payments to teen mothers; abstinence education was partly intended to be another weapon in that arsenal. Title V's eight-point definition of abstinence education includes several points whose purpose is to plant the ideal of childrearing inside marriage in young minds and to promote the idea that "bearing children out of wedlock is likely to have harmful consequences for the child, the child's parents, and society."

Moderates who eventually got behind abstinence education were also troubled by continuing high rates of teen pregnancy. True, by the early nineties, a decline in teen sexual activity, pregnancy, and abortion began, trends that continue to this day. According to the CDC's Youth Risk Behavior Survey, in 1991, 54.1 percent of high school students reported having sex; by 2001 that number was 45 percent. Those reporting multiple (more than four) partners declined from 18.7 percent to 14.2 percent. Pregnancy rates declined too—the CDC just announced that teen-birth rates decreased by another 5 percent in 2002, for a cumulative 28 percent decline since 1990. However, according to a 2001 study by the Alan Guttmacher Institute, even after the declines of the last decade, teen-birth, pregnancy, and abortion rates in the United States remain considerably higher than those in France, Sweden, Canada, and Great Britain. Moreover, American girls are more likely to start having sex before age 15 and to have multiple partners than their counterparts in those countries. In the United States, a full 25 percent of high school seniors have already had four or more partners, a much rarer phenomenon in the contrasting countries.

What also made the 1990s decline in teen pregnancy and sexual activity look less impressive was the growing incidence of sexually transmitted diseases. When most parents of today's teenagers were their age, the only widely reported sexually transmitted diseases in the United States were syphilis and gonorrhea. By the last decade of the century, common STDs grew to encompass over 20 kinds of infections. They include not just the one everyone knows, HIV-AIDS, but other viral diseases that can be asymptomatic and that while not fatal, are difficult, and in some cases impossible, to cure. While condom use among teenagers increased—in 2001, 57.9 percent of teens who had had sex reported using a condom in the three months prior to the survey, up from 46.2 percent in 1991—teenagers were still contracting three million STDs every year, far exceeding rates in other industrialized countries.

Everyone for Abstinence?

Within a short time after Title V was passed into law, it began to seem that the idea of abstinence for teenagers wasn't so radical anymore. Just about everyone connected to the business of sex education had taken to embracing the word abstinence—to the point of meaninglessness and much terminological confusion. A mere decade ago, abstinence was something of a laughingstock at places like the CDC and state departments of health. These days it is hard to find a state authority, sex-ed program, or organization, including Planned Parenthood, that doesn't promote "teaching abstinence." In using the term, educators sometimes mean they tell teens that abstaining from sex is one option to consider, much as comprehensive sex educators do. By "teaching abstinence," others mean they strongly encourage teens not to have sex, but still offer them information about how to use contraception. Both of these approaches fall under the now commonplace rubric "abstinence plus."

"Abstinence only" educators, on the other hand, teach abstinence as the only acceptable choice and discuss contraception almost entirely in terms of its failure to protect kids from pregnancy and STDs. To make matters more complicated, some abstinence supporters reject the "abstinence only" label as an overly narrow description of their goals and prefer "authentic abstinence." Meanwhile, the National Campaign Against Teen Pregnancy, the most prominent, middle-of-the-road organization in the business, has begun to promote an "abstinence first" message, apparently in order to clarify the ambiguity of "abstinence plus." Significantly, "abstinence only" programs are the only ones eligible for Title V money.

These skirmishes over terminology highlight the fact that even as American opinion leaders have grown more comfortable with the abstinence message, the handshake agreement about "teaching abstinence" only papers over a bitter, ongoing culture war. Not surprisingly, money and jobs, as well as ideology, are at stake.

For all the recent success of the abstinence forces, comprehensive sexuality education remains deeply embedded in the public-health infrastructure. While the number of schools teaching "abstinence only" has clearly grown, they are still in the minority: According to a recent article in Family Planning Perspectives, in 1988, 2 percent of school districts reported teaching abstinence as the sole way to prevent pregnancy whereas by 1999, 23 percent reported doing so. The liberal SIECUS receives money from the CDC to train teachers of curricula on HIV and AIDS that are indistinguishable from comprehensive sex-ed programs. A host of organizations including SIECUS, Planned Parenthood, the National Abortion Rights Action League, various AIDS and gay-rights organizations, as well as the National Association of County and City Health Officials, have begun a campaign entitled NoNew Money.org to stop the federal government from putting any more funds behind abstinence education.

Meanwhile, teacher unions often balk at abstinence curricula. The New Jersey Education Association has opposed a legislative proposal to "stress abstinence." The National Education Association (NEA) suggests that members in "abstinence only" districts "lobby for those funds to be used in after-school community programs so schools can be free to teach a more comprehensive program." In 2001, the NEA and 34 national organizations including Planned Parenthood, Advocates for Youth, and the ACLU, put out a joint statement declaring abstinence education "ineffective, unnecessary, and dangerous" as well as a form of "censorship" and an "affront [to the] principles of church state separation." A number of states, including California, Oregon, Missouri, and Alabama have introduced "medically accurate" laws on the books that abstinence supporters claim are backhanded attempts to sabotage their programs.

An Emotional Appeal

What is it these programs actually teach? The most common accusation against them is that they are crude, didactic efforts to get kids to "just say no." Whatever truth this generalization may have held years ago, it does not hold up to careful scrutiny today. For one thing, today's abstinence programs are extremely varied. Title V funds over 700 programs. The Abstinence Education Clearinghouse, a resource organization founded 8 years ago, has 1,300 paid affiliates and includes 74 curricula in their directory, up from 49 just 2 years ago. The early curricula funded by AFLA tended to be created with conservative middle-American communities in mind. Today, many programs—like Title V itself—are targeting lower-income kids. Some programs are aimed at preteens, some late teens, others even in their twenties. Some are community-based, others are school-based. Of those that are school-based, some are one or two sessions, others much longer. Some involve peer mentoring, some adult mentoring, some parental education. Community-based programs might use ad campaigns or cultural events or both. Some programs heavily emphasize delaying sex until marriage; others seem to be aiming to get kids to delay sex at least until they leave high school. Some programs get specific about what sexual behavior is permissible—one talks about avoiding the "underwear zone," another about going no further than holding hands and kissing—and some avoid these details altogether.

Still, today's abstinence programs share a few standard features. The first and most obvious is that they teach, as the Title V definition puts it, that "sexual activity outside the context of marriage is likely to have harmful psychological and physical effects." They aim to impress youngsters with the costs of ignoring the message, much the way drug or alcohol programs do, emphasizing the risk of pregnancy and sexually transmitted diseases. One widely used activity is a graphic slide show of the effects of STDs produced by the Medical Institute for Sexual Health in Austin, Texas. The gruesome slides of genital warts and herpes sores are reminiscent of pictures of diseased lungs shown in antismoking classes. Abstinence educators strongly emphasize—critics accuse them of actually lying about—the failure rate of condoms in protecting against pregnancy and STDs. Where comprehensive sex-ed programs promote safe sex and risk reduction—"Reducing the Risk" is the name of one well-known comprehensive program—abstinence programs are intent on risk elimination.

When critics charge abstinence education with being "fear based," they are overstating things; the newer abstinence curricula spend a relatively short amount of time on this sort of material. But there is no question that some of the warnings against sex tend toward the melodramatic. Abstinence educators are partial to stories of young people who have suffered heartbreak and misery after having sex with an unfaithful or diseased partner. In one of the more extreme examples of cautionary advice, "No Second Chance," a video sometimes shown in abstinence classes that has raised a lot of eyebrows in the media, a student asks a nurse, "What if I want to have sex before I get married?" "Well, I guess you have to be prepared to die. And you'll probably take with you your spouse and one or more of your children."

Most abstinence proponents believe premarital sex is genuinely destructive of young people's emotional and physical well-being, but some of them also cite several tactical reasons for their sensationalism. For one thing, they argue that kids should be scared. Early pregnancy does ruin lives; STDs can as well. It's not enough for kids to know how AIDS is transmitted, they argue; they need to dread the disease. For another, it makes sense to appeal to an age group partial to horror movies and gross-out reality shows—according to Health and Human Services, most programs are addressed to 9 to 14 year olds—through their emotions as well as their reason.

In fact, abstinence proponents believe that emphasizing the emotions surrounding sex sets them apart from the comprehensive sex-ed camp. They argue that comprehensive sex education gives the impression that sexual intercourse is a relatively straightforward physical transaction that simply requires the proper hygienic accessories. Abstinence proponents start with the assumption that sex elicits powerful crosscurrents of feeling that teenagers are unable to manage. Some cite new brain research showing that in adolescents the frontal lobes, the seat of judgment and self-control, are still undeveloped. They also believe that teens are not only incapable of mature, fully committed relationships but that teens have yet even to learn what such relationships are made of.

Character Counts

There is much more to these programs than an appeal to the emotions. In the later-model abstinence programs, delaying sex is treated as part of a broader effort to adopt a mindful, take-charge attitude toward life. Curricula usually incorporate goal-setting exercises; some of the more intensive also include character education. The tag line on the cover of the "Game Plan" workbook, part of a curriculum for middle schoolers sponsored by the basketball star A.C. Green from one of the oldest abstinence organizations, the Illinois-based Project Reality, says, "Everybody has one lifetime to develop your Game Plan." The booklet asks students to write down answers to questions like "What are some of your goals for the future?" "What will it take for you to reach these goals?" The workbook also tries to anticipate some of the temptations that lure kids away from their "game plan." "Describe some activities that could make it difficult for you to accomplish your goals," it asks. One section tells students to "think about how much time you spend each day on . . . TV, radio/CD's, the Internet," and asks them to analyze media messages and consider "whether those messages will help them achieve their goals."

Character education reinforces these sorts of activities. As Operation Keepsake, a Cleveland area program, puts it, the point is "to develop strong character qualities for healthy relationships to endure." Character education is also supposed to promote the autonomy that would help kids resist the unhealthy influence of a powerful peer group and glamorous media. "It's OK to stand against the crowd," Operation Keepsake urges its students. Some programs also add community-service requirements to their character component, such as reading to the elderly at nursing homes.

A Washington D.C.-based program called Best Friends, a highly regarded intervention project created by Elayne Bennett, also emphasizes character development. Bennett developed her program after working with at-risk girls and being struck by how depression and the sense of helplessness often led to sexual activity as well as drug and alcohol use. Bennett was determined to instill in drifting young women a sense of their own efficacy, or what is called in more therapeutic circles "empowerment." Best Friends' Washington D.C. program is used in schools with a large number of high-risk girls, the vast majority of them African-American. Looking at pregnancy rates of the 14 and 15 year olds in her targeted population, Bennett concluded that she had to begin her program at age 11 when "[girls'] attitudes are still forming."

What is unique about Bennett's approach is that instead of softening children's allegiance to the peer group, she tries to turn it into a force for individual improvement. "The best kind of friend is one who encourages you to be a better person," is one of the program's core messages. The girls in a selected class are designated "Best Friends" who meet at least once a month with a teacher, and once a week in a special fitness class, as well as at events like fashion shows, cultural activities, and recognition ceremonies. Once or twice a year there is a motivational speaker, a married woman with a successful career from the surrounding community who tells her life story, including how she met and married her husband, a narrative that Bennett says the girls particularly relish. The program also relies a good deal on mentoring. Each girl has a teacher-mentor from her school with whom she meets 30 to 40 minutes per week when she can complain about trouble with another teacher or talk about problems at home or with friends. Best Friends Foundation now licenses programs in 25 cities, reaching a total of 6,000 girls, and has recently started a Best Men program for boys.

Changing Hearts and Minds

The most common objection to abstinence education has always been that it turns its back on reality. Kids are going to have sex no matter what you tell them, and the best thing to do is to teach them how to be mature and responsible about it, the argument runs. What evidence do we have that it is possible to teach kids to abstain from sex?

One thing we can say with some certainty is that it is possible to change kids' attitudes on the subject. Mathematica Research, which was awarded a federal grant to examine the problem, is conducting the most rigorous study to date of abstinence education, examining 11 diverse programs each involving 400 to 700 subjects. Mathematica began following its subjects several years ago when the children's average age was 12 and one-half and will continue to do so until they are 16 or 17, so the organization will not have its final results until 2005. But its 2002 interim report confirms that teenagers are open to the abstinence message when teachers are clear about their message and appear committed to kids' wellbeing. "Youth tend to respond especially positively to programs where the staff are unambiguously committed to abstinence until marriage," the researchers write, "and when the program incorporates the broader goal of youth development." This change in attitude is not likely with less thorough curricula, which kids often view as "just another class."

Indeed, though it's not clear how much abstinence programs can claim credit for the decline in teen sexual activity since the early 1990s, this trend does appear to signal a growing conservatism among young people on sexual matters. In its annual survey of college freshman, the Higher Education Research Institute has shown a decline from 52 percent to 42 percent between 1987 to 2001 of the number of respondents who agree with the statement, "If two people really like each other, it's all right for them

to have sex if they've known each other for a very short time." The National Campaign Against Teen Pregnancy conducted a survey in which it asked, "When it comes to teens having sex over the past several years would you say that you have become more opposed, less opposed, or remained unchanged?" Twenty-eight percent of teens said they were more opposed, as compared with 9 percent who said they were less opposed.

Surveys consistently show that somewhere around two-thirds of teenagers who have had sex say they wish they had not. In the most recent example, the National Campaign asked, "If you have had sexual intercourse, do you wish you had waited longer?" Eighty-one percent of 12 to 14 year olds and 55 percent of 15 to 17 year olds answered yes. Some of these responses are undoubtedly influenced by the bedeviling "social desirability" factor, but the very fact that kids believe they should give a positive answer suggests that the abstinence message is not out of line with social attitudes. Interestingly, there are indications that adults are more likely to be skeptical of abstinence than teens. The National Campaign asked in a 2002 survey, "Do you think it is embarrassing for teens to admit they are virgins?" Thirty-nine percent of adults said yes, while only 19 percent of teens agreed, though this finding may conflict with a Kaiser Family Foundation survey showing 59 percent of kids agreeing with the statement, "There is pressure to have sex by a certain age."

What the Data Show

Regardless, wishes are not horses, and we are still left with the question of whether abstinence education actually makes kids abstain. The answer to that question is less clear. Just about everyone agrees that the decline in teen pregnancy that began in 1991 is partly attributable to a growing number of teenagers delaying sex, though there is vigorous disagreement about just how much can be chalked up to abstinence and how much to improved condom use. At any rate, a national decline in teen sexual activity cannot prove the impact of abstinence education per se, something that has been difficult to measure.

The key problem is finding well-designed research. The few early abstinence programs that did seem to show an impact on attitudes or behavior didn't use the sort of randomized control groups that more exacting researchers tend to trust. There are many studies of kids before and after attending a program, but either there is no control group, the control group comes from a different school, the sample size is too small, there was a follow-up only three months after the invention, but nothing longer term, or some combination of all of these.

"Emerging Answers," a 2001 review of the research on sex education sponsored by the National Campaign

Against Teen Pregnancy, included only those programs that had been subjected to research with a rigorous experimental or quasi-experimental design. Douglas Kirby, the report's author and a senior researcher at ETR, an education research organization that also produces comprehensive sex curricula, was able to find only three abstinence programs that satisfied the study's requirements. (By contrast, there were 19 comprehensive programs that did so, of which 5 were considered successful.) And while none of the three abstinence programs could be shown to affect either sexual initiation, pregnancy rates, or condom use, the results do not lead to generalizable conclusions about abstinence education. All three studies were of older-model programs, and as both Kirby's writings and Mathematica's research seem to confirm, straight didactic programs don't work with any message, abstinence or safe sex.

Another problem is that programs take time to test and refine. Up until two years ago there was little convincing evidence that comprehensive sex education was working. Four years before "Emerging Answers," Kirby wrote other less optimistic review of the research literature on sex education entitled "No Easy Answers," which concluded that "only a few programs have produced credible evidence that they reduced sexual risk-taking behavior," and even those results were limited to the short term.

Still, there are a few studies that provide what even the most scrupulous researchers might be willing to call "some evidence" that several abstinence programs are successful in getting kids to delay sexual initiation. One of the most intriguing, published in the Journal of Health Communication in 2001, looked at a community-based program called "Not Me, Not Now" in Monroe County, New York. In an effort to turn around high rates of teen pregnancy in and around the city of Rochester in the mid 1990s, the architects of "Not Me, Not Now" took a multifaceted approach to the problem: They spread the abstinence message through Internet sites, billboards, and community-sponsored events. Organizers also set up a youth-advisory panel, distributed 50,000 information packets for parents, and pushed abstinence curricula for middle schoolers. The results of the study show a decrease in the number of students who said they could "handle the consequences of intercourse" and a notable decline in sexual activity. Those who reported intercourse by the age of 15 dropped from 46.6 percent to 31.6 percent, and the rate of decline in teen pregnancy in Monroe surpassed that in comparison counties. But questions remain: Are students lying in their survey answers? Were there other interventions in the county that could explain the decline in teen pregnancy? These questions may yet yield firmer answers since "Not Me, Not Now" is one of the programs now being studied by Mathematica.

There are several reasons to anticipate that other abstinence programs will also have good results. The most suggestive finding in "Emerging Answers" is that service-learning programs that include time for contemplation and discussion are the most uniformly effective in getting adolescents to delay sexual initiation—even though they don't teach anything at all about sex. Kirby speculates that kids who are being supervised and mentored as they work in soup kitchens or hospitals develop close relationships with their teachers, increase their sense of competency, and gain a sense of self-respect from "the knowledge that they can make a difference in the lives of others." In general, Kirby finds that effective programs instill feelings of connectedness in kids. A number of earlier studies had shown that children who are more rooted in their peer group have earlier intercourse, while those more attached to their families and schools tend to begin having sex later. Connectedness, competency, and self-respect are precisely the goals of abstinence programs like Best Friends.

It's Not Just about Sex

But the truth is, even if evidence emerges that one particular abstinence-education program drastically reduces teen pregnancy and STDs—or conversely, of a comprehensive program that makes teenagers use condoms 100 percent of the time—sex education will remain a flashpoint in the culture wars. What a society teaches its young about sex will always be a decision founded in cultural beliefs rather than science. In the case of sex education, those beliefs are not about efficacy; they are not even only about sex. They are in part about clashing notions of adolescence. Sexuality educators emphasize teens' capacity for responsible and rational choices and their right to opportunities for self-exploration. They see their role as empowering the young to make their own decisions. Abstinence educators imagine a more impressionable and erratic adolescent. They see their role as guiding the young.

The two camps also presume different notions of identity. Comprehensive sex educators place a great deal of emphasis on gender identity and sexual orientation. Abstinence-only educators, who for the most part don't mention homosexuality, locate identity in character as reflected through qualities like respect, self-control, and perseverance. And finally, there are conflicting notions of freedom at stake. Sexuality educators see freedom as meaning individual self-expression while abstinence proponents tend to understand freedom in a more republican sense—the capacity for personal responsibility that allows individuals to become self-governing family members and citizens.

But it is likely that for most Americans outside the culture-war zone these are not absolute distinctions. One of the most striking flaws of the entire sex-ed dispute is that both sides talk about 13 year olds in the same breath as they do 18 or for that matter 23 year olds. It's unlikely that most Americans see age differences as insignificant. According to Mathematica's interim report, a good deal of Title V money is being directed toward middle schools because there is a general consensus that younger teens need a strong message that they are not ready for sex. Perhaps because they believe that as kids age they develop a firmer sense of identity and have even achieved some measure of character, Americans are not as likely to think the same about older teenagers and young adults in their twenties. Certainly, abstinence until marriage seems an improbable outcome in a society where people marry on average at the age of 26, and where acceptance of premarital cohabitation is widespread. Still, in their appeal to kids' higher aspirations and need for meaningful connections, abstinence proponents are on to something that has been missing in the lives of many children of baby boomers. "My father wasn't a very responsible man. I want to be a better father when the time is right," the 18 year old son of divorced parents told the Indianapolis Star about his decision to remain abstinent. Comprehensive sexual education promises pleasure, but abstinence education pushes honor—and a surprising number of kids seem interested in buying.

KAY S. HYMOWITZ is a contributing editor to *City Journal* and author of *Liberation's Children* (Ivan r. Dee, 2003).

Teenage Fatherhood and Involvement in Delinquent Behavior

TERENCE P. THORNBERRY, PhD, CAROLYN A. SMITH, PhD, AND SUSAN EHRHARD, MA

The human life course is composed of a set of behavioral trajectories in domains such as family, education, and work (Elder, 1997). In the domain of family formation, for example, a person's trajectory might be described as being in the following states: single, married, divorced, remarried, and widowed. Movement along these trajectories is characterized by elements of both continuity and change. Continuity refers to remaining in a certain state over time (such as being married) while change refers to transitions to a new state (such as getting divorced).

The life course is expected to unfold in a set of culturally normative, age-graded stages. In American society, for example, the culturally accepted sequence is for an individual to complete his or her high school education prior to beginning employment careers and getting married, and all the former, especially marriage, are expected to preceed parenthood. Despite these expectations, there is, in fact, a great deal of "disorder" in the life course (Rindfuss, Swicegood, & Rosenfeld, 1987). That is, many life-course transitions are out of order (i.e., parenthood before marriage) and/or off-time (i.e., either too early or too late).

A basic premise of the life-course perspective is that off-time transitions, especially precocious transitions that occur before the person is developmentally prepared for them, are likely to be disruptive to the individual and to those around the individual. Precocious transitions are often associated with social and psychological deficits and with involvement in other problem behaviors. Precocious transitions may also lead to additional problems at later developmental stages. This paper focuses on one type of precocious transition—teenage fatherhood—and investigates whether it is related to various indicators of deviant behavior.

Teen Fatherhood

Until recently, the study of teen parenthood has focused almost exclusively on becoming a teen mother, and relatively little attention has been paid to teenage fatherhood (Parke & Neville, 1987; Smollar & Ooms, 1988). Nevertheless, teen fatherhood appears to be associated with negative consequences, both to

the father and child, that are similar to those observed for teen mothers (Lerman & Ooms, 1993). These consequences include reduced educational attainment, greater financial hardship, and less stable marriage patterns for the teen parent, along with poorer health, educationally, and behavioral outcomes among children born to teen parents (Furstenberg, Brooks-Gunn, & Morgan, 1987; Hayes, 1987; Irwin & Shafer, 1992; Lerman & Ooms, 1993). Given these negative consequences, both to the young father and his offspring, it is important to understand the processes that lead some young men to become teen fathers while others delay becoming fathers until more developmentally normative ages.

One possibility is that becoming a teen father is part of a more general deviant lifestyle. If so, we would expect teen fatherhood to be associated with involvement in other problem behaviors, such as delinquency and drug use. There is some evidence for this hypothesis; teen fathering has been found to be associated with such problem behaviors as delinquency, substance use, and disruptive school behavior (Elster, Lamb, & Tavare, 1987; Ketterlinus, Lamb, Nitz, & Elster, 1992; Resnick, Chambliss, & Blum, 1993; Thornberry, Smith, & Howard, 1997). Some researchers suggest a common problem behavior syndrome underlying all these behaviors (Jessor & Jessor, 1977), a view consistent with Anderson's ethnographic data (1993). In the remainder of this paper, we explore the link between teen fatherhood and other problem behaviors, addressing two core questions:

1. Are earlier delinquency, drug use, and related behaviors risk factors for becoming a teen father?
2. Does teen fatherhood increase the risk of involvement in deviant behavior during early adulthood?

Research Methods

We examine these questions using data from the Rochester Youth Development Study, a multi-wave panel study in which adolescents and their primary caretakers (mainly mothers) have been interviewed since 1988. A representative sample from the population of all seventh- and eighth-grade students enrolled in the Rochester public schools during the 1987–1988 academic year was selected for the study. Male adolescents and students living in census tracts with high adult arrest rates were oversampled based on the premise that they were more likely than other youth to be at risk for antisocial behavior, the main concern of the original study. Of the 1,000 students ultimately selected, 73% were male and 27% were female.

Because the chances of selection into the panel are known, the sample can be weighted to represent all Rochester public school students, and statistical weights are used here. The Study conducted 12 interviews with the sample members, initially at 6-month intervals and later at annual intervals. This analysis is based on the 615 men in the study who were interviewed in Wave 11, when their average age was 21. Twenty percent of these individuals are White, 63% are African American, and 17% are Hispanic. The interviews, which lasted between 60 and 90 minutes, were conducted in private, face-to-face settings with the exception of a small number of respondents who had moved away from the Northeast and were interviewed by telephone. Overall, 84% (615/729) of the total male sample was interviewed at Wave 11. Due to missing data generated by cumulating data across interview waves, the number of cases included in the models for the analysis varies from 551 to 611. There is no evidence of differential subject loss [see Thornberry, Bjerregaard, & Miles (1993), and Krohn & Thornberry (1999) for detailed discussions of sampling and data collection methods.]

Measurement of Teen Fatherhood

In Wave 11, respondents were asked to identify all of their biological children, including the name, birth date, and primary caregiver of each child. If the respondent fathered a child before his 20th birthday, he is designated a teen father. The validity of the respondent's self-reported paternity is suggested by the 95% agreement with the report provided by the respondent's parent in their interview at Wave 11.

Problem Behavior Variables

In predicting teen fatherhood, we examine the effects of delinquent beliefs, gang membership, and three forms of delinquent behavior. These measures are based on data from early waves of the study, generally between Waves 2–5, covering ages 13.5 to 15.5, on average. As such, these indicators of problem behaviors precede the age at which fatherhood began for this sample, and they can be considered true risk factors for teen fatherhood.

Delinquent beliefs asks the respondent how wrong it is to engage in each of eight delinquent acts, with responses ranging from "not wrong at all" to "very wrong." The measure used here is a dichotomous variable denoting whether the respondent was above or below the median value on the scale. Gang membership is a self-reported measure of whether or not the respondent reported being a member of a street gang (see Thornberry, Krohn, Lizotte, Smith, & Tobin, 2003).

Three variables are used to measure deviant behavior: drug use, which is an index of the respondent's use of 10 different substances; general offending, which is an index based on 32 items reflecting all types of delinquency; and violent offending,

which is based on 6 items measuring violent crimes. For the risk factor analysis, all three indices are based on self-reported data and are trichotomized to indicate no offending, low levels of offending (below the median frequency), and high levels of offending (above the median).

These three indicators of offending are also measured during early adulthood (ages 20–22) in order to determine the effects of teen fatherhood on deviant behavior later in life. At this stage, they are simple dichotomies indicating offending versus non-offending.

Results

We present the results in three sections. The first examines the prevalence of teen fatherhood, and the second examines whether delinquency and related behaviors are significant risk factors for becoming a teen father. The final section focuses on whether the young men who became teen fathers, as opposed to those who did not, are more likely to engage in criminal behavior during early adulthood.

Prevalence of Teen Fatherhood

In the Rochester sample, 28% of the male respondents reported fathering a child before age 20. The age distribution at which they became fathers is presented in Figure 1. Seven subjects (1%) became fathers at age 15, truly a precocious transition. The rate of fatherhood increased sharply from that point on. At 16, 3% of the sample became fathers; at 17, 6% did; and at both 18 and 19 years of age, 9% entered the ranks of the young fathers.

Risk Factors

The link between delinquent behavior and becoming a teen father is evident from the results presented in Figure 2. One-third (34%) of the high-level delinquents during early adolescence fathered a child before age 20, as compared to 21% of the low-level delinquents and only 13% of the non-delinquents.

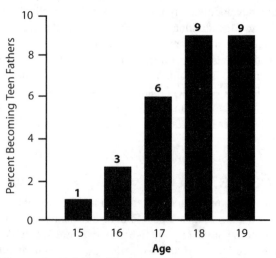

Figure 1 Relationship between age and teenage Fatherhood.

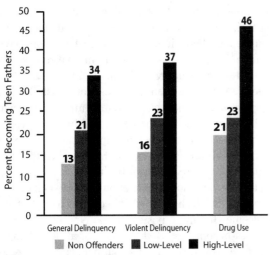

Figure 2 Relationship between early delinquent behavior and teenage fatherhood.

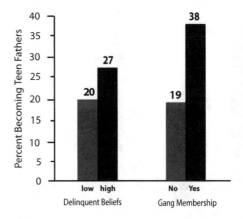

Figure 3 Relationship between delinquent beliefs and teenage Fatherhood and Between Gang Members and Teenage Fathers.

The same dose-response relationship can be seen for violent behavior: the prevalence of teen fatherhood increases from 16%, to 23%, to 37% across the three groups. The pattern is a little different for drug use. The prevalence of teen fatherhood for the non-users and the low-level users is about the same, 21% and 23% respectively, but the rate for the high-level drug users is substantially higher, 46%. All three of these relationships are statistically significant.

In Figure 3 we present bivariate results for two variables closely related to delinquency, holding delinquent beliefs and being a member of a street gang. Both relationships are statistically significant. Younger adolescents who have higher levels of pro-delinquent beliefs are more likely (27%) to become teen fathers than those who do not (20%). Finally, gang members are more likely (38%) to become teen fathers than nonmembers (19%).

To this point, we have simply investigated bivariate associations, that is, the link between delinquency, say, and teen fatherhood, without holding the effect of other potential explanatory variables constant. In a fuller investigation of this issue, Thornberry et al., (1997) examined these relationships when the following variables were controlled: race/ethnicity, neighborhood poverty and disorganization, parent's education and age at first birth, family poverty level, recent life stress, family social support, parent's expectations for son to attend college, CAT reading achievement, early onset of sexual intercourse, and depression. When this was done, delinquent beliefs were no longer significantly related to teen fatherhood, but gang membership remained a significant and sizeable predictor of becoming a teen father. These two variables—delinquent beliefs and gang membership—were then added to the above list of controls when early adolescent delinquency, drug use, and violence were considered. General delinquency was no longer significantly related to the risk of teen fatherhood, but drug use and violent behavior were (figure not included).

Overall, it appears that early problem behaviors are a risk factor for teen fatherhood. This appears to be the case especially for the more serious forms of these behaviors—violence, high-level drug use, and gang membership.

Later Consequences

The final issue we investigate is whether becoming a teen father is associated with higher rates of criminal involvement during early adulthood, ages 20–22. The results are presented in Figure 4. Teen fathers, as compared to males who delayed the onset of parenthood until after age 20, are not significantly more likely to be involved in general offending or in violent offending during their early 20s. However, there is a significant bivariate relationship between teen fatherhood and later drug use. Of the teen fathers, 66% report some involvement with drug use as compared to 47% of those who delayed fatherhood. This relationship is not statistically significant once adolescent drug use is held constant (results not shown), however. The latter finding indicates that early adult drug use is more a reflection of continuing use than a later consequence of becoming a teen father.

Conclusion

This article investigated the relationship between teenage fatherhood and involvement in delinquency and related behaviors. Based on data from the Rochester Youth Development Study, it appears that an earlier pattern of problem behaviors significantly increases the risk of later becoming a teen father. This relationship is evident bivariately for the five indicators used in this analysis. Also, three of the relationships—violence, drug use, and gang membership—remain significant when the impact of a host of other important risk factors is held constant.

While earlier involvement in deviant behavior and a deviant lifestyle is related to the odds of becoming a teen father, teen fatherhood is not significantly related to later involvement in criminal conduct. At least during their early 20s, teen fathers are not more likely than those who delayed parenthood to be involved in general offending or in violent crime. They are more likely to use drugs, although that relationship is not maintained once prior drug use is controlled.

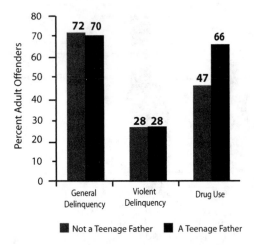

Figure 4 Relationship between teenage fatherhood and adult offending.

There is a clear link between teen fatherhood and earlier involvement in other deviant behaviors. Two kinds of explanations have been suggested for these effects. The first is that adolescent males immersed in a deviant lifestyle have many opportunities to develop a set of values and behaviors conducive to risky, adult-like adventures, some involving conquest and domination over others, including young women. This notion is supported by some ethnographic research (Anderson, 1993) and some gang studies (for example, Covey, Menard, & Franzese, 1992). Second, research has also documented that about one-fifth of teenage males feel that impregnating a young woman would make them feel "more like a man" (Marsiglio, 1993). There may be so few avenues for positive identity formation, particularly among poor adolescents and adolescents of color, that having a child is no deterrent to potential goals. Involvement in deviant behaviors, including early fatherhood, may at best be a means of achieving adult status and positive recognition or at least a means of making a mark in a world where even survival is in doubt (Burton, 1995).

Implications

It seems evident that becoming a teen father is not an isolated event in the lives of these young men. It is systematically related to involvement in a deviant lifestyle and, in a broader analysis of these data (Thornberry et al., 1997), to a variety of other deficits. These results have a number of implications for prevention programs designed to delay the transition to fatherhood and to improve the lot of these young men and their offspring. First, these programs need to be prepared to deal with this constellation of behavior problems and how teen fatherhood is intertwined with them. Focusing simply on reducing teenage fatherhood, absent a consideration of the broader context in which it occurs, may not be very effective. Second, prevention programs should include, or at least be prepared to provide access to, services to reduce involvement in antisocial behaviors for these adolescent males. Third, programs to

improve the parenting skills of these young fathers need to take into account their higher level of involvement in delinquency, drug use, and related behaviors. All of these behaviors have been shown to be related to less consistent, more erratic styles of parenting (Patterson, Reid, & Dishion, 1992) and efforts to improve effective parenting need to address these risk factors. Finally, programs and policies that try to maximize the teenage father's involvement in the rearing of his children need to be aware of the higher level of antisociality on the part of many of these young fathers. Insuring that risk to the young child is not elevated seems to be the first order of business.

Although there is a pronounced relationship between earlier antisocial behavior and the likelihood of becoming a teen father, we end on a somewhat more positive note. Not all antisocial adolescent males become teen fathers and not all teen fathers have a career of involvement in antisocial behavior. This relationship should not be painted with too broad a brush. Policies need to realistically assess the magnitude of the relationship and realistically take it into account when working with these men and their children.

References

Anderson, E. (1993). Sex codes and family life among poor inner-city youths. In R.I. Lerman & T.J. Ooms (Eds.), *Young Unwed Fathers: Changing Roles and Emerging Policies* (pp. 74–98). Philadelphia: Temple University Press.

Burton, L.M. (1995). Family structure and nonmarital fertility: Perspectives from ethnographic research. In K.A. Moore (Ed.), *Report to Congress on Out-of-Wedlock Childbearing* (pp. 147–166). Hyattsville, MD: U.S. Department of Health and Human Services.

Covey, H.C., Menard, S., & Franzese, R.J. (1992). *Juvenile Gangs.* Springfield, IL: Charles C. Thomas.

Elder, G.H., Jr. (1997). The life course and human development. In W. Damon (Ed.-in-Chief) & R.M. Lerner (Ed.), *Handbook of Child Psychology, Vol. 1: Theoretical Models of Human Development* (pp. 939–991). New York: Wiley.

Elster, A.B., Lamb, M.E., & Tavare, J. (1987). Association between behavioral and school problems and fatherhood in a national sample of adolescent fathers. *Journal of Pediatrics, 111,* 932–936.

Furstenberg, F.F., Brooks-Gunn, J., & Morgan, S.P. (1987). *Adolescent Mothers in Later Life.* New York: Cambridge University Press.

Hayes, C.D. (1987). *Risking the Future: Adolescent Sexuality, Pregnancy and Childbearing* (Vol. 1). Washington, DC: National Academy Press.

Irwin, C.E., Jr., & Shafer, M.A. (1992). Adolescent sexuality: Negative outcomes of a normative behavior. In D.E. Rodgers & E. Ginzberg (Eds.), *Adolescents at Risk: Medical and Social Perspectives* (pp. 35–79). Boulder, CO: Westview Press.

Jessor, R., & Jessor, S.L. (1977). *Problem Behavior and Psychosocial Development.* New York: Academic Press.

Ketterlinus, R.D., Lamb, M.E., Nitz, K., & Elster, A.B. (1992). Adolescent nonsexual and sex-related problem behaviors. *Journal of Adolescent Research, 7,* 431–456.

Krohn, M.D., & Thornberry, T.P. (1999). Retention of minority populations in panel studies of drug use. *Drugs & Society, 14,* 185–207.

Lerman, R.I., & Ooms, T.J. (1993). Introduction: Evolution of unwed fatherhood as a policy issue. In R.I. Lerman & T.J. Ooms (Eds.), *Young Unwed Fathers: Changing Roles and Emerging Policies* (pp. 1–26). Philadelphia: Temple University Press.

Marsiglio, W. (1993). Contemporary scholarship on fathers: Culture, identity, and conduct. *Journal of Family Issues, 14,* 484–509.

Parke, R.D., & Neville, B. (1987). Teenage fatherhood. In S.L. Hofferth & C.D. Hayes (Eds.), *Risking the Future: Adolescent Sexuality, Pregnancy, and Childbearing, Vol. 2* (pp. 145–173). Washington, DC: National Academy Press.

Patterson, G.R., Reid, J.B., & Dishion, T.J. (1992). *Antisocial Boys.* Eugene, OR: Castalia Publishing Company.

Resnick, M.D., Chambliss, S.A., & Blum, R.W. (1993). Health and risk behaviors of urban adolescent males involved in pregnancy. *Families in Society, 74,* 366–374.

Rindfuss, R.R., Swicegood, C.G., & Rosenfeld, R. (1987). Disorder in the life course: How common and does it matter? *American Sociological Review, 52,* 785–801.

Smollar, J., & Ooms, T. (1988). *Young Unwed Fathers: Research Review, Policy Dilemmas, and Options: Summary Report.* U.S. Department of Health and Human Services, Washington, DC: U.S. Government Printing Office.

Thornberry, T.P., Bjerregaard, B. & Miles, W. (1993). The consequences of respondent attrition in panel studies: A simulation based on the Rochester Youth Development Study. *Journal of Quantitative Criminology, 9,* 127–158.

Thornberry, T.P., Krohn, M.D., Lizotte, A.J., Smith, C.A., & Tobin, K. (2003). *Gangs and Delinquency in Developmental Perspective.* New York: Cambridge University Press.

Thornberry, T.P., Smith, C.A., & Howard, G.J. (1997). Risk factors for teenage fatherhood. *Journal of Marriage and the Family, 59,* 505–522.

Terence P. Thornberry, PhD, is Director of the Research Program on Problem Behavior at the Institute of Behavioral Science and Professor of Sociology, University of Colorado. He is the Principal Investigator of the Rochester Youth Development Study, an ongoing panel study begun in 1986 to examine the causes and consequences of delinquency, drug use, and other forms of antisocial behavior. Professor Thornberry is an author of *Gangs and Delinquency in Developmental Perspective* and an editor of *Taking Stock of Delinquency: An Overview of Findings from Contemporary Longitudinal Studies.* **Carolyn A. Smith,** PhD, is Professor in the School of Social Welfare, University at Albany. She holds an MSW from the University of Michigan, and a PhD from the School of Criminal Justice at the University at Albany. She has international social work practice experience in child and family mental health, and in delinquency intervention. Her primary research interest is in the family etiology of delinquency and other problem behaviors, and most recently the impact of child maltreatment on the life course. **Susan Ehrhard** holds an MA in Criminal Justice and is currently a doctoral student at the School of Criminal Justice, University at Albany, as well as a Research Assistant for the Rochester Youth Development Study. Her research interests include the sociology of crime, restorative justice, and capital punishment.

Torn between Two *Mothers*

It took 20 years and the birth of my own child for me to completely understand my feelings for my birth mother.

CHRISTINE KOUBEK

Sometimes, before the birth of my son, I wondered if it would have been easier not to have known the woman who brought me into this world. While I never wanted to sever our bond, I wished that our relationship wasn't so complex–for either of us. It wasn't that we had unpleasant experiences or memories, though. In fact, I didn't even meet my birth mother until 1987, when I was 19.

It was Mother's Day, and I was home from college for the weekend. My mother–my adoptive mother, Gail–handed me a letter that had arrived that day at our house in Albany, New York. I thought it was from a friend, until the pictures started falling out: a little girl with painted fingernails, a dark-eyed woman feeding wedding cake to a man, the same woman with someone who looked like an older version of herself, both smartly dressed in crisp black-and-white suits. I was breathless as I stared at this stranger with my own dark-brown eyes and auburn-streaked hair, then read the letter:

> *Dear Christine, The time has finally arrived. I was 17 when you were born. I remember holding you on my lap; your eyes seemed to look right into my soul. I knew I couldn't keep you and my heart was broken and still is. I visited you at the infant home but I couldn't hold you because you were behind a glass window. I named you Ann Marie. You are a five- to 10-minute drive from my house. I love you! Ann*

"Honey, who's the letter from?" Mom called from the kitchen. My face felt hot and flushed, as if I'd been caught reading someone else's diary. I had known that I was adopted since I was 13, when a neighbor let this truth slip. I had run to my babysitter in tears, and my mother rushed home from the double shift she was waitressing. I was overwhelmed to think that this woman who had always been my Mommy, and I her Chrissie, might somehow not belong to me. But then Mom, who'd planned to tell me someday, showed me an old letter from the Albany Catholic Family Services caseworker describing my birth parents. I learned that I am Irish, German and Welsh; that my birth mother was intelligent and sensitive, had taken piano lessons for years and hoped to major in music; and that my birth

father, also 17 at the time of my birth, was athletic and enjoyed playing drums.

I silently wondered whether my birth parents were the reason I was always "so sensitive," while the mother who'd raised me seemed strong-minded and pragmatic. Why, even though Mom told me not to waste time worrying about what I couldn't change, couldn't I stop myself from doing just that? I was a dreamer, the daughter who crawled out of the bedroom window at night to sit on the adjoining porch roof and gaze at the stars.

The woman I'd known all my life as my mother, Gail, had suffered enough–miscarriages, the deaths of a baby, her father and her brother, and my father's affair, which eventually left her to raise my two siblings and me alone. Mom had devoted her life to us and always made me feel loved every iota as much as my younger brother and sister, to whom she'd given birth. I wanted to do everything I could to make her life easier. Now here was another mother in my life.

Mom asked again, "Who's the letter from, honey?" Hesitantly I replied, "It's from my birth mother."

"Who the hell does she think she is?" Mom erupted. "I can't believe she didn't contact me first! How does that woman know if you're even aware that you're adopted?"

I didn't disagree with her but was studying for finals and tried to put the whole situation and all its complexities out of my mind. A few weeks later curiosity and a craving for answers got the better of me. I remember calling Ann's house, but I don't remember telling my mother ahead of time. Ann happened not to be home, but her husband and I set up a meeting a few days later after I finished work at a department store in our local mall.

That entire evening at the mall I scanned faces, wondering if one of them might be hers. After work I went to stand outside on the moonlit sidewalk in front of the store, waiting for the strangest of strangers, who might illuminate some shrouded part of me.

Suddenly a woman walked up to me, wrapped her arms around me and cried, "Oh, my baby".

Suddenly a woman walked up to me, she wrapped her arms around me and cried, "Oh, my baby." I did nothing. I felt cold. *She's my mother; I'm her baby,* crashed in my head. But what was a girl devoted to the mother she's always known to do with the yearning to find the two people responsible for a big chunk of who she is?

We went to a cozy Italian restaurant nearby and we tried to fill each other in on the last 19 years. I learned that Ann, then 36, had earned her master's in music and taught piano. After almost dying during a recent tubal pregnancy, she was trying to have a baby again. I talked about studying marketing and psychology in college. I told her about my childhood, about being the family tomboy. And I told her how my little brother had come up to me after he found out I was adopted and said, "I don't care that you're adopted, you're still my sister."

A few weeks later Ann contacted my birth father, Gregg, whom she had tracked down, and let him know she'd found me. He was a married English teacher, rock concert aficionado, poet and the father of a 13-year-old boy.

The initial lunches with Ann, as well as the separate evening get-togethers with Gregg, felt electrically charged. As the months passed, though, that initial excitement ebbed, and we each struggled with the fact that I was not baby Ann Marie any longer. I was Christine, a nearly full-grown woman, a complicated composite of all the parties involved and my own person as well. It seemed to me that just maybe they were again mourning the loss of that child.

In the meantime Mom said surprisingly little. Rightly or wrongly, I followed that cue, leaving her, I realize in hindsight, to wonder just how much time I was spending with Ann and Gregg. But I was too afraid to ask what she was feeling. And I was still trying to figure out how to balance it all at a time when a teen usually separates from her parents to begin pursuing her own life.

Several months after our meeting, Gregg put in words what we were grappling with: "I think there is such a gap between reality and the dream in this situation. . . . I want to be everything you want me to be, but, realistically, I'm not sure I have the foggiest idea what that is–do you?" I couldn't answer his question, but I found it easier to get to know Gregg, since my father wasn't around and Mom seemed okay with our relationship. Gregg and I would meet for coffee, go to U2 concerts and talk on the phone. From time to time Mom would ask me how he was doing.

It was harder to do this with Ann: I already had a mother I was close to. So, though I pursued a relationship with Ann, if anyone asked I stuck with what seemed to be socially acceptable explanations, such as: I'd wanted to know what medical conditions I could inherit, I wanted to make sure that I didn't marry my brother. But the information that mattered most to me were the discoveries of characteristics that Ann and I shared–from our spiritual philosophies to an artistic temperament–that made it easier for me to feel at home in my own skin.

So how, after all this, could I say to her and Gregg, "Hey, thanks for answering my questions, for helping me find myself. Now please go away and I'll catch up with you in another 19 years."

I couldn't. I had grown to care about them–maybe even love them. So I fumbled for several years, even though making time

for them complicated my life, especially during the holidays. I remember one weekend visit home from Boston, when I tried to divide a 48-hour stay among catching up with Mom; seeing my beloved grandmother, who had just suffered a stroke; meeting my brother's new baby; spending time with my sister; visiting Ann, who was going through a divorce; and getting together with high school friends. No matter how carefully I allocated my time, I was always wishing for more–or letting someone down. Soon I couldn't tell what I was obligated to do, capable of doing or even wanted to do.

Above all, I hated the sense that I was betraying Mom, who stepped back as best she could to give me the freedom to make my own choices and eventually worked to understand why Ann had reached out to me. I was never more awed by Mom than on my wedding day. She looked beautiful in her pink flowered dress as we rode in the limousine to the church. When we got there she sat in the place of honor in the front pew, as do all mothers of the bride, but she also graciously shared the day with her daughter's birth-parents: Ann played "All I Ask of You" from *The Phantom of the Opera* on the piano and Gregg escorted me down the aisle.

That day Mom claimed to have had a stomach bug, but I suspected it was nerves, caused by the endless questions from relatives who had never met Ann and Gregg. Yet she handled it all with grace so that I might include a part of myself by having them present. She did it because she loved me unconditionally and wanted me to be happy. And that's what makes her my mother in every sense of that word.

At my wedding it had seemed for a moment as if I could hold together all of these parts of my life. But as a newlywed I had gained not just a spouse but in-laws. I was split too many ways and I started to think life would be simpler if I could go back to thinking that maybe, if I didn't take after my mother, I took after someone else in my family. I wasn't sure I was capable of continuing to traverse the rocky terrain that being reunited with Ann and Gregg entailed.

After my son, Cameron, was born, I knew I had to make room in my life for all my parents.

Then, a few years after I married, my son, Cameron, was born. Almost immediately a deep sense of empathy washed over me for all my parents and I knew I had to continue to make room in my life for Ann and Gregg–maybe not as entrenched a place as Mom held, but still a permanent place. As I breast-fed my newborn son and stroked his pudgy legs in the middle of the night, I began to understand the desire and anticipation Mom must have felt when she first picked me up, as a baby. And I also began to understand the despair Ann felt at losing me. I couldn't imagine having to give my son away–never to cuddle him again or hear the sound of his voice or know the person he would become someday.

So I nurtured my relationships with all my parents, the contours of the associations taking shape through easy times and hard ones. After I had surgery some dozen years ago, Ann wrote me a letter that said, "Our mother–daughter relationship is indeed different from the traditional one. Gail is your traditional mother–she is there for you when you need your mother. The morning of your operation, it really struck home to me that another person is the mother of my child . . . it hit me hard–like a blow to the chest."

My son told me the other day, "Mom, you're lucky. Most adopted kids don't get to meet their real mothers." At first I cringed, as I have before, when I felt Mom was being slighted by that word "real." But I knew, and know, that there isn't an easy way to define what Ann and I are to each other.

So I replied, "Cameron, Grandma is my real mother, she raised me and mothered me in all the ways I do for you now. Annie is my birth mother, which means that I grew inside her tummy, and yes, I am very glad to know her, too." That's where we are now, and it's a good place to be.

It's been 21 years since I met Ann, and since then I've learned that just as a heart can expand to love several children, so too can it love more than one mother. Ann and I have settled into a sisterly connection of sorts. We share a genetic bond, we chat about our lives, and we turn to our respective mothers to help us over life's hurdles. Gail was there after the births of my two children; Ann's mother helped her through her first bout with breast cancer.

While standing in the card aisle last Mother's Day, I stared at the racks of cards for mothers–stepmothers, grandmothers, godmothers and "like a mother to me." The cards always include phrases like "the one constant in my life" and "since I was a child," neither of which apply to Ann. There is never a card that says, "Thank you for giving me the gift of life, for letting my mother and our family bring me up and for finding me so I can know both you and that part of me that is you." So I make my pilgrimage back to the blank-card aisle. I'll just have to keep writing in the message myself.

Staying up Late with Sue

ANNE MATTHEWS

Sue Johanson, sex guru, has three grown kids, two grandchildren, three books, a nursing degree and not one but two hit TV programs. Thirty weeks a year, live from Toronto's SkyDome, she broadcasts *The Sunday Night Sex Show,* a favorite in Canada since 1996.

In 2002 she added a second hour especially for the U.S. audience. *Talk Sex With Sue* airs late nights on the Oxygen cable network, and some 4.2 million Americans now stay up to catch her tips and quips, from the latest in lubricants to the odds of a male over 35 having a heart attack during intercourse.

Johanson, a leading sex educator in Canada for more than three decades, will discuss absolutely anything except the year she was born. "Sometime in the 20th century" is about as specific as she gets. Gray hair gives her credibility, and she knows it. "Nothing reduces inhibitions like a grandmother sitting on TV talking about whips, willies and warts," she says.

She's the Julia Child of sex, unflappable and candid. Fans know she likes to knit and sew, bake sourdough biscuits, putter at her Ontario lake cottage and go to yard sales—"I'm cheap!"

On camera, she is a born ham, especially when sharing condom advice: "If you wanna be mine, cover your vine!"; "Shroud the moose before you let loose!" Every week she delves into her Pleasure Chest—actually an old sewing basket, thriftily relined with red velvet—and offers tabletop demos of sex toys. On a live broadcast, this can be risky. Audiences have seen her battle a smoldering vibrator and a badly out-of-control vacuum pump. Sex toys that are dishwasher-safe get a special nod of approval.

The heart of her shows is the call-in segment. Erectile dysfunction, pregnancy and yeast infections are the most common worries; always, Johanson's answers reassure and teach as well as amuse. This is an international public education project that only looks like standup comedy. Her approach is slangy but never vulgar. She has never been bleeped. And you can't beat her command of statistics: What percentage of American teens have their first sexual experience in automobiles? "Twelve percent. You never see that in car commercials." What percentage of women over 80 continue to have sex? "Thirty percent. Finding a man that age with working parts is another story."

Johanson works in the tradition of the wisecracking advice columnist who uses reader queries to explain human behavior. Like Dear Abby and Ann Landers, she tackles sensitive topics head-on, and like Dr. Ruth Westheimer, she displays a frankness that can be jaw-dropping. Sex aids for quadriplegics? Bondage play after a

Getting More out of Your Love Life

Tips from Sue Johanson:

1. **Skip burgers and fries.** Good nutrition makes you feel much better, and makes for better sex. "Eat junk food," she says, "and all you want to do is fight over the remote control."
2. **Games are good.** Try phone sex—he on one extension, she on another. Try hide-and-seek, on the floor, in the dark, in the nude. "Find each other, then have fun under the coffee table."
3. **Toys work, too.** "Go to a sex store together, buy small, low-cost items to start, check them out, then invest more once you know what you like."
4. **Choose a time when both feel ready for love-making.** Wake up your partner at midnight with caresses and a sultry "Hi, big guy!" Someone with arthritis may do best in the morning, after a good night's sleep. "When we were young," Johanson points out, "we could never have sex during the day—the kids would hear."
5. **If you have a physical restriction, or just the aches and pains of aging:**
   - Take an anti-inflammatory 20 minutes ahead of time.
   - Together, take a romantic hot bath, with lights low, and candles and incense by the tub.
   - Keep extra pillows nearby in case of leg or foot cramps.
   - Have cream or gel handy.
   - Warm the bed with an electric blanket.
6. **Pleasurable positions?** Spoon-fashion. Side-by-side. The X position. Or female-on-top. Try chair sex: It's easy on the joints.
7. **And try the following books:**
   - Her latest, *Sex, Sex and More Sex,* coming out this month.
   - *The Ultimate Guide to Sex and Disability,* by Cory Silverburg, Miriam Kaufman and Fran Odette.
   - *The New Love and Sex After 60,* by Robert Butler and Myrna Lewis. "Get the book and stand well back!"

bypass? Sue covers it all. Canadians seem to love it, stopping her on the street or at the grocery store for detailed sex advice. Americans politely murmur that they really, really like the show.

Credentials and Credibility

Born in Ontario to an English-Irish family, married young to a Swedish-Canadian electrician employed by a public utility, Johanson is a registered nurse with postgraduate training in family planning, human sexuality and counseling and communications. These credentials underpin her credibility. Her ability to talk easily with teenagers about sexual issues led her to create, in 1970, the first birth control clinic in any North American high school. She still does 60 shows live and 30 lectures a year; for her countless courses, talks and media presentations on smart sex, she received in 2001 the prestigious Order of Canada award, that nation's version of knighthood.

Good sex after midlife interests Johanson—and her audience. "Who says you shouldn't have exciting sex at 70?" she asks. "If fitness and flexibility allow, do it, try it, don't limit yourself by age. 'Oh dear, I'm 50, I can't, I shouldn't.'" The key, she believes, is the quality of the relationship with one's partner. Enjoyable sex calls for drive, enthusiasm, imagination.

And understanding. "As we get older the body changes—no more firm, young, bodacious tatas. Your waistline is gone, you've got turkey neck and wrinkled skin. . . . You're not sure what a partner will think? Well, your partner has the same worries. That manly chest has slipped south. . . . Talk about it ahead of time. Say, 'I'm going to find this a little difficult—my body works, but it isn't so beautiful.' And they'll likely reply, 'Thank goodness! Me too!'"

Not Just for the Young

Arousal in both sexes takes longer with age, Johanson explains, and the need for orgasm diminishes dramatically. But the need for a sex life is evergreen, even if grown children try to interfere, or shame ("Mother! At your age!"). Sex in nursing homes and assisted-living communities is growing more common, she adds; in Canada, facilities often include a "love nest" on the premises, with double bed, flowers, candles and a good radio/CD player. Improvised intimacy works, too. "Privacy can be as simple as a Do Not Disturb sign on a room door, which means 'Meals and meds can wait. We are having fun in here.'"

Johanson's weekly call-ins still demonstrate the widespread belief that sex is the property of the young. That's changing. Aging boomers, she says, will permanently redefine post-50 sex. Women in their 70s and 80s have begun asserting their ongoing interest in a sex life. Sue calls such people "cougars"—older women who enjoy sex, always did and have no intention of giving it up. Recently she spoke to an 85-year-old woman whose male partner is 35. No complaints from either side; quite the contrary.

"So why accept arbitrary age parameters?" Johanson asks. The basic rules of sex apply at every life stage. "Use your head, plan ahead, know what you're doing, never let sex just happen." At 18 or 80, she advises, "Don't always expect multi-orgasmic bliss. Pleasure, sure. Affection, definitely. Sex should be energizing. Enjoyable. And a bit of a giggle."

ANNE MATTHEWS is a nonfiction writer in Princeton, N.J.

Women's Sexuality as They Age
The More Things Change, the More They Stay the Same

PATRICIA BARTHALOW KOCH, PhD AND PHYLLIS KERNOFF MANSFIELD, PhD

With the aging of the baby boomers and the development and hugely successful marketing of Viagra® to treat erectile dysfunction, attention from sexologists, pharmaceutical companies, and the public has become focused on the sexuality of aging women.[1]

Some of the burning questions that are currently being pursued are: Does women's sexual functioning (sexual desire, arousal, orgasm, activity, and/or satisfaction) decrease with age and/or menopausal status? And what can be done to enhance aging women's sexual functioning?

As researchers try to provide answers for women, pharmaceutical companies, and other interested parties, what is becoming crystal clear is that we (the scientific community, health care professionals, and society at large) don't understand women's sexuality as they age because we don't understand women's sexuality. Therefore, we may not even be pursuing the right questions. For example, are specific elements of sexual "functioning" the most important aspects of women's sexuality or do we need to shift our focus?

Models of Female Sexuality: The Importance of Context

Much of the information accumulated about women's sexuality has been generated from theories, research methodologies, and interpretation of data based on male models of sexuality, sexual functioning, and scientific inquiry.

As explained by Ray Rosen, Ph.D., at a recent conference on "Emerging Concepts in Women's Health," sexology has pursued a path of treating male and female functioning as similar, as evidenced by Masters and Johnson's development of the human sexual response cycle.[2]

What has resulted is a lack of appreciation for and documentation of the unique aspects of women's sexual functioning and expression. There is a growing chorus of sexologists acknowledging that women's sexuality, including their sexual response, merits different models than those developed for men.[3]

As Leonore Tiefer, Ph.D., has advocated, what is needed is a model of women's sexuality that is more "psychologically-minded, individually variable, interpersonally oriented, and socioculturally sophisticated."[4] Such models are beginning to emerge.[5]

The new models of female sexual response have been developed from quantitative and qualitative research findings and clinical practice assessments that more accurately reflect women's actual experiences than previous male-centered models.

A key component of these models is the importance of context to women's sexual expression. Context has been defined as "the whole situation, background, or environment relevant to some happening."[6] For example, unlike men whose sexual desire often is independent of context, women's sexual desire is often a responsive reaction to the context (her partner's sexual arousal, expressions of love and intimacy) rather than a spontaneous event.[7] Jordan identified the central dynamic of female adolescent sexuality as the relational context.[8] She described young women's sexual desire as actually being "desire for the experience of joining toward and joining in something that thereby becomes greater than the separate selves."[9]

So throughout women's development and the transitions in their lives (adolescence, pregnancy, parenthood, menopause) context is a key factor in their sexual expression. Thus, the more things change (their bodies, their relationships, their circumstances), the more they stay the same (the importance of context to their sexual expression).

Insights from the Midlife Women's Health Survey

Applying the new models of women's sexuality that emphasize the importance of context helps us to better understand women's sexuality as they age. Findings from the Midlife Women's Health Survey (MWHS), a longitudinal study of the menopausal transition that is part of the broader Tremin Trust Research Program on Women's Health, support these new models.[10]

The Tremin Trust is a longitudinal, intergenerational study focusing on menstrual health that first enrolled 2,350 university women in 1934 and a second cohort of 1,600 young women between 1961 and 1963. (See the Tremin Trust Web site at www.pop.psu.edu/tremin/). In 1990, an additional 347 mid-life women were enrolled in order to better study various aspects of the menopausal transition, including sexual changes.

All the participants complete a daily menstrual calendar, recording detailed information about their menstrual health.

They also complete a yearly comprehensive survey, assessing biopsychosocial information about their health and aging, life experiences, and sexuality, among other factors. These surveys collect both quantitative and qualitative data. Throughout the years, some of the women have been called upon to participate in special qualitative studies in which they have been interviewed. One hundred of the perimenopausal women who are not taking hormone replacement therapy have also supplied daily morning urine specimens so that hormonal analysis could be conducted.

The Tremin Trust participants are incredibly dedicated to the project. For example, they keep daily records throughout their lives (for some almost 70 years) and enlist participation from their daughters, granddaughters, and great-granddaughters. The study's potential for providing a greater understanding of women's sexuality throughout their lives, and the factors that affect sexual changes, is unparalleled. The greatest limitation is the lack of diversity among the participants, since over 90 percent are well-educated white women. However, data collection has been conducted with additional samples of African-American and Alaskan women as well as lesbians. More diverse cohorts may be enlisted in the future.

Analysis of the sexuality data is ongoing, with more data being collected each year. Interesting findings have emerged regarding midlife women's sexuality (ages 35 through 55 years of age) as they progress through menopausal transition. The average age of menopause is 51, with perimenopause beginning as early as the late thirties. In an open-ended question asking what they enjoyed most about their sexuality, more than two-thirds of the women referred to aspects of their relationships with their partners.[11] Most of these responses described some aspect of intimacy, including love, closeness, sharing, companionship, affection, and caring, as described below. About 15 percent of the women noted feeling comfortable and secure in their relationship, emphasizing feelings of mutual trust and honesty.

It is the most healthy relationship I've ever been in. Sex in the context of a respectful, caring, non-exploitative relationship is very wonderful.

Wow! The sexual experience is another heightened way we share the humor that comes from shared experiences such as canoeing, fine music, backyard work, scuba trips. It makes the "union" a joyous and complete one!

Many of the lesbian participants felt that the intimacy they shared in their relationships was even greater than what they had experienced or observed in male-female relationships.

Many straight women in 20-to-25-year marriages are distant and emotionally separate from their husbands. I think this is a time when lesbian women and their partners really come into their own—their best time together. There's much greater emotional intimacy with less emphasis on sex. It's very nurturing and increases the bond between us.

Another very important contextual feature that at least one in ten women enjoyed about their sexuality was a newly-found sexual freedom they experienced as they aged, either from their children leaving home or from being with a new partner.

Freedom and ability to be spontaneous with our sexual desires due to the "empty nest."

The freedom to have sex at his apartment. The growing intimacy and closeness that goes along with sex itself. The sexual playfulness and frivolity that threads itself through regular daily activities (teasing, sexual nuances, private jokes, and touches).

Approximately 20 percent of the women discussed some particular aspect to their sexual interactions, with mutual sexual satisfaction, continuing sexual interest, desire, and attraction, and lessened inhibitions and increased experimentation mentioned most often.

We seem to enjoy sex more and more as the years go by. The orgasms seem even better. We both respond well to each other sexually since we feel safe in our loving monogamous relationship.

One-third of these discussions emphasized that touching, kissing, hugging, and cuddling were the most important aspects of the sexual interactions.

You may not consider it sexual, but sleeping together in a queen-sized bed in the last year and a half. While the kids were growing up, we had twin beds. We enjoy the cuddling this provides daily.

Qualities exhibited by their sexual partners, who are most often the women's husbands, have been found to significantly impact the women's sexual responding.[12] Specifically, the more love, affection, passion, assertiveness, interest, and equality expressed by the sexual partners, the higher the women's sexual desire, arousal, frequency, and enjoyment. Women also expressed appreciation for a non-demanding partner who was responsive to their needs.

My partner is very accepting about how I feel and what I like and what I don't like even though it changes often. I also appreciate that he doesn't expect me to have an orgasm every time we make love.

Sexual Changes as Women Age

Each year the women report many changes in their sexual responding. Some women have reported enjoying sex more (8.7 percent), easier arousal (8.7 percent), desiring sexual relations more (7 percent), easier orgasm (6.7 percent), and engaging in sexual relations more often (4.7 percent).[13] The women attribute their improved sexuality most often to changes in life circumstances (new partner, more freedom with children leaving home), improved emotional well-being, more positive feelings toward partner, and improved appearance.[14]

However, two to three times more women have reported declines in their sexual responding, including: desiring sexual relations less (23.1 percent), engaging in sexual relations less often (20.7 percent), desiring more non-genital touching (19.7 percent), more difficult arousal (19.1 percent), enjoying sexual relations less (15.4 percent), more difficult orgasm (14 percent), and more pain (10 percent).

Women are much more likely to attribute declining sexual response to physical changes of menopause than to other factors.[15] Analysis of the health data has found a statistically significant relationship between having vaginal dryness and decreased sexual desire and enjoyment.[16] However, no statistically significant relationship between menopausal status and decreased sexual desire, enjoyment, or more difficulty with orgasm was found. On the other hand, sexual desire and enjoyment were significantly related to marital status, with decreases associated with being married. The woman's age was also significantly related to her sexual enjoyment, with enjoyment decreasing as the woman became older. Further, a significant relationship has been found between poor body image and decreased sexual satisfaction.[17]

Other studies among general populations of aging women have failed to find clear associations between menopausal status and declines in sexual functioning.[18] Similar to the MWHS findings, they found psychosocial factors to be more important determinants of sexual responding among midlife (perimenopausal and menopausal) women than menopausal status.[19] The factors include sexual attitudes and knowledge; previous sexual behavior and enjoyment; length and quality of relationship; physical and mental health; body image and self-esteem; stress; and partner availability, health, and sexual functioning.

Sexual Satisfaction and the Importance of Sex for Women

Even with many aging women in the MWHS identifying declines in their sexual desire, frequency, or functioning, about three-quarters of them reported overall sexual satisfaction (71 percent), including being physically and emotionally satisfied (72 percent).

> Even though sex is less frequent and it takes much longer to feel turned on, it is still very satisfying.

> I have been a very fortunate person. The man I married I still love dearly. We both respect each other and try to keep each other happy. We don't have sex as much as we used to but we kiss and hug and hold each other a lot.

The importance of sexual expression varied in the midlife women's lives and was affected by the circumstances in which they found themselves (married, divorced, widowed, in a same-sex relationship). Once again, women evaluated the importance of sexuality in the overall context of their lives. Some women who had lost their sexual partners to death or divorce reported missing a sexual relationship, mostly because of the lack of intimacy.

> I find being a widow at a young age to be very lonely. I find that I miss the desire to have a sexual closeness with a man. I also feel very sad and confused as my husband

Half of Americans over 60 Have Sexual Relations at Least Once a Month

Nearly half of all Americans over the age of 60 have sexual relations at least once a month, and 40 percent would like to have it more often. In addition, many seniors say their sex lives are more emotionally satisfying now than when they were in their forties.

These findings were part of the latest Roper-Starch Inc. survey of 1,300 men and women over the age of 60 conducted by the National Council on the Aging.

"This study underscores the enduring importance of sex among older men and women—even among those who report infrequent sexual activity," said Neal Cutler, director of survey research for the Council. "When older people are not sexually active, it is usually because they lack a partner or because they have a medical condition."

As most people might expect, the survey found that sexual relations taper off with age, with 71 percent of men and 51 percent of women in their sixties having sex once a month or more and 27 percent of men and 18 percent of women in their eighties saying they do. Cutler said women had sex less often in part because women are more likely to be widowed.

Thirty-nine percent of people said they were happy with the amount of sexual relations they currently have—even if it is none—while another 39 percent said they would like to make love more often. Only four percent of the people surveyed said they would like to have sexual relations less frequently. The people who had sex at least once a month said it was important to their relationship.

The survey also found that 74 percent of men and 70 percent of women find their sex lives more emotionally satisfying now that they are older than when they were in their forties. As to whether it is physically better, 43 percent say it is just as good as or better than in their youth, while 43 percent say sex is less satisfying.

"When it comes to knowledge about sex, older people are not necessarily wiser than their children. A third of the respondents believed it was natural to lose interest in sex as they got older," said Cutler.

was the only man I have ever been with. Having lost him, I fear beginning a new relationship.

I have been alone for 18 years after a 14 year marriage and three children. I miss regular sex, but *most* of all I miss touching, cuddling, body-to-body contact, not the sex act.

Yet many women without partners had decided that having sexual relations was not worth the price if the overall relationship was not fulfilling.

I am single by choice (heterosexual) and have never wanted children. I am finding it difficult to meet men as I get older and my relationships are further apart. My sexual response is still very strong, but I am not willing to compromise what I want in a relationship just for sex. My attitude is that if that doesn't happen, I am doing fine, and am happy with my life.

I find myself wishing for a "partner" but only if he's a real friend. My celibacy is comfortable at the moment. It has become apparent to me that our culture has taught most females to sacrifice themselves to their partner's desires and not to defend themselves. I hope I don't fall in that trap again. I find that I satisfy my physical sexual desires better than my husband ever did.

On the other hand, sexual interaction is very important to many of the aging women.

I am 58 and as horny as ever. . . . The sex urge is still with me, not much different from my earlier years. Maybe I am too physically active and healthy! I can't seem to get it into my head that I am approaching a different time of life. . . . There is little or no speaking about a situation like mine in books or media. Yet women my age say the same thing: "Where are the men? Men want only younger women. The 'good men' are married or in relationships". . . . My request to you is—listen to the voice of the horny women. When we hear each other and gain our dignity, solutions will come!

Conclusion

Results from the MWHS, some of which have been shared in this article, illustrate that women experience their sexuality as complex and holistic. Thus, it is doubtful that a particular drug or other substance or device that could improve physical functioning (increase libido or vasocongestion) would be the "magic bullet" to transform women's sexuality as they age. In order to understand and enhance women's sexuality throughout their lives, we must listen to their voices, learn from their experiences, and appreciate the importance of context to their sexual expression.

References

1. R. Basson, J. Berman, et al., "Report on the International Consensus Development Conference on Female Sexual Dysfunction: Definitions and Classifications," *Journal of Urology,* vol. 163, pp. 888–93; J. Hitt, "The Second Sexual Revolution," *The New York Times Magazine,* February 20, 2000, pp. 34–41, 50, 62, 64, 68–69; J. Leland, "The Science of Women and Sex," *Newsweek,* May 29, 2000, pp. 48–54; P. K. Mansfield, P. B. Koch, and A. M. Voda, "Qualities Midlife Women Desire in Their Sexual Relationships and Their Changing Sexual Response," *Psychology of Women Quarterly,* vol. 22, pp. 285–303.

2. R. Rosen, *Major Issues in Contemporary Research in Women's Sexuality.* (Roundtable discussion at the Women's Health Research Symposium, Baltimore, MD.)

3. R. Basson, "The Female Sexual Response: A Different Model," *Journal of Sex and Marital Therapy,* vol. 26, pp. 51–65. S. R. Leiblum, "Definition and Classification of Female Sexual Disorders," *International Journal of Impotence Research,* vol. 10, pp. S102–S106; R. Rosen, *Major Issues in Contemporary Research in Women's Sexuality.*

4. L. Tiefer, "Historical, Scientific, Clinical and Feminist Criticisms of the Human Sexual Response Cycle," *Annual Review of Sex Research,* vol. 2, p. 2.

5. R. Basson, "The Female Sexual Response: A Different Model," pp. 51–65; L. Tiefer, "A New View of Women's Sexual Problems: Why New? Why Now?," *The Journal of Sex Research,* vol. 38, no. 2, pp. 89–96.

6. *Webster's New World Dictionary of the American Language: College Edition* (New York: The World Publishing Company, 2000).

7. R. Basson, "The Female Sexual Response: A Different Model," pp. 51–65.

8. J. Jordan, *Clarity in Connection: Empathic Knowing, Desire and Sexuality,* work in progress (Wellesley, MA: Stone Center Working Papers Series, 1987).

9. J. Jordan, *Clarity in Connection: Empathic Knowing, Desire and Sexuality.*

10. A. M. Voda and P. K. Mansfield, *The Tremin Trust and the Midlife Women's Health Survey: Two Longitudinal Studies of Women's Health and Menopause.* (Paper presented at the Society for Menstrual Cycle Research Conference, Montreal, June 1995.); A. M. Voda, J. M. Morgan, et al., "The Tremin Trust Research Program" in N. F. Taylor and D. Taylor, editors, *Menstrual Health and Illness* (New York: Hemisphere Press, 1991), pp. 5–19.

11. *Midlife Women's Health Survey,* 1992, unpublished data.

12. P. K. Mansfield, P. B. Koch, et al., "Qualities Midlife Women Desire in Their Sexual Relationships and Their Changing Sexual Response," *Psychology of Women Quarterly,* vol. 22, pp. 285–303.

13. Ibid.

14. P. K. Mansfield, P. B. Koch, et al., "Midlife Women's Attributions for Their Sexual Response Changes," *Health Care for Women International,* vol. 21, pp. 543–59.

15. Ibid.

16. P. K. Mansfield, A. Voda, et al., "Predictors of Sexual Response Changes in Heterosexual Midlife Women," *Health Values,* vol. 19, no. 1, pp. 10–20.

17. D. A. Thurau, *The Relationship between Body Image and Sexuality among Menopausal Women.* (Unpublished master's thesis, Pennsylvania State University, 1996).

18. N. E. Avis, M. A. Stellato, et al., "Is There an Association between Menopause Status and Sexual Functioning?," *Menopause,* vol. 7, no. 5, pp. 297–309; K. Hawton, D. Gaith, et al., "Sexual Function in a Community Sample of Middle-aged Women with Partners: Effects of Age, Marital, Socioeconomic, Psychiatric, Gynecological, and Menopausal Factors," *Archives of Sexual Behavior,* vol. 23, no. 4, pp. 375–95.

19. N. E. Avis, M. A. Stellato, et al., "Is There an Association between Menopause Status and Sexual Functioning?," pp. 297–309; I. Fooken, "Sexuality in the Later Years—The Impact of Health and Body-Image in a Sample of Older Women," *Patient Education and Counseling,* vol. 23, pp. 227–33; K. Hawton, D. Gaith, et al., "Sexual Function in a Community Sample of Middle-aged Women with Partners: Effects of Age, Marital, Socioeconomic, Psychiatric, Gynecological, and Menopausal Factors," *Archives of*

Sexual Behavior, vol. 23, no. 4, pp. 375–95; B. K. Johnson, "A Correlational Framework for Understanding Sexuality in Women Age 50 and Older," *Health Care for Women International,* vol. 19, pp. 553–64.

PATRICIA BARTHALOW KOCH, PhD is an Associate Professor, Biobehavioral Health & Women's Studies at Pennsylvania State University State College, PA. Dr. Koch is also adjunct professor of human sexuality at Widener University in West Chester, PA. PHYLLIS KERNOFF MANSFIELD, PhD is a Professor, Women's Studies & Health Education at Pennsylvania State University State College, PA. Dr. Mansfield is director of the Tremin Trust Research Program on Women's Health. Dr. Koch is assistant director.

From *SEICUS Report,* December 2001/January 2002, pp. 5–9. Copyright © 2002 by Sex Information & Education Council of the United States. Reprinted by permission.

UNIT 4

Intimacies and Relationships

Unit Selections

Key Points to Consider

- Some people say talking about sex is harder to do with your romantic partner than with a friend or even a stranger. Do you agree or disagree with this statement? Why?

- Have you ever felt that you needed to be in a relationship? Do you currently feel this way? How have you changed in respect to your desire for a relationship?

- Have you ever felt that you couldn't survive a romantic relationship ending? Do you still feel as you once did?

- There is a lot of emphasis in our culture on intimacy, yet many complain it is difficult to achieve. What can make intimacy difficult to achieve?

- What lessons have you learned in your lifetime about intimacy in relationships?

- Which do you think is harder—finding a partner or keeping a relationship strong? Why?

- Have you ever felt "smothered" or too tightly bound in a relationship? Has anyone ever told you that you were "smothering" them with your affections? Why do you think you were doing this?

- Have you ever been in or known someone who was in a relationship that was considered "different" or "nontraditional?" What did you learn from your experiences in that relationship? Or, if you have known someone in a nontraditional relationship, what did you learn from them?

- Have you ever had a partner be "unfaithful" or have you ever been "unfaithful" to a partner? What did this feel like? What did you learn from the experience?

Student Web Site

www.mhcls.com

Internet References

American Psychological Association
   http://www.apa.org/topics/homepage.html

SexInfo: Love and Relationships
   http://www.soc.ucsb.edu/sexinfo/?article=A2J8

Bonobos Sex and Society
   http://songweaver.com/info/bonobos.html

Go Ask Alice
   http://www.goaskalice.columbia.edu

Think for a moment about the term "sexual relationship." It denotes an important dimension of sexuality—interpersonal sexuality, or sexual interactions occurring between two (or more) individuals. For most people, interpersonal contact and relationships with others form the basis for living meaningful lives. Conversely, isolation results in loneliness and depression for most human beings. People seek intimacy. Indeed, we cultivate friendships and relationships for the warmth, affection, supportiveness, and sense of trust and loyalty that they can provide. The importance of feeling connected to others can hardly be overstated. However, as this unit demonstrates, there are various kinds of relationships, intimacies, and experiences of connectedness.

Relationships often start when they are least expected. Sitting next to someone on a bus, talking to someone at a party, sending an instant message, all of these may be the possible beginnings to a relationship. Sometimes friendships may develop into intimate (and sexual) relationships. The qualifying word in the previous sentence is "may." Today many people, single as well as married, yearn for close or emotionally intimate interpersonal relationships, but fail to find them.

Despite developments in communication and technology that have led to a sense of always being "connected," discovering how and where to find potential friends or partners is reported by many to be as difficult today (if not more so) than in the past. Fear of rejection causes some to avoid interpersonal relationships, and others to present a false front or illusory self that they think is more acceptable or socially desirable. This sets the stage for a relationship that is counterproductive to genuine intimacy. For others a major dilemma may exist—the problem of balancing closeness with the preservation of individual identity in a manner that satisfies the need for both personal and interpersonal growth and integrity. In either case, partners in a relationship should be advised that the development of interpersonal awareness (the mutual recognition and knowledge of others as they really are) rests upon trust and self-disclosure—letting the other person know who you really are and how you truly feel. In American society, this has never been easy, and today some fear it may be more difficult than ever.

These considerations regarding interpersonal relationships apply equally well to achieving meaningful and satisfying sexual relationships. Three basic ingredients lay the foundation for quality sexual interaction: self-awareness, understanding and acceptance of the partner's needs and desires, and mutual efforts to accommodate both partners' needs and desires in safe and healthy ways. Without these, misunderstandings may arise, ultimately bringing anxiety, frustration, dissatisfaction, and/or resentment into the relationship. There may also be a

© Royalty-Free/CORBIS

heightened risk of sexually transmitted infections including HIV, experiencing an unplanned pregnancy, or experiencing sexual dysfunction by one or both partners. On the other hand, experience and research show that ongoing attention to these three ingredients by intimate partners contributes not only to sexual responsibility, but also to true emotional and sexual intimacy, as well as a longer and happier life.

Being in a relationship, in search of intimacy and fulfillment, involves being vulnerable. That vulnerability carries great emotional risks. One area that is a significant source of pain for many people is infidelity. Relationships and marriages can be torn apart by an "unfaithful" partner. Unfortunately, the children are often the ones who suffer the most. Although the number of married persons who have been unfaithful to their spouses may not be as high as many people may think, for those who are unfaithful, they are very unlikely to confess their unfaithfulness to their spouse/partner. If it becomes known, it is usually because the infidelity was discovered somehow, not due to a "confession."

As might already be apparent, there is much more to quality sexual relationships than our popular culture recognizes. Such relationships are not established by means of sexual techniques or beautiful bodies. Rather, it is the quality and integrity of the interaction that makes sex a celebration of our humanity and sexualities. A person-oriented (as opposed to genitally oriented) sexual awareness, coupled with an open, relaxed, even playful attitude toward exploration makes for joy and pleasure in experiencing our sexualities.

Free as a Bird and Loving It

More Americans are happy to marry later—or not at all.

SHARON JAYSON

Being single means bucking the pressure to join the married half of U.S. society.

Despite lavish celebrity weddings, a multitude of dating websites and stacks of self-help books about finding your soul mate, singles are a growing segment of the population—and increasingly say they are perfectly happy with their singlehood, thank you very much.

The Census Bureau reports about 97 million unmarried Americans age 18 and over in 2006, the most recent numbers available. That represents 44% of Americans 18 and over; a quarter have never been married; 10% are divorced, 6% widowed, and 2% separated.

"It's probably the best moment for singles in our history . . . because of the attitudes of popular support and the numbers," says Pat Palmieri, a social historian at Teachers College at Columbia University, who is writing a history of singles in America since 1870. She is 60 and has never been married.

Young adults are delaying marriage and have a longer life expectancy, experts say, so more Americans will spend more of their adult lives single. As their ranks multiply, singles aren't waiting for a partner to buy a home or even have a child. They've decided to embrace singlehood for however long it lasts.

"I don't have to be dating someone to be happy," says Jennifer MacDougall, 26, an office assistant in Wilmington, N.C. She says her friends share her outlook.

"When I was younger, I thought that was how it worked. You went to college and got married. When I got to college, I realized that was not how it worked and not how I even wanted it to work. I wouldn't mind being married someday, but I want to feel comfortable with myself and what I'm doing."

That attitude may arise from the frenetic quality dating takes on after college, says Barbara Dafoe Whitehead, co-director of the National Marriage Project, a research initiative at Rutgers University.

"It is not a bad trend that we are removing the stigma from being single and talking about alternative ways to lead a single life," she says.

Households in which no one is married now make up 47.3% of the USA's 114 million households, according to recently released Census data for 2006. (Numbers from 2005 released last year showed unmarried households at a 50.3% majority, but the percentage fluctuates year to year.)

"I don't have to be dating someone to be happy."

—Jennifer MacDougall, 26 of Wilmington, N.C.

"Unmarried here means not married right now," says Andrew Cherlin, a professor of sociology and public policy at Johns Hopkins University in Baltimore. The data reflect larger numbers of elderly singles, probably widowed or divorced, and twenty- and thirty somethings who haven't tied the knot, such as unmarried people who share living quarters or romantic partners who live together.

"Most people who are single seem to want to eventually be married," says Michael Rosenfeld, author of *The Age of Independence,* about young adults living on their own. "But they're putting it off. In the past, there just weren't that many single, young adults supporting themselves. It's a new phenomenon, post-1960, and getting stronger every day."

Singles do continue to face obstacles, from work policies and tax codes that favor married couples to extra fees lone travelers must pay. But society is beginning to recognize singles' needs: Individual servings of packaged grocery items are just one example.

Also, a Pew Research Center study released last year found that most singles aren't actively looking for a committed relationship: 55% of 3,200 adults 18 and older surveyed in 2005 reported no interest in a relationship. For ages 18–29, 38% said they weren't looking for a partner.

"When I graduated from college, I spent more time not in relationships than in relationships," says Len Sparks, 37, an engineer from Boston who says he's now in a relationship.

"Most of my 20s, I just didn't date. I had one relationship. Outside of that, I just worked. I worked really hard and was getting promotions and changing jobs and moving from city to city."

Bella DePaulo, 53, a social psychologist and author of *Singled Out: How Singles Are Stereotyped, Stigmatized, and Ignored and Still Live Happily Ever After,* says most books for singles try to teach "how to become un-single. What I love about my single life are the nearly limitless opportunities it offers," she says.

Other new books touting the solo-is-fine theme:

- *Better Single Than Sorry: A No-Regrets Guide to Loving Yourself and Never Settling* by Jen Schefft, who appeared on TV in *The Bachelor* and *The Bachelorette* and rebuffed two marriage proposals.
- *I'd Rather Be Single Than Settle: Satisfied Solitude and How to Achieve It* by Emily Dubberley, a relationship and sex writer from Brighton, England.
- *Naked on the Page: The Misadventures of My Unmarried Midlife* by Jane Ganahl, who previously wrote a newspaper column called "Single Minded."

- *On My Own: The Art of Being a Woman Alone* by Florence Falk, a "60-plus" psychotherapist in New York City.
- *Singular Existence: Because It's Better to be Alone Than Wish You Were!* by Leslie Talbot of Boston, founder of the website SingularExistence.com.

"We do have an unfortunate tendency to favor couples and perhaps disparage single people," Cherlin says. "These books are aimed at boosting the self-image of single people."

DePaulo agrees not everything is rosy. "I don't love everything about being single," she says. "I don't like the stigma or the stereotyping or the discrimination."

Talbot says she wrote her book to counter the belief that being single is "a deficiency or liability—a temporary condition that hopefully, if you're lucky, you'll get over."

She says there's a fine line between being alone and lonely. "There's nothing lonelier than being with somebody you don't want to be with."

Happily Never Married

But the legal system still favors heterosexuals who formally tie the knot.

NADIA BERENSTEIN

Retired political science professors Carol Kohfeld and John Sprague have been together 19 years, but don't plan to wed anytime soon.

"We've got a great relationship, a loving relationship," says Kohfeld. "Marriage wouldn't really add that much to it for us."

They are hardly alone in their escape from the bonds of matrimony—unmarried households (single people or partners who share an address and a "close personal relationship") have outnumbered married households in the U.S. since 2005. Some choose not to marry because of political convictions. Others feel that it would ineluctably alter the nature of their relationship. And some would like to marry but are unable to, either because they are gay or because the financial implications of marriage on taxes, pensions and other benefits would constitute an insurmountable hardship.

For example, marital status influences eligibility for social services such as public housing, food stamps and disability benefits, as married couples must file under their joint income. That can disqualify them for benefits if their joint income pushes them over a program's eligibility threshold. Also, some older people may lose Social Security survivor benefits if they remarry.

But even as some couples remain unwed to avoid financial consequences, unmarried couples in general enjoy far fewer automatic legal and civic rights (such as hospital visitation, end-of-life decisions, confidentiality rights in a trial) than those in even the flimsiest of heterosexual marriages. The most obvious inequities are in the tax code, where unmarried couples do not receive the same tax benefits as spouses with regards to inheritance, and don't receive survivor benefits from Social Security. Moreover, although growing numbers of employers, cities, counties and states offer benefits to same-sex couples—many of which are also extended to unmarried heterosexual couples—the backlash against same-sex relationships has led to public policies that privilege marriage over all other types of relationships.

According to Nicky Grist, executive director of the Alternatives to Marriage Project, a nonprofit that advocates for equal rights for unmarried people, health insurance demonstrates perfectly why marital status is the wrong way to allocate benefits.

A study conducted last year by the UCLA-affiliated Williams Institute on Sexual Orientation Law and Public Policy found that while 10 percent of married people and 15 percent of the general population are uninsured, 20 percent of people in same-sex couples and nearly one-third of those in unmarried heterosexual relationships lack insurance. Many people rely on their spouses for their benefits, and if they're unmarried or don't have domestic partnership rights, they can't get insured. Employers complain about the cost of extending benefits to domestic partners, yet the study found that if they did, health insurance enrollment would only increase in those companies a fractional amount—probably less than 2 percent.

Health insurance benefits were what motivated Phil Andrews, 28, and Rebecca Heinegg, 25, of Atlanta, to file a domestic partnership with the Service Employees International Union, where Andrews worked until recently as an organizer. He and Heinegg are uncomfortable with the oppressive history of marriage, with assumptions about gender roles within a marriage and with the very idea of entering into a contractual agreement with the government.

"We're both activists, and we both have a deep suspicion of registering things with the state," says Andrews. "We didn't feel like we needed permission from the state in order to be in a relationship with each other."

Lara Miller and Mike Finn, both 27, are also critical of the institution. "The main reason for us not wanting to get married is political," says Miller, a clothing designer in Chicago. Many of her close friends are gay, and she objects to "the general idea that our government, for the most part, will only recognize a man and a woman as being acceptable partners, and then only recognize married men and women as being acceptable parents."

That is, she objects to what Grist calls the "marriage-only" movement institutionalized as policy under the Bush administration. Most recently, on the premise that marriage is a "sacred institution," the 2005 Deficit Reduction Act allocated $100 million a year for the next five years for initiatives to encourage people—especially the poor—to marry and stay married. Over a billion dollars has been spent by the federal government on abstinence-only-until-marriage sex education programs since

2000, which teach that a "mutually faithful monogamous relationship in [the] context of marriage is the expected standard of human sexual activity." The Bush administration has actively opposed same-sex marriage laws, however.

Most state civil union and domestic partnership laws are limited to same-sex couples, although different-sex couples can enter into domestic partnerships in several places, including Washington, D.C., and New York City. Domestic partnerships in California and New Jersey, however, are open to all couples over the age of 62, recognizing the financial consequences of marriage for those earning Social Security (or pension) survivor benefits.

Gregg Greenstein, a family law attorney in Boulder, Colo., who specializes in unmarried partnership agreements, cautions that most domestic partnerships still offer scant rewards: "In the case of unmarried people living together, there are no clear regulations in most states about how property they have acquired together will be divided." He recommends that committed couples draw up cohabitation agreements specifying "who gets what and how expenses are split, both now and when the relationship ends." He warns, however, that there is no guarantee that states will honor such contracts.

This uncertainty stems in part from state constitutional amendments prohibiting same-sex marriage, some of which not only restrict marriage to certain groups of people, but also restrict certain benefits to married people. Of the 27 states with amendments banning same-sex marriage, 14 also deny all unmarried relationships any legal recognition comparable to marriage.

Deborah Widiss, staff attorney at the nonprofit women's-rights organization Legal Momentum, remarks that "the push to put gay marriage amendments into state constitutions has had far-reaching effects that were not anticipated," and the full effect of these amendments on unmarried heterosexual couples remains unclear. State universities in Michigan and Virginia, for instance, are prohibited from providing domestic partnership benefits.

Perhaps the most chilling effect has been on domestic violence laws. In Ohio, where a broadly worded no-gay-marriage constitutional amendment was passed in 2004, Legal Aid Cleveland is aware of about 80 appeals filed by people charged with domestic violence, on the grounds that equating the assault of an unmarried partner with that of a spouse would be in violation of the Constitution. The courts have been split, with some mandating that prosecutors amend the charges from felony domestic violence to misdemeanor assault.

Grist, of the Alternatives to Marriage Project, strongly opposes no-gay-marriage amendments: "People shouldn't be forced into or out of marriage because of eligibility issues. They should be allowed to define themselves and their relationships in a manner that best suits them."

Or, as Kohfeld puts it, "[John and I] don't stay together because we're forced to legally. We stay together because we love each other."

NADIA BERENSTEIN is a writer and speechwriter living in Brooklyn. She begins graduate studies at NYU this fall.

This Thing Called Love

Lauren Slater

My husband and I got married at eight in the morning. It was winter, freezing, the trees encased in ice and a few lone blackbirds balancing on telephone wires. We were in our early 30s, considered ourselves hip and cynical, the types who decried the institution of marriage even as we sought its status. During our wedding brunch we put out a big suggestion box and asked people to slip us advice on how to avoid divorce; we thought it was a funny, clear-eyed, grounded sort of thing to do, although the suggestions were mostly foolish: Screw the toothpaste cap on tight. After the guests left, the house got quiet. There were flowers everywhere: puckered red roses and fragile ferns. "What can we do that's really romantic?" I asked my newly wed one. Benjamin suggested we take a bath. I didn't want a bath. He suggested a lunch of chilled white wine and salmon. I was sick of salmon.

What can we do that's really romantic? The wedding was over, the silence seemed suffocating, and I felt the familiar disappointment after a longed-for event has come and gone. We were married. Hip, hip, hooray. I decided to take a walk. I went into the center of town, pressed my nose against a bakery window, watched the man with flour on his hands, the dough as soft as skin, pushed and pulled and shaped at last into stars. I milled about in an antique store. At last I came to our town's tattoo parlor. Now I am not a tattoo type person, but for some reason, on that cold silent Sunday, I decided to walk in. "Can I help you?" a woman asked.

"Is there a kind of tattoo I can get that won't be permanent?" I asked.

"Henna tattoos," she said.

She explained that they lasted for six weeks, were used at Indian weddings, were stark and beautiful and all brown. She showed me pictures of Indian women with jewels in their noses, their arms scrolled and laced with the henna markings. Indeed they were beautiful, sharing none of the gaudy comic strip quality of the tattoos we see in the United States. These henna tattoos spoke of intricacy, of the webwork between two people, of ties that bind and how difficult it is to find their beginnings and their elms. And because I had just gotten married, and because I was feeling a post wedding letdown, and because I wanted something really romantic to sail me through the night, I decided to get one.

"Where?" she asked.

"Here," I said. I laid my hands over my breasts and belly.

She raised her eyebrows. "Sure," she said.

I am a modest person. But I took off my shirt, lay on the table, heard her in the back room mixing powders and paints. She came to me carrying a small black-bellied pot inside of which was a rich red mush, slightly glittering. She adorned me. She gave me vines and flowers. She turned my body into a stake supporting whole new gardens of growth, and then, low around my hips, she painted a delicate chain-linked chastity belt. An hour later, the paint dry, I put my clothes back on, went home to film my newly wed one. This, I knew, was my gift to him, the kind of present you offer only once in your lifetime. I let him undress me.

"Wow," he said, standing back.

I blushed, and we began.

We are no longer beginning, my husband and I. This does not surprise me. Even back then, wearing the decor of desire, the serpentining tattoos, I knew they would fade, their red-clay color bleaching out until they were gone. On my wedding day I didn't care.

I do now. Eight years later, pale as a pillowcase, here I sit, with all the extra pounds and baggage time brings. And the questions have only grown more insistent. Does passion necessarily diminish over time? How reliable is romantic love, really, as a means of choosing one's mate? Can a marriage be good when Eros is replaced with friendship, or even economic partnership, two people bound by bank accounts?

Let me be clear: I still love my husband. There is no man I desire more. But it's hard to sustain romance in the crumb-filled quotidian that has become our lives. The ties that bind have been frayed by money and mortgages and children, those little imps who somehow manage to tighten the knot while weakening its actual fibers. Benjamin and I have no time for chilled white wine and salmon. The baths in our house always include Big Bird.

If this all sounds miserable, it isn't. My marriage is like a piece of comfortable clothing; even the arguments have a feel of fuzziness to them, something so familiar it can only be called home. And yet . . .

In the Western world we have for centuries concocted poems and stories and plays about the cycles of love, the way it morphs and changes over time, the way passion grabs us by our flung-back throats and then leaves us for something saner.

If *Dracula*—the frail woman, the sensuality of submission—reflects how we understand the passion of early romance, the *Flintstones* reflects our experiences of long-term love: All is gravel and somewhat silly, the song so familiar you can't stop singing it, and when you do, the emptiness is almost unbearable.

We have relied on stories to explain the complexities of love, tales of jealous gods and arrows. Now, however, these stories—so much a part of every civilization—may be changing as science steps in to explain what we have always felt to be myth, to be magic. For the first time, new research has begun to illuminate where love lies in the brain, the particulars of its chemical components.

Anthropologist Helen Fisher may be the closest we've ever come to having a doyenne of desire. At 60 she exudes a sexy confidence, with corn-colored hair, soft as floss, and a willowy build. A professor at Rutgers University, she lives in New York City, her book-lined apartment near Central Park, with its green trees fluffed out in the summer season, its paths crowded with couples holding hands.

Fisher has devoted much of her career to studying the biochemical pathways of love in all its manifestations: lust, romance, attachment, the way they wax and wane. One leg casually crossed over the other, ice clinking in her glass, she speaks with appealing frankness, discussing the ups and downs of love the way most people talk about real estate. "A woman unconsciously uses orgasms as a way of deciding whether or not a man is good for her. If he's impatient and rough, and she doesn't have the orgasm, she may instinctively feel he's less likely to be a good husband and father. Scientists think the fickle female orgasm may have evolved to help women distinguish Mr. Right from Mr. Wrong."

One of Fisher's central pursuits in the past decade has been looking at love, quite literally, with the aid of an MRI machine. Fisher and her colleagues Arthur Aron and Lucy Brown recruited subjects who had been "madly in love" for an average of seven months. Once inside the MRI machine, subjects were shown two photographs, one neutral, the other of their loved one.

What Fisher saw fascinated her. When each subject looked at his or her loved one, the parts of the brain linked to reward and pleasure—the ventral tegmental area and the caudate nucleus—lit up. What excited Fisher most was not so much finding a location, an address, for love as tracing its specific chemical pathways. Love lights up the caudate nucleus because it is home to a dense spread of receptors for a neurotransmitter called dopamine, which Fisher came to think of as part of our own endogenous love potion. In the right proportions, dopamine creates intense energy, exhilaration, focused attention, and motivation to win rewards. It is why, when you are newly in love, you can stay up all night, watch the sun rise, run a race, ski fast down a slope ordinarily too steep for your skill. Love makes you bold, makes you bright, makes you run real risks, which you sometimes survive, and sometimes you don't.

I first fell in love when I was only 12, with a teacher. His name was Mr. McArthur, and he wore open-toed sandals and sported a beard. I had never had a male teacher before, and I thought it terribly exotic. Mr. McArthur did things no other

teacher dared to do. He explained to us the physics of farting. He demonstrated how to make an egg explode. He smoked cigarettes at recess, leaning languidly against the side of the school building, the ash growing longer and longer until he casually tapped it off with his finger.

What unique constellation of needs led me to love a man who made an egg explode is interesting, perhaps, but not as interesting, for me, as my memory of love's sheer physical facts. I had never felt anything like it before. I could not get Mr. McArthur out of my mind. I was anxious; I gnawed at the lining of my cheek until I tasted the tang of blood. School became at once terrifying and exhilarating. Would I see him in the hallway? In the cafeteria? I hoped. But when my wishes were granted, and I got a glimpse of my man, it satisfied nothing; it only inflamed me all the more. Had he looked at me? Why had he not looked at me? When would I see him again? At home I looked him up in the phone book; I rang him, this in a time before caller ID. He answered.

"Hello?" Pain in my heart, ripped down the middle. Hang up.

Call back. "Hello?" I never said a thing.

Once I called him at night, late, and from the way he answered the phone it was clear, even to a prepubescent like me, that he was with a woman. His voice fuzzy, the tinkle of her laughter in the background. I didn't get out of bed for a whole day.

Sound familiar? Maybe you were 30 when it happened to you, or 8 or 80 or 25. Maybe you lived in Kathmandu or Kentucky; age and geography are irrelevant. Donatella Marazziti is a professor of psychiatry at the University of Pisa in Italy who has studied the biochemistry of lovesickness. Having been in love twice herself and felt its awful power, Marazziti became interested in exploring the similarities between love and obsessive-compulsive disorder.

She and her colleagues measured serotonin levels in the blood of 24 subjects who had fallen in love within the past six months and obsessed about this love object for at least four hours every day. Serotonin is, perhaps, our star neurotransmitter, altered by our star psychiatric medications: Prozac and Zoloft and Paxil, among others. Researchers have long hypothesized that people with obsessive-compulsive disorder (OCD) have a serotonin "imbalance." Drugs like Prozac seem to alleviate OCD by increasing the amount of this neurotransmitter available at the juncture between neurons.

Marazziti compared the lovers' serotonin levels with those of a group of people suffering from OCD and another group who were free from both passion and mental illness. Levels of serotonin in both the obsessives' blood and the lovers' blood were 40 percent lower than those in her normal subjects. Translation: Love and obsessive-compulsive disorder could have a similar chemical profile. Translation: Love and mental illness may be difficult to tell apart. Translation: Don't be a fool. Stay away.

Of course that's a mandate none of us can follow. We do fall in love, sometimes over and over again, subjecting ourselves, each time, to a very sick state of mind. There is hope, however, for those caught in the grip of runaway passion—Prozac. There's nothing like that bicolored bullet for damping down the sex drive and making you feel "blah" about the buffet. Helen

Fisher believes that the ingestion of drugs like Prozac jeopardizes one's ability to fall in love—and stay in love. By dulling the keen edge of love and its associated libido, relationships go stale. Says Fisher, "I know of one couple on the edge of divorce. The wife was on an antidepressant. Then she went off it, started having orgasms once more, felt the renewal of sexual attraction for her husband, and they're now in love all over again."

Psychoanalysts have concocted countless theories about why we fall in love and with whom we do. Freud would have said your choice is influenced by the unrequited wish to bed your mother, if you're a boy, or your father, if you're a girl. Jung believed that passion is driven by some kind of collective unconscious. Today psychiatrists such as Thomas Lewis from the University of California at San Francisco's School of Medicine hypothesize that romantic love is rooted in our earliest infantile experiences with intimacy, how we felt at the breast, our mother's face, these things of pure unconflicted comfort that get engraved in our brain and that we ceaselessly try to recapture as adults. According to this theory we love whom we love not so much because of the future we hope to build but because of the past we hope to reclaim. Love is reactive, not proactive, it arches us backward, which may be why a certain person just "feels right." Or "feels familiar." He or she is familiar. He or she has a certain look or smell or sound or touch that activates buried memories.

Love and obsessive-compulsive disorder could have a similar chemical profile. Translation: Love and mental illness may be difficult to tell apart. Translation: Don't be a fool. Stay away.

When I first met my husband, I believed this psychological theory was more or less correct. My husband has red hair and a soft voice. A chemist, he is whimsical and odd. One day before we married he dunked a rose in liquid nitrogen so it froze, whereupon he flung it against the wall, spectacularly shattering it. That's when I fell in love with him. My father, too, has red hair, a soft voice, and many eccentricities. He was prone to bursting into song, prompted by something we never saw.

However, it turns out my theories about why I came to love my husband may be just so much hogwash. Evolutionary psychology has said good riddance to Freud and the Oedipal complex and all that other transcendent stuff and hello to simple survival skills. It hypothesizes that we tend to see as attractive, and thereby choose as mates, people who look healthy. And health, say these evolutionary psychologists, is manifested in a woman with a 70 percent waist-to-hip ratio and men with rugged features that suggest a strong supply of testosterone in their blood. Waist-to-hip ratio is important for the successful birth of a baby, and studies have shown this precise ratio signifies higher fertility. As for the rugged look, well, a man with a good dose of testosterone probably also has a strong immune system and so is more likely to give his partner healthy children.

Perhaps our choice of mates is a simple matter of following our noses. Claus Wedekind of the University of Lausanne in Switzerland did an interesting experiment with sweaty T-shirts. He asked 49 women to smell T-shirts previously worn by unidentified men with a variety of the genotypes that influence both body odor and immune systems. He then asked the women to rate which T-shirts smelled the best, which the worst. What Wedekind found was that women preferred the scent of a T-shirt worn by a man whose genotype was most different from hers, a genotype that, perhaps, is linked to an immune system that possesses something hers does not. In this way she increases the chance that her offspring will be robust.

It all seems too good to be true, that we are so hardwired and yet unconscious of the wiring. Because no one to my knowledge has ever said, "I married him because of his B.O." No. We say, "I married him (or her) because he's intelligent, she's beautiful, he's witty, she's compassionate." But we may just be as deluded about love as we are when we're *in* love. If it all comes down to a sniff test, then dogs definitely have the edge when it comes to choosing mates.

W hy doesn't passionate love last? How is it possible to see a person as beautiful on Monday, and 364 days later, on another Monday, to see that beauty as bland? Surely the object of your affection could not have changed that much. She still has the same shaped eyes. Her voice has always had that husky sound, but now it grates on you—she sounds like she needs an antibiotic. Or maybe you're the one who needs an antibiotic, because the partner you once loved and cherished and saw as though saturated with starlight now feels more like a low-level infection, tiring you, sapping all your strength.

Studies around the world confirm that, indeed, passion usually ends. Its conclusion is as common as its initial flare. No wonder some cultures think selecting a lifelong mate based on something so fleeting is folly. Helen Fisher has suggested that relationships frequently break up after four years because that's about how long it takes to raise a child through infancy. Passion, that wild, prismatic insane feeling, turns out to be practical after all. We not only need to copulate; we also need enough passion to start breeding, and then feelings of attachment take over as the partners bond to raise a helpless human infant. Once a baby is no longer nursing, the child can be left with sister, aunts, friends. Each parent is now free to meet another mate and have more children.

Biologically speaking, the reasons romantic love fades may be found in the way our brains respond to the surge and pulse of dopamine that accompanies passion and makes us fly. Cocaine users describe the phenomenon of tolerance: The brain adapts to the excessive input of the drug. Perhaps the neurons become desensitized and need more and more to produce the high—to put out pixie dust, metaphorically speaking.

Maybe it's a good thing that romance fizzles. Would we have railroads, bridges, planes, faxes, vaccines, and television if we were all always besotted? In place of the ever evolving technology that has marked human culture from its earliest tool use, we would have instead only bonbons, bouquets, and birth control. More seriously, if the chemically altered state induced by romantic love is akin to a mental illness or a drug-induced euphoria, exposing yourself for too long could result in psychological damage. A good sex life can be as strong as Gorilla Glue, but who wants that stuff on your skin?

Once upon a time, in India, a boy and a girl fell in love without their parents' permission. They were from different castes, their relationship radical and unsanctioned. Picture it: the sparkling sari, the boy in white linen, the clandestine meetings on tiled terraces with a fat, white moon floating overhead. Who could deny these lovers their pleasure, or condemn the force of their attraction?

Their parents could. In one recent incident a boy and girl from different castes were hanged at the hands of their parents as hundreds of villagers watched. A couple who eloped were stripped and beaten. Yet another couple committed suicide after their parents forbade them to marry.

Anthropologists used to think that romance was a Western construct, a bourgeois by-product of the Middle Ages. Romance was for the sophisticated, took place in cafés, with coffees and Cabernets, or on silk sheets, or in rooms with a flickering fire. It was assumed that non-Westerners, with their broad familial and social obligations, were spread too thin for particular passions. How could a collectivist culture celebrate or in any way sanction the obsession with one individual that defines new love? Could a lice-ridden peasant really feel passion?

Easily, as it turns out. Scientists now believe that romance is panhuman, embedded in our brains since Pleistocene times. In a study of 166 cultures, anthropologists William Jankowiak and Edward Fischer observed evidence of passionate love in 147 of them. In another study men and women from Europe, Japan, and the Philippines were asked to fill out a survey to measure their experiences of passionate love. All three groups professed feeling passion with the same searing intensity.

But though romantic love may be universal, its cultural expression is not. To the Fulbe tribe of northern Cameroon, poise matters more than passion. Men who spend too much time with their wives are taunted, and those who are weak-kneed are thought to have fallen under a dangerous spell. Love may be inevitable, but for the Fulbe its manifestations are shameful, equated with sickness and social impairment.

In India romantic love has traditionally been seen as dangerous, a threat to a well-crafted caste system in which marriages are arranged as a means of preserving lineage and bloodlines. Thus the gruesome tales, the warnings embedded in fables about what happens when one's wayward impulses take over.

Today love marriages appear to be on the rise in India, often in defiance of parents' wishes. The triumph of romantic love is celebrated in Bollywood films. Yet most Indians still believe arranged marriages are more likely to succeed than love marriages. In one survey of Indian college students, 76 percent said they'd marry someone with all the right qualities even if they weren't in love with the person (compared with only 14 percent of Americans). Marriage is considered too important a step to leave to chance.

Studies around the world confirm that, indeed, passion usually ends. No wonder some cultures think selecting a lifelong mate based on something so fleeting is folly.

Renu Dinakaran is a striking 45-year-old woman who lives in Bangalore, India. When I meet her, she is dressed in Western-style clothes—black leggings and a T-shirt. Renu lives in a well-appointed apartment in this thronging city, where cows sleep on the highways as tiny cars whiz around them, plumes of black smoke rising from their sooty pipes.

Renu was born into a traditional Indian family where an arranged marriage was expected. She was not an arranged kind of person, though, emerging from her earliest days as a fierce tennis player, too sweaty for saris, and smarter than many of the men around her. Nevertheless at the age of 17 she was married off to a first cousin, a man she barely knew, a man she wanted to learn to love, but couldn't. Renu considers many arranged marriages to be acts of "state-sanctioned rape."

Renu hoped to fall in love with her husband, but the more years that passed, the less love she felt, until, at the end, she was shrunken, bitter, hiding behind the curtains of her in-laws' bungalow, looking with longing at the couple on the balcony across from theirs. "It was so obvious to me that couple had married for love, and I envied them. I really did. It hurt me so much to see how they stood together, how they went shopping for bread and eggs."

Exhausted from being forced into confinement, from being swaddled in saris that made it difficult to move, from resisting the pressure to eat off her husband's plate, Renu did what traditional Indian culture forbids one to do. She left. By this time she had had two children. She took them with her. In her mind was an old movie she'd seen on TV, a movie so strange and enticing to her, so utterly confounding and comforting at the same time, that she couldn't get it out of her head. It was 1986. The movie was *Love Story*.

"Before I saw movies like *Love Story,* I didn't realize the power that love can have," she says.

Renu was lucky in the end. In Mumbai she met a man named Anil, and it was then, for the first time, that she felt passion. "When I first met Anil, it was like nothing I'd ever experienced. He was the first man I ever had an orgasm with. I was high, just high, all the time. And I knew it wouldn't last, couldn't last, and so that infused it with a sweet sense of longing, almost as though we were watching the end approach while we were also discovering each other."

When Renu speaks of the end, she does not, to be sure, mean the end of her relationship with Anil; she means the end of a certain stage. The two are still happily married, companionable, loving if not "in love," with a playful black dachshund they bought together. Their relationship, once so full of fire, now seems to simmer along at an even temperature, enough to keep them well fed and warm. They are grateful.

"Would I want all that passion back?" Renu asks. "Sometimes, yes. But to tell you the truth, it was exhausting."

From a physiological point of view, this couple has moved from the dopamine-drenched state of romantic love to the relative quiet of an oxytocin-induced attachment. Oxytocin is a hormone that promotes a feeling of connection, bonding. It is released when we hug our long-term spouses, or our children. It is released when a mother nurses her infant. Prairie voles, animals with high levels of oxytocin, mate for life. When scientists block oxytocin receptors in these rodents, the animals don't form monogamous bonds and tend to roam. Some researchers speculate that autism, a disorder marked by a profound inability to forge and maintain social connections, is linked to an oxytocin deficiency. Scientists have been experimenting by treating autistic people with oxytocin, which in some cases has helped alleviate their symptoms.

In long-term relationships that work—like Renu and Anil's—oxytocin is believed to be abundant in both partners. In long-term relationships that never get off the ground, like Renu and her first husband's, or that crumble once the high is gone, chances are the couple has not found a way to stimulate or sustain oxytocin production.

"But there are things you can do to help it along," says Helen Fisher. "Massage. Make love. These things trigger oxytocin and thus make you feel much closer to your partner."

Well, I suppose that's good advice, but it's based on the assumption that you still want to have sex with that boring windbag of a husband. Should you fake-it-till-you-make-it?

"Yes," says Fisher. "Assuming a fairly healthy relationship, if you have enough orgasms with your partner, you may become attached to him or her. You will stimulate oxytocin."

This may be true. But it sounds unpleasant. It's exactly what your mother always said about vegetables: "Keep eating your peas. They are an acquired taste. Eventually, you will come to like them."

But I have never been a peas person.

It's 90 degrees on the day my husband and I depart, from Boston for New York City, to attend a kissing school. With two kids, two cats, two dogs, a lopsided house, and a questionable school system, we may know how to kiss, but in the rough and tumble of our harried lives we have indeed forgotten how to *kiss*.

The sky is paved with clouds, the air as sticky as jam in our hands and on our necks. The Kissing School, run by Cherie Byrd, a therapist from Seattle, is being held on the 12th floor of a run-down building in Manhattan. Inside, the room is whitewashed; a tiled table holds bottles of banana and apricot nectar, a pot of green tea, breath mints, and Chapstick. The other Kissing School students—sometimes they come from as far away as Vietnam and Nigeria—are sprawled happily on the bare floor, pillows and blankets beneath them. The class will be seven hours long.

Byrd starts us off with foot rubs. "In order to be a good kisser," she says, "you need to learn how to do the foreplay before the kissing." Foreplay involves rubbing my husband's smelly feet, but that is not as bad as when he has to rub mine. Right before we left the house, I accidentally stepped on a diaper the dog had gotten into, and although I washed, I now wonder how well.

"Inhale," Byrd says, and shows us how to draw in air.

"Exhale," she says, and then she jabs my husband in the back. "Don't focus on the toes so much," she says. "Move on to the calf."

Byrd tells us other things about the art of kissing. She describes the movement of energy through various chakras, the manifestation of emotion in the lips; she describes the importance of embracing all your senses, how to make eye contact as a prelude, how to whisper just the right way. Many hours go by. My cell phone rings. It's our babysitter. Our one-year-old has a high fever. We must cut the long lesson short. We rush out. Later on, at home, I tell my friends what we learned at Kissing School: We don't have time to kiss.

A perfectly typical marriage. Love in the Western world.

Luckily I've learned of other options for restarting love. Arthur Aron, a psychologist at Stony Brook University in New York, conducted an experiment that illuminates some of the mechanisms by which people become and stay attracted. He recruited a group of men and women and put opposite sex pairs in rooms together, instructing each pair to perform a series of tasks, which included telling each other personal details about themselves. He then asked each couple to stare into each other's eyes for two minutes. After this encounter, Aron found most of the couples, previously strangers to each other, reported feelings of attraction. In fact, one couple went on to marry.

Novelty triggers dopamine in the brain, which can stimulate feelings of attraction. So riding a roller coaster on a first date is more likely to lead to second and third dates.

Fisher says this exercise works wonders for some couples. Aron and Fisher also suggest doing novel things together, because novelty triggers dopamine in the brain, which can stimulate feelings of attraction. In other words, if your heart flutters in his presence, you might decide it's not because you're anxious but because you love him. Carrying this a step further, Aron and others have found that even if you just jog in place and then meet someone, you're more likely to think they're attractive. So first dates that involve a nerve-racking activity, like riding a roller coaster, are more likely to lead to second and third dates. That's a strategy worthy of posting on Match.com. Play some squash. And in times of stress—natural disasters, blackouts, predators on the prowl—lock up tight and hold your partner.

In Somerville, Massachusetts, where I live with my husband, our predators are primarily mosquitoes. That needn't stop us from trying to enter the windows of each other's soul. When I propose this to Benjamin, he raises an eyebrow.

"Why don't we just go out for Cambodian food?" he says.

"Because that's not how the experiment happened."

As a scientist, my husband is always up for an experiment. But our lives are so busy that, in order to do this, we have to make a plan. We will meet next Wednesday at lunchtime and try the experiment in our car.

On the Tuesday night before our rendezvous, I have to make an unplanned trip to New York. My husband is more than happy to forget our date. I, however, am not. That night, from my hotel room, I call him.

"We can do it on the phone," I say.

"What am I supposed to stare into?" he asks. "The keypad?"

"There's a picture of me hanging in the hall. Look at that for two minutes. I'll look at a picture I have of you in my wallet."

"Come on," he says.

"Be a sport," I say. "It's better than nothing."

Maybe not. Two minutes seems like a long time to stare at someone's picture with a receiver pressed to your ear. My husband sneezes, and I try to imagine his picture sneezing right along with him, and this makes me laugh.

Another 15 seconds pass, slowly, each second stretched to its limit so I can almost hear time, feel time, its taffy-like texture, the pop it makes when it's done. Pop pop pop. I stare and stare at my husband's picture. It doesn't produce any sense of startling intimacy, and I feel defeated.

Still, I keep on. I can hear him breathing on the other end. The photograph before me was taken a year or so ago, cut to fit my wallet, his strawberry blond hair pulled back in a ponytail. I have never really studied it before. And I realize that in this picture my husband is not looking straight back at me, but his pale blue eyes are cast sideways, off to the left, looking at something I can't see. I touch his eyes. I peer close, and then still closer, at his averted face. Is there something sad in his expression, something sad in the way he gazes off?

I look toward the side of the photo, to find what it is he's looking at, and then I see it: a tiny turtle coming toward him. Now I remember how he caught it after the camera snapped, how he held it gently in his hands, showed it to our kids, stroked its shell, his forefinger moving over the scaly dome, how he held the animal out toward me, a love offering. I took it, and together we sent it back to the sea.

Pillow Talk

A conversation with Stephen and Ondrea Levine about lust, the meaning of marriage, and true intimacy.

NINA UTNE

What is a good long-term relationship? *When we asked the question around the office and among our friends, we heard a lot of fear and even more relief. Fear because asking questions inevitably rocks the boat of marriage and family. Relief because after we admit that there are few long-term relationships to emulate, we can begin an honest exploration of how to do it differently. Stephen and Ondrea Levine, with three marriages behind them, have made their marriage work for 26 years and have raised three children. They work as counselors and writers, with a focus on death and dying as well as relationship issues. Good relationships are entirely idiosyncratic, they say, but self-respect, clarity of intent, and commitment to growth are the key elements. Ondrea says each of us has to start by answering the question "What do you want out of this very short life?" But ultimately, Stephen says, it's about "when you get to just loving the ass off that person and you still don't know what love means."*

Nina: We hear a lot about how relationships begin, and plenty about how they end. But there's not a lot of honest talk about how to make them last—or, for that matter, why they should.

Ondrea: Once the lust of the first couple of years wears off, once the other person is off the pedestal, and you're off the pedestal, and you're facing each other and you see each other's craziness, frailties, vulnerabilities—that's when the work really starts. The initial intensity of the passion cools, and love comes to a middle way, a balance. You have to have something more than the fact that you're in love to keep it going and keep it growing.

Nina: And what is that something?

Stephen: I think relationships persevere because you're interested in what's going to happen the next day and your partner is an interesting person to share it with.

O: Also, the people with the best relationships often have some kind of practice. It can be religious practice, love practice, nature practice, whatever, but they have something that's so essentially helpful in their growth that it keeps the relationship going.

S: People who get into a relationship who don't already have something that's more important to them than themselves—generally spiritual practice and growth, or maybe service work—are less liable to stay with the process when the relationship doesn't give them exactly what their desire system wishes for.

N: Someone wrote that 35 percent of his relationship comes from the fact that he brings his wife a cup of coffee in bed every morning.

S: What a weak relationship! Boy, that's a miserable relationship. This guy better get himself another hobby!

O: I was just thinking how very thoughtful that is. Serving each other is exceptionally important.

S: Growth. Growth is also important.

O: Yes, various levels of growth, but certainly heart expansion. Everybody would define growth so differently, but love has to grow, your heart has to open more, you have to get clearer about your intentions, clearer about what you really want out of this very short life.

And it's so individual; it depends so much on life experience. Love and simple human kindness are of huge value to me, and I find that I'm drawn to people who are thoughtful and kind. I used to be drawn to people who were only wise.

N: It seems like the bottom line is the level of consciousness and openheartedness that we bring to a long-term relationship.

S: In a relationship, we're working on a mystical union. That's a term that came from the Christian tradition, but it's part of almost all devotional traditions. And it means uniting at a level way beyond our separation. After 26 years, the line between Ondrea and the Beloved is very, very blurred. In that context, you may ask what happens when two people's goals change. Well, if they're working on becoming whole human beings, they'll change in a whole way, whether it means being together or separate.

N: Growth and service and practice are important. But what happens if you have those intentions but there are kids and hectic lives and petty annoyances and betrayals? How does mystical union accommodate that?

S: But that's what everybody has to work with. I mean, if you can't get through that stuff, there is no mystical union. If only mystical union were so easy—if people could just lean into each other's soul space, as it were. In fact, people think they're doing that, and it's actually lust, generally. We say that love is as close as you get to God without really trying. When people live together, maybe they do feel each other's soul, maybe they do feel the Beloved, maybe they both enter the Beloved. But mind arises, preference arises, attitude arises, inclination arises.

O: We raised three kids, and we certainly had our share of times when our hearts were closed to each other and we felt separate, but our commitment was to work on that and to work with it by trying to stay open, trying to understand the other person's conditioning, because our conditionings were so different.

For instance, what you might think of as betrayal I might not think is betrayal, so all of that has to be defined in a relationship. How I might work with betrayal, you might not be willing to, and that's part of what you have to work out with your partner. Some levels of betrayal are workable, and some are not worth putting in the energy for some relationships. There's no right way other than your way.

S: And *betrayal* is a loaded word. A lot of people naturally feel resentment in a relationship because there are two people with two desire systems. Sometimes they're complementary and sometimes contradictory. And when someone doesn't get what he or she wants—it can be something so simple, like not enough gas in the car, little things—the feeling of betrayal may arise. Now, sexual betrayal, that's something else entirely.

N: What do you think about the possibility of open marriages?

S: Raging bullshit. Well, it's fine for young people who don't want a committed relationship. But you might as well kiss your relationship good-bye once you open it. I don't think there is such a thing. People who open their relationships open them at both ends. The relationship becomes something you're just passing through. There's no place for real trust. There's no place where you're concerned about the other person's well-being more than your own, which is what relationship is, which is what love is. I've never, ever seen it work, and we've known some extremely conscious people.

N: But when I look at the carnage in so many marriages, I think maybe we need to step back and look at the whole agreement. There are many, many different kinds of love, and maybe we're just being too narrow.

O: We've known a couple of people who have had multiple relationships within their marriage and it's worked out for them, but it takes a certain inner strength and a depth of self-trust. Part of why marriage has been set up is because of trust, and keeping track of lineage and money and paternity and all that stuff. I think it's all based on trust, and we don't seem to have the capacity to trust deeply unless it's just one other person.

S: Then again, for some, sexual betrayal is like an active catapult. It can throw them right into God. It can clarify their priorities.

N: So you're saying that an open arrangement undercuts intimacy?

O: So many people nowadays run to divorce court because it's easier than trying to work it through. And it's so exciting to go on to that next new relationship, where someone really loves you and doesn't know your frailties. I know many people who keep going from relationship to relationship because it's easier. Although they wouldn't say that. They wouldn't even think of the children. They would only think of themselves, and that's okay too, but I don't think you get as much growth.

S: That sex thing, that's way overrated. Way, way overrated. Because if two people love each other, the part that becomes most interesting in sex is the part that may be the least interesting in the beginning. It's the quality of taking another person internally. I don't think people realize, with our loose sexual energy, the enormity of letting someone inside your aura, so to speak. To let someone closer to you than a foot and a half, you are already doing something that is touching on universal wonders and terrors.

As the intimacy becomes more intimate, though the sex may not be as hot, the intimacy becomes much hotter. Much more fulfilling. Sexual relationships actually become more fulfilling the longer they go on if you start getting by all the hindrances to intimacy—all your fears, your doubts, your distrust. Sex has an exquisite quality to support a relationship, not because of the skin sensory level, but because of heart sensory level.

N: What significance is there in the formality of marriage? The contract?

O: That depends on your conditioning. For us, marriage meant that we were going to work as hard as we could. But we both said that if the other person wanted to go another way or had a major epiphany or wanted a change in life, we would honor that.

The contract gives you a sense of security that both people are willing to work as hard as they can. I certainly don't know that the marriage contract is for everyone, although I think it can be helpful with kids. Then again, I'm 60, and that's an old style of thinking. That's why I think nowadays maybe a six-month marriage contract might be more skillful. The most important thing is to be honest about how you see your relationship: Do you see it as 'til death do you part, do you see it as until you just can't stand each other, do you see it as until the kids are 18? Anything is workable.

N: I'm thinking about children, this container we call family. For me, there's a certain mystical union in families. Sometimes "staying together for the sake of the children" is actually about honoring this idea of family.

O: Of course we didn't stay together for the children, because we're both divorced and had children.

S: It's only my third marriage . . . I'm working at it!

O: I got married for the old reason that many women in my generation did. I was pregnant. I didn't really want to get married, but I would've been a *puta,* a prostitute—looked at as a lesser woman in those days.

I think that it mostly is an empty relationship when you're staying together for the kids, but we have known some people whose love for their kids was so great that they became more brotherly and sisterly, and it worked very well for them, but that's pretty rare.

S: And usually when people are in that kind of disarray, the children do not benefit from their staying together.

N: Are there other options than the train wreck to divorce?

S: Depends on the individuals. It depends on their spiritual practice. I think it has a lot to do with their toilet training.

O: Oh, we're screwed.

S: What I mean is that our earliest self-esteem and self-image comes into play. The most beautiful thing about love—and the most difficult—is that it makes us go back to our unfinished places and relationships and, maybe, finish them. Your partner is the person who helps you do that, not by serving you, but by serving as a mirror for you, by his or her own honesty. By observing our partners' struggle to be honest we learn to be honest ourselves.

N: I just see so many people who are either rushing to divorce or living in dead marriages. They seem afraid to ask these deep kinds of questions and have these kinds of conversations.

O: I have worked with thousands of people who are dying, and I have heard several common complaints on the deathbed. The first was: "I wish I had got a divorce." Mostly it was fear: They didn't want to start all over again with someone else. Oh, some people were happy. They said marriage was the most wonderful ride of their lives. But many were unhappy. They wished that they hadn't let fear get in the way. But, you know, to wait until you're on your deathbed to start reflecting on what your needs are—it's not too late, but it's awfully late.

N: That's a lot of procrastination.

To learn more about the ideas of counselors, teachers, and writers Stephen and Ondrea Levine, visit their website at www.warmrocktapes.com.

Behind the Cloak of Polygamy

What's life for the women and children in the Texas fundamentalist Mormon cult like? Ask the women who have escaped similar communities.

ANDREA MOORE-EMMETT

In 1953, Gov. John Howard Pyle of Arizona tried to rescue 263 children living in the fundamentalist Mormon polygamist community of Short Creek, near the Utah border of Arizona. His effort failed, as the press and public sentiment turned against him. Children who had been removed from their families were returned, and the governor's political career effectively ended.

Rena Mackert's mother, part of a fundamentalist Mormon polygamist family in Short Creek, was pregnant with her during that period in 1953. "If they hadn't reunited our family, I would never have suffered the continuous sexual abuse by my father," says Mackert, a bookkeeper.

In the 55 years since the abortive Short Creek incident, politicians in Arizona and Utah have been reluctant to challenge the Fundamentalist Church of Jesus Christ of Latter-day Saints (FLDS), a polygamy-practicing group that broke away from the Mormon Church (formally, the Church of Jesus Christ of Latter-day Saints). But in early April, a similar sort of child-rescue effort took place, this time at the Yearning for Zion Ranch near Eldorado, Texas—reportedly the new headquarters of the FLDS. Texas child-welfare authorities, acting on an abuse complaint from an anonymous caller, eventually removed more than 400 children from the property and put them in foster care.

The women of the Yearning for Zion Ranch quickly became subjects of empathy, even if their long, high-necked prairie dresses and sky-high bouffant hairdos were disconcerting. No one is immune to the grief of a parent having her child wrenched away, or can fail to be moved by the sight of children taken from what seems to be their safe maternal haven.

And the FLDS knows this. The group immediately launched a public relations campaign—complete with photo ops of the sad-looking mothers—accusing Texas Child Protective Services of violating their parental rights and for targeting them on account of religion. But people like Mackert know what is really happening behind the walls of the YFZ compound.

My own research, which includes interviews with dozens of women, adolescents, children and men who formerly lived or are currently living in fundamentalist Mormon and polygamous Christian families, shows the very dark reality of these communities. It uncovers how claims of religious and parental rights can be a cloak for abusive and criminal behavior. And it suggests that deference to religion and parental rights must sometimes be overweighed in favor of protecting the safety and human rights of women and children.

Before the 1,700-acre yearning for zion compound was settled into four years ago, FLDS members had already been thriving for a century within isolated towns in Utah, Arizona, Mexico and British Columbia, Canada. The polygamous group has also recently built compounds in Colorado, Idaho and South Dakota.

The church now boasts between 10,000 to 15,000 members, led by 52-year-old Warren Jeffs, who, in 2007, was convicted in Utah on two felony counts as an accomplice to rape. Jeffs still faces trial in Arizona on four charges of sexual conduct with a minor, incest and conspiracy.

But that's "man's law," in which bigamy/polygamy and sex with minors are prohibited. FLDS members believe they are commanded to live "God's law" of "patriarchal marriage"—polygamy—as directed by early Mormon founder Joseph Smith. (The mainstream Mormon Church, however, discontinued the practice of polygamy over a century ago, although it remains in their scriptures as doctrine.) Males are to marry at least three wives. Some acquire many more.

According to a review of the literature and his own work with women from polygamous families, Salt Lake City psychologist Larry Beall, director of the Trauma Awareness Treatment Center, has been able to outline the basic structure of fundamentalist Mormon polygamy. He describes it as male-centered and authoritarian, with a leader—known as the "prophet"—who is to be worshipped as God and not to be questioned. A select number of bishops presides over separate congregations (72-year-old Merril Jessop serves as bishop in Eldorado). Although the prophet leads the entire group in "one-man rule," with bishops second in authority, individual men act as "God of the home." Males are endowed at age 12 with priesthood, which positions them next to God.

According to numerous women I have spoken with, the prophet, through the father, controls decisions of who will marry whom and when, where the family will live, what education children will receive and what work they will do. At any point, the leader can remove a child, a father or mother, and reassign those individuals to a different family. In some polygamous communities, children are rotated among the wives of one husband so as not to cause mothers and children to bond with one another.

The women who escaped from FLDS have also related to me that they were conditioned not to have feelings of love, because that would bring jealousy and is a sign of weakness. Laura Chapman, a 45-year-old consultant in Colorado who escaped from FLDS as a young adult, told me in a recent phone conversation, "All the mothers were called mother so-and-so; I had to call my own mother 'Mother Myra' like the other children. I couldn't say 'Mom,' or she'd ignore me."

Women are mere property within this structure, born for the single purpose of bearing children. Many of the women I spoke with told me that they are expected to have a child per year, serving as "vessels to be worn out in childbirth." When a wife reaches the age of 40, or is no longer able to bear children, the husband is given permission from the prophet to replace her with two wives under age 20.

Girls are typically married to much older men, some by age 12 or even younger. They also are often trafficked to and from the other compounds, across state lines and national borders. The girls may or may not know whom they are marrying; it may be a relative, due to the belief that, as a chosen people, the FLDS must intermarry to preserve the royal bloodline.

As could be predicted, incest-resultant births have caused numerous genetic defects within this group, including the world's highest prevalence of a rare disease known as fumarase deficiency. The disorder causes severe mental retardation, epileptic seizures and debilitating muscle-control problems. But this is not necessarily considered a tragedy within the FLDS, as the U.S. government pays additional subsidies to families caring for a disabled child, thus contributing to the FLDS practice of "bleeding the beast." (The idea is to get the U.S. to subsidize the FLDS, thus draining resources so that the government can eventually be brought down. FLDS members believe that when this happens, their prophet will rule over all.) According to the *Salt Lake Tribune*, in 2002 the neighboring FLDS strongholds of Hildale, Utah, and Colorado City, Ariz. (formerly Short Creek), received $8 million in public aid for their less than 6,000 residents. Sixty-six percent of Hildale residents were on Medicaid, compared to 6.5 percent of all Utahans.

Indoctrination begins in the FLDS cradle, with babies being "broken" by such means as spanking them until they are too exhausted to cry, according to many women I've interviewed, including Mackert. They've told me that other techniques to stop crying include immersing babies in water, or holding them under the faucet. Crying is not to be tolerated in babies, children or women, as it is viewed as a sign that one has an evil spirit, according to Beall's research.

Beall also notes that violence is seen as a necessary strength by FLDS men. Women have no concept of what constitutes abuse: They must submit cheerfully to their husband and are admonished to "keep sweet." No woman has a right to complain about what is done to her or to her children, since a father "can all but kill a child for deliberately disobeying," says Chapman.

With females as objects owned by men, girls are often sexually abused by their fathers. "It would be difficult to pull a girl out of [the FLDS] who hasn't been sexually abused," says Chapman. She adds that girls also suffer from sexual abuse by other men in the community, as well as by their own brothers—who are often taught to be sexual predators and are sexually abused themselves.

"When I confided to my mom what my brothers were doing, we had to go to my father about it," Chapman remembers. "He told my mom he wanted to talk to her alone. When she came out, she said, 'Your father says we have to let [brothers] be who they're going to be.'"

According to my interviews, both girls and boys face lives of servitude and hard labor from very young ages, with girls putting in their time within the home and boys on farms or in construction. "It's hard to explain to someone what it feels like to be enslaved," says Rena's sister Kathleen Mackert, 50, who grew up in the FLDS in Utah and Arizona but escaped as a young woman and is now a bartender in Las Vegas. As early as she can remember, she was a surrogate parent to younger children, sewed clothes, washed clothes with a wringer washer, made bread, canned fruit, churned butter, plucked and cleaned chickens, and cooked for the entire family of multiple wives and more than 30 children.

At puberty, girls become chattel for the men's harems and boys become the older men's competition for marriageable girls. Young boys who come from well-placed families can look forward to a future of collecting their own harem and rising within the priesthood ranks, but less fortunate boys are thrown out of the FLDS. These "Lost Boys," as they are called, rove about society trying to make a life for themselves, forever banished by their families and community.

To ensure secrecy and isolation as a means of control over FLDS members, the outside world is portrayed as an evil and fearful place. This fear further compounds existence for girls and women who may have escaped. Says Mackert, "I was terrified. I had nothing and no one. I only knew that I was damned."

Another factor making life difficult for those who leave is the lack of an education. Teaching certain topics, such as science, is actually viewed as a crime by the FLDS, according to Beall, who has helped a number of women and children after their escape from polygamist communities. A typical polygamous home- or church-schooled education consists of basic math and reading. Most literature is forbidden, as is discussion of the human body. Other cultures have no value, and racism is taught as religious doctrine. Racist rhetoric from Jeffs to his followers leaked out to news media in 2005, which led the Southern Poverty Law Center to put the FLDS on its list of general hate groups.

For decades, the towns on the Utah/Arizona border have been a law unto themselves, violating the rights of women and children while authorities looked the other way. I have attended town hall meetings on polygamy where I have heard the attorney general of Utah say that there aren't enough resources to go after polygamists—so polygamy should be reduced to a misdemeanor.

> ## "American court systems are quick to turn the other way when abusive practices are enthroned in religious dogma."
>
> —Cult expert, Steve Eichel

"American court systems are quick to turn the other way when abusive practices are enthroned in religious dogma and the trappings of religious organization," says psychologist and cult expert Steve Eichel. Indeed, when testifying in court on cult-related cases, he has to avoid mentioning religious beliefs because judges will disallow testimony about cults or the impact of religious coercion on children or adult behavior.

Only recently, through the work of women's and children's activist organizations, have state authorities taken notice. Even then, action has been slow in coming, spurred by media attention and directed toward only a small fraction of those individuals responsible for crimes.

In the recent Texas case, the state's Department of Child Protective Services stirred up a hornet's nest of legal maneuvering.

Within weeks after the children from the Yearning for Zion compound were taken into foster care, the 3rd District Court of Appeals ruled that the department had failed to prove an urgent need to remove the children, and that the state did not provide ample evidence in extending abuse allegations to the entire community. In response, the state of Texas appealed to the Texas Supreme Court who, in a divided opinion, upheld the appeals court but stipulated provisions the FLDS must follow to gain back their children. As of this writing, court-ordered DNA testing to untangle parent-child ties has still not been completed and the case could still be appealed to the U.S. Supreme Court.

"Individualized hearings could still result in state custody if the findings are strong enough," says Marci Hamilton, a Princeton public affairs professor and most recently author of *Justice Denied: What America Must Do to Protect Its Children* (Cambridge, 2008).

At the time of the raid in 1953, there were 263 children in danger. In 2008, there were more than 400 children, and they came from just one of several FLDS compounds around the country. How many more women and children will have their civil and human rights violated under the cloak of patriarchy and religion? How many more generations will continue to be abused?

ANDREA MOORE-EMMETT is author of *God's Brothel: The Extortion of Sex for Salvation in Contemporary Mormon and Christian Fundamentalist Polygamy and the Stories of 18 Women Who Escaped* (Pince-Nez Press, 2004).

Love at the Margins
Extreme Relationships Demand Extreme Commitment

Nontraditional couples may be seen as weird, discomfiting or even sinful by others, but if they survive the crucible of social censure and self-doubt they can forge powerful bonds—and teach others about enduring love.

MARK TEICH

It's not easy being a lesbian couple in a suburban New Jersey community. "We're surrounded by married couples and families, and we stand out," says Allison. Madeleine adds, "By now I'm sure the neighbors can guess our situation. I feel comfortable with a few, but I'd rather keep things secret from the rest."

When they first dated, Allison, an artist, was in her element in Manhattan. Madeleine spent weekends at Allison's place. "In the city, no one noticed us," Allison says. "I never felt we were marginalized until I moved to New Jersey." Ultimately she'd felt she had to make the commitment to move in with Madeleine, because her girlfriend was the major breadwinner then, with a stable job as a computer software engineer 20 minutes from home.

"I love my work," notes Madeleine. "But there's a lot of prejudice in this field, so I don't mention Allison. I'd never bring her to an office party."

Sustaining a relationship is a challenge for anyone, but couples deemed inappropriate or abnormal by traditional social norms must forge their unions in the face of both internal and external pressures. Walking down the street or dining out, a gay or interracial couple or, say, a 50-year-old man embracing a 27-year-old woman (or vice versa) may be stared at, or viewed as suspect or even unnatural. More important, they may often face the wrath and rejection of their families, colleagues and friends. Couples considered marginal can encounter impediments from the law or organized religion—any institution built on traditional belief. No wonder they often hesitate to invest emotionally in one another, balking at moving in together or taking their partners to Christmas gatherings with their friends or families.

Nonetheless, many nontraditional couples end up thriving for decades. How do they move past the stigmas, ridicule and rejection to build some of the most enduring unions?

The answer lies in a kind of emotional trifecta. First, somewhere amid the prejudice, resentment and doubt they face, they find a support system that sustains them and confirms their relationship; second, like Romeo and Juliet, they discover an us-against-them inner strength that defies all naysayers; third, they simply stand the test of time, until both they and those who doubted them come to be believers.

The Glue That Binds

The question is: Why do it—especially with all the extra stress from such disapproval? Why begin a romance with so many strikes against you?

Certainly, physical attraction can override social concerns. Floridians Ken and Sara Benjamin were immediately drawn to one another at a computer conference 18 years ago, even though she had just turned 40 (a blond, young-looking 40) and he was only 24. "I thought she was an attractive female with great legs," he remembers. "But I also felt something deeper almost immediately. I wanted something much more than a one-night stand."

For some nontraditional couples, friendship comes first. Steven and Joyce Boro, a Jewish-American married to a black emigrant from Dominica, were roommates and buddies at Brooklyn College in New York well before they became involved. "We knew one another a full year first," says Steven. "We hung out, hitchhiked around together

Steven and Joyce Boro, Portland, Oregon

Couples on the margins of society may discover that a relationship frowned on in one locale is encouraged elsewhere. For Steven and Joyce Boro, a white Jewish man and a black Caribbean woman, that meant moving their show west—far from the disapproving eyes of family and friends in New York—to a commune. "I'd mainly dated white guys, but I never brought them to meet my mother," says Joyce. "It was probably intentional, because I wanted to avoid the racial issue with her. And Steven's mother thought blacks were the scum of the earth." By moving to the commune, they simultaneously limited their contact with their parents and gained a network of supportive friends. Ultimately they moved to Portland, where they raised their two children and have remained happily married for more than 30 years. Of course, like all interracial couples, they have been subject to some negative scrutiny. "Just the other day, I got angry looks from a black guy when we were walking together in Seattle," says Steven. "We've had our share of looks from whites, too. But none of that means anything to me. I've never really seen Joyce's color. It looks good on her, though."

Steven Pearl and Gino Grenek, Brooklyn, New York

Steven, a 40-year-old editor, and Gino, a 33-year-old dancer, finish each other's sentences with an edgy intimacy. They met at a party six years ago, felt an instant simpatico and attraction, and soon became a pair. Today they share an apartment in Brooklyn and consider themselves official domestic partners even if New York rejects same-sex marriage. This barrier notwithstanding, Steven and Gino find New York City especially accepting ("It's not Brokeback Mountain out here," Gino says)—so much so that their greatest relationship challenges come not from their same-sex status but from religion and involvement with work. Steven is Jewish, while Gino is Russian Orthodox. Both come from observant families. "We have learned to celebrate these differences and participate in each other's rituals," Steven explains. Gino travels with his troupe, while Steven works regular hours as an editor. "I told him that dance comes first and he comes second, but I've softened a bit on that," Gino states. According to Steven, the one complexity that may rear its head in the future involves having a family. "A lot of gay men and women don't often think of themselves as having children," he comments, "and to some degree I've internalized that." Yet, growing their family is something they consider. Says Gino, "If we decide to have a family I think we'll both be fantastic fathers and role models for our kids."

and became good friends before anything romantic happened. I always felt good being with her."

While relatives usually react badly at first to these unions, in some cases family acceptance launches the relationship. Stephanie, a young Chinese-American from California, who planned a career in medicine, met Juan, a poor construction worker, in a little town in Honduras when she was serving as a Peace Corps health worker. His family was the initial glue; Stephanie actually met them first, when Juan was working out of town. His mother, a coworker, kept inviting her home. "He has a big family, with 10 brothers and sisters, and lots of cousins, and they interact every day. They were all so nice, and kind of adopted me."

By the time Juan arrived on the scene, she was already a fixture. "We never really dated, we just spent a lot of time together," she recalls.

Vive La Difference

Marginalized couples come together for many of the same reasons as other couples. But the very extremity of their differences may give their relationship an extra dimension. "The primary thing people look for in relationships is to expand themselves," asserts Arthur Aron, psychologist at the State University of New York at Stony Brook. "Those we grow close to become part of who we are, widening our social resources and our perspective. We want someone different from ourselves to increase our efficacy and range of influence. If you're black and they're white, if you're older and they're younger, if you're one nationality and they're another, you've expanded your knowledge and opportunities."

The more you and your partner differ, the better—until the stress exceeds the thrill.

As a same-sex couple fairly close in age, Allison and Madeleine clearly don't have these kinds of disparities. But their personalities couldn't be more different. Allison is a free-spirited artist, Madeleine a meticulous software expert. Allison is comfortable living hand to mouth, while Madeleine thrives on the security of a lucrative career; Allison is assertive and public about being gay, displaying her pictures online with other lesbian artists; Madeleine likes to keep her sexual orientation off the radar. "When I met Allison, she would blatantly flirt with me so that everyone knew she had a crush on me, and I was horrified," Madeleine says.

The more radical your choices in a partner, the better—until the stress exceeds the thrill. "The key to a successful relationship is the tension between similar and opposite," says Aron. "Difference increases excitement and resources, but similarity ups the chance of maintaining the relationship long-term."

Allison's free-spiritedness and openness (as well as a slinky black dress) helped win Madeleine over, while Madeleine's intelligence, seriousness and solidity did the trick for Allison. Ultimately they learned that despite major personality differences, they had lots in common.

Coming to the Crossroads

The tension between commonality and difference eventually brings most nontraditional couples to a crossroads. Families' and communities' initial reactions reflect age-old cultural fears of letting the invaders in, of polluting and depleting the race. That's why, for example, Hasidic Jewish families traditionally hold funerals when a family member marries outside the faith.

Faced with such strong disapproval, even the happiest partners experience serious reservations early on, which can lead to moments of reckoning. Purdue University social psychologists Justin Lehmiller and Christopher Agnew have shown that at the start, nontraditional couples invest less of themselves in their relationships and are less committed than traditional couples, probably for this very reason.

Differences increase excitement, but similarity ups the chance of maintaining the relationship long-term.

Steven Boro, whose father (a Holocaust survivor) and mother were appalled that he was dating a black woman, simply set off without Joyce, hitching around the U.S. and Canada the moment he graduated from college, though Joyce and he had been involved for months. He had no plans of coming back. "I was committed not to her but to what I saw as my 'spiritual journey,' " Steven recalls. "Really I was floating like a leaf on a stream. On my 22nd birthday, I vowed that I wouldn't marry until I was 30 and that I'd never have kids.' "

It took Joyce to save the relationship. When she received a letter from Steven that he had settled on a commune in the Washington wilderness—and was involved with another woman there—she sought out his brother Fred to help her go after her boyfriend. "I hadn't been in this country that long, and I was still very naive. I didn't

Ken and Sara Benjamin, Taverna, Florida

When Ken and Sara were dating 18 years ago, they faced problems: Ken wanted to marry, but Sara was twice divorced. Ken, then 24, was interested in having children, but Sara, then 40, already had two going off to college, "I liked marriage, but I was at the end of child-rearing and wanted to stretch my wings," Sara recalls. Adding insult to injury, people kept mistaking Sara for Ken's mother.

They found a unique way to solve their dilemmas: They backpacked around the world for two years. "I wouldn't say we went on the trip to escape the problems," says Sara. "We just needed to get into a neutral area to work things out." They went to India and Nepal, stayed in hostels and hiked mountains. "In these places, where people's life spans were very contracted, we would tell people we were a couple, and they would respond flat out: 'That's not possible; she's too old,'" remembers Ken.

There was no escaping the issues, but the longer they were together, the more they loved one another. So they compromised: On their return, Sara agreed to marry Ken and he passed up having children. "I didn't want children as a concept, I just wanted her children," says Ken. In fact, it all worked out. "Even though I'm only five years older than Sara's daughter, she needed support and I was glad to fill that role."

even know what a commune was, and I almost headed for Washington, D.C.,' " says Joyce. "Fred put me on the right bus. I was still in school, and I thought I was going for the weekend, but it took me four days just to cross the country."

"Halfway there, in Nebraska, she called to tell me she was coming," says Steven. "I was really happy. I told her the other relationship was over."

Neither of them ever came back. They settled, along with 30 other people, on 120 acres of rolling hills and forests. Within a few weeks, their commune friends began suggesting they get married. " 'You look so good together. You're such a great couple,' they kept telling us," says Steven. "I thought about it, and I realized they were right. Joyce was wonderful. So I said sure." Two months later, they were married. Three decades later, their two grown children are now out on their own, and the couple no longer live on the commune.

"Despite investing less in their relationship at first, marginalized partners ultimately tend to be significantly more committed than nonmarginalized couples," Lehmiller notes.

Tracie and Leo Auguste, Miami, Florida

Tracie Auguste, 30, is Chinese, and her husband, Leo, 31, is Haitian—but cultural and racial differences have never stood in their way. One reason: At North Miami Senior High, where they met when she was a junior and he a senior, they were simply fellow minority students in the multicultural melting pot that was their school. "People might have noticed if Tracie were white," comments Leo, "but we were both minorities and no one batted an eye." Even their families were accepting. "Leo's family wouldn't have cared if I was purple, they loved me like a daughter," says Tracie. Though Tracie's parents were more standoffish, they have heartily embraced Leo since the arrival of the couple's two children, ages four and one. By living and working in Miami (he's a carpenter and she's an assistant policy director for the mayor of Miami Dade) Leo and Tracie have continued to escape stigma. Leo is mindful, however, of the judgments his children may face. "America still teaches us to view people based on appearance," he says. "The best thing we can do for our children is to teach them to be proud of who they are."

Stephanie and Juan Carlos Valderramos, Bronx, New York

Serving as a Peace Corps volunteer in Honduras in 1998, Stephanie, an educated Chinese-American, was "adopted" by the family of a friendly coworker who happened to have a son named Juan. "I didn't have a TV, so I'd go to their house after work and watch it there. I had most of my meals there, "Stephanie recalls. Meeting Juan in the bosom of his nurturing family showed her just what she was getting, and their relationship took off.

To outsiders, they seemed mismatched: Stephanie had already applied to medical school, while Juan, who needed to work to pay the bills, was still in high school. But the differences didn't bother them. "Juan is really smart. We talk about everything—at first in Spanish, now more in English—and he always has an opinion," says Stephanie, who notes that Juan served as her cultural guide during their time in Honduras. Juan concurs: "I'm proud of who I am, and I liked her the way she was. If she wanted to be with me, it made no difference that she had more money or education."

Stephanie now works as a physician and Juan is studying at Bronx Community College and plans to become an environmental engineer.

Family Feuds

Often it takes every bit of that commitment for these couples to survive the extreme pressures their families impose on them; no other stressor is typically as great.

Like Steven and Joyce, Stephanie and Juan came to a crossroads relatively early in their relationship, in their case because of issues with *both* families. It started when Stephanie's Peace Corps stint was ending. She had to return home, and though she and Juan had been together a year and a half, he wasn't ready to go with her.

"Stephanie meant a lot to me, but I didn't want to leave my family," he says. They weren't dying to lose him either, even though they loved Stephanie. His parents were divorced. As the oldest brother, Juan was seen as "Papi" at home. So Stephanie headed back to the States thinking the relationship was over.

They kept communicating, though, and soon realized they missed each other too badly to stay apart. Juan applied for a fiancé visa, and that's when the trouble with Stephanie's father began.

When he learned she was planning to marry Juan, he felt disrespected. He pointed to all the egregious differences between her and Juan: She was Chinese-American, he was Hispanic; she had been raised Buddhist, he was Catholic; she was a well-off medical school candidate, and he hadn't completed high school. What's more, Juan

didn't speak English. "He's just using you to get a green card," her father said. When Stephanie married Juan and moved with him to the Bronx, New York, her father didn't talk to her for years.

Stephanie lived with a pang in her heart for her lost family. "I was with Juan for three and a half years before my family met him, and I'd never spoken to my father in all that time. I've always been close to my family, so it was awful," she says. "Juan is such a good, honest man, such a gentle soul, that I knew they would love him if they ever met him."

Marginalized partners ultimately tend to be significantly more committed than mainstream couples.

Finally, the couple was invited home one Christmas, and the response to Juan was everything Stephanie had hoped for: Her father was nice to him from the moment he met him. And after five years of marriage, Juan, now preparing to become an environmental engineer, has shown that he deserved the trust Stephanie always placed in him.

Advice for the Rest of Us

Nontraditional couples who make it have a lot to teach us. Here's what we can learn from their success.

- The more you trust your gut instinct and the more comfortable you feel in your own skin, the less outsiders will be able to interfere.
- When partners bring different skills to a relationship, they enhance each other's positions in the world.
- You may be attracted to your opposite, but if you want the relationship to last, you need lots in common as well.
- Don't let outside disapproval of your partner determine the way you feel about him or her.
- Extended family or a close circle of friends can nurture your relationship.
- Friends and family who initially disapprove may change their minds as your relationship stands the test of time. But accept the possibility that they may not. Be prepared to reduce contact and forge new ties with others.
- If in-laws interfere in your relationship or take a strong stance on how you must raise your children, it may be time to limit their role.
- If you can deal with it together as a team, adversity will strengthen the relationship.
- Traditional couples can enhance their bonds by introducing exciting challenges. Climbing a mountain or building a company together can spice up the love.

The advent of children typically brings a whole new level of familial turmoil to marginalized couples, as the in-laws are now involved. For the Boros, for instance, Steven's mother was a continual irritant whenever she visited, "as much because Joyce wasn't Jewish as because she was black," Steven explains. "She was concerned about what faith the children would be raised in." Joyce recalls, "She'd tell my friends how disappointed she was that Steven was married to me, and though she grew to love the kids very much she felt embarrassed to be seen with them because they were dark."

When the World Rushes In

While families cause the most havoc, the censure of the world contributes its own share of trouble. The mixed-race Boro children, for instance, received some of the same rejection in school that they got from their grandmother. Trying to give the kids an ethnic identity and please Steven's parents, Joyce had converted to Judaism and enrolled the children in Jewish schools, but the schools never fully accepted them. Feeling rejected by Jewish people, they've committed themselves to black culture and are exclusively dating African-Americans. "But the black community tends to see them as white and hasn't embraced them either," Joyce says.

Partners with wide age differences experience a subtler form of marginalization, but social pressures can still be great. While they're not discriminated against in housing or social services, and not barred from marrying as gays are, they may make their families, friends and neighbors uneasy, and are often the butt of insulting misunderstandings or jokes.

"It's so nice that you brought your mother with you" is a typical comment that Ken, now 42, hears about his 58-year-old wife Sara. In the early days of their relationship it bothered them, but they had larger hurdles to worry about: Sara was reluctant to marry for a third time, and Ken had to accept that they might never have a biological child. (Sara was already the mother of teenagers.) Three years ago, Sara had a stroke that left her weak on her left side, in need of a cane and prone to epilepsy-related blackout seizures. "I can't imagine any physical infirmity that would test my commitment. The stroke is a life challenge, not a relationship challenge," says Ken.

Ever since, they have remained so secure in their relationship that rude comments roll off their backs. "We always understood we were abnormal in society's eyes," Sara says, "but what anybody else thinks about our relationship is far less important to us than the relationship itself."

"She's the love of my life," Ken says.

Staying the Course

In their research, Lehmiller and Agnew found that the key reason most marginal couples stayed together was not deep satisfaction in their relationships, but a sense of limited alternatives. In other words, they didn't think they could do better, so they settled for what they had.

But when told about these findings, the couples we interviewed couldn't have disagreed more.

"Joyce and I have been blessed to be as close as we are, and I can't imagine any couple being closer," asserts Steven Boro. "That sounds conceited," chides Joyce. "But we are extremely close."

"I liked and learned from my first two husbands, but neither was my soulmate," says Sara.

Having settled for less is the furthest thing from these couples' minds.

"Lehmiller and Agnew argue that people who stay in marginalized relationships feel they have worse options, but I'm not fully convinced," says Douglas T. Kenrick, Ph.D., professor of evolutionary psychology at Arizona State University. "We all make trade-offs. Maybe these couples just happened to land on partners who were well worth the trade-offs." You might not automatically put a poor construction worker from Honduras on your checklist of potential partners, but then you run into him and he has a wealth of other characteristics that are wonderful to you. If you have confidence in your feelings, you see that instinct through.

In fact, the chance to be true to yourself may be one of the greatest surprises—and rewards—of these relationships.

"You find a lot of freedom at the margins," says Joshua Gamson, a Jew married to a biracial man. "When you're at the center of society, you feel forced to obey the norms. Marginalized couples have a lot of disadvantages, but since they're already outcasts in a sense, they're far freer to do what they really want, to put on their own show and be purely themselves."

MARK TEICH, a freelance writer living in Connecticut, has written for *Sports Illustrated, Redbook* and other magazines.

My Cheatin' Heart

When love comes knocking, do you answer the door?

DAPHNE GOTTLIEB

Let's just get this out in the open.

I was 14 and madly in love for the first time. He was 21. He made me suddenly, unaccustomedly beautiful with his kisses and mix tapes. During the year of elation and longing, he never mentioned that he had a girlfriend who lived across the street. A serious girl. A girl his age. A girl he loved. Unlike inappropriate, high school, secret me.

The next time, I was 15 and visiting a friend at college. It was a friend's friend's boyfriend who looked like Jim Morrison and wore leather pants and burned candles and incense. She was at work and I wanted him to touch me. She found out. I don't know what happened after that.

I was 19 and he was my boyfriend's archrival. I was 20 and it was my lover's girlfriend and we had to lie because otherwise he always wanted to watch. I was 24 and her girlfriend knew about it but then changed her mind about the open relationship. We saw each other anyway. I was 30 when we met—we wanted each other but were committed to other people; the way we look at each other still scorches the walls. I turned thirtysomething and pointedly wasn't invited to a funeral/a wedding/a baby shower because of a rumor.

I am a few years older now and I know this: That there are tastes of mouths I could not have lived without; that there are times I've pretended it was just about the sex because I couldn't stand the way my heart was about to burst with happiness and awe and I couldn't be that vulnerable, not again, not with this one. Waiting to have someone's stolen seconds can burn you alive, and there is nothing more frightening than being willing to take this free fall. It is not as simple as we were always promised. Love—at least the pair-bonded, prescribed love—does not conquer all. It does not conquer desire.

Arrow, meet heart. Apple, meet Eve.

Call me Saint Sebastian.

Out there in self-help books, on daytime television shows, I see people told that they're wrong to lust outside their relationships. That they must heal what's wrong at home and then they won't feel desire "inappropriately." I've got news. There's nothing wrong. Desire is not an illness. We who are its witnesses are not infected. We're not at fault. Not all of us are running away from our relationships at home, or just looking for some side action. The plain fact about desire is that sometimes it's love.

If it were anything else, maybe it would be easier. But things are not as simple as we were always promised: Let's say you're a normal, upstanding, ethical man (or woman) who has decided to share your life with someone beloved to you. This goes well for a number of years. You have a lot of sex and love each other very much and have a seriously deep, strong bond. Behind door number two, the tiger: a true love. Another one. (Let's assume for the moment that the culture and Hollywood are wrong—we have more than one true love after all.)

The shittiest thing you can do is lie to someone you love, yet there are certain times you can choose either to do so or to lie to yourself. Not honoring this fascination, this car crash of desire, is also a lie. So what do you do? Pursue it? Deny it? It doesn't matter: The consequences began when you opened the door and saw the tiger, called it by its—name: love. Pursue it or don't, you're already stuck between two truths, two opportunities to lie.

The question is not, as we've always been asked, the lady—beautiful, virtuous, and almost everything we want—or the tiger—passionate, wild, and almost everything we want. The question is, what do we do with our feelings for the lady *and* the tiger? The lady is fair, is home, is delight. The tiger is not bloodthirsty, as we always believed, but, say, romantic. Impetuous. Sharing almost nothing in common with the lady. They even have a different number of feet. But the lady would not see it this way. You already know that.

You can tell the second love that you can't do this—banish the tiger from your life. You can go home to the first, confess your desire, sob on her shoulder, tell her how awful you feel, and she (or he) will soothe you. Until later, when she wonders if you look at all the other zoo animals that way, and every day for a while, if not longer, she will sniff at you to see if you've been near the large cat cages. Things will not be the same for a long time. And you've lost the tiger. Every time the housecat sits on your lap, you tear up thinking of what might have been, the love that has been lost. Your first love asks you what's wrong and you say "nothing." You say nothing a lot, because there's nothing left, nothing inside.

So instead, let's say you go home and tell your first love, *This new love is a love I can't live without. What can we do?* She will say, *All right, I want to meet her right away. I get all holidays and weekends with you, and there will be no sleepovers with the new love, and I expect the same for myself, and you are never to call her any of the nicknames you have ever used for me,* and the whole thing starts to remind you of a high school necking session—under the sweater; over the bra, but not under it.

You feel like an inmate all the time, and, moreover, where is your first love tonight? She's out with someone you've never met while you're out with your second love, who once had been amenable to an affair. She looks at you sadly and says, "So you think I'm only a half-time tiger?" Her fangs are yellowed and sharp and she finds herself unable to stop staring at the clock, which shows when you will have to leave her to return to the lady.

Maybe there is no "happily ever after" here, but I think there's an "after." I have been the first love; I have been the second; and I have tried to decide between my own firsts and seconds. I have walked through each ring of fire, and I've found no easy answers. It could be that hearts are dumb creatures, especially mine. It could be that there are no good answers. Whether we're admitting desire, lying about it, denying it, or fulfilling it, the consequences are staggering, sometimes ruinous.

So, heart firmly sewn onto sleeve, assured that there is an "after," what can we do but stride forth? It seems clear that no system—polyamory, monogamy, or stand-on-your-head-for-me—will sanitize the astonishing highs and the bereft lows of desire and betrayal. And even if they did, who wants a sanitized heart? So it's up to us: to work together, to love what's so human about us, to understand that the risk of love is loss, and to try to grant desire without eviscerating ourselves. I'm not sure how to do this, but I'm still trying. Because above all, I know this: It's grace to try, and fail, and try again.

A version of this essay appeared as the introduction to *Homewrecker: An Adultery Reader* (Soft Skull Press, 2005), edited by **Daphne Gottlieb.**

UNIT 5

Gender and Sexual Diversity

Unit Selections

Key Points to Consider

- What are the major causes of gender differences? Have you ever thought about this before?

- Do boys and girls learn differently? Why/why not?

- How do media images of sex and sexuality impact our self-concepts? Do these images impact males and females differently? If so, how?

- What challenges do transgendered people face in our society?

- Have you ever wondered what causes heterosexuality? If not, why not?

- Why are some people heterosexual, others bisexual, and yet others gay or lesbian?

- Are lesbian, gay, bisexual, and transgendered people significantly different from non-transgendered, heterosexual people in most aspects of their lives?

- Is there really such a thing as "the gay lifestyle" that we seem to hear so much about?

- Is there such a thing as "the heterosexual lifestyle?" Or, are there multiple ways of living, and different kinds of lives possible for heterosexual people? Could the same be said for lesbian, gay, bisexual, and transgendered people?

- Are the children of gay or lesbian parents any different from those raised by heterosexual parents?

- How are lesbian, gay, bisexual, and transgendered people represented in the media? What media examples did you think of first? Why those particular examples?

Student Web Site

www.mhcls.com

Internet References

SocioSite: Feminism and Women's Issues
http://www.sociosite.net/topics/women.php
Woman in Islam: Sex and Society
http://www.jamaat.org/islam/WomanSociety.html
Women's Human Rights Resources
http://www.law-lib.utoronto.ca/Diana/

The Intersex Society of North America (ISNA)
http://www.isna.org/
Parents, Families, and Friends of Lesbians and Gays
http://www.pflag.org
The Gay, Lesbian & Straight Education Network
http://www.glsen.org/cgi-bin/iowa/all/home/index.html

© BananaStock/Punchstock

In *Unit 5,* we consider *Gender and Sexual Diversity.* We begin in *Part A: Perspectives on Gender,* with articles on gender. Here we explore differences between males and females. What we know from research is that although there are some interesting differences between men and women, there are many more similarities. It is important to realize that when we talk about gender differences from a research perspective, we are usually talking about differences that are "statistically significant." The actual lived experiences of individual men and women may or may not match the "statistically significant differences" reported in scientific research literature.

Perhaps the importance of gender is hard for many of us to recognize. There are so many things about gender that we take for granted. Its importance may only become apparent when a social expectation is somehow not met, or when a social norm is broken. When we are born, we are born into a world of norms, expectations, and sometimes conflicting attitudes and beliefs surrounding gender. The first thing most new parents want to know, other than if the baby is healthy, is the gender of the new addition to their family. So many decisions are made, almost automatically, by the gender of the child. The color of clothes that are chosen, the colors of the baby's room, the types of toys the baby is given to play with–all of this is decided for most parents at the moment they find out if their new bundle of joy is a boy or a girl. The words used to describe the little one, the interactions that the parent(s) have with their child, and how others view him or her–all of these things are determined by the label "male" or "female." If someone can't tell what gender a child is because of his or her dress, not knowing may actually cause feelings of discomfort or distress. In other words, if a baby is dressed in yellow, green, and white, some people may actually become upset that they cannot tell right away if the baby is a boy or a girl. This will almost surely lead to questions. Of course, the baby couldn't care less about all this silly gender chaos that seems to constantly swirl around him or her. Only later will these things be internalized.

In this unit, we also explore the issue of transgenderism, also often called transsexuality. For transgendered people, there is a disconnect between anatomical/biological sex and gender identity. This can produce a very complicated life situation. Hormone therapies, sex reassignment, and related surgeries are all options for transgendered people who have the resources to pursue bringing their outside appearance in line with their identity. How various states and countries deal with the legalities of changing one's sex differs significantly. In some places, the form to change one's gender is easily located at the local Department of Motor Vehicles. In other places, there may be significant obstacles.

In *Part B,* we explore *Perspectives on Sexual Orientation.* Why we humans feel, react, respond, and behave sexually can be quite complex. This is especially true regarding the issue of sexual orientation. Perhaps no other area of sexual behavior is as misunderstood. Although experts do not agree about what causes our sexual orientations—homosexuality, heterosexuality, or bisexuality—growing evidence suggests multiple possible developmental pathways for each sexual orientation. Some factors that may contribute to sexual orientation include biological factors, sociocultural influences, and free choice. While most gay people seem to report that there is no point in time when they chose to be gay, there are some who have reported that they made a conscious choice. Whether we are heterosexual,

gay, lesbian, or bisexual, who we are is fixed at a very early age for most of us. For others, there may be fluidity to their sexual attractions and expression.

In the mid-1900s, biological scientist and sex researcher Alfred Kinsey introduced his seven-point continuum of sexual orientation known as the Kinsey scale. It placed exclusive heterosexual orientation at one end, exclusive homosexual orientation at the other, and identified the middle range as where most people would fall if society and culture were unprejudiced. Since Kinsey, many others have added their research findings and theories to what is known about sexual orientation, including some apparent differences in the contributions of biological, psychological, environmental, and cultural factors for males versus females. In addition, further elaboration of the "middle" range on the Kinsey scale has included some distinction between bisexuality—the attraction to males and females, and ambisexuality—representing individuals for whom gender is no more relevant than any other personal characteristic, such as height, hair color, right- or left-handedness, with respect to sexual attraction and/or orientation.

Research on sexual orientation has certainly come a long way since the time of Kinsey. Today, researchers examine many aspects of sexual orientation; from biological, to psychological, to sociocultural. Anthropological and historical evidence suggests that homosexuality has existed across cultures and times. Political scientists and sociologists have conducted research on such topics as the lesbian and gay movement, public opinion, same-sex marriage, lesbian and gay communities, among many other interesting topics.

The birth of lesbian and gay studies has been an exciting new development in academia. This multidisciplinary area of inquiry grew out of the diverse body of research conducted (especially) since the late 1960s, on the lives of lesbian, gay, and bisexual men and women. As this research has documented, there has been significant social change over the past several decades. There are more possibilities today than ever before for lesbian, gay, bisexual, and transgendered people to fully participate as "out" citizens with greater expectations for truly equal rights as those of their heterosexual counterparts. It will be interesting to see the social, political, and legal changes that occur over the next several decades. These changes surely will have a significant impact on the lives of many people and their families. A number of issues that are likely to continue to be important well into the future are explored in this unit.

A Case for Angry Men and Happy Women

Observers are quicker to see anger on men's faces and happiness on women's. A simple case of gender stereotyping, or something more deeply rooted?

Beth Azar

It might not be surprising that people find it easier to see men as angry and women as happy. Women do tend to be the nurturers and men—well—men do commit 80 to 90 percent of all violent crimes. More surprising, perhaps, is new research suggesting that the connection between men and anger and women and happiness goes deeper than these simple social stereotypes, regardless of how valid they are.

Our brains automatically link anger to men and happiness to women, even without the influence of gender stereotypes, indicate the findings of a series of experiments conducted by cognitive psychologist D. Vaughn Becker, PhD, of Arizona State University at the Polytechnic Campus, with colleagues Douglas T. Kenrick, PhD, Steven L. Neuberg, PhD, K.C. Blackwell and Dylan Smith, PhD. They even turned it around to show that people are more likely to think a face is masculine if it's making an angry expression and feminine if its expression is happy. In fact, their research, published in February's *Journal of Personality and Social Psychology* (Vol. 92, No. 2, pages 179–190), suggests that the cognitive processes that distinguish male and female may be co-mingled with those that distinguish anger from happiness, thereby leading to this perceptual bias.

Becker proposes that this bias may stem from our evolutionary past, when an angry man would have been one of the most dangerous characters around, and a nurturing, happy female might have been just the person to protect you from harm. Evolutionary psychologist Leda Cosmides, PhD, agrees.

"If it's more costly to make a mistake of not recognizing an angry man, you would expect the [perceptual] threshold to be set lower than for recognizing an angry female," says Cosmides, of the University of California, Santa Barbara (UCSB).

More than a Stereotype

Becker first noticed that people find it easier to detect anger on men and happiness on women a couple years ago while working on his dissertation at Arizona State. He was testing whether viewing an angry or happy expression "primes" people to more quickly identify a subsequent angry or happy expression. Becker confirmed his initial hypothesis, but when he ran an additional analysis to test whether the gender of the person making the facial expression affected his results, he found that gender was, by far, the biggest predictor of how quickly and accurately people identified facial expressions.

Becker couldn't find any mention of this gender effect in the literature. So he set out to confirm that people more quickly link men to anger and women to happiness and figure out why that might be.

In the first of a series of studies, 38 undergraduate participants viewed pictures of faces displaying prototypical angry and happy expressions. They pressed "A" or "H" on a computer keyboard to indicate whether the expression was angry or happy, and the researchers recorded their reaction times. As expected, participants were quicker to label male faces "angry" and female faces "happy."

The researchers then used a version of the "Implicit Association Test" to uncover unconscious biases that study participants may have linking men to anger and women to happiness. The well-documented test allows researchers to examine the strength of connections between categories, which lead to unconscious stereotypes. Becker tested whether study participants unconsciously linked male names with angry words and female names with happy words. Most did.

However, 13 students showed the opposite association (male-happy, female-angry), implying that their unconscious gender stereotypes run counter to those of the general public. It was an ideal opportunity to determine whether gender stereotypes are at the heart of the emotion/gender bias. They weren't: Just like the main group of participants, this subgroup more quickly and accurately categorized male faces as angry and female faces as happy.

"While gender stereotypes clearly influence perception, the implicit association test results made us think the effect is not solely a function of stereotypes," says Becker.

Overlapping Signals

Since gender stereotypes don't seem to be the culprit, Becker looked toward more deeply rooted causes.

For example, perhaps we see more men with angry faces—on television, in movies—than we see women with angry faces, so our brains are well practiced at recognizing an angry expression on a man. To investigate this possibility, one of the co-authors, Arizona State University graduate student K.C. Blackwell, suggested they flip the experiment around. Instead of asking people to identify facial expressions while the experimenters manipulated gender, they asked them to identify whether a face was male or female while manipulating facial expressions.

"While you can argue that the majority of angry faces we see are male, it's tough to argue that the majority of male faces we see are angry," says Becker. So, if the relationship between emotional expression and gender is simply a matter of how frequently we see anger on men and happiness on women, the effect should disappear when researchers flip around the question. What they found, on the contrary, was that people were faster to identify angry faces as male and happy faces as female.

To follow-up on this finding, they conducted another study in which they used computer graphics software to control not only the intensity of facial expressions, but also the masculinity and femininity of the facial features, creating faces that were just slightly masculine or feminine. As predicted, people were more likely to see the more masculine faces as angrier, even when they had slightly happier expressions than the more feminine faces.

These findings suggest that the brain begins to associate emotions and gender very early in the cognitive process, says Becker. One possible explanation is that the brain has an "angry male detection module" enabling fast and accurate detection of what would have been one of the most dangerous entities in our evolutionary past. But Becker thinks there's a more parsimonious explanation.

"I'm more inclined to think that we've got a situation where the signals for facial expressions and those for masculinity and femininity have merged over time," he says.

In particular, features of masculinity—such as a heavy brow and angular face—somewhat overlap with the anger expression, and those of femininity—roundness and soft features—overlap with the happiness expression.

To test this hypothesis, Becker and his colleagues used computer animation software to individually manipulate masculine and feminine facial features of expressively neutral faces. As predicted, a heavier brow caused participants to see faces as both more masculine and more angry, implying that the mental processes for determining masculinity and anger may be intertwined.

"These results make a lot of sense," says University of Pittsburgh behavioral anthropologist and facial expression researcher Karen Schmidt, PhD. "Faces have always had gender, so if we're always activating gender and affect at the same time then the processing is likely highly coordinated."

The paper raises new and interesting questions about gender, says UCSB postdoctoral student Aaron Sell, PhD, who studies the evolution of gender. "Specifically," he says, "why do male and female faces differ, and what is the nature of emotion detection?"

The data appear to suggest that the anger expression has evolved to make a face seem more masculine, says Sell. Even female faces may communicate anger more effectively the more masculine they appear, says Becker. Future studies will have to tackle questions about the intentions expressed by the angry face and why looking more male would be an evolutionary advantage in communicating these intentions.

"I see this article as opening the book on a new research topic more than having the final say on the issue," says Sell.

BETH AZAR is a writer in Portland, Ore.

Learning and Gender

By paying attention to the differences between boys and girls, schools can gain new perspectives on teaching all children.

MICHAEL GURIAN

On the day your district administrators look at test scores, grades, and discipline referrals with gender in mind, some stunning patterns quickly will emerge.

Girls, they might find, are behind boys in elementary school math or science scores. They'll find high school girls statistically behind boys in SAT scores. They might find, upon deeper review, that some girls have learning disabilities that are going undiagnosed.

Boys, they'll probably notice, make up 80 to 90 percent of the district's discipline referrals, 70 percent of learning disabled children, and at least two-thirds of the children on behavioral medication. They'll probably find that boys earn two-thirds of the Ds and Fs in the district, but less than half the As. On statewide standardized test scores, they'll probably notice boys behind girls in general. They may be shocked to see how far behind the boys are in literacy skills; nationally, the average is a year and a half.

The moment an administrator sees the disparity of achievement between boys and girls can be liberating. Caring about children's education can now include caring about boys and girls specifically. New training programs and resources for teachers and school districts are opening cash-strapped school boards' eyes, not just to issues girls and boys face but also to ways of addressing gender differences in test scores, discipline referrals, and grades.

In the Edina School District, outside Minneapolis, Superintendent Ken Dragseth and district staff implemented a gender initiative that has helped close achievement gaps and improve overall education for students. In 2002, Dragseth and his staff analyzed district achievement data. They found that girls were doing much better than boys on most academic indicators, showing that they needed to address this achievement gap. They discovered areas of need for girls as well.

Edina officials decided to work on gaining greater knowledge on how boys and girls learn differently. Over the last three years, the district has seen qualitative and quantitative improvement in student performance.

Dragseth says that the gender-specific techniques and gender-friendly instructional theory he and his staff learned at the Gurian Institute helped the district significantly improve student achievement. For example, he says, they have seen higher seventh- and 10th-grade state reading and math mean scores for both boys and girls.

"We have also found that teacher- and parent-heightened awareness of gender differences in learning styles and appropriate strategies has been well received by students themselves," he says.

Brain Research

Gender training and resources used by Edina and other districts rely on information gained from PET, MRI, and other brain scans. This brain-based approach to gender was conceived in the early 1990s when it became clear that teachers were leaving college, graduate school, and teacher certification programs without training in how boys and girls learn differently. Educational culture was struggling to serve the needs of children—the needs of girls were most publicly discussed in the early 1990s—without complete knowledge of the children themselves.

When I wrote *The Wonder of Boys* in 1996, I hoped to bring a brain-based approach to gender issues into a wider public dialogue. In 1998, I joined the Missouri Center for Safe Schools and the University of Missouri-Kansas City in developing a two-year program to academically test the links among brain science, gender, and teacher education.

In six school districts in Missouri, teachers and staff integrated information from various fields and technologies and developed a number of strategies for teaching boys and girls. Gender disparities in achievement began to disappear in these districts. After one year, the pilot elementary school in the St. Joseph School District finished among the top five in the district after testing at the bottom previously. Discipline referrals diminished as well. In Kansas City's Hickman Mills School District, discipline referrals were cut by 35 percent within six months.

In the five years following the Missouri pilot program, more than 20,000 teachers in 800 schools and districts have received training in how boys and girls learn differently. More and more teachers are using this knowledge in the classroom.

Increasingly, universities and teacher certification programs are training young teachers in the learning differences between boys and girls.

Different Learning Styles

As with so many things of value in life, a teacher's innovations on behalf of children begins with an epiphany. A fourth-grade teacher recently told me, "When I saw the brain scans and thought about my class, I just went 'aha.' So much made sense now. The boys and their fidgeting; the girls and their chatting; the girls organizing their binders colorfully; the boys tapping their pencils; the girls writing more words in their essays than the boys; even the way the boys end up in the principal's office so much more frequently than the girls. We were all told long ago that every child should be taught as an individual, so gender didn't matter—but it really matters! Knowing about it has completely changed the way I teach, and the success my students are having."

On your way home this afternoon, stop by your local elementary school and see some of these differences for yourself. Walk down the hallway and find a classroom in which the teacher displays students' written work. Stand for a moment and look at the stories.

With all exceptions noted, you will probably find that the girls on average write:

- More words than the boys,
- Include more complex sensory details like color and texture, and
- Add more emotive and feeling details ("Judy said she liked him" "Timmy frowned").

If you could look with X-ray glasses into the brains of the boys and girls who wrote those stories, you would see:

- More blood flow in the verbal centers (in the cerebral cortex) of the girls' brains;
- More neural connections between the verbal centers and emotive centers in the limbic systems of the girls' brains; and
- More blood flow in sensorial centers (for instance in the occipital lobe), with more linkage between those centers and the verbal centers in the girls' brains.

A Visual Link to Learning

My example of the differences in boys and girls writing has a visual link. The female visual system (optical and neural) relies more greatly than the male on P cells. These are cells that connect color variety and other sensory activity to upper brain functioning. Boys rely more on M cells, which make spatial activity and graphic clues more quickly accessible.

This difference is linked significantly to a gender-different writing process for boys and girls. Boys tend to rely more on pictures and moving objects for word connections than girls. Girls tend to use more words that describe color and other fine,

sensory information. Not surprisingly, gender gaps in writing are often "detail" gaps.

Girls use more sensorial detail than boys, receiving better grades in the process. However, when elementary school teachers let boys draw picture panels (with colored pens) during the brainstorming part of story or essay writing, the boys often graphically lay out what their story will be about. After that, they actually write their "word brainstorming" because they can refer to a graphic/spatial tool that stimulates their brains to greater success in writing.

Watch a fourth-grade classroom led by a teacher untrained in male/female brain differences. You'll probably see the teacher tell students to "take an hour to write your brainstorming for your paper." Five to 10 of the boys in a classroom of 30 kids will stare at the blank page.

But when teachers are trained in male/female brain differences, they tell students to draw first and write later. Students who need that strategy will end up writing much more detailed, organized, and just better papers.

The Rest State and Discipline Problems

Another area where you'll see gender differences is classroom behavior. Boys tend to fidget when they are bored. In a boy's brain, less of the "calming chemical," serotonin, moves through the pre-frontal cortex (the executive decision-maker in the brain). Boys thus are more likely to fidget, distract themselves and others, and become the objects of the teacher's reprimands.

Furthermore, the male brain naturally goes into a rest state many times per day and is not engaged in learning. Thus the boy "zones out," "drifts off," or "disappears from the lesson."

Sometimes he begins to tap his pencil loudly or pull the hair of the kid in front of him. He's not trying to cause trouble; in fact, he may be trying to wake up and avoid the rest state. Girls' brains do not go to this severe rest state; their cerebral cortices are always "on." They more rarely need to tap, fidget, or talk out of turn in order to stay focused.

Teachers can learn how to organize classrooms so that any boys (and girls) who need it can physically move while they are learning and keep their brains engaged. The rest state and boredom issues begin to dissolve. Discipline referrals decrease exponentially.

Brains on Math

Both boys and girls can do math and science, of course, but their brains perform these tasks differently. Girls fall behind boys in complex math skills when their lesson plans rely solely or mainly on abstract formulations specified in symbols on the blackboard.

However, when words, essay components, and active group work are added to the toolbox of teacher strategies, girls reach a parity of performance. Brain-based innovations to help girls in math and science over the last decade have brought more verbal elements into math and science teaching and testing: more words, more word-to-formula connections, and more essay answers in math tests.

The results in both math and science achievement have been stunning, with girls closing the math/science gap in many school districts.

Different Reactions to Competition

Because of neural and chemical differences in levels and processing of oxytocin, dopamine, testosterone, and estrogen, boys typically need to do some learning through competition. Girls, of course, are competitive too, but in a given day, they will spend less time in competitive learning and less time relating successfully to one another through "aggression-love"—the playful hitting and dissing by which boys show love.

The current emphasis on cooperative learning is a good thing, and the basis of a diversity-oriented educational culture. However, because they are not schooled in the nature of gender in the brain, teachers generally have deleted competitive learning, and thus de-emphasized a natural learning tool for many boys. We've also robbed girls of practice in the reality of human competitiveness.

When teachers receive training on how competitive learning can be integrated into classrooms (without chaos ensuing)

they actually come to enjoy seeing both boys and girls challenge one another to learn better. Many girls who avoided leadership before now step forward to lead.

Learning to Their Potential

Our children are children, of course—but they are also girls and boys. This is something we all know as parents. When a school board makes the decision to focus on how the girls and boys are doing, all children gain. Students learn more, teachers are more productive, test scores and behavior improve, and parents and the community are happier.

A school board member in North Carolina told me, "Ten years ago, it was almost scary to talk about hard-wired gender differences. There were a lot of Title IX concerns, fears of reprisal. Now it's not scary, the brain research has caught up, and now it's so necessary. In fact, it just feels right."

It does indeed feel right to help boys and girls learn to their potential. Ten years ago, our girls were behind our boys in math and science; now, we see that our boys are far behind our girls in literacy. Neither of these gaps need exist anymore, as we engage in best practices on behalf of both boys and girls.

MICHAEL GURIAN, co-founder of the Gurian Institute, is author of 21 books, including *The Minds of Boys* (with Kathy Stevens), *The Wonder of Girls*, and *Boys and Girls Learn Differently* (with Patricia Henley and Terry Trueman).

Goodbye to Girlhood

As pop culture targets ever younger girls, psychologists worry about a premature focus on sex and appearance.

STACY WEINER

Ten-year-old girls can slide their low-cut jeans over "eye-candy" panties. French maid costumes, garter belt included, are available in preteen sizes. Barbie now comes in a "bling-bling" style, replete with halter top and go-go boots. And it's not unusual for girls under 12 to sing, "Don't cha wish your girlfriend was hot like me?"

American girls, say experts, are increasingly being fed a cultural catnip of products and images that promote looking and acting sexy.

"Throughout U.S. culture, and particularly in mainstream media, women and girls are depicted in a sexualizing manner," declares the American Psychological Association's Task Force on the Sexualization of Girls, in a report issued Monday. The report authors, who reviewed dozens of studies, say such images are found in virtually every medium, from TV shows to magazines and from music videos to the Internet.

While little research to date has documented the effect of sexualized images specifically on *young* girls, the APA authors argue it is reasonable to infer harm similar to that shown for those 18 and older; for them, sexualization has been linked to "three of the most common mental health problems of girls and women: eating disorders, low self-esteem and depression."

Said report contributor and psychologist Sharon Lamb: "I don't think because we don't have the research yet on the younger girls that we can ignore that [sexualization is] of harm to them. Common sense would say that, and part of the reason we wrote the report is so we can get funding to prove that."

Boys, too, face sexualization, the authors acknowledge. Pubescent-looking males have posed provocatively in Calvin Klein ads, for example, and boys with impossibly sculpted abs hawk teen fashion lines. But the authors say they focused on girls because females are objectified more often. According to a 1997 study in the journal Sexual Abuse, 85 percent of ads that sexualized children depicted girls.

Even influences that are less explicitly erotic often tell girls who they are equals how they look and that beauty commands power and attention, contends Lamb, co-author of "Packaging Girlhood: Rescuing Our Daughters from Marketers' Schemes" (St. Martin's, 2006). One indicator that these influences are reaching girls earlier, she and others say: The average age for adoring the impossibly proportioned Barbie has slid from preteen to preschool.

When do little girls start wanting to look good for others? "A few years ago, it was 6 or 7," says Deborah Roffman, a Baltimore-based sex educator. "I think it begins by 4 now."

While some might argue that today's belly-baring tops are no more risque than hip huggers were in the '70s, Roffman disagrees. "Kids have always emulated adult things," she says. "But [years ago] it was, 'That's who I'm supposed to be as an adult.' It's very different today. The message to children is, 'You're already like an adult. It's okay for you to be interested in sex. It's okay for you to dress and act sexy, right now.' That's an entirely different frame of reference."

It's not just kids' exposure to sexuality that worries some experts; it's the kind of sexuality they're seeing. "The issue is that the way marketers and media present sexuality is in a very narrow way," says Lamb. "Being a sexual person isn't about being a pole dancer," she chides. "This is a sort of sex education girls are getting, and it's a misleading one."

Clothes Encounters

Liz Guay says she has trouble finding clothes she considers appropriate for her daughter Tanya, age 8. Often, they're too body-hugging. Or too low-cut. Or too short. Or too spangly.

Then there are the shoes: Guay says last time she visited six stores before finding a practical, basic flat. And don't get her started on earrings.

"Tanya would love to wear dangly earrings. She sees them on TV, she sees other girls at school wearing them, she sees them in the stores all the time. . . . I just say, 'You're too young.'"

"It's not so much a feminist thing," explains Guay, a Gaithersburg medical transcriptionist. "It's more that I want her to be comfortable with who she is and to make decisions based on what's right for her, not what everybody else is doing. I want her to develop the strength that when she gets to a point where kids are offering her alcohol or drugs, that she's got enough self-esteem to say, 'I don't want that.'"

Some stats back up Guay's sense of fashion's shrinking modesty. For example, in 2003, tweens—that highly coveted marketing segment ranging from 7 to 12—spent $1.6 million on thong underwear, Time magazine reported. But even more-innocent-seeming togs, toys and activities—like tiny "Beauty Queen" T-shirts, Hello Kitty press-on nails or preteen make-overs at Club Libby Lu—can be problematic, claim psychologists. The reason: They may lure young girls into an unhealthy focus on appearance.

Studies suggest that female college students distracted by concerns about their appearance score less well on tests than do others. Plus, some experts say, "looking good" is almost culturally inseparable for girls from looking sexy: Once a girl's bought in, she's hopped onto a consumer conveyor belt in which marketers move females from pastel tiaras to hot-pink push-up bras.

Where did this girly-girl consumerism start? Diane Levin, an education professor at Wheelock College in Boston who is writing an upcoming book, "So Sexy So Soon," traces much of it to the deregulation of children's television in the mid-1980s. With the rules loosened, kids' shows suddenly could feature characters who moonlighted as products (think Power Rangers, Care Bears, My Little Pony). "There became a real awareness," says Levin, "of how to use gender and appearance and, increasingly, sex to market to children."

Kids are more vulnerable than adults to such messages, she argues.

The APA report echoes Levin's concern. It points to a 2004 study of adolescent girls in rural Fiji, linking their budding concerns about body image and weight control to the introduction of television there.

In the United States, TV's influence is incontestable. According to the Kaiser Family Foundation, for example, nearly half of American kids age 4 to 6 have a TV in their bedroom. Nearly a quarter of teens say televised sexual content affects their own behavior.

And that content is growing: In 2005, 77 percent of prime-time shows on the major broadcast networks included sexual material, according to Kaiser, up from 67 percent in 1998. In a separate Kaiser study of shows popular with teenage girls, women and girls were twice as likely as men and boys to have their appearance discussed. They also were three times more likely to appear in sleepwear or underwear than their male counterparts.

Preteen Preening

It can be tough for a parent to stanch the flood of media influences.

Ellen Goldstein calls her daughter Maya, a Rockville fifth-grader, a teen-mag maniac. "She has a year's worth" of Girls' Life magazine, says Goldstein. "When her friends come over, they pore over this magazine." What's Maya reading? There's "Get Gorgeous Skin by Tonight," "Crush Confidential: Seal the Deal with the Guy You Dig," and one of her mom's least faves: "Get a Fierce Body Fast."

"Why do you want to tell a kid to get a fierce body fast when they're 10? They're just developing," complains Goldstein. She

also bemoans the magazines' photos, which Maya has plastered on her ceiling.

"These are very glamorous-looking teenagers. They're wearing lots of makeup. They all have very glossy lips," she says. "They're generally wearing very slinky outfits. . . . I don't think those are the best role models," Goldstein says. "When so much emphasis is placed on the outside, it minimizes the importance of the person inside."

So why not just say no?

"She loves fashion," explains Goldstein. "I don't want to take away her joy from these magazines. It enhances her creative spirit. [Fashion] comes naturally to her. I want her to feel good about that. We just have to find a balance."

Experts say her concern is warranted. Pre-adolescents' propensity to try on different identities can make them particularly susceptible to media messages, notes the APA report. And for some girls, thinking about how one's body stacks up can be a real downer.

In a 2002 study, for example, seventh-grade girls who viewed idealized magazine images of women reported a drop in body satisfaction and a rise in depression.

Such results are disturbing, say observers, since eating disorders seem to strike younger today. A decade ago, new eating disorder patients at Children's National Medical Center tended to be around age 15, says Adelaide Robb, director of inpatient psychiatry. Today kids come in as young as 5 or 6.

Mirror Images

Not everyone is convinced of the uglier side of beauty messages.

Eight-year-old Maya Williams owns four bracelets, eight necklaces, about 20 pairs of earrings and six rings, an assortment of which she sprinkles on every day. "Sometimes, she'll stand in front of the mirror and ask, "Are these pretty, Mommy?"

Her mom, Gaithersburg tutor Leah Haworth, is fine with Maya's budding interest in beauty. In fact, when Maya "wasn't sure" about getting her ears pierced, says Haworth, "I talked her into it by showing her all the pretty earrings she could wear."

What about all these sexualization allegations? "I don't equate looking good with attracting the opposite sex," Haworth says. Besides, "Maya knows her worth is based on her personality. She knows we love her for who she is."

"Looking good just shows that you care about yourself, care about how you present yourself to the world. People are judged by their appearance. People get better service and are treated better when they look better. That's just the way it is," she says. "I think discouraging children from paying attention to their appearance does them a disservice."

Magazine editor Karen Bokram also adheres to the beauty school of thought. "Research has shown that having skin issues at [her readers'] age is traumatic for girls' self-esteem," says Bokram, founder of Girls' Life. "Do we think girls need to be gorgeous in order to be worthy? No. Do we think girls' feeling good about how they look has positive effects in other areas of their lives, meaning that they make positive choices academically, socially and in romantic relationships? Absolutely."

Some skeptics of the sexualization notion also argue that kids today are hardier and savvier than critics think. Isaac Larian, whose company makes the large-eyed, pouty-lipped Bratz dolls, says, "Kids are very smart and know right from wrong." What's more, his testing indicates that girls want Bratz "because they are fun, beautiful and inspirational," he wrote in an e-mail. "Not once have we ever heard one of our consumers call Bratz 'sexy.'" Some adults "have a twisted sense of what they see in the product," Larian says.

"It is the parents' responsibility to educate their children," he adds. "If you don't like something, don't buy it."

But Genevieve McGahey, 16, isn't buying marketers' messages. The National Cathedral School junior recalls that her first real focus on appearance began in fourth grade. That's when classmates taught her: To be cool, you needed ribbons. To be cool, you needed lip gloss.

Starting around sixth grade, though, "it took on a more sinister character," she says. "People would start wearing really short skirts and lower tops and putting on more makeup. There's a strong pressure to grow up at this point."

"It's a little scary being a young girl," McGahey says. "The image of sexuality has been a lot more trumpeted in this era. . . . If you're not interested in [sexuality] in middle school, it seems a little intimidating." And unrealistic body ideals pile on extra pressure, McGahey says. At a time when their bodies and their body images are still developing, "girls are not really seeing people [in the media] who are beautiful but aren't stick-thin," she notes. "That really has an effect."

Today, though, McGahey feels good about her body and her style.

For this, she credits her mom, who is "very secure with herself and with being smart and being a woman." She also points to a wellness course at school that made her conscious of how women were depicted. "Seeing a culture of degrading women really influenced me to look at things in a new way and to think how we as high school girls react to that," she says.

"A lot of girls still hold onto that media ideal. I think I've gotten past it. As I've gotten more comfortable with myself and my body, I'm happy not to be trashy," McGahey says. "But most girls are still not completely or even semi-comfortable with themselves physically. You definitely still feel the pressure of those images."

STACY WEINER writes frequently for Health about families and relationships. Comments: health@washpost.com.

(Rethinking) Gender

A growing number of Americans are taking their private struggles with their identities into the public realm. How those who believe they were born with the wrong bodies are forcing us to re-examine what it means to be male and female.

DEBRA ROSENBERG

Growing up in Corinth, Miss., J. T. Hayes had a legacy to attend to. His dad was a well-known race-car driver and Hayes spent much of his childhood tinkering in the family's greasy garage, learning how to design and build cars. By the age of 10, he had started racing in his own right. Eventually Hayes won more than 500 regional and national championships in go-kart, midget and sprint racing, even making it to the NASCAR Winston Cup in the early '90s. But behind the trophies and the swagger of the racing circuit, Hayes was harboring a painful secret: he had always believed he was a woman. He had feminine features and a slight frame—at 5 feet 6 and 118 pounds he was downright dainty—and had always felt, psychologically, like a girl. Only his anatomy got in the way. Since childhood he'd wrestled with what to do about it. He'd slip on "girl clothes" he hid under the mattress and try his hand with makeup. But he knew he'd find little support in his conservative hometown.

In 1991, Hayes had a moment of truth. He was driving a sprint car on a dirt track in Little Rock when the car flipped end over end. "I was trapped upside down, engine throttle stuck, fuel running all over the racetrack and me," Hayes recalls. "The accident didn't scare me, but the thought that I hadn't lived life to its full potential just ran chill bumps up and down my body." That night he vowed to complete the transition to womanhood. Hayes kept racing while he sought therapy and started hormone treatments, hiding his growing breasts under an Ace bandage and baggy T shirts.

Finally, in 1994, at 30, Hayes raced on a Saturday night in Memphis, then drove to Colorado the next day for sex-reassignment surgery, selling his prized race car to pay the tab. Hayes chose the name Terri O'Connell and began a new life as a woman who figured her racing days were over. But she had no idea what else to do. Eventually, O'Connell got a job at the mall selling women's handbags for $8 an hour. O'Connell still hopes to race again, but she knows the odds are long: "Transgendered and professional motor sports just don't go together."

To most of us, gender comes as naturally as breathing. We have no quarrel with the "M" or the "F" on our birth certificates. And, crash diets aside, we've made peace with how we want the world to see us—pants or skirt, boa or blazer, spiky heels or sneakers. But to those who consider themselves transgender, there's a disconnect between the sex they were assigned at birth and the way they see or express themselves. Though their numbers are relatively few—the most generous estimate from the National Center for Transgender Equality is between 750,000 and 3 million Americans (fewer than 1 percent)—many of them are taking their intimate struggles public for the first time. In April, L.A. Times sportswriter Mike Penner announced in his column that when he returned from vacation, he would do so as a woman, Christine Daniels. Nine states plus Washington, D.C., have enacted antidiscrimination laws that protect transgender people—and an additional three states have legislation pending, according to the Human Rights Campaign. And this month the U.S. House of Representatives passed a hate-crimes prevention bill that included "gender identity." Today's transgender Americans go far beyond the old stereotypes (think "Rocky Horror Picture Show"). They are soccer moms, ministers, teachers, politicians, even young children. Their push for tolerance and acceptance is reshaping businesses, sports, schools and families. It's also raising new questions about just what makes us male or female.

Born female, he feels male. 'I challenge the idea that all men were born with male bodies.'

—Mykell Miller, age 20

What is gender anyway? It is certainly more than the physical details of what's between our legs. History and science suggest that gender is more subtle and more complicated than anatomy. (It's separate from sexual orientation, too, which determines which sex we're attracted to.) Gender helps us organize the world into two boxes, his and hers, and gives us a way of quickly sizing up every person we see on the street. "Gender is a way of making the world secure," says feminist scholar Judith Butler, a rhetoric professor at University of California, Berkeley. Though some scholars like Butler consider gender largely a social construct, others increasingly see it as a complex interplay of biology, genes, hormones and culture.

She kept her job as a high-school teacher. 'Most people don't get this fortunate kind of ending.'

—Karen Kopriva, age 49

Genesis set up the initial dichotomy: "Male and female he created them." And historically, the differences between men and women in this country were thought to be distinct. Men, fueled by testosterone, were the providers, the fighters, the strong and silent types who brought home dinner. Women, hopped up on estrogen (not to mention the mothering hormone oxytocin), were the nurturers, the communicators, the soft, emotional ones who got that dinner on the table. But as society changed, the stereotypes faded. Now even discussing gender differences can be fraught. (Just ask former Harvard president Larry Summers, who unleashed a wave of criticism when he suggested, in 2005, that women might have less natural aptitude for math and science.) Still, even the most diehard feminist would likely agree that, even apart from genitalia, we are not exactly alike. In many cases, our habits, our posture, and even cultural identifiers like the way we dress set us apart.

Now, as transgender people become more visible and challenge the old boundaries, they've given voice to another debate—whether gender comes in just two flavors. "The old categories that everybody's either biologically male or female, that there are two distinct categories and there's no overlap, that's beginning to break down," says Michael Kimmel, a sociology professor at SUNY-Stony Brook. "All of those old categories seem to be more fluid." Just the terminology can get confusing. "Transsexual" is an older term that usually refers to someone who wants to use hormones or surgery to change their sex. "Transvestites," now more politely called "cross-dressers," occasionally wear clothes of the opposite sex. "Transgender" is an umbrella term that includes anyone whose gender identity or expression differs from the sex of their birth—whether they have surgery or not.

Gender identity first becomes an issue in early childhood, as any parent who's watched a toddler lunge for a truck or a doll can tell you. That's also when some kids may become aware that their bodies and brains don't quite match up. Jona Rose, a 6-year-old kindergartner in northern California, seems like a girl in nearly every way—she wears dresses, loves pink and purple, and bestowed female names on all her stuffed animals.

But Jona, who was born Jonah, also has a penis. When she was 4, her mom, Pam, offered to buy Jona a dress, and she was so excited she nearly hyperventilated. She began wearing dresses every day to preschool and no one seemed to mind. It wasn't easy at first. "We wrung our hands about this every night," says her dad, Joel. But finally he and Pam decided to let their son live as a girl. They chose a private kindergarten where Jona wouldn't have to hide the fact that he was born a boy, but could comfortably dress like a girl and even use the girls' bathroom. "She has been pretty adamant from the get-go: 'I am a girl,'" says Joel.

Male or female, we all start life looking pretty much the same. Genes determine whether a particular human embryo will develop as male or female. But each individual embryo is equipped to be either one—each possesses the Mullerian ducts that become the female reproductive system as well as the Wolffian ducts that become the male one. Around eight weeks of development, through a complex genetic relay race, the X and the male's Y chromosomes kick into gear, directing the structures to become testes or ovaries. (In most cases, the unneeded extra structures simply break down.) The ovaries and the testes are soon pumping out estrogen and testosterone, bathing the developing fetus in hormones. Meanwhile, the brain begins to form, complete with receptors—wired differently in men and women—that will later determine how both estrogen and testosterone are used in the body.

After birth, the changes keep coming. In many species, male newborns experience a hormone surge that may "organize" sexual and behavioral traits, says Nirao Shah, a neuroscientist at UCSF. In rats, testosterone given in the first week of life can cause female babies to behave more like males once they reach adulthood. "These changes are thought to be irreversible," says Shah. Between 1 and 5 months, male human babies also experience a hormone surge. It's still unclear exactly what effect that surge has on the human brain, but it happens just when parents are oohing and aahing over their new arrivals.

Here's where culture comes in. Studies have shown that parents treat boys and girls very differently—breast-feeding boys longer but talking more to girls. That's going on while the baby's brain is engaged in a massive growth spurt. "The brain doubles in size in the first five years after birth, and the connectivity between the cells goes up hundreds of orders of magnitude," says Anne Fausto-Sterling, a biologist and feminist at Brown University who is currently investigating whether subtle differences in parental behavior could influence gender identity in very young children. "The brain is interacting with culture from day one."

So what's different in transgender people? Scientists don't know for certain. Though their hormone levels seem to be the same as non-trans levels, some scientists speculate that their brains react differently to the hormones, just as men's differ from women's. But that could take decades of further research to prove. One 1997 study tantalizingly suggested structural differences between male, female and transsexual brains, but it has yet to be successfully replicated. Some transgender people blame the environment, citing studies that show pollutants have disrupted reproduction in frogs and other animals. But those links are so far not proved in humans. For now, transgender issues are classified as "Gender Identity Disorder" in the psychiatric manual DSM-IV. That's controversial, too—gay-rights activists spent years campaigning to have homosexuality removed from the manual.

Gender fluidity hasn't always seemed shocking. Cross-dressing was common in ancient Greece and Rome, as well as among Native Americans and many other indigenous societies, according to Deborah Rudacille, author of "The Riddle of Gender." Court records from the Jamestown settlement in 1629 describe the case of Thomas Hall, who claimed to be both a man and a woman. Of course, what's considered masculine or feminine has long been a moving target. Our Founding Fathers wouldn't be surprised to see men today with long hair or earrings, but they might be puzzled by women in pants.

Transgender opponents have often turned to the Bible for support. Deut. 22:5 says: "The woman shall not wear that which pertaineth unto a man, neither shall a man put on a woman's garment: for all that do so are abomination unto the Lord thy God." When word leaked in February that Steve Stanton, the Largo, Fla., city manager for 14 years, was planning to transition to life as a woman, the community erupted. At a public meeting over whether Stanton should be fired, one of many critics, Ron Sanders, pastor of the Lighthouse Baptist Church, insisted that Jesus would "want him terminated." (Stanton did lose his job and this week will appear as Susan Stanton on Capitol Hill to lobby for antidiscrimination laws.) Equating gender change with homosexuality, Sanders says that "it's an abomination, which means that it's utterly disgusting."

Not all people of faith would agree. Baptist minister John Nemecek, 56, was surfing the Web one weekend in 2003, when his wife was at a baby shower. Desperate for clues to his long-suppressed feelings of femininity, he stumbled across an article about gender-identity disorder on WebMD. The suggested remedy was sex-reassignment surgery—something Nemecek soon thought he had to do. Many families can be ripped apart by such drastic changes, but Nemecek's wife of 33 years stuck by him. His employer of 15 years, Spring Arbor University, a faith-based liberal-arts college in Michigan, did not. Nemecek says the school claimed that transgenderism violated its Christian principles, and when it renewed Nemecek's contract—by then she was taking hormones and using the name Julie—it barred her from dressing as a woman on campus or even wearing earrings. Her workload and pay were cut, too, she says. She filed a discrimination claim, which was later settled through mediation. (The university declined to comment on the case.) Nemecek says she has no trouble squaring her gender change and her faith. "Actively expressing the feminine in me has helped me grow closer to God," she says.

Others have had better luck transitioning. Karen Kopriva, now 49, kept her job teaching high school in Lake Forest, Ill., when she shaved her beard and made the switch from Ken. When Mark Stumpp, a vice president at Prudential Financial, returned to work as Margaret in 2002, she sent a memo to her colleagues (subject: Me) explaining the change. "We all joked about wearing panty hose and whether 'my condition' was contagious," she says. But "when the dust settled, everyone got back to work." Companies like IBM and Kodak now cover trans-related medical care. And 125 Fortune 500 companies now protect transgender employees from job discrimination, up from three in 2000. Discrimination may not be the worst worry for transgender people: they are also at high risk of violence and hate crimes.

Perhaps no field has wrestled more with the issue of gender than sports. There have long been accusations about male athletes' trying to pass as women, or women's taking testosterone to gain a competitive edge. In the 1960s, would-be female Olympians were required to undergo gender-screening tests. Essentially, that meant baring all before a panel of doctors who could verify that an athlete had girl parts. That method was soon scrapped in favor of a genetic test. But that quickly led to confusion over a handful of genetic disorders that give typical-looking women chromosomes other than the usual XX. Finally, the International Olympic Committee ditched mandatory lab-based screening, too. "We found there is no scientifically sound lab-based technique that can differentiate between man and woman," says Arne Ljungqvist, chair of the IOC's medical commission.

The IOC recently waded into controversy again: in 2004 it issued regulations allowing transsexual athletes to compete in the Olympics if they've had sex-reassignment surgery and have taken hormones for two years. After convening a panel of experts, the IOC decided that the surgery and hormones would compensate for any hormonal or muscular advantage a male-to-female transsexual would have. (Female-to-male athletes would be allowed to take testosterone, but only at levels that wouldn't give them a boost.) So far, Ljungqvist doesn't know of any transsexual athletes who've competed. Ironically, Renee Richards, who won a lawsuit in 1977 for the right to play tennis as a woman after her own sex-reassignment surgery, questions the fairness of the IOC rule. She thinks decisions should be made on a case-by-case basis.

'We all joked about wearing panty hose and whether "condition" was contagious.'

—Margaret Stumpp, age 54

Richards and other pioneers reflect the huge cultural shift over a generation of gender change. Now 70, Richards rejects the term transgender along with all the fluidity it conveys. "God didn't put us on this earth to have gender diversity," she says. "I don't like the kids that are experimenting. I didn't want to be something in between. I didn't want to be trans anything. I wanted to be a man or a woman."

But more young people are embracing something we would traditionally consider in between. Because of the expense, invasiveness and mixed results (especially for women becoming men), only 1,000 to 2,000 Americans each year get sex-reassignment surgery—a number that's on the rise, says Mara Keisling of the National Center for Transgender Equality. Mykell Miller, a Northwestern University student born female who now considers himself male, hides his breasts under a special compression vest. Though he one day wants to take hormones and get a mastectomy, he can't yet afford it. But that doesn't affect his self-image. "I challenge the idea that all men were born with male bodies," he says. "I don't go out of my way to be the biggest, strongest guy."

Nowhere is the issue more pressing at the moment than a place that helped give rise to feminist movement a generation ago: Smith College in Northampton, Mass. Though Smith was one of the original Seven Sisters women's colleges, its students have now taken to calling it a "mostly women's college," in part because of a growing number of "transmen" who decide to become male after they've enrolled. In 2004, students voted to remove pronouns from the student government constitution as a gesture to transgender students who no longer identified with "she" or "her." (Smith is also one of 70 schools that have antidiscrimination policies protecting transgender students.) For now, anyone who is enrolled at Smith may graduate, but in order to be admitted in the first place, you must have been born a female. Tobias Davis, class of '03, entered Smith as a woman, but graduated as a "transman." When he first told friends over dinner, "I think I might be a boy," they were instantly behind him, saying "Great! Have you picked a name yet?" Davis passed as male for his junior year abroad in Italy even without taking hormones; he had a mastectomy last fall. Now 25, Davis works at Smith and writes plays about the transgender experience. (His work "The Naked I: Monologues From Beyond the Binary" is a trans take on "The Vagina Monologues.")

As kids at ever-younger ages grapple with issues of gender variance, doctors, psychologists and parents are weighing how to balance immediate desires and long-term ones. Like Jona Rose, many kids begin questioning gender as toddlers, identifying with the other gender's toys and clothes. Five times as many boys as girls say their gender doesn't match their biological sex, says Dr. Edgardo Menvielle, a psychiatrist who heads a gender-variance outreach program at Children's National Medical Center. (Perhaps that's because it's easier for girls to blend in as tomboys.) Many of these children eventually move on and accept their biological sex, says Menvielle, often when they're exposed to a disapproving larger world or when they're influenced by the hormone surges of puberty. Only about 15 percent continue to show signs of gender-identity problems into adulthood, says Ken Zucker, who heads the Gender Identity Service at the Centre for Addiction and Mental Health in Toronto.

In the past, doctors often advised parents to direct their kids into more gender-appropriate clothing and behavior. Zucker still tells parents of unhappy boys to try more-neutral activities— say chess club instead of football. But now the thinking is that kids should lead the way. If a child persists in wanting to be the other gender, doctors may prescribe hormone "blockers" to keep puberty at bay. (Blockers have no permanent effects.) But they're also increasingly willing to take more lasting steps: Isaak Brown (who started life as Liza) began taking male hormones at 16; at 17 he had a mastectomy.

For parents like Colleen Vincente, 44, following a child's lead seems only natural. Her second child, M. (Vincente asked to use an initial to protect the child's privacy), was born female. But as soon as she could talk, she insisted on wearing boy's clothes. Though M. had plenty of dolls, she gravitated toward "the boy things" and soon wanted to shave off all her hair. "We went along with that," says Vincente. "We figured it was a phase." One day, when she was 2 ½, M. overheard her parents talking about her using female pronouns. "He said, 'No—I'm a him. You need to call me him,'" Vincente recalls. "We were shocked." In his California preschool, M. continued to insist he was a boy and decided to change his name. Vincente and her husband, John, consulted a therapist, who confirmed their instincts to let M. guide them. Now 9, M. lives as a boy and most people have no idea he was born otherwise. "The most important thing is to realize this is who your child is," Vincente says. That's a big step for a family, but could be an even bigger one for the rest of the world.

This story was written by **DEBRA ROSENBERG,** with reporting from Lorraine Ali, Mary Carmichael, Samantha Henig, Raina Kelley, Matthew Philips, Julie Scelfo, Kurt Soller, Karen Springen and Lynn Waddell.

Finding the Switch

Homosexuality may persist because the associated genes convey surprising advantages on homosexuals' family members.

Robert Kunzig

If there is one thing that has always seemed obvious about homosexuality, it's that it just doesn't make sense. Evolution favors traits that aid reproduction, and being gay clearly doesn't do that. The existence of homosexuality amounts to a profound evolutionary mystery, since failing to pass on your genes means that your genetic fitness is a resounding zero. "Homosexuality is effectively like sterilization," says psychobiologist Qazi Rahman of Queen Mary College in London. "You'd think evolution would get rid of it." Yet as far as historians can tell, homosexuality has always been with us. So the question remains: If it's such a disadvantage in the evolutionary rat race, why was it not selected into oblivion millennia ago?

Twentieth-century psychiatry had an answer for this Darwinian paradox: Homosexuality was not a biological trait at all but a psychological defect. It was a mistake, one that was always being created anew, in each generation, by bad parenting. Freud considered homosexuality a form of arrested development stamped on a child by a distant father or an overprotective mother. Homosexuality was even listed by the American Psychiatric Association as a mental disorder, and the idea that gays could and should be "cured" was widely accepted. But modern scientific research has not been kind to that idea. It turns out that parents of gay men are no better or worse than those of heterosexuals. And homosexual behavior is common in the animal kingdom, as well—among sheep, for instance. It arises naturally and does not seem to be a matter of aloof rams or overbearing ewes.

More is known about homosexuality in men than in women, whose sexuality appears more fluid. The consensus now is that people are "born gay," as the title of a recent book by Rahman and British psychologist Glenn Wilson puts it. But for decades, researchers have sought to identify the mechanism that *makes* a person gay.

Something seems to flip the sexuality switch before birth—but what? In many cases, homosexuality appears to be genetic. The best scientific surveys put the number of gays in the general population between 2 and 6 percent, with most estimates near the low end of that range—contrary to the 10 percent figure that is often reported in the popular media.

But we know gayness is not entirely genetic, because in pairs of identical twins, it's often the case that one is gay and the other is not. Studies suggest there is a genetic basis for homosexuality in only 50 percent of gay men.

No one has yet identified a particular gay gene, but Brian Mustanski, a psychologist at the University of Illinois at Chicago, is examining a gene that helps time the release of testosterone from the testes of a male fetus. Testosterone masculinizes the fetal genitalia—and presumably also the brain. Without it, the fetus stays female. It may be that the brains of gay men don't feel the full effects of testosterone at the right time during fetal development, and so are insufficiently masculinized.

But if that gene does prove to be a gay gene, it's unlikely to be the only one. Whatever brain structures are responsible for sexual orientation must emerge from a complex chain of molecular events, one that can be disrupted at many links. Gay genes could be genes for hormones, enzymes that modify hormones, or receptors on the surface of brain cells that bind to those hormones. A mutation in any one of those genes might make a person gay.

Having some gay genes might promote feminine traits in straight men, making them kinder, gentler, more nurturing—and as a result, women may be more likely to choose them as mates.

More likely it will take mutations in more than one gene. And that, as Rahman and Wilson and other researchers have suggested, is one solution to the Darwinian paradox: Gay genes might survive because so long as a man doesn't have enough of them to make him gay, they increase the reproductive success of the woman he mates with. Biologists call it "sexually antagonistic selection," meaning a trait survives in one sex only because it is useful to the other. Nipples—useless to men, vital to women—are one example, and homosexuality maybe another. By interfering with the masculinization of the brain, gay genes might promote feminine behavior traits, making men who carry them kinder, gentler, more nurturing—"less aggressive and psychopathic than the typical male," as Rahman and Wilson put it. Such men may be more likely to help raise children rather than kill them—or each other—and as a result, women may be more likely to choose them as mates.

In this way, over thousands of generations of sexual selection, feminizing genes may have spread through the male population. When the number of such genes exceeds a certain threshold in a man, they may flip the switch and make him want to have sex with other men. Evolutionarily speaking, that is bad for him. But for the women who are doing the selecting, the loss of a small number of potential mates maybe a small price to pay for creating a much larger number of the kind of men they want.

Some gay genes may benefit women more directly—to the detriment of their own sons. The evidence comes from groundbreaking studies by Andrea Camperio-Ciani, a researcher at the University of Padua in Italy. Camperio was interested in understanding the evolutionary paradox and began by replicating a family-tree study done in the early 1990s by geneticist Dean Hamer of the National Institutes of Health. Hamer had concluded that some cases of homosexuality are passed down on the X chromosome, which a boy receives from his mother. Camperio and his colleagues compared the family trees of gay men to those of straight men, and confirmed that homosexuals had more gay male relatives on their mother's side than on their father's side—which suggests an X-linked trait. But the Italian researchers also found something more intriguing: Compared with the straight men, the gay men had more relatives, period.

Camperio did not quite know at first what to make of these results—or how they might help him understand the Darwinian paradox of homosexuality. Then one day, he was driving through the forest with his daughter, on the way to their country house. Their tradition was to play mathematical games to keep themselves entertained. This time, he began talking about a different puzzle. "I began explaining my research," Camperio recalls. "I explained to her that we found out that homosexuals come from large families. I told her that there is an inheritance from the mother—she's giving the homosexual genes to her son. I said, This is impossible—how can they be surviving?"

His daughter, 15, replied, "But Dad, did you check if this factor that makes sons homosexual is not the same factor that makes the mother produce more children and have big families?"

Camperio stopped the car, looked her in the eyes, and said, "Shit! What is this? It's a great suggestion!"

The next day he left his daughter in the country and went back to the lab to investigate the idea. Sure enough, the mothers of homosexuals in the study did indeed have between a quarter and a third more children than the mothers of heterosexuals. Camperio also uncovered another dramatic finding: In families with gay sons, the aunts from the mother's side had many more children than the aunts on the father's side—the large families, in other words, were on the maternal side. Camperio realized his daughter was right. "There was something in the genes that, in the male, changed his sexual orientation, and in the female, increased her probability of having children," he says.

What could it be? Camperio spent the next few years going to gay men and begging them to let him interview their mothers

and aunts—a daunting task in deeply Catholic Italy. In the end, it took him three years to get 30 subjects. When he interviewed the women, though, he found they had fewer miscarriages, fewer infections, and used fewer contraceptives than the mothers and aunts of heterosexuals, though the differences were only slight. One difference, though, was not slight at all: The homosexuals' mothers and aunts had had between *three and four times* as many sexual partners. They seemed to really like having sex with men.

Perhaps mothers of gays have a "man-loving" gene—that makes them more sexually active, and makes their sons gay.

Camperio's explanation for all this relies, like Rahman and Wilson's hypothesis, on sexually antagonistic selection. Perhaps, he suggests, the mothers of some homosexuals have a "man-loving" gene. In women, it would be adaptive, causing them to have more sex and more children. But in men, the "man-loving" gene would be expressed differently, causing homosexuality. To the gay sons, that would be an evolutionary disadvantage—but one outweighed by the advantage to the mothers, who would have more than enough other children to compensate. And so gayness in men would persist in these families—as a side effect of a trait that is beneficial to the women.

But even Camperio says his results can explain no more than 20 percent of the incidence of homosexuality. "The more we study, the more we find there will be other mechanisms," he says. His research confirms that there are many ways to become gay—including, perhaps, one way that is much stranger than the rest.

The gay men in Camperio's study didn't just have larger families than the straight men. They also had more older brothers—and not just because they came from larger families. It's true across the board: The more older brothers a man has, the more likely he is to be gay. The "fraternal birth order effect" was first uncovered by Ray Blanchard and Anthony Bogaert of the Center for Addiction and Mental Health in Toronto, and has since been replicated by a dozen other studies.

For every older brother a man has, his chances of being gay go up by around a third. In other words, if you have two older brothers, you're nearly twice as likely to be gay—regardless of whether the older brothers are themselves gay. It is not possible to explain that as an effect of genetics.

Some researchers have tried to explain it as an effect the older brothers have on their sibling's environment. Perhaps a boy grows up homosexual, one argument goes, because the presence of older brothers means more incestuous sex play early in life. Or perhaps their presence makes his parents treat him differently.

But in another study, Bogaert found that it was only *biological* older brothers that contributed to the effect. Men who grew up with older stepbrothers or adopted brothers—brothers born of different wombs—were no more likely to become gay. Meanwhile, men with biological older brothers who died in infancy or who were raised separately—including brothers they had never even met and sometimes didn't even know about—*did* manifest the effect. In other words, the effect could not be explained through upbringing.

If it wasn't genetic and it wasn't upbringing, then what could it possibly be? The answer is the prenatal environment—the result of something that occurs as the fetus develops in the womb.

So what happens in the womb to make a fetus gay? Researchers can only speculate, but Blanchard and Bogaert suggest the older-brother effect could result from a mother's immune reaction against her male fetuses. During her first male pregnancy, the mother's body reacts against some factor related to male fetal development. Her immune system detects male-specific proteins produced by the boy's Y chromosome—perhaps proteins located on the surface of his brain cells—and deems them foreign invaders. As a result, her body generates antibodies against them. Each successive male pregnancy strengthens this immune response. The next time she's pregnant, the anti-male antibodies cross through the placenta and influence the fetus's brain, interfering with the masculinization of his brain and making him gay.

It may even be that women with strong immune systems are more likely to produce gay sons. The reproductive advantages to her of having such a healthy constitution might outweigh the disadvantages of occasionally producing a son who will have no kids himself. Even if the immunization scenario is true, however, it explains only 15 to 30 percent of the cases of male homosexuality. "My theory is not meant to explain homosexuality in all males—obviously not in firstborn males," says Blanchard. "And it does not explain homosexuality in women at all." It's really just a "working hypothesis," says Bogaert, for a strange and puzzling phenomenon.

Most recently, Bogaert, Blanchard, and their colleagues have found that older brothers increase the likelihood of homosexuality only in men who are right-handed—even though left-handed men are more likely to be gay in general. "We don't really know what that means," says Bogaert It's one more piece of evidence, though, that homosexuality is determined biologically, before birth—just like handedness. As often happens with science, the mystery deepens and becomes more complicated before the ultimate pattern finally reveals itself.

S o how do the pieces fit together? So far, they don't. Rather, they exist side by side. "There is no all-inclusive explanation for the variation in sexual orientation, at least none supported by actual evidence," says geneticist Alan Sanders of Northwestern University. It's one of the most consistent themes to emerge from the literature on homosexuality: the idea that there are many different mechanisms, not a single one, for producing homosexuality. Neither Camperio nor Bogaert sees much of a connection between the female-fecundity theory and the older-brother effect "They are somewhat disparate," Bogaert says. "But that is compatible with the idea that there are multiple biological pathways affecting sexual orientation."

The biggest gap in the science of homosexuality concerns lesbians: Much less research has been done on them than on men. That's because women's sexuality seems to be more complicated and fluid—women are much more likely to report fantasizing about both sexes, or to change how they report their sexual orientation

The Gay Science

Test your knowledge about breaking research on homosexuality.

True or False

1. 10 to 12 percent of men are gay.
2. Gay men have longer, thicker penises than straight men, on average.
3. As children, most gay men display gender-bending behavior, like dressing up in their sisters' clothes or playing with dolls.
4. In general, gay men are worse than straight men at certain cognitive skills, like reading maps, spatial orientation, finding missing objects, and packing trunks.
5. Lesbians are better than straight women at certain spatial, navigational, and language tasks.
6. Men with the most masculine voices tend to be straight.
7. Gay men often have distant fathers, suggesting that levels of childhood affection have an effect on sexual orientation.
8. The more older brothers you have, the more likely you are to be gay.
9. Sexual orientation correlates with whether you are right- or left-handed.
10. The ratio of the lengths of the second to fourth fingers predicts sexual orientation.

ANSWERS: **1.** False: 2 to 6 percent of men are gay. **2.** True. **3.** True. **4.** True. **5.** True. **6.** False. The voices rated as most masculine are those of gay men (and the most feminine are those of lesbians). **7.** False, though some fathers may become distant in reaction to childhood gender nonconformity of boys who are born gay. **8.** True. **9.** True. Homosexuals are 39 percent more likely to be left-handed or ambidextrous. **10.** True.

---

over time—which makes it harder to study. "Maybe we're measuring sexual orientation totally wrong in women," says Mustanski. Rahman and Wilson suggest that lesbianism might result from "masculinizing" genes that, when not present to excess, make a woman a more aggressively protective and thus successful mother—just as feminizing genes might make a man a more caring father.

Right now, there is no one all-inclusive solution to the Darwinian mystery of why homosexuality survives, and no grand unified theory of how it arises in a given individual. Homosexuality seems to arise as a result of various perturbations in the flow from genes to hormones to brains to behavior—as the common end point of multiple biological paths, all of which seem to survive as side effects of various traits that help heterosexuals pass along their genes.

"It's the fundamental question for the next 10 years," says Mustanski. "How do these things interact? What is the model that explains all these things?"

ROBERT KUNZIG is a freelance writer living in France and Alabama.

Children of Lesbian and Gay Parents

Does parental sexual orientation affect child development, and if so, how? Studies using convenience samples, studies using samples drawn from known populations, and studies based on samples that are representative of larger populations all converge on similar conclusions. More than two decades of research has failed to reveal important differences in the adjustment or development of children or adolescents reared by same-sex couples compared to those reared by other-sex couples. Results of the research suggest that qualities of family relationships are more tightly linked with child outcomes than is parental sexual orientation.

CHARLOTTE J. PATTERSON

Does parental sexual orientation affect child development, and if so, how? This question has often been raised in the context of legal and policy proceedings relevant to children, such as those involving adoption, child custody, or visitation. Divergent views have been offered by professionals from the fields of psychology, sociology, medicine, and law (Patterson, Fulcher, & Wainright, 2002). While this question has most often been raised in legal and policy contexts, it is also relevant to theoretical issues. For example, does healthy human development require that a child grow up with parents of each gender? And if not, what would that mean for our theoretical understanding of parent–child relations? (Patterson & Hastings, in press) In this article, I describe some research designed to address these questions.

Early Research

Research on children with lesbian and gay parents began with studies focused on cases in which children had been born in the context of a heterosexual marriage. After parental separation and divorce, many children in these families lived with divorced lesbian mothers. A number of researchers compared development among children of divorced lesbian mothers with that among children of divorced heterosexual mothers and found few significant differences (Patterson, 1997; Stacey & Biblarz, 2001).

These studies were valuable in addressing concerns of judges who were required to decide divorce and child custody cases, but they left many questions unanswered. In particular, because the children who participated in this research had been born into homes with married mothers and fathers, it was not obvious how to understand the reasons for their healthy development. The possibility that children's early exposure to apparently heterosexual male and female role models had contributed to healthy development could not be ruled out.

When lesbian or gay parents rear infants and children from birth, do their offspring grow up in typical ways and show healthy development? To address this question, it was important to study children who had never lived with heterosexual parents. In the 1990s, a number of investigators began research of this kind.

An early example was the Bay Area Families Study, in which I studied a group of 4- to 9-year-old children who had been born to or adopted early in life by lesbian mothers (Patterson, 1996, 1997). Data were collected during home visits. Results from in-home interviews and also from questionnaires showed that children had regular contact with a wide range of adults of both genders, both within and outside of their families. The children's self-concepts and preferences for same-gender playmates and activities were much like those of other children their ages. Moreover, standardized measures of social competence and of behavior problems, such as those from the Child Behavior Checklist (CBCL), showed that they scored within the range of normal variation for a representative sample of same-aged American children. It was clear from this study and others like it that it was quite possible for lesbian mothers to rear healthy children.

Studies Based on Samples Drawn from Known Populations

Interpretation of the results from the Bay Area Families Study was, however, affected by its sampling procedures. The study had been based on a convenience sample that had been assembled by word of mouth. It was therefore impossible to rule out the possibility that families who participated in the research were especially well adjusted. Would a more representative sample yield different results?

To find out, Ray Chan, Barbara Raboy, and I conducted research in collaboration with the Sperm Bank of California

(Chan, Raboy, & Patterson, 1998; Fulcher, Sutfin, Chan, Scheib, & Patterson, 2005). Over the more than 15 years of its existence, the Sperm Bank of California's clientele had included many lesbian as well as heterosexual women. For research purposes, this clientele was a finite population from which our sample could be drawn. The Sperm Bank of California also allowed a sample in which, both for lesbian and for heterosexual groups, one parent was biologically related to the child and one was not.

We invited all clients who had conceived children using the resources of the Sperm Bank of California and who had children 5 years old or older to participate in our research. The resulting sample was composed of 80 families, 55 headed by lesbian and 25 headed by heterosexual parents. Materials were mailed to participating families, with instructions to complete them privately and return them in self-addressed stamped envelopes we provided.

Results replicated and expanded upon those from earlier research. Children of lesbian and heterosexual parents showed similar, relatively high levels of social competence, as well as similar, relatively low levels of behavior problems on the parent form of the CBCL. We also asked the children's teachers to provide evaluations of children's adjustment on the Teacher Report Form of the CBCL, and their reports agreed with those of parents. Parental sexual orientation was not related to children's adaptation. Quite apart from parental sexual orientation, however, and consistent with findings from years of research on children of heterosexual parents, when parent–child relationships were marked by warmth and affection, children were more likely to be developing well. Thus, in this sample drawn from a known population, measures of children's adjustment were unrelated to parental sexual orientation (Chan et al., 1998; Fulcher et al., 2005).

Even as they provided information about children born to lesbian mothers, however, these new results also raised additional questions. Women who conceive children at sperm banks are generally both well educated and financially comfortable. It was possible that these relatively privileged women were able to protect children from many forms of discrimination. What if a more diverse group of families were to be studied? In addition, the children in this sample averaged 7 years of age, and some concerns focus on older children and adolescents. What if an older group of youngsters were to be studied? Would problems masked by youth and privilege in earlier studies emerge in an older, more diverse sample?

Studies Based on Representative Samples

An opportunity to address these questions was presented by the availability of data from the National Longitudinal Study of Adolescent Health (Add Health). The Add Health study involved a large, ethnically diverse, and essentially representative sample of American adolescents and their parents. Data for our research were drawn from surveys and interviews completed by more than 12,000 adolescents and their parents at home and from surveys completed by adolescents at school.

Parents were not queried directly about their sexual orientation but were asked if they were involved in a "marriage, or marriage-like relationship." If parents acknowledged such a relationship, they were also asked the gender of their partner. Thus, we identified a group of 44 12- to 18-year-olds who lived with parents involved in marriage or marriage-like relationships with same-sex partners. We compared them with a matched group of adolescents living with other-sex couples. Data from the archives of the Add Health study allowed us to address many questions about adolescent development.

Consistent with earlier findings, results of this work revealed few differences in adjustment between adolescents living with same-sex parents and those living with opposite-sex parents (Wainright, Russell, & Patterson, 2004; Wainright & Patterson, 2006). There were no significant differences between teenagers living with same-sex parents and those living with other-sex parents on self-reported assessments of psychological well-being, such as self-esteem and anxiety; measures of school outcomes, such as grade point averages and trouble in school; or measures of family relationships, such as parental warmth and care from adults and peers. Adolescents in the two groups were equally likely to say that they had been involved in a romantic relationship in the last 18 months, and they were equally likely to report having engaged in sexual intercourse. The only statistically reliable difference between the two groups—that those with same-sex parents felt a greater sense of connection to people at school—favored the youngsters living with same-sex couples. There were no significant differences in self-reported substance use, delinquency, or peer victimization between those reared by same- or other-sex couples (Wainright & Patterson, 2006).

Although the gender of parents' partners was not an important predictor of adolescent well-being, other aspects of family relationships were significantly associated with teenagers' adjustment. Consistent with other findings about adolescent development, the qualities of family relationships rather than the gender of parents' partners were consistently related to adolescent outcomes. Parents who reported having close relationships with their offspring had adolescents who reported more favorable adjustment. Not only is it possible for children and adolescents who are parented by same-sex couples to develop in healthy directions, but—even when studied in an extremely diverse, representative sample of American adolescents—they generally do.

These findings have been supported by results from many other studies, both in the United States and abroad. Susan Golombok and her colleagues have reported similar results with a near-representative sample of children in the United Kingdom (Golombok et al., 2003). Others, both in Europe and in the United States, have described similar findings (e.g., Brewaeys, Ponjaert, Van Hall, & Golombok, 1997).

The fact that children of lesbian mothers generally develop in healthy ways should not be taken to suggest that they encounter no challenges. Many investigators have remarked upon the fact that children of lesbian and gay parents may encounter anti-gay sentiments in their daily lives. For example, in a study of 10-year-old children born to lesbian mothers, Gartrell, Deck, Rodas, Peyser, and Banks (2005) reported that a substantial minority had encountered anti-gay sentiments among their peers. Those who had had such encounters were likely to report having felt angry, upset, or sad about these experiences. Children of lesbian and gay parents may be exposed to prejudice against their parents in some settings, and this may be painful for them, but evidence for the idea that such encounters affect children's overall adjustment is lacking.

Conclusions

Does parental sexual orientation have an important impact on child or adolescent development? Results of recent research provide no evidence that it does. In fact, the findings suggest that parental sexual orientation is less important than the qualities of family relationships. More important to youth than the gender of their parent's partner is the quality of daily interaction and the strength of relationships with the parents they have.

One possible approach to findings like the ones described above might be to shrug them off by reiterating the familiar adage that "one cannot prove the null hypothesis." To respond in this way, however, is to miss the central point of these studies. Whether or not any measurable impact of parental sexual orientation on children's development is ever demonstrated, the main conclusions from research to date remain clear: Whatever correlations between child outcomes and parental sexual orientation may exist, they are less important than those between child outcomes and the qualities of family relationships.

Although research to date has made important contributions, many issues relevant to children of lesbian and gay parents remain in need of study. Relatively few studies have examined the development of children adopted by lesbian or gay parents or of children born to gay fathers; further research in both areas would be welcome (Patterson, 2004). Some notable longitudinal studies have been reported, and they have found children of same-sex couples to be in good mental health. Greater understanding of family relationships and transitions over time would, however, be helpful, and longitudinal studies would be valuable. Future research could also benefit from the use of a variety of methodologies.

Meanwhile, the clarity of findings in this area has been acknowledged by a number of major professional organizations. For instance, the governing body of the American Psychological Association (APA) voted unanimously in favor of a statement that said, "Research has shown that the adjustment, development, and psychological well-being of children is unrelated to parental sexual orientation and that children of lesbian and gay parents are as likely as those of heterosexual parents to flourish" (APA, 2004). The American Bar Association, the American Medical Association, the American Academy of Pediatrics, the American Psychiatric Association, and other mainstream professional groups have issued similar statements.

The findings from research on children of lesbian and gay parents have been used to inform legal and public policy debates across the country (Patterson et al., 2002). The research literature on this subject has been cited in amicus briefs filed by the APA in cases dealing with adoption, child custody, and also in cases related to the legality of marriages between same-sex partners. Psychologists serving as expert witnesses have presented findings on these issues in many different courts (Patterson et al., 2002). Through these and other avenues, results of research on lesbian and gay parents and their children are finding their way into public discourse.

The findings are also beginning to address theoretical questions about critical issues in parenting. The importance of gender in parenting is one such issue. When children fare well in two-parent lesbian-mother or gay-father families, this suggests that the gender of one's parents cannot be a critical factor in child development. Results of research on children of lesbian and gay parents cast doubt upon the traditional assumption that gender is important in parenting. Our data suggest that it is the quality of parenting rather than the gender of parents that is significant for youngsters' development.

Research on children of lesbian and gay parents is thus located at the intersection of a number of classic and contemporary concerns. Studies of lesbian- and gay-parented families allow researchers to address theoretical questions that had previously remained difficult or impossible to answer. They also address oft-debated legal questions of fact about development of children with lesbian and gay parents. Thus, research on children of lesbian and gay parents contributes to public debate and legal decision making, as well as to theoretical understanding of human development.

References

American Psychological Association (2004). Resolution on sexual orientation, parents, and children. Retrieved September 25, 2006, from http://www.apa.org/pi/lgbc/policy/parentschildren.pdf

Brewaeys, A., Ponjaert, I., Van Hall, E.V., & Golombok, S. (1997). Donor insemination: Child development and family functioning in lesbian mother families. *Human Reproduction, 12,* 1349–1359.

Chan, R.W., Raboy, B., & Patterson, C.J. (1998). Psychosocial adjustment among children conceived via donor insemination by lesbian and heterosexual mothers. *Child Development, 69,* 443–457.

Fulcher, M., Sutfin, E.L., Chan, R.W., Scheib, J.E., & Patterson, C.J. (2005). Lesbian mothers and their children: Findings from the Contemporary Families Study. In A. Omoto & H. Kurtzman (Eds.), *Recent research on sexual orientation, mental health, and substance abuse* (pp. 281–299). Washington, DC: American Psychological Association.

Gartrell, N., Deck., A., Rodas, C., Peyser, H., & Banks, A. (2005). The National Lesbian Family Study: 4. Interviews with the 10-year-old children. *American Journal of Orthopsychiatry, 75,* 518–524.

Golombok, S., Perry, B., Burston, A., Murray, C., Mooney-Somers, J., Stevens, M., & Golding, J. (2003). Children with lesbian parents: A community study. *Developmental Psychology, 39,* 20–33.

Patterson, C.J. (1996). Lesbian mothers and their children: Findings from the Bay Area Families Study. In J. Laird & R.J. Green (Eds.), *Lesbians and gays in couples and families: A handbook for therapists* (pp. 420–437). San Francisco: Jossey-Bass.

Patterson, C.J. (1997). Children of lesbian and gay parents. In T. Ollendick & R. Prinz (Eds.), *Advances in clinical child psychology* (Vol. 19, pp. 235–282). New York: Plenum Press.

Patterson, C.J. (2004). Gay fathers. In M.E. Lamb (Ed.), *The role of the father in child development* (4th ed., pp. 397–416). New York: Wiley.

Patterson, C.J., Fulcher, M., & Wainright, J. (2002). Children of lesbian and gay parents: Research, law, and policy. In B.L. Bottoms, M.B. Kovera, & B.D. McAuliff (Eds.), *Children, social science and the law* (pp. 176–199). New York: Cambridge University Press.

Patterson, C.J., & Hastings, P. (in press). Socialization in context of family diversity. In J. Grusec & P. Hastings (Eds.), *Handbook of socialization.* New York: Guilford Press.

Stacey, J., & Biblarz, T.J. (2001). (How) Does sexual orientation of parents matter? *American Sociological Review, 65,* 159–183.

Wainright, J.L., & Patterson, C.J. (2006). Delinquency, victimization, and substance use among adolescents with female same-sex parents. *Journal of Family Psychology, 20,* 526–530.

Wainright, J.L., Russell, S.T., & Patterson, C.J. (2004). Psychosocial adjustment and school outcomes of adolescents with same-sex parents. *Child Development, 75,* 1886–1898.

Address correspondence to **CHARLOTTE J. PATTERSON,** Department of Psychology, P.O. Box 400400, University of Virginia, Charlottesville, VA 22904; e-mail: cjp@virginia.edu.

Broadcast News: The Insider Is Out

In 2006 a blog announced to the world that Thomas Roberts is gay, and the then CNN anchor instantly became the poster boy for a very rare breed: the out news anchor. But as Sean Kennedy reports, the success of Roberts and other out anchors and on-air talent may finally shatter their industry's glass ceiling for gays—and usher in the future of broadcast news.

GREG ENDRIES

It's the first hot day of 2008 in Los Angeles—upward of 90 degrees, and it's only April—and I'm hiking in dusty Runyon Canyon in the Hollywood hills with Thomas Roberts, the former CNN anchor turned *Insider* correspondent. Halfway up a moderately rugged climb, both wheezing a bit, we spot a secluded ridge off the main path, safely removed from the dogs and owners and shirtless runners enjoying the late-afternoon sunshine. We stand still for a moment and take in the commanding view from downtown in the east to the Pacific in the west. The vast metropolis, bustling with kinetic dreams up close, lies before us in a state of startling clarity. The only thing moving is an airplane in the distance.

The peaceful tableau is a good match for the calm, confident demeanor of Roberts, a major talent who's weathered some career turbulence of late. It started in 2006, when his appearance on a panel of gay broadcast journalists was picked up by a blog. The "news" quickly turned into a coming-out of the first order—even though Roberts was already out at CNN. Never mind: He was now an official gay celebrity, and along with the affection came the opposite—the rumors, innuendos, and downright trash talk hurled at anyone in the public eye these days. When Roberts left CNN a year ago this May, people speculated that the cable news behemoth parted ways with him because of his sexuality. Then, when he started on the air at *The Insider* a few months later, in September 2007, a blogger posted pictures that were purportedly from Roberts's Manhunt profile—a nasty hit that was splashed across the top of the *New York Post* gossip column Page Six.

A tall, muscular, classic hunk of a man, Roberts is the all-American matinee-idol version of a broadcaster, as opposed to, say, Anderson Cooper's effete, almost European vibe. But Roberts isn't talking to me today to name names or speculate about other people's careers and choices. He's here simply to talk about his own experience being gay in broadcasting—which, for the most part, has been positive, despite what you may think.

"It's funny that people think I got fired from CNN," he says, addressing the prevailing rumor about him. "I left CNN on my accord: I resigned from my contract because of personal reasons." During his six years at the channel, he says, "I never dealt with anything but respect and kindness. There's a great misconception."

Indeed, Roberts says, being gay has never held him back. "I've worked my ass off, I've been fortunate, and luck doesn't hurt either," he says. "If people don't like that I'm gay or that I talk about being gay, I'm sorry. Because that's not my problem."

The glaring absence of openly gay television anchors at the networks, on cable, and in local markets across the country is most obvious in the case of the CNN and *60 Minutes* silver fox, who delivers the facts on everything except his sexuality. But when you turn your attention away from him and scan the ranks of America's newsreaders, you notice Cooper has lots of company.

According to longtime industry talent agent Mendes J. Napoli, there are only two openly gay main news anchors currently working in the top 20 U.S. television markets: Randy Price at Boston's WHDH and Craig Stevens at Miami's WSVN. On cable news there's one: Jason Bellini of CBS News on Logo. And on the networks? None.

In the correspondent and reporter corps, the numbers are higher—NBC News's John Yang and ABC News's Jeffrey Kofman and Miguel Marquez are a few of the big names, though there are countless others at all levels of TV. (And—let's get this out of the way—there's CNN's Richard Quest, recently busted on charges of loitering in Central Park after hours with meth in his pocket.)

Yet when it comes to being the face of a news division, the glass ceiling is barely smudged. "You can be a morning anchor, a weekend anchor, an afternoon anchor, a reporter—they love gay reporters now because they're so animated, they're not stiff," says Napoli, who represents Stevens. "But a primary male anchor who's gay? It's an issue."

The reason, he says, is simple: The decision makers are middle-aged white men. "Ninety-nine percent of main anchor decisions end up on the desk of an older white male manager, who is not going to view gay men the same way other people might." Plus, Napoli says, "There's a fear that the audience will reject them."

"It's uncharted territory," says "Jake," an anchor in a major media market who, in exchange for anonymity, spoke to me candidly about his experience being gay but not out. "Maybe I should have the attitude of 'I am gay—take it or leave it.' But in the back of your mind, there's always that thing: the culture of the industry." The business is rife with gay talent, from executives on down—"tons," according to Jake. But television is also a fundamentally conservative, risk-averse world. "It's OK if they know within the company," Jake says, "but you wouldn't do a cover story with *The Advocate* without warning your media-relations person."

Indeed, when I first inquired about an interview with Roberts before he started at *The Insider,* a spokesperson for the show instantly said no. When I followed up two months later, it was no dice again. Roberts says he doesn't recall being contacted either time.

This January, though, he got involved directly, when I learned through a mutual contact that he was interested in talking. Yet when he ran the idea up the flagpole, he too was denied. Roberts won't cite the reasons on the record, but he was clearly disappointed by the decision. When I asked him how he felt about it, there was a long pause while he considered his response. "I won't attach a negative to it," he finally says diplomatically, "but I will say that I was flattered by the offer and thought that it would be great to be included." It wasn't until this February, when his contract was unexpectedly optioned—meaning he was cut from the show—that he was free to talk.

Roberts doesn't want to knock anyone. He's not that kind of guy. "Quote me: I am flawed! I make mistakes! I do things that are stupid! Hopefully this interview won't be one of them!" But he also knows he's making a difference, as hackneyed as that sounds. "I heard this phrase the other night: You can always tell the pioneers by the number of arrows in their back," he says, chuckling. "It's not that I want to be a pioneer—I'm certainly a reluctant role model—but it's like, Come out already. There's just no reason not to."

"I can state unequivocally that we would be a thousand percent supportive of any employee who wanted to come out publicly," says ABC News senior vice president Jeffrey Schneider, who is gay. And yet, none of the highest-profile gays on the air at ABC News (think *Good Morning America,* which is reportedly called "Gay-MA" by its rivals at *Today*) wanted to come out for this story, since they declined to be interviewed. Nevertheless, Schneider says, being openly gay isn't a career breaker: "Are people good broadcasters? Are they aggressive and great journalists? How do they do their job? Those are the things that people talk about in terms of the on-air talent."

For Roberts, 35, and Jake, who's around the same age, it wasn't always that way. "When I went into this business 14 years ago, I had the sense that coming out would probably hurt my career," says Jake, who like many broadcast journalists got his start in a small market and worked his way up to a network. (He stepped down from that gig to take his current job at a prominent affiliate for another network, where he's being groomed to return to the big league.) "There were no openly gay news anchors or reporters," he says. "You don't want to be judged before you've even had a career. You don't know what the personal bias of a general manager or a news director is. I thought, It's something I'll feel more comfortable being open about down the road."

Now he does: His colleagues, including his executive producer, all know he's gay, and he assumes the executives who hired him know—though they haven't mentioned anything to him. "I know the people who hired me are not stupid. You can Google my name and stuff pops up all over the place." It makes him a little paranoid. "I hate to bring up the 'don't ask, don't tell' thing, but I've been hired by middle-aged, conservative, married men. You think, *I know you accept the fact that I'm gay, but you don't want me to be out. I'm just going to keep that private.*"

What's actually said is far more coded. "They'll tell you, 'You're playing to Middle America. Our stories are going to be built around what a housewife in Wichita would want to see.'" Translation: Don't let it show.

Roberts too was skittish early in his career. For one thing, he wasn't out at all. "I didn't know how best to deal with that professionally, or personally for that matter," he says, as flies buzz around us and the occasional dog trots by. "I thought it would be a roadblock—or a brick wall—to advancement." So whenever he arrived in a new market, like San Diego or Lincoln, Neb., "I would automatically date a girl and have everyone at the station see it. We'd date for a little while and then I'd break up with them or do something to make them break up with me." Later, when his friends would offer to set him up with another girl, Roberts would say he was "too hurt." "That would get me out of the whole meet-my-sister thing."

He didn't make his first gay friend until he was almost 26 and working at WFTX in Fort Myers, Fla. The guy worked at a rival station, and Roberts met him through journalist friends. "It was great for me because I finally had somebody I could talk to or josh around with," he says. "He knew that I wasn't out and he made no big deal about it. He didn't go blabbing. He respected the fact that I wasn't in a place emotionally or psychologically" to come out.

That soon changed. "I was 26—you can only lie to yourself so long," Roberts says. During his next stint, at Virginia Beach, Va.'s WAVY, he met his current partner, Patrick. Then, right before he was called up to CNN, he came out to his colleagues. "I had already come out to my family by that point, so the next logical step was work," he says. And everyone was "so cool. They started to meet Patrick and they loved him. I mean, they're some of my dearest friends still today."

Former colleagues were next, a long list of people who had moved on to bigger and better things just as he did. "Broadcasting is a small world, and news travels quickly—I wanted everyone to hear from me," he says. "And I never lost a friend."

In 2001, Roberts joined CNN as an anchor for its Headline News channel, part of a revamp aimed at attracting younger viewers. Altogether, the new Hollywood-ready faces—*NYPD Blue* star Andrea Thompson, Miles O'Brien, and Robin Meade among them—were like *Saved by the Bell: The New Class,* Roberts jokes. But the pressure was considerably greater than in high school.

"I remember getting to CNN and the place is just ginormous—there's so many people," he says. "I didn't know how I would be received—you kind of catch yourself. But my comfort level grew and grew, and then I told people." Again, the reaction was unremarkable. "They weren't a gossipy bunch, like, 'Oh, did you hear about Thomas?' It just wasn't that type of place."

He never felt unwelcome at CNN because of his sexual orientation. In fact, six years later, when Patrick was offered a great job in Washington, D.C., and Roberts decided to quit to be with him—a transfer from Atlanta wasn't possible—his bosses tried to talk him out of it. "They were like, 'Are you sure you want to do this? We'd love to have you stay,'" he remembers. "They were fantastic."

Miguel Marquez, Roberts's friend and former colleague at CNN, says his experience in broadcasting has also been uniformly positive. The dapper Los Angeles correspondent for ABC News often reports from Baghdad for the network. When he called me from his office outside the Green Zone last fall, I asked if he ever worried about being out in the biz. "I'm not that smart," deadpanned Marquez, every bit as handsome and dashing as the late Peter Jennings. "I guess I figured if someone didn't want to hire me because I was gay, then I probably wouldn't want to work for them. There's a lot of people who are worried about that, and to me it's sort of a self-fulfilling prophecy."

Jane Velez-Mitchell would say much the same thing. A veteran anchor at prominent affiliates in New York (WCBS) and Los Angeles (KCAL), the youthful, sexy 51-year-old is best known these days for her stint as a correspondent on the now-defunct syndicated crime show *Celebrity Justice,* for which she covered Michael Jackson's 2005 child-molestation trial. (That and other cases are the subject of her 2007 book *Secrets Can Be Murder.*) She also guest-hosts for Nancy Grace on her CNN Headline News show and appears as a commentator on radio and TV. While doing such a gig on L.A. radio station KABC last September, Velez-Mitchell decided to come out. She had been inspired by financial guru Suze Orman's acknowledgment earlier that year that she's gay, and she was looking for a convenient opening to announce her own news. She found it with a toe-tapping senator from Idaho.

> ## "Opinionating about Larry Craig and his apparent hypocrisy, it would have been hypocritical for me not to be honest with the listeners about who I am."
>
> —Jane Velez-Mitchell

"Opinionating about Larry Craig and his apparent hypocrisy, it would have been hypocritical for me not to be honest with the

listeners about who I am," she told me a few weeks after the fact at the home she shares with her partner, Sandra, in Marina del Rey, Calif., just south of Venice and less than a block from the beach. "So I just came out and said it: 'I want to be honest. I live with a woman and have been in a relationship with a woman.'"

No one she knew blinked an eye—though on the air, a listener called in and asked if she was a "hypocrite" for not revealing her sexual orientation during her two decades as an anchor. In fact, Velez-Mitchell had been in relationships with men until she met Sandra five years ago, though she says she always had "gay tendencies." "My answer was, 'Probably,'" she says. "I really like those kinds of questions. Let's move society forward by having a dialogue about this."

Of course, Velez-Mitchell would be the first to point out that she had a certain freedom to talk about her sexuality, given her freelance status and role as a pundit. She concedes she sometimes noticed unease about out talent during her anchoring days—"like, 'We don't really care, but we don't want you leading the parade,' that kind of thing"—but she also gives the public "a lot more credit" on this issue than most broadcast folks seem to. "I've always found that people in the 'liberal' areas aren't quite as liberal as they say they are, and people in the 'conservative' areas aren't quite as rigid as they say they are," she observes. "Everybody in America knows somebody who is gay: They have a family member or know somebody who knows somebody. The vice president's daughter is gay. Who cares?"

Indeed, Velez-Mitchell sees her coming-out as part of a trend. "I think the logjam has opened," she says. "We're at a point now where, in a couple of years, everybody's going to come out. It's a trickle, and it becomes a stream, and it becomes a river."

No one is more responsible for that rising tide than Boston's Randy Price, the first openly gay anchor in America. He came out publicly in the early 1990s in an interview with a New England gay periodical, and a mainstream paper picked it up. At the time, people in his professional life questioned his choice to be so open, but it has only paid off for Price: In 1997 he was hired at WHDH, and in 1998 he began to co-anchor the evening broadcasts, which regularly top the ratings. Today he's not only Boston's most popular news anchor but one of its most admired public figures.

"Wouldn't you rather be a little distinctive even if it's unpopular in a few quarters?" Price says about coming out. "Is it really going to hurt you? Is your career going to erode? Honestly not. We've been watching gay-friendly entertainment for years, *Will & Grace* and this and that. It's not a big deal." He offers a pointed question to those gay journalists who claim they don't want to become the story themselves or risk access to sources who may not be gay-friendly: "In a business based on honesty, when do you eventually become yourself?"

Steve Kmetko, the longtime E! anchor, saw no damage to his career either when he came out publicly on the cover of this magazine in 1999. Though he left the channel in 2002 after an acrimonious contract dispute, he says he had a great experience there and has never regretted the decision. "Quite frankly, age is more of a hindrance at this point in my career than being gay," he says.

But instead of following the lead of Price or Roberts, Jake and his closeted peers seem to be taking their cues from the Coop, whose publicists—no surprise—did not respond to interview requests for this story. "When CNN hired Anderson, especially among the industry, it was just known that he's gay. I guess nobody cared. He made the choice, much like I have, not to talk about it,'" says Jake, who in the past has worked in proximity to him.

The most celebrated anchor of his generation, Cooper is also the object of intense fascination vis-à-vis his sexual orientation. Media critics, bloggers, viewers, my mom—people are dying to penetrate his opaque exterior and find out what makes him tick. Whom does he date? Why won't he come out? Has he discussed strategy with CNN? Is it all just a deliberate ruse to keep the buzz going?

Indeed, his glass closet may well be a canny marketing move, judging from the informal advice that Jake himself once received from an executive during a business dinner. "He said to me, 'It's better if people don't know one way or the other,'" he recalls. "'Let the people who think you're gay think you're gay, and let the people who think you're straight think you're straight. Then we have it both ways. A little mystery never hurts.'"

"You give an article to *Vanity Fair,* and [your sexual orientation] is the one issue skirted. Did Cooper think, Now I'm in a star position, I'm doing these personal articles, but I'm going to omit that?"

—Jake

No one begrudges Jake—or Cooper—if he feels hemmed in by forces beyond his control. "To talk about reporters and anchors—I'm not doing that anymore, so I can't put myself in the shoes of someone who is," Velez-Mitchell tells me. "They have all these other variables that I don't have to contend with." But Jake is an interesting proxy for the silver-haired one, given their similar circumstances, and he's watched his predecessor's rise with keen interest. "It presents an interesting conundrum that I haven't been faced with yet, which is: You give an article to *Vanity Fair,* you talk about every single personal thing, and [your sexual orientation] is the one issue that's skirted," says Jake. "Did he think, *OK, now I'm really in a star position, I'm doing all these personal articles, but I'm going to omit that?*

"I'm not there yet—I may never get there. But if you want to be judged by your work, then how much do you share?" He pauses to consider the question. "I don't know if I'm ready for that."

But Jake is worried about more than that—he's also scared of the hawks in the gay community who circle celebrities with killer intent, none more so than their own. By pure coincidence, I interviewed Jake in his apartment on the very day that Roberts's Manhunt "scandal" hit. It was

clearly on his mind—he brought the subject up unprompted. "What is it the community says it wants?" he asked rhetorically. "Well, it would be nice to have some role models in various industries: lawyers, doctors, anchors, reporters, actors, whoever. Well, Roberts came out. He's open. He's landed another job. In your mind, you think, *OK, people know and they don't really care.*

"But then the gossip starts: Who has he slept with? Who has he been with? Where does he hang out? What does he do? What's he like? It's like, Jesus, is that necessary? It's become this weird witch hunt."

Jake has already been burned by innuendos. Early in his anchoring career, after he'd made a guest appearance on a local radio show, someone left a message at the station outing him. As Jake remembers it, "It said, 'Hi, this is so-and-so. I don't know if you're aware. Everyone knows. He's gay and he has a boyfriend. Just thought you should know.'" That people might be out to get him was an alarming revelation. "I thought, *Oh, my gosh, there's a weird thing going on here.* If you're gay and want to keep it a secret—if you're on TV—you can't. It felt like an attack." As a public figure, he learned, one's sexuality can be used as "ammunition."

It was probably a foregone conclusion that Roberts was in for similar treatment as soon as word hit the blogosphere that he was gay. In September 2006 he had appeared on a panel called "Off Camera: The Challenges for LGBT TV Anchors" at the National Lesbian and Gay Journalists Association convention in Miami Beach, Fla. A blogger in attendance wrote about the event, and though he mentioned other participants like Stevens, for some reason—his comely appearance?—Roberts's name ripped through the gay media (including this magazine's website).

It was a total shock to him. "It was the worst-kept secret, I guess," Roberts says about his sexual orientation. "Everyone at CNN knew Patrick, knew my life. I'd go out, I'd support gay restaurants or bars. It was no big secret in Atlanta. But sitting on a panel—people took that as some great step." He wasn't trying to come out; he did the panel to show younger broadcast journos "that you can have a career, don't be afraid. Just keep your head down and work hard. Like anything in this business, it's about skill, luck, and timing."

Roberts made headlines again the following March, when Cooper interviewed him on his show about the molestation he suffered by a priest as a kid growing up in Maryland. Given all the attention he was receiving, Roberts had become a bona fide celebrity in the gay world. It was all too predictable when someone tried to topple him from his pedestal.

It was September 6, Roberts's fourth day at *The Insider,* when the Manhunt photos were posted online last year. The next day, a Page Six item dripping with homophobia detailed the whole thing. The headline? "New Sex Mess Jolts *Insider.*" Roberts had come out to California excited about the new gig—he had spent the summer looking for a good opportunity like this—and now he was faced with potential disaster.

His response to the incident is honest, if reticent. "I never put inappropriate pictures of myself on a public website," he says by way of explanation. "For me it was really hurtful, for Patrick and I it was terribly painful, and I'm sure anyone reading this will realize that what happened was something that we needed to deal with on a personal level. And we've dealt with it—we've closed the book on that issue and moved on."

I ask him if he was angered by what was clearly meant to be a personal take-down. "The only thing I'll say is that it is a nonissue for me anymore. It's not active in my life, nor do I want it to be. But respectfully"—he smiles broadly—"I thank you for asking."

A statement by *The Insider* called the event "a malicious personal attack," and Roberts says he was pleased with the show's response. "They handled that situation like a class act," he says. "They rallied the wagons and fought back against the allegations and did everything they could to show me kindness and respect." But although *The Insider,* like any celebrity-obsessed show, loves a good scandal, the team there couldn't have been happy with the development. "They said 'We are not throwing the baby out with the bathwater'" is all Roberts will say.

Does he think the incident had anything to do with his being cut from the show? "You'll have to ask them. I've heard it could be budgetary decisions—I don't know. I was just told that I wasn't part of the future direction of the show. And I have to respect their decision."

Was being gay a factor? "They hired me knowing I was gay—that's all I'll say to that question. They hired me knowing I was out and gay."

A spokesperson for the show concurred: "We were aware of Thomas's sexuality when we hired him and it had nothing to do with our decision to make a change."

So Roberts was out of a job—but the blogger had made a name for himself. Funny thing is, if you go to his site now (and, full disclosure, he once discussed writing for *The Advocate* with me, though nothing came of it), you can't find the original item without some assiduous searching. Instead, you'll see links to the coverage it got—and an undated photo of the blogger with Roberts at an event, both smiling. It's a paradox of contemporary fandom not unique to the gays: We love our stars, but we also love to tear them down.

Tom Brokaw thinks there's no reason there can't be an openly gay anchor. "No," says the retired NBC News lion, and "I've been saying that for years, by the way." And yet when he talked to *The Advocate* in January in connection with his book *Boom! Voices of the Sixties,* he inadvertently revealed the kind of subtle discomfort about gays that Jake senses at high levels in the industry. "We have someone—I'm not going to say [her] name because I haven't checked with her on this—who is a terrific advocate for gay rights in the NBC Nightly News room. It's well-known, and she is an important voice," Brokaw said. An entirely appropriate response: He clearly didn't want to out his colleague against her wishes. But the very fact that one's sexuality requires such delicacy confirms the stigma that still exists.

Nevertheless, people like Velez-Mitchell are coming out all the time in the broadcast news business. "If it does impact my career, well, so be it," she says. "Life's short. When you're lying on your deathbed, are you going to remember that you had two more years working in a cubicle, or are you going to remember that you were true to yourself and maybe encouraged some other people to be true to themselves?"

> **"It's what you make of it. Had I been reserved and so forth, then it would have been a taboo issue. But if you are who you are, you have no problems with it. [It's] a win-win situation."**
>
> —Chris Saldaña

That's already happening, as the new generation of broadcast talent coming up sees being gay as an asset, not baggage. Take Chris Saldaña, the cute 31-year-old who co-anchors the weekend broadcasts at KLAS in Las Vegas. Out virtually from the start of his career, the Texas native says that his experience as a gay person is one of many areas of expertise for him as a journalist. "Whenever there's a gay issue, I'm on it; whenever there's a Latino issue, I'm on it—a Catholic issue, they put me on it," Saldaña says about reporting stories for broadcast. Indeed, being gay and being involved in the local LGBT community has been a "win-win situation" for him. "It's what you make of it. Had I been reserved and so forth, then it would have been a taboo issue. But if you are who you are, you have no problems with it."

In the new world of television news, diversity is key to success. Ask Harvey Levin, the energetic force behind TMZ.com and its hit TV spin-off. Granted, the subject matter is down-market celebrity fluff, but it's well-done—and it's attracting demographically desirable viewers by the droves. In part that's due to a young staff filled with personalities that Levin happily lets shine. "Everybody brings something to the table with their personality," says Levin, a onetime investigative reporter for Los Angeles's KCBS who can frequently be seen on *Larry King Live,* filling in for the host or providing commentary on the latest Hollywood scandal. "There are people on my staff who are gay, there are people who are straight, and that absolutely filters into what we do. I like that there's diversity, that sometimes you can tell whether a woman wrote [a piece], whether a man wrote it, somebody gay, somebody straight. It's all part of the diet."

Levin himself has been out for years. "Everybody I work with knows, everybody in the television business knows. We'll make jokes about it: I'll say things in meetings [like] 'That's the gayest thing I've ever said!' It doesn't matter."

Sooner or later, a household name will realize that and come out publicly. Someone will notice that nothing too bad has be-fallen Roberts or Velez-Mitchell or Price. Based on recent comments, even Cooper seems to be inching out of his fragile enclosure. He's made a habit of bantering knowingly with his newsreader, Erica Hill, like the time she pointed out baby blankets imprinted with the names ERICA and COOPER in a catalog. "Did your husband get a little nervous, a little jealous?" Cooper asked, before joking, "Clearly [he] doesn't have anything to be nervous about." Of course, it could all just be more grist for the buzz machine.

One thing's for sure: Whenever he comes out—and he will, eventually—Cooper has lost the opportunity to lead on the issue, to be as brave as he's been while dropping in and out of war zones. He's surely aware of the stakes, and of the courage it takes to be out. If he wonders how it's done, he only has to look to Thomas Roberts.

"We are covered in bugs!" Roberts nearly shouts toward the end of our interview that warm April day in Los Angeles. Little yellow flowers surround us—along with the view and the weather, annoying insects can hardly diminish the beautiful atmosphere. And Roberts seems to be enjoying the ride. He may be out of a job with nothing definite lined up (though he is developing a secret project of his own), but the anchorman remains optimistic, almost impossibly so.

"You're so self-actualized," I say with a laugh. He quickly replies with a serious look in his eyes. "I'm just getting to a point where it's like, Who cares?" he says. "I'm getting too old. The sun is going to come up tomorrow; bills are going to be paid." About being gay in broadcast news, he says, "I think everybody's looking for somebody else to do something. Well, it's just you. All it takes is you."

UNIT 6

Sexual Health and Well-Being

Unit Selections

Key Points to Consider

- How would you define the terms healthy sexuality? What does sexual health mean to you?

- What do you know about various cancers, such as breast cancer, ovarian cancer, cervical cancer, and testicular cancer?

- In what ways is breast cancer an issue for both men and women?

- How knowledgeable are you about various sexual disorders and dysfunctions (including their treatments)?

- How comfortable are you to honestly discuss your past sexual history with a new sexual partner? Is there anything you wouldn't want to mention about your sexual past? If so, what and why?

- How knowledgeable are you about HIV disease? Do you perceive yourself to be at-risk for infection? Have you ever known anyone who is HIV positive?

- What treatments are currently available to treat HIV? How does post-exposure prophylaxis work?

- What needs to be done to keep people vigilant in the fight against HIV, and in preventing infections from occurring?

- What are some of the current challenges in the fight against HIV?

Student Web Site

www.mhcls.com

Internet References

World Health Organization: Sexual Health
http://www.who.int/topics/sexual_health/en/

National Cancer Institute: Breast Cancer
http://www.cancer.gov/cancertopics/types/breast

National Cancer Institute: Ovarian Cancer
http://www.cancer.gov/cancertopics/types/ovarian

National Cancer Institute: Testicular Cancer
http://www.cancer.gov/cancertopics/types/testicular/

SexInfo: Sexually Transmitted Infections
http://www.soc.ucsb.edu/sexinfo/?article=VN5j

The Johns Hopkins University HIV Guide Q&A
http://www.hopkins-hivguide.org/q_a/index.html?
categoryId=9352&siteId=7151#patient_forum

The Body: The Complete HIV/AIDS Resource
http://www.thebody.com/index.html

The readings found in *Unit 6* all focus on *Sexual Health and Well-Being.* Health, including sexual health, now receives a significant amount of attention in the mainstream media. Over the past two decades, the general public's awareness of, and interest and involvement in, their own health care has dramatically increased. We want to stay healthy and live longer, and we know that to do so, we must learn more about our bodies, including how to prevent problems, recognize danger signs, and find the most effective treatments. By the same token, if we want to stay sexually fit—from robust youth through a healthy, happy, sexy old age—we must be knowledgeable about sexual health care. This is one of the most important and fundamental topics covered in any human sexuality course. The urgency of this topic is demonstrated by the fact that this is one area of the sexuality curriculum in which all adult students seem highly interested.

Healthy sexualities are multifaceted and influenced by biological, psychological, and social factors. The World Health Organization (WHO) defines sexual health as follows:

> Sexual health is a state of physical, emotional, mental and social well-being in relation to sexuality; it is not merely the absence of disease, dysfunction or infirmity. Sexual health requires a positive and respectful approach to sexuality and sexual relationships, as well as the possibility of having pleasurable and safe sexual experiences, free of coercion, discrimination and violence. For sexual health to be attained and maintained, the sexual rights of all persons must be respected, protected and fulfilled.

Many people seem to think of sexual health as simply "the absence of disease," but as the WHO definition indicates, it is so much more than that. Simply not having a sexually transmitted infection or a reproductive cancer is not enough. Cognitive, behavioral, and emotional components are important as well. The meanings given to sexual behaviors and interactions will greatly influence the ways in which sexualities are experienced. Anxiety, fear, and shame are hardly conducive to healthy sexualities. The WHO definition makes mention of variables such as discrimination, violence, and sexual rights. Institutionalized discrimination and culturally validated violence are profoundly social in nature. The notion of sexual rights is hardly universal. Social and cultural processes play an important role in the sexual health of everyday people. To go back to a theme that has been present in readings throughout this book, we are simultaneously biological, psychological, and social beings. The area of sexual health is, in this way, no different from many other topics we have considered in this book.

The above discussion in no way minimizes the important and perhaps central role that disease (or lack thereof) plays in sexual health. In fact, many of the readings in this unit focus squarely on infections and disease; cancers and sexually transmitted infections being the primary interest. Even with physical disease states, there are often behavioral, psychological, and

© The McGraw-Hill Companies, Inc./Christopher Kerrigan, photographer

sociocultural components that must be understood. This unit addresses all of this.

There are many potential threats to our sexual health and well-being. Sexual or reproductive cancers, such as breast cancer, cervical cancer, ovarian cancer, male breast cancer, penile cancer, testicular cancer, among many others, threaten the health of affected people around the world. In industrialized nations, many treatment options exist. Often, people in developing countries simply have no access to life-saving treatments that so many in Western countries take for granted.

Some strains of the human papilloma virus (HPV), an extremely common infection, can lead to cancers. In addition to cancer, there are other life threatening infections that can be sexually transmitted. Hepatitis B Virus, which can be transmitted through sexual activities, can be deadly. Untreated syphilis can lead to death, although with the common use of antibiotics, this has become quite uncommon in Western Countries. However, there are still many thousands of people who die of syphilis infection worldwide, every year. HIV has killed over 25 million people worldwide over the past three decades.

Over the years, HIV has certainly received much attention in the media. The fear of HIV has lessened somewhat since the 1980s, but among some people who are at high risk of infection through unprotected sexual behaviors, "HIV apathy" has taken hold. This is partly because HIV disease has gone from being almost always fatal to a long-term chronic infection for some, at least for those who have access to effective antiretroviral medications and are highly compliant with their drug regimens. Sex educators are trying to find ways to fight the apathy among some people who are engaging in the highest risk sexual behaviors.

Because of the behavioral and social dimensions of sexually transmitted infections, educators and scientists have long been interested in understanding high risk behaviors and situations. We have learned much from sexual risk-taking behavior research. Sex researchers Janice and John Baldwin at the University of California have found that knowing about the risks is simply not enough. Other components that may influence behavior include things like worry and perceptions of individual risk. Those who worry about becoming infected with an STI are more likely to be cautious in their behaviors. Also, those who perceive themselves to be potentially at risk may be less likely to engage in risky behaviors. Again, knowledge alone is not enough. On the other hand, too much worry can be paralyzing. This is the kind of research science that has immediate application, and can provide the foundation for public health education efforts to prevent the spread of STIs and HIV. With no cure for HIV in sight, education and public health prevention efforts remain our very best hope.

In addition to cancers and STIs, other sexual health problems are explored in this unit, including: erectile dysfunction, premature ejaculation, orgasm difficulties, lack of sexual desire, and painful intercourse. Some treatment options are also discussed in this unit. Whether we are talking about cancers, STIs, or other sexual health concerns, one of the biggest concerns we have in the field of human sexuality is the prevention and alleviation of pain and suffering. The ultimate goal is that we make this information our own. We need to go beyond knowledge alone to accepting personal responsibility, and accurately assessing personal risk. By taking responsibility, we help to create a world of possibilities, where sexualities may be expressed in healthy and satisfying ways. Ultimately, that is what this unit is all about.

Sex, Health & Happiness

Love lives keep getting longer and better. Yours can, too.

Deborah Kotz

Comedian George Burns once cracked that "sex at age 90 is like trying to shoot pool with a rope." Clearly, he was speaking for his own generation. Today's seniors, their sex lives liberated long ago by one pill and extended indefinitely by another, have every intention of staying in the game. The scope of the sexual shifts launched by Viagra a decade ago—perhaps as monumental as those triggered by the birth control pill—is now becoming apparent. A July study published in the *British Medical Journal* found that considerably more 70-year-olds are enjoying sex regularly than 30 years ago: 57 percent of men and 52 percent of women today versus 40 percent and 35 percent back then. (And that's before the baby boomers arrive with their outsize expectations.) About one quarter of those ages 75 to 85 are now sexually active, according to recent research from the University of Chicago. "We used to think seniors didn't have sexuality at all," says Helen Fisher, a professor of anthropology at Rutgers University and author of *Why We Love.* "Viagra has caused many older people to put sex way up front in their relationships."

That could explain why U.S. sales of the little blue pill and two newer drugs have skyrocketed to more than $1.5 billion—or 19 million prescriptions—a year, causing drug companies to salivate over the possibility—still distant—of a "pink Viagra" for women. Further along in the pipeline: a testosterone gel to reverse libido loss after menopause and a pill that boosts desire by acting on serotonin receptors in the brain.

Sales of the little blue pill and two similar drugs have hit more than $1.5 billion, or 19 million prescriptions, a year.

The merits of staying sexually active through the years are obvious and plentiful: joy and excitement, connectedness, and a host of health benefits. Scientists have shown that having sex regularly boosts the immune system and releases hormones that lower stress levels, improve sleep, and might even hold off wrinkles: A Scottish study found that people who enjoy sex every other day looked about seven to 12 years younger than their peers, on average.

Beyond Drugs

But it's also clear that fulfillment depends on far more than pharmaceutical fixes. "Erectile dysfunction drugs are marketed to suggest that older men will get back the kinds of erections they had in their 20s," and that's simply not the case, says Barry McCarthy, a professor of psychology at American University in Washington, D.C., and author of *Men's Sexual Health.* Clinical trials show that about 65 to 85 percent of men with erectile dysfunction find their problem improves with Viagra or one of the other two ED drugs, Levitra or Cialis. Yet, one third of men responding to a recent *Consumer Reports* survey said they experienced side effects from the drugs like headaches, heartburn, or, in rarer cases, prolonged painful erections. And men tempted to try drugs just for a little boost will most likely be disappointed at what Viagra *can't* do. "It's not an aphrodisiac and won't make a man bigger," says Abraham Morgentaler, an associate clinical professor of urology at Harvard Medical School and author of *The Viagra Myth.* "It also won't make a guy's erection any better if he doesn't have a problem in the first place."

When pills do fix the mechanical problems, reliving the passionate and soul-melding sex of younger days appears possible, too—assuming creativity and commitment. Passionate feelings are certainly more associated with the early throes of love, but researchers now believe they can be stirred in long-married folks, too. The proof lies in brain scans: Stony Brook University researchers recently performed functional magnetic resonance imaging on couples claiming to still be head over heels after 20-plus years of marriage and found remarkable similarities to scans of euphoric young lovers. "They both show substantial increases in those 'excitement' areas of brain that produce dopamine," a brain chemical associated with sexual arousal, winning the lottery, and cocaine highs, says Stony Brook social psychologist Arthur Aron.

Turns out the older set may even have an advantage. Whereas early love activates brain regions thought to be responsible for those can't-stop-thinking-about-you love pangs, more mature passion lights up areas where the "bonding" or "cuddle" hormone oxytocin is active. "Sexual liveliness can be equally strong for both," says Aron, "but long-term love doesn't have the jealousy or obsession that occurs when you've just fallen in love."

No one has yet determined exactly how to light up the brain's passion centers. But research shows that couples feel more attracted to one another after they've engaged in novel, challenging activities—like being tied together in a three-legged race—than after taking part in a routine pleasurable activity like sharing an ice-cream sundae. Fisher says it probably has something to do with challenge that causes a surge in dopamine. Rock climbing isn't necessary; Aron and his wife recently found it quite arousing to go to a bar for the first time in 10 years. "It was challenging for us just to walk in and figure out what to order," he says. Making it a point to celebrate good things together, like job promotions or prestigious awards, also has been shown to fuel passion, probably because of that shared dopamine surge. Practice helps, too. "Any kind of sexual stimulation drives up dopamine in the brain," Fisher explains, "and orgasms release oxytocin to trigger feelings of deep attachment."

Still, as baby boomers heading into their 60s are just beginning to realize, Mother Nature makes them feel less driven for sex when reproduction is no longer on the agenda. Testosterone levels naturally decline in both men and women, making them feel less in the mood, and less often. And common middle-age medical problems like diabetes, enlarged prostate, and heart disease can disrupt blood flow to sex organs, making it difficult for men to achieve and maintain erections even with Viagra or Cialis. (Guidance on managing sexual problems can be found on Page 54.) A host of medications, too, can interfere with sexual functioning.

Prostate cancer treatments, which can permanently damage nerves that cause erections, present the biggest challenge in terms of robbing men of their sexuality. "At best, Viagra helps about half of those with no function," Morgentaler says. But perseverance can pay off. "Susan," 65, a writer in Manhattan who prefers to remain anonymous, donned "black lace teddies and stiletto heels worthy of a 20-year-old" and initiated oral sex twice a week for several years after her husband's prostate surgery. "At first, he looked at me hopelessly," she recalls, "trying to get to that place where his libido had been. Last year, we were finally able to have intercourse again."

For women, the plunging estrogen levels that occur during menopause often lead to vaginal wall thinning and dryness, which can make sex uncomfortable or downright painful. Menopausal mood swings can also be a mood killer. Susan has had to contend with both of these problems but worked with her doctor to find solutions; they opted to slowly lower her dose of hormone replacement therapy instead of her going cold turkey, for example, and she experimented with different over-the-counter lubricants. But many women are uncomfortable broaching the subject of sexual difficulties, and more than 90 percent of doctors don't ask, according to a 2007 survey conducted by the Women's Sexual Health Foundation.

Speak Up

"Most gynecologists say they have very little training in the area of intimacy and sexual function," says Lisa Martinez, the foundation's executive director, "yet women expect these doctors to take the lead." After being treated for breast cancer last year, Martinez, 53, initiated conversations with her doctors about her mastectomy scar, vaginal dryness caused by an antiestrogen drug, and the extreme fatigue she felt from chemotherapy—all of which put a big damper on her sex life. She included her husband in these discussions to put him at ease.

Among the best concrete ways to extend a pleasurable sex life: Stay in peak form as long as possible. "I suspect just as good sex promotes good health, good health promotes good sex," says gynecologist Stacy Tessler Lindau, whose findings in the University of Chicago study showed that diabetics, for instance, were more likely to experience lack of pleasure or difficulty maintaining erections. The study also found that a man's physical health was the most common reason couples gave up. Sexually transmitted diseases can lead to painful intercourse and lubrication problems years later, according to a study published last month in the *Journal of Sexual Medicine.* Beyond the obvious—practicing safe sex—McCarthy recommends such healthful lifestyle habits as keeping regular sleep patterns, maintaining a healthy body weight, and following a nutritious diet of whole grains, lean protein, and fruits and vegetables. Plus, avoid excess alcohol, known to interfere with sexual function, and exercise regularly to improve blood flow and increase energy.

At any age, of course, it's being in a relationship that's cherishing and intimate on many levels that matters most in elevating sex beyond mere mechanics. Joan Price, the 64-year-old author of *Better Than I Ever Expected: Straight Talk About Sex After Sixty,* says that she had the best sex of her life after meeting her late husband seven years ago. "He saw me as beautiful, and I thought, if he thinks it, it must be so."

Fighting the Cancer a Mammo Can't Catch

This mom found her diagnosis—a rare, stealthy form of breast cancer—online. Now, she's using the power of the Web and the love of her family to fight it.

MARGARET RENKL

It was a long night, and Susan Niebur was feeling low. Normally, this working mom in Silver Spring, Maryland, can keep a shocking number of balls in the air and still smile. She's a physicist who works part-time as a consultant to NASA; an at-home mom to Matt, 1, and Andrew, 3; an animal-rescue volunteer; and a daily blogger. But Niebur, 35, is also a full-time cancer patient, and one night last fall her characteristic attitude of resolve and optimism failed her. After nearly six months of chemotherapy, the treatment's side effects—which are cumulative—were brutal. She was in constant pain, couldn't sleep or eat, and had just developed a case of temporary nerve damage that rendered her unable to walk or even get out of bed without help. So while her husband, Curt, 35, and their little boys slept, Niebur did the only thing she could do to feel more in control of a terrible situation: She booted up her laptop, logged on to her blog, and wrote about what had happened earlier that night.

Because the meds weren't taking away the pain, my husband lifted me into a hot, steaming bath (my legs still aren't working) to relax the muscles. The pain dissipated a bit, and I began to feel better. Then, after the water cooled off, we added bubbles and a baby. I began to gently wash his back with soapy hands, and he looked up at me and giggled. I giggled back, briefly, and then, as he turned away to splash a bit, it struck me again. This is the baby we waited for. This is the last baby I'll ever have. This is the baby I'm living for. And I began to cry. Great big gobs of tears, actually, and I turned on the water again so no one else in the house would hear it. I'm not good at talking about these feelings, you see, and I really still don't want to talk about it, but, in truth, I am sad.

Six months earlier Niebur had been diagnosed with inflammatory breast cancer, or IBC, the deadliest form of the disease. The best hope for survival is early diagnosis combined with aggressive treatment: chemotherapy, followed by mastectomy, followed by radiation. It's a devastating regimen that lasts for nearly a year, and one of the ways Niebur copes is by writing it

all down—her research, her experiences, her fears, her hopes—and sharing it through her blog, Toddler Planet.

The First Hint of Trouble

For Niebur, the initial sign that something was wrong came after her youngest son was born in January 2007. It had taken some time for his older brother to get the hang of nursing, too, but weeks passed and still baby Matt rejected the right breast. Visits to the pediatrician and lactation specialist turned up no trouble with his latch or sucking reflex. He's just a stubborn baby, the pediatrician finally decided—"And if you know me, that's not so hard to believe," Niebur laughs.

By May her right breast had swollen and the skin on it had thickened a little and developed an unusual dimpled texture, almost like the skin of an orange. The changes were subtle at first, and Niebur didn't give them much thought. "Who would, when you're busy breast-feeding and helping a newborn survive?" she asks. She'd never found a lump during her monthly self-exams, so she didn't worry.

Then came a diagnosis of breast cancer—not Niebur's but her mother-in-law's. Like any good scientist, Niebur immediately began to research the disease and its treatments. After Googling "infiltrating ductile carcinoma," her mother-in-law's diagnosis, she came across a term she'd never heard before: inflammatory breast cancer. *My heart sank,* she wrote in her blog. *There, staring me in the face, were symptoms like "thickness of the breast," "dimpling," "redness," and "looks like an orange." I looked down. And back up at the screen. And then it hit me: I should get myself checked out, too.*

Facing the Worst

Within 10 days, Niebur had been diagnosed with IBC, a highly aggressive breast cancer that's very different from other forms of the disease. About 85 percent of breast-cancer patients have ductal carcinoma, which begins in the milk ducts and slowly infiltrates the surrounding tissue. By the time the cancer has formed a palpable lump, it has been growing for years. (That's why doctors urge women older than 40 to get yearly mammograms, so breast tumors can be discovered before they've grown large enough to be detected by hand.)

But IBC rarely produces a lump. Instead, it grows rapidly in sheets of cells that quickly infect the whole breast. The inflammation marches across the surface of the skin in a way that's visible to the naked eye, and there may be a constant itching or pain (either a dull ache or stabbing sensation) in the affected breast, as well as swollen lymph nodes on the neck or under the arm. In some cases, the earliest symptom is a bruise or a sore that looks like a bug bite but doesn't go away.

Though IBC is more common in younger women than other forms of the disease, overall it's very rare, affecting only 6,000 to 10,000 American women each year and accounting for only 1 to 5 percent of all breast cancers. Most OB-GYNs and even many cancer specialists have never seen a case, so in women of childbearing age—like Niebur—it's frequently misdiagnosed as mastitis, a common (and benign) complication of breast-feeding. Because IBC spreads so rapidly, misdiagnosis can be deadly. Of the 100,000 American women who suffer from it today, nearly half weren't diagnosed until the disease had already metastasized. And when cancer spreads from its original site to other organs—such as the liver, lungs, bone, or brain—it's too late for a cure. That's one reason why the five-year survival rate is only around 40 percent—less than half that of other breast cancers.

When Niebur brought her symptoms to her OB-GYN, he immediately referred her to a cancer specialist who biopsied a section of her skin, as well as seven core samples. The next day Niebur learned that she had breast cancer—and the one of the worst kinds of all.

Treating IBC varies by whether the patient is pre- or post-menopausal, whether the cancer has already metastasized, and whether estrogen makes it grow more rapidly. But all IBC patients receive chemotherapy (though the specific drugs and timing may vary), possibly along with hormone therapy, to shrink the cancer. If an MRI indicates a surgeon can remove it all, the patient has a mastectomy followed by radiation. They will likely need further treatment in future years; however, up to 70 percent of IBC patients suffer a recurrence in the opposite breast or elsewhere in the body if the cancer has reached the lymph nodes.

In addition to early diagnosis, the right treatment plan is crucial, says Massimo Cristofanilli, MD, an IBC researcher and co-director of the IBC clinic at the University of Texas' M.D. Anderson Cancer Center. "Every patient with IBC should be going to a specialized center, because this disease requires care from teams that know exactly how it behaves," Cristofanilli says. Patients who don't live in a major research area may need to travel to find a doctor who can develop an appropriate treatment plan with the help of their local oncologists.

Raising Awareness—and Her Own Spirits

Susan Niebur was lucky. Thanks to her "stubborn" baby and her mother-in-law, she got her diagnosis early, before the cancer had metastasized, so she has the best possible shot at beating this deadly disease. Determined to help other young women, she began writing about the illness on Toddler Planet, a blog she started keeping when her first child began walking. She explained the symptoms of IBC and urged women to get checked out if they noticed any change in their breasts. "I was caught off guard by the fact that I'd never even *heard* of IBC and, here it was, trying to kill me," Niebur says. "Spreading the word became very important to me."

So far, dozens of women have had their breasts checked after reading Niebur's blog. ("Thankfully, all but one have turned out to be negative," she says.) But they come back for the wisdom and honesty they find at Toddler Planet, which gets viewed about 1,500 times a day. The blog has also become a critical tool in Niebur's survival kit. After she was diagnosed, she wasn't sure whom to talk to. "I didn't want to burden my friends—they all have two or three young children of their own to worry about. I didn't want to burden my family—my mother-in-law's diagnosis needed everyone's attention. I just wanted to talk it through, and the blog was a natural outlet for me," she says. On the day she announced her diagnosis, she wrote, *I will continue to post every day so I don't slip into sadness over here. Help me stay focused and positive, OK? I will need you all.*

In post after post, Niebur chronicled what it's like to live with cancer and care for two small children at the same time. The details can be heart-wrenching, as in one post about 3-year-old Andrew: *It breaks my heart that he tells me sometimes, "Me sad" or "Me sick." Because he's not sick. I am. And it makes him sad.* But for every post that honestly names the fear and pain of cancer treatment, there's another in which Niebur points out the beauty in her life—like the time she and Curt coped with a long wait for chemo by slow dancing in the cancer ward. She's even able—on good days—to find the blessings in cancer itself: *When I'm really down, I think, I could have been hit by a bus and died instantly. Instead, I was hit by the cancer bus and given a chance to fight for my life.*

"I blog for me, for an honest record, and for that one woman who sees changes in her breast and is Googling what might be wrong," Niebur says. "I hope I can help her, now or years from now. Hopefully, all this won't be in vain."

"If I'm sad about the cancer, I just log on and there are friends waiting for me. The blogosphere is saving my life."

Readers respond with encouragement, prayers, and silly jokes to take her mind off the effects of chemotherapy. "If I'm up in the middle of the night and feel alone and sad about the cancer,

Blogging for Health

There are no stats on the number of bloggers who face a major health challenge, but the impulse to write your way through a crisis (as Susan Niebur does at www.toddlerplanet.wordpress.com) is very healthy, says Kelly McGonigal, PhD, a Stanford University psychologist who studies the psychological benefits of expressive writing. Writing about a stressful experience is one way to feel in control of it, which in turn lessens stress. "It's one of the most effective ways of making sense of what often feels senseless and overwhelming," McGonigal says.

But a blog offers a benefit that writing in private doesn't: a way to reach out. Patients who keep a blog "hope that others in similar situations will read their stories and have hope or simply feel less alone," McGonigal says. And feeling you have something to give even when life is beating you down is healing, physically and psychologically. To meet some of *Health*'s bloggers, visit Health.com/poked.

I just log on and there are friends waiting for me," Niebur says. "The blogosphere is saving my life."

Niebur has a lot of practical help, as well. Curt, also a NASA scientist, works a flexible schedule that allows him to be home if needed, and one set of parents or the other—Curt's mother has finished her own treatment and is doing well—has cared for the children while he accompanies Niebur to treatment.

But the blog has been a unique source of help, Curt says. "Susan expected it to be just an outlet and perhaps a way she could alert a few other people to this disease. But it also provided something unexpected and wondrous. I hope everyone who reads it realizes just how precious their support is. Cancer is a lonely disease: You're the only person in the chemo chair, and you're losing your hair, feeling pain pierce your bones. But Susan knows she's not alone, and that helps her every single day."

Looking to the Future

Last Christmas Eve, after six grueling months of chemotherapy, Niebur got the news she had been hoping for: Her cancer had responded to the chemo, and it was now operable. To reduce her risk of recurrence, she opted to have a double mastectomy. After the surgery, followed by seven weeks of daily radiation, she would be cancer-free. *An unbelievable lightness accompanies me these days,* Niebur wrote on Toddler Planet. *I've moved away from the scariest thoughts about cancer and am enjoying the present and looking to the future.*

Her readers responded joyfully: "I usually don't comment. But *this* deserves a huge *hallelujah!*" wrote one. "I am crying I am so happy for you!" wrote another.

In the past few months Niebur has enjoyed things most people take for granted: *Planting seeds. The forsythia bursting yellow. The trees filling out with leaves.* In other words, beginning life anew. As she reminds her readers, *Every day can be magical.*

When Sex Hurts

If lovemaking is more agony than ecstasy, the problem may be medical. Now there's help.

LISA COLLIER COOL

Thanks to recent advances, doctors have more effective treatments than ever for sexual pain. But zeroing in on the right diagnosis may be tricky, says Susan McSherry, M.D., who is affiliated with Tulane Medical School, in New Orleans. "If the first treatment doesn't help, keep working with your doctor. Painful sex isn't something you have to grit your teeth and tolerate. It's usually very treatable." Below are some common problems—and solutions.

Infections

Vaginal infections (collectively known as vaginitis) are so common that more than 75 percent of women can expect to develop at least one during their lifetime. The usual culprits are bacteria (bacterial vaginosis), yeast, and *Trichomonas* microorganisms, which are responsible for trichomoniasis, a sexually transmitted infection.

Symptoms. With some infections, you may have an unpleasant-smelling discharge, painful urination, and, in some cases, lower abdominal discomfort—plus itching and burning of the vagina and outer labia. But with other forms of vaginitis, there may be no special symptoms, says Erica V. Breneman, M.D., an obstetrician-gynecologist at Kaiser Permanente in Oakland, California.

During sex. The irritation may worsen when you're having intercourse or afterward.

Diagnosis. If itching is your main symptom and you have been diagnosed with a yeast infection in the past, try an over-the-counter medication. But if the problem doesn't clear up in a few days, see a gynecologist; left untreated, some forms of vaginitis can lead to more serious problems, including infertility. Your doctor will do a pelvic exam and examine your vaginal fluid for microorganisms.

Treatment. Depending on the cause, antibiotics, antifungal drugs, or medicated vaginal creams or suppositories. (For some infections, both partners need to be treated.) Symptoms should clear up—and sex should be comfortable—within several days.

Endometriosis

This disorder occurs when cells from the uterine lining (the endometrium) migrate to other parts of the abdomen, then swell and bleed during your period but aren't discharged as the uterine lining is. Over time, this misplaced tissue often causes chronic inflammation, scars, and weblike adhesions, most commonly on the ovaries or fallopian tubes, on the outer surface of the uterus, or on the internal area between your vagina and rectum.

Symptoms. Pain in the abdomen or lower back, severe menstrual cramps, fatigue, diarrhea, and/or painful bowel movements during your period.

During sex. Often there is deep, burning pain in the pelvis, abdomen, or lower back.

Diagnosis. In a procedure called laparoscopy, a gynecologist examines your pelvic organs using a lighted tube inserted through a small incision in your abdomen. Small lesions can usually be removed during the same procedure.

Treatment. For mild or moderate endometriosis, pain medication may be enough. But if you have severe cramping, or if the condition is interfering with your ability to become pregnant, or in order to suppress further growth of the lesions, you may need surgery or hormone treatment that temporarily stops your period. Neither of these is a cure, but two thirds of women improve after surgery; for the hormone treatment, the rate is a little more than half.

As for sex, you may find it's more comfortable during the week or two after your period rather than later in your cycle. And choosing a position that avoids deep penetration—side by side, for example, or with the woman on top—may help too.

"Painful sex isn't something you have to grit your teeth and tolerate," says one expert.

Fibroids

An estimated 20 to 30 percent of American women are affected by these noncancerous masses of muscle and fibrous tissue that grow inside the uterus (or, occasionally, outside). No one knows why some women are more prone, but a report from the National Institute of Child Health and Development shows that women who have had two or more children are far less likely to develop fibroids than those who have never given birth.

Symptoms. Some women are never bothered by their fibroids. But others may have heavy and painful periods, midmonth bleeding, a feeling of fullness in the lower abdomen, frequent urination, constipation, bloating, and lower back pain.

During sex. Your husband's thrusting can set off deep pelvic pain, due to pressure on your uterus.

Diagnosis. A routine pelvic exam. If a fibroid is detected, your doctor may use ultrasound or magnetic resonance imaging to check its size and location.

Treatment. For mild or occasional pelvic pain—including during sex—ibuprofen or other analgesics may be enough. If your fibroids need to be treated, there are several surgical approaches, as well as a new nonsurgical technique called fibroid embolization.

Interstitial Cystitis (IC)

Unlike "regular" cystitis, which is caused by a bacterial infection, the cause of IC is a mystery. This chronic inflammation of the bladder wall strikes women almost exclusively.

Symptoms. Very frequent urination (up to 30 times a day) and/or burning and pressure before urination; chronic lower abdominal pain that may intensify before your period.

During sex. Intercourse frequently triggers painful flare-ups, "like a severe headache all over your pelvis," says Dr. McSherry. Some women also have vaginal spasms, lower back pain, or pain that radiates down the thighs.

Diagnosis. First, your doctor will rule out other causes. Then she'll perform a test called cystoscopy—in which the bladder is filled with fluid and examined for tiny hemorrhages (a telltale sign of IC).

Treatment. Elmiron is the only oral medication specifically approved for IC. But many other drugs are available to relieve symptoms: Some women are helped by certain antidepressants that have pain-blocking effects (such as Elavil) or anti-inflammatory drugs that are inserted into the bladder. The good

A Mysterious Disorder

Imagine pain so piercing you can't even tolerate pantyhose rubbing against your genitals, much less sex. That's what vulvodynia can feel like, say sufferers, who may seek help from doctor after doctor, only to be dismissed as hypochondriacs. Part of the problem is that everything usually looks normal; women have no symptoms beyond persistent pain in the vulva, the skin folds around the vagina. (In a few cases, however, there may be inflammation.)

Experts don't know for sure what causes vulvodynia, though they theorize that nerve injury may play a role. Interestingly, over-the-counter products can trigger the condition in women who are pre-disposed, says Howard Glazer, Ph.D., associate professor in the department of obstetrics and gynecology at Cornell University Medical Center in New York City and codirector of the New York Center for Vulvovaginal Pain. "Some 85 percent of my patients tell me they treated what they thought was a yeast infection with an OTC cream or douche—and then developed pain that never went away." It may be they're re-acting to an irritant in the cream, Glazer suggests.

To diagnose the condition, your doctor may do what's called a Q-Tip Test, in which a cotton swab is used to gently check the vulva and the vaginal entrance for areas of pain and hypersensitivity. You may be able to relieve symptoms with medication (antidepressants, nerve blocks, or anticonvulsant drugs that also combat pain) or with biofeedback. In severe cases, surgery to remove the affected tissue may help.

news is that 85 percent of patients can be successfully treated with one or more of these therapies, says Dr. McSherry. As for sex, women may find it's more comfortable side by side and when they're fully aroused.

Vaginal Dryness

The most common reason for this annoying (though not medically serious) problem is the drop in estrogen that takes place at menopause or during perimenopause—the three to six years before your periods actually stop. Some women also experience a decrease in lubrication after having a baby or while breastfeeding. Allergies, too, can trigger dryness. Soap is probably the biggest offender, but laundry detergent, fabric softeners, bubble bath, vaginal-hygiene products, and spermicidal creams or foams can all be culprits as well.

Symptoms. Chafing, irritation, and itching. At menopause, falling estrogen levels also cause the walls of your vagina to become thinner and less elastic.

During sex. Friction may leave you quite sore. Discomfort may occur only at penetration or during thrusting.

Diagnosis. Fairly self-evident, but check with your doctor if you suspect an allergy.

Treatment. Over-the-counter lubricants, such as Replens or Astroglide. At menopause, talk to your gynecologist about hormone replacement therapy or estrogen cream. For allergic dryness, try using mild liquid bath soaps and fragrance-free or hypoallergenic brands of laundry and cosmetic products. Try different brands of spermicides until you find a nonirritating one. And ask your doctor about taking antihistamines: That might be wise until you figure out what you are allergic to.

Pelvic Congestion Syndrome (PCS)

There's some controversy about this syndrome: Not all doctors are convinced that it is a cause of pain during sex. Those who believe it is say that the disorder is triggered by varicose veins in the pelvis, a condition similar to varicose veins in the legs (and, indeed, about half the women with PCS also have the leg problem). In both cases, valves that normally keep the blood moving forward become leaky, allowing blood to flow backward and pool. As a result of the pressure, veins become large and bulgy. Most women develop the disorder after pregnancy, says Luis Navarro, M.D., director of The Vein Treatment Center, in New York City.

Symptoms. Aching, heaviness, pressure, or throbbing in the pelvis; sometimes visibly protruding veins in the genital area.

During sex. The discomfort intensifies during or after intercourse (as well as before or during your menstrual period).

Diagnosis. Several noninvasive tests, including the recently developed venography. During this procedure, a thin catheter is used to inject special dye into the pelvic veins, allowing the doctor to map blood flow with X rays.

Treatment. Tiny metal coils or a gluelike liquid are used to block off the affected area. The procedure has a success rate of 80 to 90 percent, says Dr. Navarro. But it can take a couple of weeks for symptoms to clear up.

Popping the *Other* Question

Before you hit the sheets, *hit the clinic* and be ready to prove your results.

ADRIENNE P. SAMUELS

"Honey, Do You Have an STD?"

It's the one question no one really wants to ask, but everyone should.

Why? Because sexually transmitted diseases affect Blacks at disproportionately higher rates than any other race in America. In fact, one of every two Black women has herpes, one in 10 Blacks carries syphilis and hundreds of thousands of us have the human papillomavirus that causes genital warts and can lead to cervical cancer. That makes asking the question more than a matter of etiquette. It's a safety imperative!

The issue is bigger than AIDS and HIV. Consider that many other STDs—if left unchecked—can destroy your womb, damage your spine and potentially kill or blind a newborn baby. Some of those viruses, like herpes, cannot be stopped by a condom and do not have a cure. And some others, like chlamydia, are becoming resistant to medications.

"You have to just ask. You can't sugarcoat it," says LaTanya Hines, a Pasadena, Calif.-based obstetrician/gynecologist who is also president of the Association of Black Women Physicians. Hines recently diagnosed a married woman who contracted a disease from her new husband a mere six weeks after the marriage was consummated. The couple had never had sex before tying the knot. "Before you get to the next point, you must say 'I've had my HIV test, have you?'"

This is easier said than done. Yet when you consider that half of your co-workers, most of your church and a third of your bowling league likely have or have had an STD, it becomes easier. Just remember, you can't take anyone's word for it. And men, just because you don't see a lump or a bump doesn't mean you're clean, especially given that men in particular might not show physical symptoms but can well be carrying one or more diseases.

Rejection Issues

"I had to emotionally deal with the fact that I had been diagnosed with Herpes II, and I hadn't talked to anybody about it," says Nicole Scott, a 36-year-old Chicagoan. Since her diagnosis, she has since told every boyfriend about her condition, which is being suppressed with drugs, but will never go away.

STD Conversation Clip 'n Save Script

Make sure you are in a safe, comfortable place. Have this conversation in private, with few distractions and not on your first date. Remember that this only works with someone who respects you and respects intimacy. If they freak out, get angry, get violent or try to flip the script, that's a RED FLAG.

You: Rashawn, I'm really feeling you, and I can't wait for us to make love. However, given today's ugly sexual environment, I think we should talk about our health.

Rashawn: OK. What are you saying?

You: Well, you should know that I have asthma, and I'm allergic to goose feathers. So we gotta get our freak on without those supersoft pillows. Also, I've been tested for HIV, herpes and gonorrhea. My tests came back negative, and I can show you the receipts. When's the last time you were tested?

Rashawn: I'm clean, baby. No bumps, no nothing.

You: OK. That's good to hear, but I was thinking that maybe we could be tested together. If we're sure about this STD thing, we'll have better, more uninhibited sex. We can go to an anonymous clinic, and it would be free.

Rashawn: You think I'm lying? This is uncomfortable.

You: No. I don't think you're lying. But sometimes you just never know. And honestly, you don't know much about me either. I don't want to catch something that'll give me cervical cancer or kill my chance of having babies. I'm sure you don't want that either.

Rashawn: Talk about a buzz killer. Let me think about it.

You: OK. We got plenty of time. Sex ain't going nowhere.

At first she thought that men might not consider her to be marriage material. But she was wrong.

"I did sit him down and say there's something I want to talk to you about," says Scott. "His [her husband-to-be's] response was basically that it didn't change his mind. He was still like, 'I still see you as wife material and mother material.'"

Couples with incurable STDs can still have sex, they just have to be careful, doctors say. And when pregnancy is involved, a woman is not advised to give vaginal birth if she has herpes lesions or bumps on her thighs, legs or in the vaginal area. Men with STDs must be mindful to wash their hands after using the bathroom.

The homosexual population has an easier time dealing with these questions, says Robinson Y., 30, a gay marketing and sales representative who lives in the Midwest. Robinson's first boyfriend was HIV-positive and they continued to have sex, just very carefully. The two dated for seven years before breaking up. Now he makes a habit of asking every man he dates about his STD history.

"I'll usually start off asking about the status," explains Robinson. "And I have had people up front tell me, 'Hey, I have herpes.' And if so, I'm willing to limit the things I do with [them] to things like heavy petting . . . And certainly anything and everything needs to have a condom at that point, even if it's oral sex, especially oral sex."

Lying about It

It's all well and good to talk about coming clean, but there are folks out there who just won't.

Take Tony S., 42, of Atlanta. Tony belongs to an online social group that's designed for people who have genital warts and herpes. He's open with his group members about his status, but sometimes he doesn't tell women that he has acquired the virus. It's pretty easy, he says, because women believe him when he says he is virus-free.

"I rarely have breakouts, and they [the women] don't really know," says Tony, who is aware that herpes can be spread to sexual partners even if symptoms aren't present. "I am careful, though, when it comes to oral sex. And, I don't have sex if I think I might be having an outbreak."

That's a dangerous precedent, says Debra W. Haffner, a minister and director of the Connecticut-based Religious Institute on Sexual Morality, Justice, and Healing.

"Women are really at risk because their husbands [or boyfriends] are not honest about their STD status," says Haffner. "Unfortunately people lie to have sex."

Seniors Have Sex Too

Sexually transmitted diseases affect everybody, not just teenyboppers.

According to the federal government, some 19 percent of senior citizens have HIV/AIDS. The adult children of senior citizens might want to have a discussion with their parents about safer sex, say experts.

"Viagra has changed the world with respect to HIV," says Hines. "We have a growing population of elderly women who are HIV-positive because they didn't think they could get it. They're having sex with men who previously weren't able to perform."

Adds Hines: "Sex is sex, whether you're 20 or 50. Just wear a condom."

Sex, Drugs, Prisons, and HIV

SUSAN OKIE, MD

One recent morning at a medium-security compound at Rhode Island's state prison, Mr. M, a middle-aged black inmate, described some of the high-risk behavior he has witnessed while serving time. "I've seen it all," he said, smiling and rolling his eyes. "We have a lot of risky sexual activities. . . . Almost every second or minute, somebody's sneaking and doing something." Some participants are homosexual, he added; others are "curious, bisexual, bored, lonely, and . . . experimenting." As in all U.S. prisons, sex is illegal at the facility; as in nearly all, condoms are prohibited. Some inmates try to take precautions, fashioning makeshift condoms from latex gloves or sandwich bags. Most, however, "are so frustrated that they are not thinking of the consequences except for later," said Mr. M.

Drugs, and sometimes needles and syringes, find their way inside the walls. "I've seen the lifers that just don't care," Mr. M said. "They share needles and don't take a minute to rinse them." In the 1990s, he said, "needles were coming in by the handful," but prison officials have since stopped that traffic, and inmates who take illicit drugs usually snort or swallow them. Tattooing, although also prohibited, has been popular at times. "A lot of people I've known caught hepatitis from tattooing," Mr. M said. "They use staples, a nail . . . anything with a point."

Mr. M had just undergone a checkup performed by Dr. Josiah D. Rich, a professor of medicine at Brown University Medical School, who provides him with medical care as part of a long-standing arrangement between Brown and the Adult Correctional Institute in Cranston. Two years ago, Mr. M was hospitalized with pneumonia and meningitis. "I was scared and in denial," he said. Now, thanks to treatment with antiretroviral drugs, "I'm doing great, and I feel good," he reported. "I am HIV-positive and still healthy and still look fabulous."

U.S. public health experts consider the Rhode Island prison's human immunodeficiency virus (HIV) counseling and testing practices, medical care, and prerelease services to be among the best in the country. Yet according to international guidelines for reducing the risk of HIV transmission inside prisons, all U.S. prison systems fall short. Recognizing that sex occurs in prison despite prohibitions, the World Health Organization (WHO) and the Joint United Nations Program on HIV/AIDS (UNAIDS) have recommended for more than a decade that condoms be made available to prisoners. They also recommend that prisoners have access to bleach for cleaning injecting equipment,

that drug-dependence treatment and methadone maintenance programs be offered in prisons if they are provided in the community, and that needle-exchange programs be considered.

Prisons in several Western European countries and in Australia, Canada, Kyrgyzstan, Belarus, Moldova, Indonesia, and Iran have adopted some or all of these approaches to "harm reduction," with largely favorable results. For example, programs providing sterile needles and syringes have been established in some 50 prisons in eight countries; evaluations of such programs in Switzerland, Spain, and Germany found no increase in drug use, a dramatic decrease in needle sharing, no new cases of infection with HIV or hepatitis B or C, and no reported instances of needles being used as weapons.[1] Nevertheless, in the United States, condoms are currently provided on a limited basis in only two state prison systems (Vermont and Mississippi) and five county jail systems (New York, Philadelphia, San Francisco, Los Angeles, and Washington, DC). Methadone maintenance programs are rarer still, and no U.S. prison has piloted a needle-exchange program.

The U.S. prison population has reached record numbers—at the end of 2005, more than 2.2 million American adults were incarcerated, according to the Justice Department. And drug-related offenses are a major reason for the population growth, accounting for 49% of the increase between 1995 and 2003. Moreover, in 2005, more than half of all inmates had a mental health problem, and doctors who treat prisoners say that many have used illicit drugs as self-medication for untreated mental disorders.

In the United States in 2004 (see table), 1.8% of prison inmates were HIV-positive, more than four times the estimated rate in the general population; the rate of confirmed AIDS cases is also substantially higher (see graph).[2] Some behaviors that increase the risk of contracting HIV and other bloodborne or sexually transmitted infections can also lead to incarceration, and the burden of infectious diseases in prisons is high. It has been estimated that each year, about 25% of all HIV-infected persons in the United States spend time in a correctional facility, as do 33% of persons with hepatitis C virus (HCV) infection and 40% of those with active tuberculosis.[3]

Critics in the public health community have been urging U.S. prison officials to do more to prevent HIV transmission, to improve diagnosis and treatment in prisons, and to expand programs for reducing high-risk behavior after release. The

HIV–AIDS among Prison Inmates at the End of 2004*

Jurisdictions with the Most Prisoners Living with HIV–AIDS	No. of Inmates Living with HIV–AIDS	Prevalence of HIV–AIDS %
New York	4500	7.0
Florida	3250	3.9
Texas	2405	1.7
Federal system	1680	1.1
California	1212	0.7
Georgia	1109	2.2

*Data are from Maruschak.[2]

debate over such preventive strategies as providing condoms and needles reflects philosophical differences, as well as uncertainty about the frequency of HIV transmission inside prisons. The UNAIDS and WHO recommendations assume that sexual activity and injection of drugs by inmates cannot be entirely eliminated and aim to protect both prisoners and the public from HIV, HCV, and other diseases.

But many U.S. prison officials contend that providing needles or condoms would send a mixed message. By distributing condoms, "you're saying sex, whether consensual or not, is OK," said Lieutenant Gerald Ducharme, a guard at the Rhode Island prison. "It's a detriment to what we're trying to enforce." U.S. prison populations have higher rates of mental illness and violence than their European counterparts, which, some researchers argue, might make providing needles more dangerous. And some believe that whereas European prison officials tend to be pragmatic, many U.S. officials adopt a "just deserts" philosophy, viewing infections as the consequences of breaking prison rules.

Studies involving state-prison inmates suggest that the frequency of HIV transmission is low but not negligible. For example, between 1988—when the Georgia Department of Corrections began mandatory HIV testing of all inmates on entry to prison and voluntary testing thereafter—and 2005, HIV seroconversion occurred in 88 male inmates in Georgia state prisons. HIV transmission in prison was associated with men having sex with other men or receiving a tattoo.[4] In another study in a southeastern state, Christopher Krebs of RTI International documented that 33 of 5265 male prison inmates (0.63%) contracted HIV while in prison.[5] But Krebs points out that "when you have a large prison population, as our country does . . . you do start thinking about large numbers of people contracting HIV."

Studies of high-risk behavior in prisons yield widely varying frequency estimates: for example, estimates of the proportion of male inmates who have sex with other men range from 2 to 65%, and estimates of the proportion who are sexually assaulted range from 0 to 40%.[5] Such variations may reflect differences in research methods, inmate populations, and prison conditions that affect privacy and opportunity. Researchers emphasize that classifying prison sex as either consensual or forced is often overly simplistic: an inmate may provide sexual favors to another in

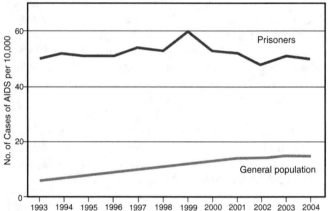

Rates of Confirmed AIDS Cases in the General Population and among State and Federal Prisoners, 1993–2004.

Data are from Maruschak.[2]

return for protection or for other reasons. Better information on sexual transmission of HIV in prisons may eventually become available as a result of the Prison Rape Elimination Act of 2003, which requires the Justice Department to collect statistics on prison rape and to provide funds for educating prison staff and inmates about the subject.

Theodore M. Hammett of the Domestic Health, Health Policy, and Clinical Research Division of Abt Associates, a Massachusetts-based policy research and consulting firm, acknowledged that for political reasons U.S. prisons are unlikely to accept needle-exchange programs, but he said adoption of other HIV-prevention measures is long overdue. "Condoms ought to be widely available in prisons," he said. "From a public health standpoint, I think there's little question that that should be done. Methadone, also—all kinds of drug [abuse] treatment should be much more widely available in correctional settings." Methadone maintenance programs for inmates have been established in a few jails and prisons, including those in New York City, Albuquerque, and San Juan, Puerto Rico. Brown University's Rich is currently conducting a randomized, controlled trial at the Rhode Island facility, sponsored by the National Institutes of Health, to determine whether starting methadone maintenance in heroin-addicted inmates a month before their release will lead to better health outcomes and reduced recidivism, as compared with providing either usual care or referral to community methadone programs at the time of release.

At the Rhode Island prison, the medical program focuses on identifying HIV-infected inmates, treating them, teaching them how to avoid transmitting the virus, addressing drug dependence, and when they're released, referring them to a program that arranges for HIV care and other assistance, including methadone maintenance treatment if needed. The prison offers routine HIV testing, and 90% of inmates accept it. One third of the state's HIV cases have been diagnosed at the prison. "These people are a target population and a captive one," noted Rich. "We should use this time" for health care and prevention. Nationally, 73% of state inmates and 77% of federal inmates surveyed in 2004 said they had been tested for HIV in prison. State policies vary, with 20 states reportedly testing all inmates and the rest offering tests for high-risk groups, at inmates' request, or in specific situations. Researchers said inmate acceptance rates also vary widely, depending on how the test is presented. Drugs for treating HIV-infected prisoners are not covered by federal programs, and prison budgets often contain inadequate funding for health services. "You can see how, in some cases, there could be a disincentive for really pushing testing," Hammett said.

Critics of U.S. penal policies contend that incarceration has exacerbated the HIV epidemic among blacks, who are disproportionately represented in the prison population, accounting for 40% of inmates. A new report by the National Minority AIDS Council calls for routine, voluntary HIV testing in prisons and on release, making condoms available, and expanding reentry programs that address HIV prevention, substance abuse, mental health, and housing needs as prisoners return to the community. "Any reservoir of infection that is as large as a prison would warrant, by simple public health logic, that we do our best . . . to reduce the risk of transmission" both inside and outside the walls, said Robert E. Fullilove of Columbia University's Mailman School of Public Health, who wrote the report. "The issue has never been, Do we understand what has to happen to reduce the risks? . . . It's always been, Do we have the political will necessary to put what we know is effective into operation?"

Notes

1. Dolan K, Rutter S, Wodak AD. Prison-based syringe exchange programmes: a review of international research and development. *Addiction* 2003;98:153–158.

2. Maruschak LM. HIV in prisons, 2004. Washington, DC: Bureau of Justice Statistics, November 2006.

3. Hammett TM, Harmon MP, Rhodes W. The burden of infectious disease among inmates of and releasees from US correctional facilities, 1997. *Am J Public Health* 2002;92: 1789–1794.

4. HIV transmission among male inmates in a state prison system—Georgia, 1992–2005. *MMWR Morb Mortal Wkly Rep* 2006;55:421–6.

5. Krebs CP. Inmate factors associated with HIV transmission in prison. *Criminology Public Policy* 2006;5:113–36.

DR. SUSAN OKIE MD is a contributing editor of the *Journal.*

Silent Treatment

HIV Plan B

JUSTINE SHARROCK

One winter night in 2000, Danny, who was 21 at the time, went home with a guy he met at a crowded bar in San Francisco. Random hookups weren't out of the ordinary for Danny, but this one ended badly: As he was buttoning up to go home, his new friend mentioned he was HIV positive. Usually conscientious about safe sex, Danny hadn't been, and he panicked. "I was in shock," he says. "I just couldn't believe it." He vaguely remembered reading about an emergency treatment that could prevent infection, so when he got home he called the California AIDS hotline. Memory served. A monthlong regimen known as post-exposure prophylaxis treatment (PEP)—usually given to health care workers who have been stuck with needles—was available at local clinics and emergency rooms to people who had recently been exposed to HIV. The side effects of debilitating nausea and fatigue were a small price to pay for its potential benefits: A study of health care workers published in the *New England Journal of Medicine* linked the rapid administration of the drag to an 81 percent decrease in the risk of contracting the virus.

Danny went to a city clinic, where after a consultation, he was given a prescription for two antiretroviral drugs—the same kind that HIV-positive patients have taken since the '80s. As preventative medicine, the drugs work with a one-two punch: The first intercepts the virus' initial attachment to DNA, and the second stops infected cells from spreading the virus.

Danny was lucky that California is one of the few states (along with New York, Massachusetts, New Mexico, and Rhode Island) where policies ensure that the general public—not just hospital workers who have been exposed on the job—can access the drugs. Elsewhere, the decision is up to individual hospitals, clinics, and doctors. Surveying all 50 state health departments and more than 50 ERs nationwide, I encountered STD clinicians and workers at AIDS hotlines and Planned Parenthoods who did not know PEP could be prescribed to the public. An Alabama health department official told me, "It's not available." A nurse at a North Dakota clinic said he all but encouraged patients to fly to San Francisco.

Since the virus must be intercepted before it attaches to cells and reaches the lymph nodes, it is crucial that PEP be administered immediately—each passing hour means decreased effectiveness.

"It needs to be treated like a gunshot wound or a stabbing," says Antonio Urbina, a medical director at St. Vincent Catholic Medical Center's HIV clinic in New York City. Yet of the largest hospitals in each state, only a quarter offer PEP in their emergency rooms. In a 2005–06 CDC survey taken at gay pride parades around the country, less than 20 percent of HIV-negative respondents knew about PEP. "When I tell people that I used it, they say they've never heard of it," says Danny. "You see signs about crystal meth or syphilis, but even in the gay publications, you never see ads for PEP."

PEP is FDA approved, commercially available, and even often covered by insurance (though for the uninsured the drugs run upward of $1,000). In 2005, the CDC recommended that PEP be administered to all patients on a case-by-case basis within 72 hours of a high-risk exposure, followed up by testing and counseling. But for reasons that are more political than scientific, there is no federal funding for the treatment. Some public health officials claim that public availability of PEP will encourage risky behavior—the same argument used against RU-486, abortions, and condom distribution. Robert Janssen, director of the Division of HIV/AIDS Prevention at the CDC, explains, "Biomedical interventions raise concerns that people would feel, 'Oh, I have these pills, they will keep me from getting it.'"

Yet 73 percent of non-hospital-worker PEP recipients in a San Francisco study decreased high-risk sex over the following year. And since PEP drugs are so toxic, most doctors would be careful about overprescribing. "I'm concerned with two things," says Urbina. "Is the person that exposed them either HIV positive or at high risk for HIV, and is there potential contact with infectious body fluid? If both are yes, in my equation, you give PEP." Peter Leone, medical director of North Carolina's HIV department, who hasn't received the necessary support to institute a public PEP program in his state, believes the benefits of PEP outweigh the risks. "Nationally, there is a 'Don't Ask, Don't Tell' policy," he says. "We're okay to say it's a good idea, as long as we don't know about it and don't do anything to support it. We don't deny care to smokers or people who didn't buckle their seat belts. It says a lot about the political climate around sexuality and homophobia." For the 40,000 people infected with HIV in the United States each year, the knowledge of a lost opportunity for prevention is devastating. In Britain, an HIV-positive couple has filed suit against the government for withholding lifesaving information.

Two months after he finished his treatment, Danny tested negative for HIV—whether because he hadn't contracted the virus from the encounter or because the PEP worked, he'll never know. Since a randomized clinical trial is unethical, researchers have to rely on observational and tangential research. "At least if you test positive after PEP, you'll know you did everything you could," says Danny. He keeps his medication label as a token of how a little bottle may have saved his life.

From *Mother Jones,* May/June 2008, pp. 15–18. Copyright © 2008 by Foundation for National Progress. Reprinted by permission.

HIV Apathy

New drugs have changed HIV from a terminal to a chronic illness. To counter complacency, health officials are pushing to make testing more widespread.

ZACH PATTON

On a rainy day last June, local officials in Washington, D.C., gathered under tents erected on a public plaza to be tested for HIV. The District of Columbia's health department was kicking off a sweeping new effort to encourage city residents to take action against the disease. With banners, music and mobile-testing units, officials hoped the launch event and the campaign would help raise local awareness about HIV—and help the city address its most pressing health concern.

Washington has the nation's highest rate of new AIDS cases, and the city's goal—HIV testing for every resident between the ages of 14 and 84, totaling over 400,000 people—was unprecedented in its scope. City officials said the campaign, which also included distributing an initial 80,000 HIV tests to doctors' offices, hospitals and health clinics, would enable them to get a better idea of how many residents are infected with HIV. And making such screenings routine, they hoped, would help erase the stigma against getting tested for the disease.

Six months later, though, the effort was faltering. Fewer than 20,000 people had been tested. Many of the HIV test kits expired before they were distributed, forcing the city to throw them away. Others were donated to the Maryland health department to use before they went bad. And the city still lacked a comprehensive plan for ensuring effective treatment for those residents who test positive for the disease.

It's not all bad news. The District nearly tripled the number of sites offering free HIV screenings, and the Department of Corrections began screening all inmates for HIV. And the city improved its disease-surveillance technique, recording information on behaviors and lifestyles, in addition to counting the number of new HIV cases.

But D.C.'s struggle to meet its goals underscores a challenge common to local health officials across the country. More than a million U.S. residents are infected with HIV, and one-quarter of them don't know it, experts estimate. Diagnosis rates of HIV have stabilized in recent years, but large cities continue to grapple with much higher rates. They're dealing with higher incidents of the risky behaviors—drug use and unprotected sex, particularly gay sex—that tend to spread the disease. But they're also trying to battle something less tangible: complacency. Antiretroviral drugs have largely changed HIV from a terminal

illness into a chronic one. And the fears associated with AIDS have faded over the past 20 years. As health officials work to combat HIV, they're finding that their hardest fight is the one against apathy.

Testing Laws

The first test for the human immunodeficiency virus was licensed by the FDA in March 1985. It was quickly put into use by blood banks, health departments and clinics across the country. But HIV testing at that time faced some major obstacles, which would continue to thwart HIV policies for much of the following two decades. For one, it usually took two weeks to obtain lab results, requiring multiple visits for patients waiting to see if they had HIV. Many patients—in some places, as many as half—never returned for the second visit. Another barrier was that, at the time, a diagnosis of the disease was a death sentence. With no reliable drugs to slow the progression of HIV into AIDS, and with an attendant stigma that could decimate a person's life, many people just didn't want to know if they were HIV-positive. "The impact of disclosure of someone's HIV-positive status could cost them their job, their apartment and their social circle," says Dr. Adam Karpati, assistant commissioner for HIV/AIDS Prevention & Control for the New York City health department. "In a basic calculus, the value to the patient was questionable. Knowing their status could only maybe help them, but it could definitely hurt them."

Because of that stigma and the seriousness of a positive diagnosis, many cities and states developed rigorous measures to ensure that testing was voluntary and confidential, and that it included a full discussion of the risks associated with the disease. That meant requiring written consent in order to perform tests, and mandatory pre- and post-test counseling. "A lot of the laws were, appropriately, concerned with confidentiality and protecting people's rights," Karpati says.

Two major developments have since changed the method—and the purpose—of HIV testing. First, the development of antiretroviral drugs in the mid-1990s has lessened the impact of HIV as a fatal disease. And in the past two or three years, advancements in testing technology have effectively eliminated the wait time for receiving results. Rapid tests using a finger-prick or an oral swab can be completed in 20 minutes, meaning nearly everyone can receive results within a single visit.

Those changes, along with aggressive counseling and education about risk-prevention measures, helped stabilize the rate of HIV diagnosis. After peaking in 1992, rates of AIDS cases leveled off by 1998. Today, about 40,000 AIDS cases are diagnosed every year. Data on non-AIDS HIV infection rates are much harder to come by, but they seem to have stabilized as well.

The problem, however, remains especially acute in urban areas. While health experts take pains to stress that HIV/AIDS is no longer just a "big city" problem, the fact is that 85 percent of the nation's HIV infections have been in metropolitan areas with more than half a million people. "Urban areas have always been the most heavily impacted by the HIV epidemic, and they continue to be," says Jennifer Ruth of the Centers for Disease Control and Prevention. Intravenous drug use, risky sexual behavior and homosexual sex all contribute to higher HIV rates, and they are all more prevalent in urban areas. But cities face other complicating factors as well, including high poverty rates and residents with a lack of access to medical care, which exacerbate the challenges of HIV care.

Prevention Fatigue

Nowhere is that more evident than in Washington, D.C., where an estimated one in every 20 residents is HIV-positive. That's 10 times the national average. But that figure is only a rough guess. The truth is that health officials don't even know what the city's HIV rate is. Last year's campaign was supposed to change that. By setting a goal to test nearly all city residents, District health officials hoped to make HIV screening a routine part of medical care. In the process, the health department hoped it could finally get a handle on just how bad the crisis was. "We've had problems in the past, I'll be the first to say," says D.C. health department director Dr. Gregg A. Pane. "But we have galvanized interest and action, and we've highlighted the problem in a way it hasn't been before."

The effort stumbled, though. The Appleseed Center for Law and Justice, a local public advocacy group, has issued periodic report cards grading the District's progress on HIV. The most recent assessment, published six months into last year's testing push, found mismanagement and a lack of coordination with the medical community. The District was testing substantially more people than it had been, but the number was still falling far short of officials' goal. "D.C. took a great step forward, but it takes more than just a report announcing it," says Walter Smith, executive director for the Appleseed Center. "You have to make sure there's a plan."

What D.C. did achieve, however, was a fundamental shift in the way health officials perceive the HIV epidemic. "This is a disease that affects everyone," says Pane. "It's our No. 1 public health threat, and treating it like a public health threat is the exact right thing to do."

That paradigm change has been happening in health departments across the country. Last year, the CDC made waves when it announced new recommendations for treating HIV as an issue of public health. That means testing as many people as possible, making HIV testing a routine part of medical care, and removing the barriers to getting tested. Washington was the first city to adopt the CDC's recommendations for comprehensive testing, but other cities have also moved to make testing more routine. San Francisco health officials dropped their written-consent and mandatory-counseling requirements for those about to be tested. New York City has been moving in a similar direction, although removing the written-consent rule there will require changing state law. Many health officials think that since testing has become so easy and social attitudes about the disease have shifted, the strict testing regulations adopted in the 1980s are now cumbersome. The protections have become barriers.

Officials also are moving away from "risk-assessment testing," in which doctors first try to identify whether a patient falls into a predetermined high-risk category. "What has evolved is that, with an epidemic, risk-based testing is not sufficient," says New York City's Karpati. "Now there's a general move toward comprehensive testing." Privacy advocates and many AIDS activists oppose the shift away from individual protections. Yes, the stigma isn't what it used to be, they say, but it still exists. HIV isn't like tuberculosis or the measles, so they believe health officials shouldn't treat it like it is.

But even if officials could strike the perfect balance between public health and private protection, there's another factor that everyone agrees is thwarting cities' efforts to combat HIV. Call it burnout or complacency or "prevention fatigue." In an age when testing consists of an oral swab and a 20-minute wait, and an HIV-positive diagnosis means taking a few pills a day, health officials are battling a growing sense of apathy toward the disease. "The very successes we've made in the past 20 years have hurt us, in a sense," Karpati says. "We don't have hospital wards full of HIV patients. We don't have people dying as much. There's a whole new generation of folks growing up who don't remember the fear of the crisis in the 1980s."

That casual attitude toward the disease can lead to riskier behavior and, in turn, more infections. With HIV and AIDS disproportionately affecting low-income residents, any increase in infections places an additional burden on governments. And while prescription drugs have made the disease more manageable, the fact is that 40 percent of the new HIV diagnoses in the nation are still made within a year of the infection's progressing to AIDS—which is usually too late for medicine to do much good. As cities try to fight HIV complacency through refined testing policies and a focus on comprehensive testing, residents will have increasingly widespread access to tests for the disease. But for health officials, the greatest challenge will be getting the right people to care.

ZACH PATTON can be reached at zpatton@governing.com

UNIT 7

Sexualities and Social Issues

Unit Selections

Key Points to Consider

- What is your view on abortion? Would you be willing to have an abortion (or offer support to someone who chooses to have an abortion)?

- Would you be willing to use Plan B to avoid a possible pregnancy?

- Does your college or university have a rape awareness/prevention program?

- At your college or university, do you know how a report of an assault is supposed to be handled? How do you think these issues should be handled on college and university campuses?

- What do you recommend as safeguards against misunderstanding, confusion, and sexual assault?

- What are your criteria for consent when two (or more) people have a sexual encounter? What age must the partners be? Why this age?

- How do you think you would react to finding out that your partner is logging on to "adult" websites?

- How do you think you would react if your partner asked you to watch explicit "adult" videos together?

- How would you react if you found out your 8 year old was accessing pornographic websites? Imagine the same scenario with the ages being 10, 12, 14, and 16. What do you think your reaction would be at these different ages?

- Should prostitution be legal? If yes, under what circumstances?

Student Web Site

www.mhcls.com

Internet References

Planned Parenthood
   http://www.plannedparenthood.org
Rape, Abuse and Incest National Network (RAINN)
   http://www.rainn.org/
The Child Rights Information Network (CRIN)
   http://www.crin.org
Child Exploitation and Obscenity Section (CEOS)/U.S. Department of Justice
   http://www.usdoj.gov/criminal/ceos/trafficking.html

This final unit deals with several topics that are of interest for different reasons. These topics have a common denominator—they have all taken positions of prominence in the public's awareness. Some of the topics explored in this unit are much less controversial than others. Yet even with the least controversial among them, there are debates and significant disagreement in how we, as a society, should deal with these issues. Controversies abound around almost anything to do with topics such as sex, sexuality, sex education, contraception, and abortion. Indeed, sex in one way or another has very much been at the heart of the "culture wars" in the United States.

Clearly, many people are having sex. This regularly leads to unplanned pregnancies. In our age of supposed sexual enlightenment, some individuals, possibly in the heat of the moment, fail to understand the likelihood of pregnancy with unprotected intercourse. Even with our astounding medical technologies,

there is no 100 percent effective, safe, or aesthetically acceptable method of birth control. Before sex can become safe as well as enjoyable, people must receive thorough and accurate information regarding conception and contraception, birth, and birth control. However, we have learned that information about, or even access to, birth control is not enough. We still have some distance to go to make every child one who is planned and wanted.

Despite the relative simplicity of the above assertion, abortion and birth control remain emotionally charged issues in American society. While opinion surveys indicate that most of the public supports family planning and abortion, at least in some circumstances, there are certain individuals and groups strongly opposed to some forms of birth control and abortion. Voices for and against birth control and abortion—traditional and newer methods—remain passionate, and face-offs range from academic debates and legislative hearings to work stoppages by pharmacist, and protests with or without violence. The Supreme Court's, the legislative's, and the medical community's efforts are at times at odds; some seek to restrict the right or access to abortion or the availability of birth control methods, while others seek to mandate freer access to contraceptive and reproductive choice options. Voices on both sides are raised in emotionally and politically charged debate between "we must never go back to the old days" (of illegal and unsafe back-alley abortions) and "the baby has no choice." Abortion remains a fiercely debated topic. Because of that, legislative efforts for and against it abound. This is likely to continue for a very long time to come.

This unit explores other emotionally charged and difficult topics as well. We know that sexual abuse and violence permeate our society. For centuries, a strong code of silence surrounded sexual abuse and violence. Many now agree that the silence has increased not only the likelihood of sexual abuse and violence, but the harm to the victims of these acts.

Beginning in the middle of the twentieth century, two societal movements helped to begin eroding this code of silence. The child welfare/child rights movement exposed child abuse and mistreatment. This movement sought to improve the lives of children and families. Soon after, and to a large extent fueled by the emerging women's movement, primarily "grass-roots" organizations that became known as "rape crisis" groups or centers became catalysts for altering the way we looked at (or avoided looking at) rape and sexual abuse.

Research today suggests that these movements have accomplished many of their initial goals and brought about significant social change. The existence and prevalence of rape and other sexual abuse is much more accurately known today than ever before. Many of the myths previously believed (rapists are strangers that jump out of bushes, sexual abuse only occurs in poor families, all rapists are male and all victims are female, and so on) have been replaced with more accurate information. The code of silence has been recognized for the harm it can cause, and millions of friends, parents, teachers, counselors, and others have learned how to be approachable, supportive listeners to victims disclosing their abuse experiences. Also, we

have come to recognize the role that power, especially unequal power, plays in rape, sexual abuse, sexual violence, and sexual harassment. However, as current events have shown, the battle is far from over, and sexual abuse continues to have serious devastating consequences for victims, and those who love them, as well as society as a whole.

As we, as a society, have sought to expose and reduce abusive sex, it has become increasingly clear that all of society and each of us as individuals and potential partners must grapple with the broader issue of what constitutes consent. What is non-abusive sexual interaction? How can people communicate interest, arousal, desire, and/or propose sexual interaction, when remnants of unequal power, ignorance, misinformation, fear, adversarial sex roles, and inadequate communication skills still exist?

Finally, another layer of perplexing questions that confront the proactive/reactive dilemma: What is, or should be, the role of employers, school personnel, or simply any of us who may be seen as contributing on some level due to lack of awareness or complicity to an environment that allows uncomfortable, abusive, or inappropriate sexual interactions? Conversely, is it possible that we could become so "sensitive" to the potential for abuse that combined with our discomfort, anger, and fear we could become hysterical vigilantes pushing an eager legal system to indict "offenders" who have not committed abuse or harassment? These are just some of the many issues that you may grapple with as you process the information included in this unit.

As we have seen throughout this book, human sexuality is biology, behavior, society, culture and much, much more. Our sexual beliefs, behaviors, choices, even feelings and comfort levels are profoundly affected by what our culture prescribes and proscribes, which has been transmitted to us by the full range of social institutions with which we interact. We are biological organisms living in many complex social worlds. We each have a long road ahead of us as we try to understand human sexualities. This book has been part of your journey for sexual knowledge. It is important to continue on that journey, always asking questions, and seeking answers and accurate knowledge. This is a journey that will truly take a lifetime.

Flower Grandma's Secret

Physician Susan Wicklund had never told her grandmother about her medical specialty: reproductive health and abortion. She finally decided to divulge the truth just before appearing on a national television program that would reveal the constant harassment and danger she faced from anti-abortion fanatics. Before Wicklund could say much, Grandma offered her own heartbreaking disclosure. Here, from Wicklund's new memoir.

SUSAN WICKLUND

When I drove into Grandma's driveway all I could think about was how she would react. I had started out to tell her many times over the last years. On so many visits I had meant to have that conversation, but had never found a way. Something had always intervened. Some other errand had always come up. I had found a way not to face her judgment.

It didn't matter that I was rock solid in my resolve and in my chosen profession. This was my grandma. My Flower Grandma. What she thought of me mattered a lot, and I had no idea how she'd take it.

It was February of 1992, a Saturday afternoon. The next day the *60 Minutes* segment I'd done with Leslie Stahl would air. Grandma never missed *60 Minutes*. I had to tell her before she saw it—before she saw her oldest granddaughter talking about the death threats and stalking and personal harassment my family and I were enduring.

The harassment wasn't the issue that mattered now. It was the fact that I was, as a physician, traveling to five clinics in three states to provide abortion services for as many as one hundred women every week, and that I had been doing this work for four years already.

I wasn't at all ashamed of my career. In fact, I always considered it an honor to be involved in reproductive choices, this most personal and intimate realm for women. I just never felt the need to make it public. Very few of my family and friends were aware of what I did.

Within a day, however, everyone I had grown up with, everyone who knew my family, and every member of my family would know the truth. Would I be isolated and ostracized? Would I get support or condemnation?

I pulled off the highway and into the drive leading to the house I'd grown up in. Mom and Dad still lived in the white, two-story wood-frame home.

Dad had worked as a precision machinist in the town of Grantsburg, 10 miles away. His love had been the gunsmithing, hunting and fishing he did in his free time. My three siblings and I had always been included. We were as competent with firearms, field dressing a deer or catching a batch of sunfish as anyone in the area. Dad was retired now and not feeling well. It was painful to watch him, the strong man who starred in my memories, struggling with simple tasks.

Mom was retired too, from her elected position as Clerk of Court for our county. She was the one everyone—especially women—turned to for advice and support. Mom had been instrumental, many years earlier, in starting a shelter for victims of domestic abuse. In her job she had seen so many situations where women and children had nowhere to go for help. It was just like Mom to tackle a need that everyone else ignored.

I grew up in the unincorporated village of Trade Lake, Wis., a small gathering of about six houses, several of which were the homes of my relatives. The only business left was one small gas station/grocery store. When I was a kid there had been a feed store and creamery and a meat market, but those had been gone for better than 30 years. Only rotten shells of buildings remained.

Even now, Trade Lake is a very rural place. People still raise chickens in backyards, drive tractors to the little grocery store. Chimneys puff wood smoke in the winter.

The small river that wound its way through our yard came into view. Behind it, the woods where I'd built forts and climbed oak trees with my sister. She and I each had a horse and spent the bulk of our summers out of doors. Grandma and Grandpa had lived just down the road. We picked mayflowers every spring with Grandma. In the summer we fished with Grandpa for sunfish and crappies with cane poles baited with worms dug out of the garden.

Mine had been a good childhood. This was a safe place. Turning in the driveway had always been a good thing—a coming home. This time was different.

I felt myself sweating under my coat. My racing heart pushed against my throat. I had to reveal something to my dear grandma that could change everything she believed and loved about me.

Grandma had moved into a trailer house in the backyard of the family home. Grandpa died 15 years earlier and Mom wanted her mother even closer—just steps across the yard. I saw the clothesline filled with rugs, the twine still strung up on the porch to hold the morning glories that filled the railings in the summer.

Flower Grandma. My daughter, Sonja, gave her the name when she was 3 and there were too many grandmas to keep track of. Sonja spent many days baking cookies with her great-grandmother and playing outside, just as I had as a young girl. She ran back and forth constantly between the houses of her two grandmothers. This grandma always had flowers growing in every nook and cranny, inside and out.

Flower Grandma she became, and Flower Grandma she stayed. Before long my entire extended family called her Flower Grandma, and even her friends at the local senior center fell into the habit.

I coasted to a stop at the bottom of the slope. I sat there long enough to take a deep breath and fight back a few unexpected tears. I didn't know where the sadness came from. The car engine ticked. I was alone, vulnerable, aching. Was I longing for those simple childhood days, whipping down the hill on my sled? How far I'd come from that.

I peeled myself out of the car, shed my coat and left it on the seat. It was unusually warm for February in Wisconsin. The hardwood forest was all bare sticks and hard lines. I knew it would soon be time to tap the maple trees and cook the wonderful syrup we all loved on Grandma's Swedish pancakes.

I turned and deliberately moved up the steps to the trailer house. I was terrified of what Grandma would say, but there was no avoiding this moment.

The big door was already open by the time I got to the top step. Out peeked her welcoming smile. She was giggling.

"Hi, Grandma!"

"Oh my goodness! What a surprise! What a sweet, sweet surprise! Did I know you were coming today?"

I hugged her in the doorway, held her tight, stepped inside.

"Did you somehow know I was making ginger snaps?" she teased as she set a plate full on the kitchen table. She poured me a glass of milk and I sat down on the wooden chair next to hers. I tried to bury myself in the smell of her place, a mixture of ginger cookies, Estée Lauder perfume (the one in the blue, hourglass bottle always on her dresser), and home permanents. She and Mom always gave each other perms, trying to get just the right curl in their hair. The smell never left the place.

I think she sensed that I had come to talk about something important. I started talking a few times about other, inconsequential things, then, finally, I plunged in.

"Grandma, you know I work as a doctor."

"Of course. And we are all so proud of you."

"Yes, but I don't think you know the whole story. I'm a doctor who works mostly for women, helping women with pregnancy problems."

Flower Grandma hesitated just a second, pushed back her chair, stood and held out her hand for me to follow. She went to sit in her rocker, the same one sitting in my living room today. The rocker I have sat in so many hours since. The rocker I sit in right now, writing this down and trembling as I do.

She seemed distant. I moved to the old leather hassock beside her. She took my hand and placed it on top of one of hers, then covered it with her other one. Our hands made a stack on the arm of the rocker—old skin, young skin. We sat in silence a minute. She turned to look directly at me. Her eyes, framed by gentle wrinkles, were full of some deep trouble.

After a moment, she stared straight ahead and started to speak. Slowly. Deliberately. In a very quiet voice. At the same time she began stroking my hand. It was as if the gentle stroking was pushing her to talk.

"When I was 16 years old my best friend got pregnant," she said. A chill went through me.

"I always believed it was her father that was using her," she went on, "but I never knew for sure. She came to my sister, Violet, and me, and asked us to help her."

While I listened, my thoughts whirled through my head. Stories I had read of women self-aborting and dying of infections when a safe, legal option was not available. The many women who came to the clinics where I worked, many of whom still had to overcome huge difficulties to end an unwanted pregnancy.

It isn't uncommon to have patients confide in me that prior to coming in for an abortion, they had used combinations of herbs to try to force a miscarriage. These home remedies can be extremely dangerous and have caused the deaths of many women.

I felt myself tighten and withdraw, anticipating what Flower Grandma was going to tell me. I wanted to see her eyes, but she kept them straight ahead. And she kept stroking my hand. So soft. I only wanted to think about those hands. Hands embracing and caressing mine—strong, gentle, soft.

"The three of us were so naive. We knew very little about these things, but we had heard that if you put something long and sharp 'up there,' in the private place, sometimes it would end the pregnancy."

In spite of myself I conjured the modest room: a dresser in the corner with a kerosene lamp and maybe a hairbrush or hand mirror beside it. I saw three young, scared girls, still children, acting on old wives' tales and whispered instructions.

My stomach turned. Was this my Grandma? Was I really here in her trailer house hearing this? I could barely breathe. She kept talking, all the while stroking the top of my hand, her eyes looking off into space, traveling back in time. Occasionally a pat-pat with her hand would break the rhythm of the stroking. Such old skin, full of brown age spots and paper thin. Stroking my hand in perfect measure with her words.

Please just stop, Grandma. Don't tell me anymore. Just hold my hand and let's talk about what you'll plant in the spring. Tell me about the oatmeal bread you baked yesterday. Are there many birds coming to the birdfeeder? I was flushed all over. And still she stroked while she talked. Pat-pat, stroke.

"We closed ourselves, the three of us, in one of the bedrooms late one morning. We didn't talk much, and she didn't ever cry out in pain. It took a few tries to make the blood come. None of us spoke. We didn't know what to expect next, or what to do when the blood kept coming. It was all over the sheets. All over us. So bright red. It was awful. It just wouldn't stop."

She was still stroking my hand. I was shaking uncontrollably. I stared at the African violets under the plant light, trying to make them the focus of my attention. Her voice was a monotone, never a pause.

"We put rags inside of her to try to stop the bleeding, but they soaked full. We all three stayed in her bed. We just didn't know what to do."

My hand was trembling so hard it was all I could do to keep it on top of hers. She grasped it briefly, held it tight, patted it a few times and then went on.

"We stayed there together, unable to move, even after she was dead. Her father found us, all three of us, in the bed. He stood in the doorway, staring. No words for a long time. When he did speak, he told my sister and me to leave and that we were never, ever to speak of this. We were not to tell anyone, ever. Ever."

She stopped stroking my hand and sat still before turning to look directly at me. "That was 72 years ago. You are the first person I have ever told that story. I am still so ashamed of what happened. We were just so young and scared. We didn't know anything."

Terrible sadness welled up inside me. And anger. I couldn't picture my Grandma as someone responsible for the death of anything, much less her best friend at the age of 16. She had carried this secret all her life, kept it inside, festering with guilt and shame.

I wondered if the pregnancy was indeed the result of incest. Would it have made a difference? What were friends and family told about the death? What had they actually used to start the bleeding? What had the doctor put on the death certificate as the cause of death?

I knew, through the patients I had met, that no one has to look very far into their family history to find these stories tucked away, hidden from view. But it didn't lessen the shock of finding it here, so close, in the heart of my own family.

Flower Grandma sighed and held my hand tight. Tears welled in her eyes.

"I know exactly what kind of work you do, and it is a good thing. People like you do it safely so that people like me don't murder their best friends. I told you how proud I am of what you do, and I meant it."

Susan Wicklund has worked in the field of women's reproductive health for more than 20 years. For much of that time she has been on the front lines of the abortion war, both as a doctor and as a spokesperson for women's rights.

You Can't Do That on Television

Why abortion doesn't show up on the small screen anymore.

RACHEL FUDGE

On any given evening, you can turn on the TV and surf past images that just a few decades ago were considered too shocking for national broadcast: interracial couples, visibly pregnant women, actual autopsies. You might even catch a comic skit that openly mocks Jesus and God. But there's one thing you're almost guaranteed not to see on television: abortion, despite many of the old you-can't-do-that-on-television taboos have fallen away, abortion, despite being one of the most common medical procedures in the United States, is the one hot-button issue that simply remains too hot for TV.

Robert Thompson, director of the Center for the Study of Popular Culture and Television at Syracuse University, says the portrayal of abortion on TV is "conspicuous by its absence," while in a recent *New York Times* article writer Kate Arthur calls it an "aberration." Although *Roe v. Wade* established a woman's right to choose in 1973, the discourse around abortion and reproductive rights has actually narrowed over the past 30 years, to the point where it has become more difficult to introduce the issue of abortion on a television show than it once was.

The best-known and most widely viewed pop-culture abortion took place in 1972 on *Maude,* a sitcom starring Bea Arthur as a liberal feminist. When 47-year-old Maude, who was married and had a grown daughter, unexpectedly became pregnant, she opted for an abortion, which was legal in New York state at the time. (In a sign of just how different the times were, *Maude's* producers cooked up the abortion storyline in response to a challenge from the group Zero Population Growth—now called Popular Connection—which was sponsoring a $10,000 prize for sitcoms that tackled the issue of population control.)

In the wake of the *Roe* decision, as the basic tenets of second-wave feminism seeped into the American mainstream, serious adult-oriented dramas like *Hill Street Blues* and *St. Elsewhere* featured abortions every season or so, as did the occasional soap opera. (Shortly after *Roe,* Susan Lucci's *All My Children* character had soap opera's first legal abortion, with none of the health or psychosocial aftereffects-sterility, insanity, murder-that would come to, characterize soap abortions in the future.) In the real world, the annual number of abortions steadily increased until 1985, when they leveled off. In the late 1980s and early 1990s, in the face of a growing number of legal challenges to *Roe,* a smattering of storylines revisited the specter of illegal abortions, as if to remind us of what was at stake. On the Vietnam War drama *China Beach,* a young nurse named Holly had an illegal abortion; the show's moral center, leading character Colleen McMurphy, was a staunch Catholic who disapproved of Holly's actions. The popular show *thirtysomething* addressed the issue more obliquely, often using flashbacks to provide distance from the controversial event.

13 percent of unwanted pregnancies end in miscarriage, but on television that number is much, much higher.

With the rise of the prime-time teen soap *(Beverly Hills 90210, Party of Five, Dawson's Creek)* in the mid1990s, it was inevitable that sexually active teen and young adult characters would be confronted with pregnancy, often in the guise of the Very Special Episode. Enter the convenient miscarriage. In the real world, according to the Alan Guttmacher Institute, a nonprofit organization that studies sexual and reproductive health issues, some 13 percent of unwanted pregnancies end in miscarriage, but on television that number is much, much higher. The convenient miscarriage goes something like this: Sympathetic lead character gets knocked up. Agonizing over what to do, SLC sometimes goes so far as to visit an abortion clinic. SLC decides that although she believes in a woman's right to choose, she's going to keep her baby. Moral dilemma resolved, SLC spontaneously miscarries. SLC is sad but realizes that in the end she wasn't really ready to be a mother anyway. Alternatively, the pregnancy turns out to be a false alarm, an even tidier wrap-up to the dilemma. The convenient "miscarriage and the false alarm remain the most popular strategies for dodging abortion since they allow television producers to congratulate themselves for tackling the tough topics without actually having to take a stand.

Recently, however, a handful of shows have approached the issue head-on, even allowing characters to go through with the abortion. HBO's *Six Feet Under* depicted teenage lead Claire matter-of-factly getting an abortion, without endless agonizing or moral anguish. And last year, a two part episode of the made-in-Canada teen soap *Degrassi: The Next Generation* made headlines when 14-year-old lead character Manny got pregnant, had an abortion (saying, "I'm just trying to do the right thing here. For me. For everyone, I guess"), and didn't express any regret afterward. Alas, U.S. viewers didn't get to see the show: The Viacom-owned cable channel N, which airs *Degrassi* in the United States, refused to show it.

While Maude's abortion was truly ground breaking, it inadvertently galvanized the anti-choice movement. When CBS reran the episode six months later, some 40 affiliates refused to air it, and national advertisers shied away from buying ad time, establishing a pattern that remains in effect today. Even more significantly, after the episode first aired, anti-abortion leaders took their case to the Federal Communications Commission, arguing that the fairness doctrine—which mandated equal time for opposing views—ought to cover not just editorials and public affairs but entertainment programming too. Because Maude had an abortion on CBS, they argued, they should have the right to reply on CBS. They lost the case but won the attention of the networks. In 1987 the fairness doctrine itself was struck down, but by that point it didn't matter: The networks had established a pattern of covering their asses by presenting some semblance of balance as a way of diffusing potentially volatile subjects.

In the landmark episode, Maude agonized over the decision, but her daughter reassured her, speaking in the language of the growing feminist movement: "When you were young, *abortion* was a dirty word. It's not anymore." But more than 30 years later, as many of the tenets of the women's liberation movement have become accepted parts of mainstream American culture, *abortion* is a messy, if not exactly dirty, word. Back in 1992, when the sitcom *Murphy Brown* was hailed for its overt feminism and its main character found herself unmarried and unexpectedly pregnant, the *a-word* was never uttered. Diane English, the show's producer, said in a June 1992 *Houston Chronicle* article, "She would have used the word many times, but I wanted a lot of people to watch, and certain words have become inflammatory and get in the way of people hearing what we wanted her to say." In the end, Brown had the baby, igniting the ire of Vice President Dan Quayle (who viewed the character's decision

not to wed as an assault on American values) and disappointing many feminists.

During the battle for abortion rights that culminated in the *Roe* ruling, public declarations were an integral tactic of the movement. In an effort to overcome the shame and silence surrounding abortion, women organized public speakouts, at which they talked openly about their illegal abortions. Abortion is a fact of life, they asserted, and it affects women of all colors, classes, and religious and political beliefs. Over the years, as the anti-abortion movement has grown stronger and more organized, the pro-choice movement has struggled to regain this clarity of speech. Young women who were born after *Roe* assert that abortion is a private decision, a private choice that needn't be broadcast—true, but also extremely naive politically.

Veteran TV producer English acknowledged this back in February 2001, when she said to *The New York Times:* "Maybe women . . . only had to think about their Manolo Blahniks for the past eight years under the Clinton administration. If women start to wonder if they will lose the right to have an abortion, perhaps that attitude may change during the next four years."

While poll after poll indicates that a majority of Americans support upholding *Roe v. Wade,* it's also clear that a majority of Americans have deep concerns and moral conflicts about abortion. This ambivalence is reflected in the pro-choice movement, too, as nationally recognized feminist leaders speak of the need to recognize the agony and shame that accompany abortion. Given this roiling mass of conflicting feelings and politics, it's no wonder that a one-hour drama can't get a handle on the issue. As Syracuse University's Thompson points out, "A lot of people strongly feel that there's too much sex on TV, but they will have no trouble watching an episode of *Blind Date* or *Desperate Housewives* in their own home. With abortion, those feelings aren't so easily eliminated in one's TV viewing. No [networks] want to run the risk of powerfully offending people on either side [of the issue]."

As a result, what we see on television isn't likely to satisfy anyone, no matter where they stand. Producers strive for a form of balance by always ensuring that there's a dissenting voice of some sort—friend, relative, or authority figure who ardently asserts the anti-abortion point of view. To pro-choice folks, TV's take on abortion seems unnecessarily harsh, moralizing, and punitive. Rarely, they say, do you see a character undertake an abortion the way many women actually do: with utter confidence that they're doing the right thing in a difficult situation. For now, it's unlikely that TV viewers will ever see one of the desperate housewives unapologetically opting for a second-trimester abortion when she realizes her fetus has profound genetic anomalies, or one of the lissome gals on *The O.C.* sporting one of Planned Parenthood's "I had an abortion" baby tees, proclaiming that ending her pregnancy was the best decision she ever made.

The trashy, ephemeral landscape of pop culture may seem like an unimportant front in the battle for women's rights. But as the 2004 election has shown, the United States is in the midst of an all-out culture war in which public language and pop images are playing a crucial role in shaping the terms of the debate. Thus, the reproductive-rights movement, like the rest of the progressive movement, needs to find new ways to present its case openly and frankly. After all, of the 6 million U.S. pregnancies each year, half are unintended, and some 47 percent of those unintended pregnancies result in abortion. And as history has shown, not talking about it won't make it go away.

Sex, Politics, and Morality at the FDA: Reflections on the Plan B Decision

Frank Davidoff

On September 3, 2005, I resigned my consultant position with the Food and Drug Administration. I did this to protest the agency's August 26, 2005, decision to delay a final ruling on over-the-counter availability of Plan B, the emergency contraceptive, and I wasn't alone: Susan Wood, the FDA's assistant commissioner for women's health and director of the agency's Office of Women's Health, also resigned at about the same time. What in the world has been going on at the FDA?

Plan B consists of two relatively large doses of a single ingredient, levonorgestrol, a constituent of many birth control pills. Taken twelve hours apart within seventy-two hours after unprotected intercourse, the drug is about 75 percent effective in preventing pregnancy. Importantly for the question of over-the-counter availability, the drug's contraceptive efficacy decreases dramatically during this seventy-two hour window.

Plan B has been available by prescription since 1999. In April 2003, Women's Capital Corporation, which produces Plan B, filed an application with the FDA for approval of over-the-counter marketing of the drug. (Women's Capital Corporation later transferred ownership of the drug to Barr Laboratories.) As it often does in considering such applications, the agency then convened a joint meeting of its Nonprescription Drug and Reproductive Health Drug Advisory Committees (NDAC and RHDAC, respectively) in December 2003 to obtain independent expert opinion on the application. The briefing materials for the meeting were more extensive than usual; they weighed eighteen pounds.

During two days of intensive hearings and discussion, the committees carefully examined the pros and cons of over-the-counter availability; they also heard comments from several dozen members of the public, nearly all in support of approval. In the course of their deliberations, the committees voted twenty-eight to zero that the drug was safe (one member of NDAC commented that the single ingredient of Plan B, levonorgestrol, is the safest drug the committee had yet considered); they voted twenty-seven to one that consumers could properly use Plan B as recommended on the proposed labeling (as judged from the "actual use study" that was part of

the sponsor's application); they voted twenty-eight to zero that women were unlikely to use Plan B as a regular form of contraception; and they voted twenty-seven to one that the actual use study data were generalizable to the overall population of over-the-counter users, including adolescents. At the end of the day, they voted twenty-three to four in favor of approval for over-the-counter availability (I was one of the twenty-three).

In sum, the committees agreed that Plan B met all of the FDA's criteria for over-the-counter availability: 1) an acceptable safety profile based on prescription use and experience; 2) a low potential for abuse; 3) an appropriate safety and therapeutic "index" (the ratio between the toxic and the therapeutic dose); 4) a positive benefit-risk assessment; and 5) demonstrable need for treatment of a condition or illness that is self-recognizable, self-limiting, and requires minimal intervention by a health care practitioner.

While all of that is true, the committees spent most of their time during the hearings considering several complex social, behavioral, and ethical issues—both benefits and side effects or "toxicities"—associated with over-the-counter availability of emergency contraception. FDA advisory committees do occasionally take up issues of that kind; in other meetings, for example, the NDAC struggled at length with the problem that acetaminophen, the active ingredient in Tylenol, is often used for suicidal overdose. But many of the issues raised in connection with the proposed over-the-counter switch of Plan B differed, both quantitatively and qualitatively, from the usual biological and clinical concerns raised by other over-the-counter switches. To start with, the proposed benefits for the switch of Plan B—and the primary explicit rationale for the over-the-counter switch application—were as much social, behavioral, and ethical as they were clinical. They included the likelihood that over-the-counter availability would prevent a large number of unwanted pregnancies and, consequently, a substantial proportion of elective abortions; that it would be of particular importance on weekends, since much unprotected intercourse probably takes place on Friday and Saturday nights, when it is particularly difficult to find a doctor to write a prescription; and that it would cut down on inappropriate, and dauntingly expensive, emergency room visits as a source of prescriptions on short notice for the many women who have no established relationship with a doctor.

But the list of potential social, behavioral, and ethical side effects and toxicities of Plan B's over-the-counter availability was also substantial. First, some members of the RHDAC suggested that requiring a prescription for emergency contraception forces women to see doctors, who can then provide medical evaluations plus education and counseling on contraception. These members argued that over-the-counter availability of Plan B would deprive women of that presumed benefit. Second, because the mechanism by which the drug prevents pregnancy isn't definitely known, some on the committees argued that levonorgestrol could, at least at times, prevent implantation of a fertilized ovum, which some view as a form of abortion, hence unacceptable. Third, easy availability of Plan B could have the social side effect of increased promiscuity, since impulsive sexual encounters might be seen as not having the consequence of an unplanned pregnancy. A related, secondary effect might be an increase in sexually transmitted disease. Fourth, over-the-counter availability might discourage the use of other means of regular contraception. Finally, and importantly, some committee members were concerned about the possibility that the social and behavioral side effects and toxicities associated with over-the-counter availability might be greater in women aged sixteen and younger because women in that age group may be less capable of understanding and following instructions and making appropriate judgments.

During the discussion the committees dealt with each of these issues in considerable depth. As is evident from the votes, the overwhelming majority of committee members appeared to be convinced, largely by the rather extensive published evidence and by the special studies submitted by the sponsor, that the overall benefits of over-the-counter availability of emergency contraception far outweighed its potential risks and harms, whether social, behavioral, or clinical.

The increased control that easier availability would give women over their reproductive lives appeared to most committee members to outweigh concerns about women bypassing doctor visits. After all, women generally consult doctors for contraceptive advice when their sexual activity is to some degree planned. But not all sexual activity is planned, so many women who have had no reason to seek out contraception from a doctor are inevitably exposed to the risk of unplanned and unwanted pregnancy.

As is evident from the twenty-three to four vote, the majority of committee members appeared convinced that the benefits of over-the-counter emergency contraceptive availability far outweighed its potential risks and harms, whether social, behavioral, or clinical.

The available evidence on mechanism of action, limited as it is, strongly indicates that levonorgestrol is a contraceptive, rather than an abortifacient; that is, it appears to prevent fertilization rather than preventing implantation of the fertilized ovum. Among other evidence, the drug is known to be ineffective once pregnancy is established; moreover, as one member of the RHDAC pointed out, this is the same drug that is given to preserve pregnancies in women with spontaneous "threatened abortion."

A variety of clinical studies, some in the United States and others in countries where contraception is available without prescription (there are many), indicate that promiscuity or sexually transmitted diseases do not increase when emergency contraception is available over the counter, nor does use of conventional, preventive contraception decrease. In addition, Plan B frequently produces nausea and vomiting, and repeated use leads to menstrual irregularity, so it is unlikely that women will depend exclusively on it for contraception. Finally, although relatively few women aged sixteen and younger were included in the actual use studies of Plan B, the data that were presented indicated that the youngest women who were studied actually used the drug correctly about as often as older women.

As I thought about the hearings after getting home, I realized that the discussion hadn't considered the issue of spontaneous abortion, a serious omission that in my view prevented the committees from reaching a clear and balanced understanding of the whole abortion issue. Accordingly, several days after the hearings I wrote a letter to the agency, to be included in the public record, which laid out the following concerns. The best studies, using sensitive hormonal assays, have shown that about 30 percent of all pregnancies in women who are using no contraception are spontaneously lost very early after conception, well before the woman knows she is pregnant. Assuming that Plan B prevents pregnancy by preventing fertilization—an entirely reasonable assumption, given current evidence—the over-the-counter availability of Plan B could therefore result in a large decrease in the loss of fertilized ova; in effect, use of Plan B could actually decrease the overall number of "abortions" that would otherwise have occurred (in this case, spontaneously). Moreover, since levonorgestrol is, in fact, a progestational agent that is used to prevent threatened abortion, it is even possible that many, and perhaps most, of the 25 percent of pregnancies that occur despite the use of Plan B (Plan B "failure") could be those that would have otherwise been spontaneously lost early on if the woman had not taken the drug. In this latter case, emergency use of levonorgestrol could, at least in theory, virtually eliminate very early spontaneous "abortion." These considerations suggest that even if Plan B were to prevent as many as 30 percent of pregnancies by preventing implantation of fertilized ova, rather than by preventing fertilization, the overall early loss of fertilized ova in any group of women using Plan B would be no greater than if the drug was not used at all, although drug-induced early loss would replace spontaneous early loss—a tradeoff of uncertain moral significance.

Advisory committee recommendations are not binding on the agency, but the FDA rarely makes decisions that are contrary to those recommendations. Moreover, as a high-level FDA staffer explained to me informally, in the few instances in which the agency's approval decisions went against advisory committee votes, the votes (for reasons that were usually not clear) had been inconsistent with the sense of the committees' own discussions—clearly not the case in the Plan B hearings. It was therefore a considerable surprise, not to mention a serious disappointment, to many of us when the FDA announced its decision in May 2004 that Plan B was "not approvable" for over-the-counter use. The decision seemed to me to be so obviously inconsistent with the evidence that I seriously considered resigning at that time, but I decided not to. I felt an obligation to finish my full term.

It was anyone's guess in May 2004 what drove the FDA to behave in such a seemingly irrational way. True, we had learned during the Plan B committee hearings that some members of Congress had written to the FDA opposing over-the-counter availability, apparently on the grounds that it might foster promiscuity, and some statements in the public hearings had raised concern about the social and behavioral side effects. Moreover, two or three members of the RHDAC had made it clear that they had serious moral concerns because of the possibility, however remote, that in some women Plan B might be acting as an abortifacient. But there was no "smoking gun" to indicate that the agency had actually yielded to direct political pressure from social conservatives. On the other hand, there was no other obvious explanation, either.

In fact, the FDA's May 2004 "not approvable" decision for Plan B did not close the door entirely on the over-the-counter option. The agency offered the sponsor the option of "two tier," age-dependent marketing—that is, making Plan B available over the counter to women over age sixteen, but only by prescription to younger women. As pointed out later, this option is very limited: it would discriminate not only against younger women, but also against those over sixteen who do not have drivers' licenses—usually poor women and those from inner-city neighborhoods.[1] Moreover, being "carded" by a pharmacist in order to buy the drug—a very public process—would be a serious and humiliating invasion of privacy that would intimidate many women and prevent them from obtaining the drug. Despite these disturbing concerns, and despite the fact that such marketing for over-the-counter drugs is virtually unprecedented (nicotine preparations for smoking cessation are not approved for over-the-counter availability to people under age eighteen, but that restriction is consistent with the age restriction for tobacco sales), Barr Laboratories apparently decided it was better to settle for half a loaf and refiled their over-the-counter switch application, which included a plan for dual-level availability.

While this was happening, the FDA's then newly appointed commissioner, Lester Crawford, made a public commitment as a condition of his appointment that the agency would make a definite decision on Plan B's over-the-counter approvability by September 1, 2005. On August 26, 2005, however, the FDA, apparently as the result of a sudden and unexpected *crise de nerfs* over the unprecedented nature of a two-tier marketing

system, announced that it would require a ninety-day comment period before it could make a final ruling on over-the-counter availability. Those familiar with the FDA's rulemaking recognized immediately that this nondecision ruling meant the agency could put off a decision on over-the-counter approvability almost indefinitely. There's an old saying that seemed to capture the situation very well: "Fool me once, shame on you; fool me twice, shame on me." At that point, therefore, I decided that the irrationality of the FDA's decision process had crossed the line, and the time had come for me to resign. (Since my term on the NDAC officially ended in May 2005, the position I resigned was actually as a consultant.)

O ther information that has surfaced along the way strengthens the inference that the presumed inability of younger women to use Plan B correctly was a smoke screen (or, perhaps more appropriately, a "fig leaf ") used to obscure the real pressures for nonapproval. First, it became increasingly clear that many people confuse Plan B with mifepristone, or RU-486—the "French pill"—which is a progesterone antagonist used explicitly to induce abortion.[2] Second, as reported in *Time* magazine, prior to the FDA's August 2005 decision, socially conservative organizations were encouraging their members to flood the White House and Congress with letters and calls opposing over-the-counter approval. Third, W. David Hager, an obstetrician-gynecologist recruited directly by the Bush White House to serve on the RHDAC and one of the four committee members who voted against over-the-counter availability, confirmed that after the committee hearings he had sent the FDA a "minority report" at the behest of "someone at the FDA," whose name he says he is not at liberty to reveal, asking for "more studies" and for "more data on the use of Plan B by young girls."[3] It was also later revealed that in speaking about Plan B to an audience at a Christian college, Hager had said "God has used me to stand in the breach for the cause of the Kingdom."

These suspicions of social conservative pressure received further strong support from the report of the Government Accountability Office released in November 2005.[4] Produced in response to a request by forty-eight members of the U.S. Senate and House of Representatives, the report documents four unusual aspects of the initial "not approvable" Plan B decision process. First, the FDA staff who would normally have been responsible for signing the not-approvable letter disagreed with the decision and refused to sign. Second, high-level FDA management was more involved in the review of Plan B than in the review of any other over-the-counter switch application. Third, the decision not to approve the application may have been made before the scientific reviews were completed. And lastly, the rationale for the decision (the presumed inability of younger women to use the drug appropriately) did not follow the FDA's usual practices—it normally considers extrapolating data from older to younger adolescents to be scientifically appropriate. The exercise of such pressures should not be surprising, however, when we recognize that the FDA is part of the executive branch of government. The FDA commissioner therefore reports to the secretary of the Department of Health and Human Services who, in turn, reports directly to the president; and the current president makes no secret of his determination to implement a socially conservative agenda by whatever means necessary.

The distressing history of Plan B teaches lessons on at least two points: the special vulnerabilities of the FDA, and the vagaries of resignation as a form of social protest. As a regulatory agency, the FDA is caught in crossfire from several sources. There is pressure from free market advocates, most obviously those in industry, for whom the agency—like all Federal regulators—is anathema; free marketeers truly believe that the economy, medicine, and the public interest would all be better off without the FDA's "paternalistic" control. Accordingly, industry has worked hard, and with considerable success, to reshape the FDA's regulatory role to be more in line with its own interests.[5] Industry has exerted its influence largely through Congress, both because many members of Congress share its free market perspective, and because Congress in turn does possess some control over the shape, size, and function of the FDA. On the other hand, when it perceives that the FDA has allowed the public to be exposed to preventable risks and harms, Congress apparently sees no internal (and political) contradiction in taking the opposite position, coming down hard on the agency and pushing for more stringent regulation. The 1962 Kefauver-Harris amendments mandating that drugs must be shown to be effective as well as safe before they can be marketed came about because of the thalidomide tragedy. The FDA is also subject to direct political pressure from the executive branch, as was apparently the case with the Plan B decision. And finally, the FDA is under constant, detailed, and intensive scrutiny by the media and, consequently, the public. The public's judgments can be swift and harsh, particularly when it perceives that the agency is roiled by conflict of interest, bureaucratic paralysis, and lack of transparency.

It was anyone's guess in May 2004 what drove the FDA to decide Plan B was not approvable for over-the-counter use. While there was no smoking gun to indicate it yielded to direct political pressure, there was no other obvious explanation, either.

Managing these pressures while trying to get its basic scientific and administrative job done is a huge challenge for the agency. Its priority, then, is to manage relationships with the outside world, and for that it requires public trust. Unfortunately, corruption of the decision-making process by political forces, as has happened in the case of Plan B, squanders that trust and tarnishes the agency's image.[6] But the FDA also needs to manage the effects of those pressures internally, particularly their impact on its own employees. Virtually all the FDA staff who worked with the advisory committees struck me as being knowledgeable, professional, competent, and hard working. And although I suspect many FDA staff could have made considerably larger incomes in industry or even academia, several made it clear to me that they chose to stay with the agency because they felt their work was both rewarding and important. I found it particularly distressing, therefore, to be told in September 2005 by a high-level agency official that the staff had become "demoralized and depressed" by the Plan B decision, and to learn that Susan Wood had resigned.

Resigning from an organization is hardly as visible as signing a petition or taking out an ad, nor is it as strident as rioting in the streets; but resigning in protest is certainly a time-honored practice. I had never before resigned in protest, however, and since no one ever taught me in school how to go about it, I was on my own. At first, I wondered whether to do it at all. I would be withholding my expertise, such as it was, from the FDA at a time when it probably needed outside expert help more than ever, and I did feel I had something useful to offer. I knew that, by resigning, I would be letting down my colleagues on the NDAC. And I also knew that my leaving might lead to the appointment of someone worse—someone who believed that social and religious values should trump a rational decision process, based on scientific evidence, which is the agency's mandate.

In the end, I simply decided that the potential value of such a protest outweighed the down side. At the same time, however, just resigning quietly made no sense at all. (As one of my friends put it, "If an FDA committee member falls in the forest and no one hears it, does it make a noise?") In my resignation letter, I therefore told the FDA that I was resigning "publicly," thus declaring my intention to use my resignation actively as leverage for reconsideration of the Plan B decision. (I also told them I would encourage other members of the NDAC to resign, but later reconsidered that decision after a colleague persuaded me that the potential damage to the FDA of multiple simultaneous resignations might be greater than the value of the protest.) Having no clear idea how to turn my resignation into an active protest—how to get the word out, use it for some leverage, "make a fuss"—I fell back on the storied method of social protest: writing a letter to the *New York Times*. Unfortunately, my letter got to the *Times* two days after Hurricane Katrina hit New Orleans, and like so much else, it was washed away in the flood.

It was only when, about two weeks later, I got a call from a *Hartford Courant* reporter asking for an interview that it seemed my protest might gain some traction. The reporter's interest, it turns out, came about only because I had mentioned my resignation to a colleague, and the conversation was passed on through a network of personal connections—the vagaries of chance. The resulting article appeared a few days later as the cover story in *Northeast,* the *Courant*'s Sunday magazine.[7] Since the media seems to find blood in the water irresistible, the *Courant* story was immediately followed by an intense but short-lived media frenzy, which included tapings by National Public Radio, Fox news, and ABC news, not to mention Associated Press and Reuters stories in various newspapers (including the *New York Times*), as well as reports in "The Tan Sheet" and the *British Medical Journal*. But it was only when I began getting e-mail a few days later from friends and colleagues in far-flung places— London, Rome, and Bangkok—that I appreciated fully the reach and power the Internet has given to the media. A number of advocacy groups also approached me, offering to put on press conferences in which I could talk about the Plan B "debacle." That idea seemed attractive at first, but when I considered the possibility of getting tangled up in the agendas of groups I knew nothing about, I decided against it.

> **In my view, what has brought out the harsh, controlling streak in so many is that emergency contraception has to do with sex, and the resultant co-mingling of sex with politics and morality is highly corrosive.**

Has my resignation made any difference at all? It's hard to say. It did lead directly to my being contacted by staffers of two U.S. senators who had questions about "decision-making at the FDA," and this gave me an opportunity to talk at length with them about the Plan B decision. When the GAO report was released, I was invited to discuss it on *The NewsHour with Jim Lehrer* (which I unfortunately couldn't do). I did learn in passing about one or more bills being considered by Congress that would require a definitive decision, up or down, from the FDA on Plan B by "date certain," the default being that over-the-counter availability would be automatically approved if the decision weren't forthcoming by that date. Any relief I felt from the prospect that rationality might be restored to the Plan B decision was quickly extinguished, however, by the realization that such a law would set the terrible precedent of drug approval directly by the unruly politics of Congress, rather than by sober and balanced review of the evidence by the FDA.

How did we get ourselves into such a mess? In my view, what has brought out the harsh, controlling streak in so many people is that emergency contraception has to do with sex, and that the resultant commingling of sex with politics and morality is highly corrosive. Why does sex get people's backs up? Like all powerful forces—terrorism, hurricanes, pandemics—the power of sex can seem appalling, terrifying, something that must therefore be controlled at all costs. And since men exert most organized social control, the control over sexuality is asserted primarily by controlling the sexual and reproductive lives of women. A small number of women apparently also share these views. Furthermore, although several other serious and legitimate concerns—including interests of the state and society, as well as personal, humanistic issues—attach to abortion, one can argue that the abortion issue—particularly not permitting very early abortion—is also in substantial part an expression of the need to control women's sexual lives.

How can we get ourselves out of this mess? It may be both necessary and possible to "fight back" against political attacks on science,[8] but that strategy is likely to be successful only in the short run; deeper structural changes are probably required in the long run to keep from having to fight those battles over and over again. Although a simple solution is unlikely, at least two approaches might help. The first is a greatly increased reliance on transparency. That is, rather than imposing rigid and

absolutist control over the availability of a safe and effective drug like Plan B, both doctors and patients would be better off if the public had greater access to the drug, but only on condition that everyone is fully informed about the issues associated with its use. For example, providing everyone with full information about the facts on spontaneous early abortion and possible effects of Plan B on early pregnancy loss would allow those doctors and those women who have serious moral concerns about abortion to make informed choices about using the drug. At the same time, access would not be limited for women for whom these concerns are not a serious barrier to the drug's use. Providing this information through appropriate wording on the package label should be quite possible; I suggested such wording in my December 2005 follow-up letter to the FDA.

The second approach would be to find a way to protect the FDA without diluting its effectiveness. The agency, like all regulators, is currently caught in the crossfire precisely because, by design, it is positioned in the no man's land between the commercial and "guardian" (governmental, academic, legal, religious, and military) worlds. It is therefore subject to the contrasting, often clashing and conflicting "moral syndromes" and pragmatic interests of these two worlds. As the social critic Jane Jacobs has argued, both worlds are necessary for a healthy and well-functioning society.[9] But when one world takes over the functions of the other, the result is a "monstrous hybrid"—think of the Soviet Union's effect on commerce, or, conversely, the effect of commercialism on managed care and HMOs in the United States.[10] However, although each of these worlds needs to keep well within its own domain, they need to interact closely with one another, balancing their interests and working out mutually acceptable solutions if the larger society is to prosper.

That balancing act is a tough one for everyone, and particularly for regulatory agencies, all of which are caught in the middle; moreover, the FDA carries a large added burden because protection of the public health is such a sensitive issue. It has occurred to me, therefore, that it would make sense to convert the FDA into a quasigovernmental agency, like the Federal Reserve and the National Academy of Sciences—supported by public funds and with binding decision-making power over both the standards of scientific evidence and the flow of commerce, but largely out of reach of direct political pressure. I made that suggestion during my discussions with the senate staffers. Unfortunately, they didn't seem impressed.

Notes

1. A.J.J. Wood, J.M. Drazen, and M.F. Greene. "A Sad Day for Science at the FDA," *New England Journal of Medicine* 352 (2005): 1197–99.

2. *60 Minutes,* "The Debate over Plan B," http://www.cbsnews.com/stories/2005/11/22/60minutes/main1068924.shtml.

3. Ibid.

4. United States Government Accountability Office, "Decision Process to Deny Initial Application for Over-the-Counter Marketing of the Emergency Contraceptive Drug Plan B Was Unusual," Report GAO-06-109, http://www.gao.gov/cgi-bin/getrpt?GAO-06-109.

5. M. Angell, *The Truth about the Drug Companies: How They Deceive Us and What to Do about It* (New York: Random House, 2004).

6. Wood, Drazen, and Greene, "A Sad Day for Science at the FDA."

7. R. Buck, "Plan B Casualties," *Northeast Magazine,* October 2, 2005: 3–5.

8. L. Rosenstock and L.J. Lee, "Attacks on Science: The Risks to Evidence-Based Policy," *American Journal of Public Health* 92 (2002): 14–18.

9. J. Jacobs, *Systems of Survival: A Dialogue on the Moral Foundations of Commerce and Politics* (New York: Random House, 1992).

10. F. Davidoff, "Medicine and Commerce. 1: Is Managed Care a 'Monstrous Hybrid'?" [Editorial] *Annals of Internal Medicine* 128 (1998): 496–99; J.G. Coombs, *The Rise and Fall of HMOs: An American Health Care Revolution* (Madison: University of Wisconsin Press, 2005).

FRANK DAVIDOFF, "Sex, Politics, and Morality at the FDA: Reflections on the Plan B Decision," *Hastings Center Report* 36, no. 2 (2006): 20–25.

Guess Who's Watching Porn

These days it's kids as young as eight or 10. As boys get hooked ever earlier, Net porn is reshaping youth sexuality.

MONIQUE POLAK

Marc first looked at Internet porn when he was in Grade 4. "We were at a Pokémon birthday party," he recalled. His 10-year-old host had something better than Pokémon cards to show his guests: a website full of naked busty blonds. Now 19, and a recent graduate of a Montreal college, Marc checks out Internet porn sites about as often as he brushes his teeth. "I look at least twice a day," he says.

Marc and his friend Christian, 18, visit sites with names like Bookworm Bitches, My Sister's Best Friend and My First Sex Teacher. Having a girlfriend with whom he regularly has sex doesn't deter Marc from visiting porn websites. "I have a girlfriend, but hey, we've been together three years," he says. "Besides, this is good quality HD. It's fun and it helps you sleep."

The pornification of culture is something that we encounter at every turn: it's in Snoop Doggy and Pussycat Dolls videos; it keeps the *Girls Gone Wild* franchise going strong; it guides the fashion trends of females six to 60; and it's behind prime-time reality shows, like the E! Network's *The Girls Next Door* chronicling the life of Hugh Hefner. But when it comes to explicit materials, nothing compares to the Wild West of cyberporn. There's been an explosion of pornographic websites in the last decade, with tens of millions of sites literally a click away, according to Frederick S. Lane, author of *Obscene Profits: The Entrepreneurs of Pornography in the Cyber Age.* Lane estimates the North American cyperporn industry brings in about $2 billion dollars a year.

More than just big business, this wave of easy-to-access online images, videos and chat rooms is shaping the way young people indulge their sexual curiosity. Back when parents of today's teens were growing up, porn meant girlie magazines like *Playboy* or *Hustler.* And accessing porn took effort—and courage. Magazine stands weren't supposed to sell pornography to minors. Curious teens had to sneak into their older brothers' bedrooms—or their dads' tool sheds—to find their secret stashes.

Today, airbrushed Playboy playmates are tame compared to what's out there: oral sex, anal sex, same-sex sex, sex with animals and vegetables, ménages à trois, quatre and many more—all of this going on right under the parental roof. Although it's hard to quantify exactly what and how much online porn kids are looking at, a report from the London School of Economics found that nine out of 10 children between the ages of eight and 16 have viewed at least something that qualifies. According to a 2004 Columbia University study, 25 per cent of 12- and 13-year-old girls, and 37 per cent of boys the same age, say they have friends who regularly view and download Internet pornography.

A Columbia study found 37 per cent of boys view porn

And these are only approximations—probably lowball ones. "I don't think we know anywhere near as much as we need to know," says Gary Brooks, a professor of psychology at Baylor University in Waco, Texas, who studies the effects of pornography on men. "In my writing, I say that we knew a little bit about the amount of usage and the amount of damage before cyberspace—and now we have no clue."

In the majority of cases, the London School of Economics report says, children's exposure to online pornography is inadvertent—the result of misspelled words and Web addresses, or confusing a .com suffix for a .net. In her book *Pornified: How Pornography is Transforming*

Our Lives, Our Relationships and Our Families, journalist Pamela Paul reports that 94 per cent of the porn images children ages 10 to 17 encountered accidentally were of naked people, 38 per cent were of people having sex, and eight per cent involved sexual violence. Forty-five per cent of kids who stumble upon porn in this way report being upset by what they saw.

But a great many others, at ever-younger ages, are far from upset about it. In fact, a 2001 Kaiser Family Foundation Study found that almost one-third of kids in Grades 7 through 12 have lied about their ages in order to access adult-only websites.

Which begs the question: to what extent can—and should—parents be monitoring what their teenage sons are up to when they're supposedly surfing the Web or doing their homework? Like many young people (roughly a fifth of eight- to 18-year-olds), Christian and Marc have their own computers. "My parents have no idea," Marc says. How could they? Monitoring what kids are up to in cyberspace has become virtually impossible since most of them have Internet access in multiple venues: at home, at school, at friends' houses, in public libraries, and Internet cafés, for instance.

'My parents have no idea,' A teen says. How could they?

Patricia, who lives in Montreal and has a 13-year-old son, has a pretty good idea about what he's been up to at home on Saturday nights after she and her husband go to bed. One recent Sunday morning, Patricia checked out the history on the family computer. "I spotted some very explicit titles that were obviously way out there. I said to my husband, 'What is this?'" she said.

"I almost chuckled," she said, "because my son's so not like that. The girls like him because he's not macho at all. Other parents always say how nice and polite he is. But he's growing up. He's sprouting body hair and he takes longer showers than he used to." Patricia and her husband decided not to confront their son. Instead, they came up with another solution: "We changed the code to log on to the computer. Now he can only use it when we're around."

Jane, another Montreal mom, had a similar experience five years ago. The mother of three sons, now aged between 18 and 25, she happened to be looking at the history on the family computer when she came across a link to a pornographic website. "You can tell from the titles, like Wet and Wild P . . . ies or whatever, and my sons aren't animal lovers."

Jane didn't realize that by clicking on the link, she'd access the website. "I'd been married a long time," she

said, "but I saw stuff I'd never seen or dreamt of. There was everything. Sex between old people. People defecating on other people." She was traumatized. "I was trying to close the website with my eyes closed," she said. (Getting trapped in a sort of smutty hall of mirrors online is a common experience. A 2003 study in the journal *Youth & Society* found that, in a quarter of cases where youth accidentally opened pornographic websites, they were exposed to multiple sex sites when they tried to close the first one.)

Jane and her husband confronted their sons. "No one confessed, but I did get a written confession later from one," she said. "He was absolutely horrified I was so upset. He told me the sites keep opening to stuff that's disturbing even for him."

The couple also took action. They moved the computer from the basement den. "It's on an Ikea desk—right in the middle of the kitchen," she said. Now with only her youngest son still living at home, Jane occasionally monitors his Internet use. She's also become more computer savvy. "Smart kids erase the history. But on our computer, I can look up something called, 'recently changed,'" she said. She admits she's still anxious about her sons' use of Internet porn. How can she be sure they won't do something that might bring the police to her door—like download child porn? "It's kind of terrifying. Let's face it, any parent has to be concerned," she said.

It's not only parents dealing with this kind of trouble at home. Devon, a Grade 12 student in Calgary, recently discovered her 13-year-old brother was visiting porn websites. She made the discovery when she typed in a Web address on her parents' laptop and another website popped up. "There were these weird sexual positions. I thought, 'This isn't where I want to be.' I checked the history and there were tons of porn websites mixed in with skateboard sites, so I knew it was him."

Devon, who is 17, talked with her brother. "I told him, 'If you want to be looking at that stuff, it's not the smartest way to be looking on your parents' computer.' He said it was his friends daring him. I knew that wasn't true."

Devon herself has seen her fair share of Internet porn. "I've had it happen quite a few times that I'm at a guy's house and he says, 'Come look at this!' or 'Isn't this hilarious?'" According to Paul's book, *Pornified,* 41 per cent of 15- to 17-year-olds now say viewing porn online underage is "no big deal." "Now I'm totally desensitized to the issue," she says. "I just laugh it off with them."

But her boyfriend, who is 18, isn't like that. "He claims he doesn't look at porn at all, that it disgusts him and that porn is demeaning and icky," she said. Still, Devon is skeptical. "I can't tell if that's him trying to be the opposite of the guys I laugh about or if it's really true. I swear to God, all boys look. That's my experience," she said.

For parents, when it comes to Internet porn, not only do they have to deal with logistical concerns—how can they monitor their kids' activity—they also have to ask themselves what, if any, are the long-term effects of all of this exposure? "Pornography in all its permutations affects developing sexuality," writes Paul in *Pornified*. "The younger the age of exposure and the more hard-core the material, the more intense the effects." These effects can include everything from a skewed sense of sexual norms to difficulty maintaining a healthy, loving relationship; an unrealistic view of women; and potentially, pornography addiction, which can interfere with school work, friendships and family relationships.

Sex therapists, like Toronto-based Robert Burgoyne, have a term for what these young men are up to: cyber-sexual auto-eroticism. In itself, says Burgoyne, it's not a problem. The danger with pornography in general is that it encourages users to isolate sexuality from emotional intimacy. "It becomes problematic if it interferes with other aspects of life such as school, work and relationships or if these young men are getting harmful information or locked into objectifying women sexually," he said.

Most of Burgoyne's clients are grown men seeking help for sexual addiction. But lately, he's been counselling several young men struggling with a cybersexual habit that began in early adolescence and continues to occupy far too much of their time and attention. As a result, Internet porn is interfering with their relationships. "Some want support or coaching to reduce or manage this habit," he says.

David Marcus, a psychologist at the San Jose Marital and Sexuality Center in California, who treats men of all ages struggling with pornography addiction, says one of biggest problems with Internet porn in particular is that people's tolerance to it becomes accelerated. "What people really, really don't get is that what was enough yesterday—and exciting yesterday—is not enough today," he says. In other words, very soon a naked woman is old news, and users are seeking out different, increasingly graphic, and in extreme cases criminal, content—things that will continue to shock and arouse. "They have to keep getting more and more, so it becomes this insatiable thirst for it."

Marcus says that when the men he sees look back on their own childhoods, there are often two common indicators of future trouble. The first is early exposure to particularly graphic or disturbing sexual images. "As an analogy, it's like trauma in that people can only tolerate a certain degree of intensity," says Marcus. Especially for very young or immature children. "Their central nervous system can only take in so much. And so if the experience is so intense or so mind-altering, what happens is it really affects their sense of social norms—what they can

expect from a partner and what their own desires are get so flooded that they can't really make contact with what would be a more 'normal' progression of sexual desire."

Of course, just because a kid is exploring pornography online doesn't mean he will develop an addiction, or become more likely to engage in "deviant" behaviour. "With the Internet, the images are interacting with whatever the person brings to the table," Marcus says. "If there's a lot of rage in the person that's not being dealt with then it's going to find its expression there."

But the combination of unbridled Internet access and a predilection toward, for instance, violent sexuality or images of children is a recipe for trouble. "It's sort of like whatever is latent in a person is going to get aroused and supercharged through the Internet images," he says. "People could live their whole lives without knowing they have that propensity or that desire and then all of a sudden they go online and it finds a voice and expression and Pandora's box opens."

Another indicator, he says, is that men with addiction often report having used pornography from a young age as a form of self-help—something they do to soothe themselves in the face of stress or anxiety. "I have people who will talk about getting into it because they didn't like what was going on at school, so they got onto chat rooms and websites with pornography," he says. "And they continued that through college every time they had a problem and now they're finished college and they're struggling because they want to be in certain types of relationships but the pornography is messing up those relationships for them."

It often becomes a self-esteem issue for the women involved, says Marcus. "They say, 'If you expect that from me, then forget it. I can't compete with how that girl looks, what that girl does, what you see online.'"

So how are parents—particularly of boys—supposed to know the difference between healthy curiosity and the early signs of a problem? Therapists say the standard signs of addiction apply: they're spending more and more time on it; they use it to cope with external problems; they become isolated; and they try to keep it a secret. "The more of a secret it is," says Marcus, "the more of a problem."

While conclusive data is impossible to come by, many sex therapists believe pornography addiction is growing exponentially with the Internet. In health centres on university campuses, it has become a growing concern. "I have some students at Baylor involved with a 'Christian responsibility group,'" says Brooks, "and they have 'accountability partners,' which is very much like having a sponsor in Alcoholics Anonymous to help them kick the pornography habit."

Of course, the majority continue to see a little bit of pornography, even among young people, as good, healthy fun.

Burgoyne, for instance, is not surprised to hear that teenagers like Christian and Marc openly compare notes about which porn sites offer the "hottest" images, or that Devon's male friends ask her to view pornographic images with them. For Burgoyne, this is all part of growing up male in the digital age: they're unlikely to talk "love" with each other. "If teenage boys admit to having romantic fantasies it could be social suicide," he says, "like saying you're passionate about your stamp collection."

Burgoyne believes parents should discuss sexuality and issues like Internet porn with their teenagers. He does not think parents who discover that their sons are accessing pornographic websites should necessarily panic. "We shouldn't assume that a teen boy who self-pleasures while looking at erotica on the Internet isn't, at heart, just a hopeless romantic," he said.

With Lianne George.

Breeder Reaction

Does everybody have the right to have a baby? And who should pay when nature alone doesn't work?

ELIZABETH WEIL

Guadalupe Benitez and her partner, Joanne Clark, had been buying frozen sperm at a bank in Los Angeles and trying to get pregnant at home for two years when Benitez finally sought out the services of a fertility specialist. Not at all uncommon—infertility affects more than 6 million Americans, and about 20 percent of them seek help through assisted reproductive technology, or ART. At that point, 1999, Benitez was 27 years old, Clark was 40 years old, and the couple had been together for eight years, since Benitez emigrated from Culiacán, Mexico. Benitez, a medical assistant, had some infertility benefits at a nearby OB/GYN clinic, the North Coast Women's Care Medical Group. There, Dr. Christine Brody put Benitez on a hormonal drug called Clomid, to treat her polycystic ovarian syndrome, and also told her that she was willing to oversee her treatment but not to perform inseminations because, as a Christian, she disapproved of lesbians having children.

"When she said that," Benitez told me, "I was so upset, but she made it better by saying the other doctors would do it for us." Benitez and Clark tried home inseminations for a few more months, and Brody even did some exploratory surgery. But when the time came to schedule a more effective in utero insemination—a procedure that involves injecting sperm directly into the uterus—an assistant from North Coast Women's Care called to inform Benitez that no one in the practice would do the procedure, nor would they refill her prescriptions. Benitez demanded to speak with the head of the clinic, who responded by telling her that he, too, objected to helping lesbians have children and would not further her care. "They had just lied and lied to me, trying to brush me aside to do inseminations at home as some form of excuse. But once they found themselves against the wall, they had no choice but to tell me they flat-out wouldn't do it." So Benitez sued.

Benitez's is far from the only case brought by a woman turned down for fertility services. Kijuana Chambers, a single blind woman living in Denver, Colorado, was eventually turned away from her fertility clinic. Among the reasons cited at trial by one of the clinic's doctors: She was prone to emotional outbursts; she had dirty underwear. Chambers lost her trial in the U.S. District Court in Denver in November 2003. Last summer, the 10th Circuit Court of Appeals declined to rehear her case.

Screening at fertility clinics is not just a concern for gays, lesbians, and the disabled. Women over 39 and women with severely compromised fertility are commonly turned down for services or told they won't be treated unless they agree to use donor eggs. This is largely a matter of economics. Assisted reproduction is a $4 billion-a-year business. The average cost of a single cycle of in vitro fertilization, including medications, egg retrieval, sperm washing, fertilization, incubation, and embryo transfer, is $12,400. Given all the failures and repeat attempts, the average amount spent per baby born through IVF in the United States is much higher: $100,000. Few insurance companies pick up the tab, so patients themselves decide where to spend their considerable money, and they do this largely based on a clinic's success rate. As a result, many doctors try to game the system, producing high "live birth" success rates by cherry-picking patients. Before being accepted by a clinic, a woman must submit to a battery of tests to determine things like the level of follicle-stimulating hormone on day three of her menstrual cycle. Get a number over 12, and she's out of luck.

According to Dr. Geoffrey Sher, founder and medical director of the Sher Institute of Reproductive Medicine, the

---

Amount that Americans spend each year on assisted reproductive technology: $4 billion.

Chances that ART will be successful: 1 in 3.

Average cost of a single cycle of in vitro fertilization: $12,400.

Average amount spent per baby born through IVF in the United States: $100,000.

largest chain of privately owned fertility clinics in the world, almost any clinic that can afford to turn down patients does. "I'd like to think most doctors try to be honest. The problem is, you're confronted with the reality that if you don't get high success rates, patients don't come to you."

"How much selecting is going on?" I asked.

"A lot."

"How much is a lot?"

"A *lot*."

The practice of screening at fertility clinics poses a simple yet difficult-to-answer question: Should there be a right to reproductive assistance? The very fact that we're asking this question shows how radically things have changed. Up until the birth of Louise Brown, the first test-tube baby, in 1978, if you couldn't reproduce, you couldn't reproduce. You adopted or went childless or spent a lot of time with other people's kids, and that was the end of that. Now, of course, if you want children and they aren't happening naturally, there are many procedures to try: in vitro fertilization, blastocyst transfer, gestational surrogates, donor eggs, donor sperm, donated embryos—the list goes on and on. In recent years, our legal system has had to grapple with such novel, ART-related issues as the parenting rights of the egg donor who is also the ex-live-in lover of the birth mom, the gestational surrogate who refuses to give up the baby, and the couple who refuses to take the delivery of twins from the surrogate. Embryos have been implanted in and carried by the wrong mothers—who gets to bring up the resulting children? In one very sad case, a bachelor hired a gestational surrogate. After delivery, the baby cried an awful lot. The father killed the child in just six weeks.

Amazingly, in the United States, almost no public policy exists around assisted reproduction: what procedures should be legal, how many babies a woman should be allowed to carry at one time, how old is too old for a woman to conceive. The Vatican, on grounds that creating a baby outside of a woman's body is playing God, opposes all IVF. In Europe, the enterprise of technology-enhanced baby-making is subsidized and also well regulated. (Different countries stipulate different benefits: A woman is entitled to two cycles of IVF, a woman is entitled to four cycles of IVF, a doctor will implant one embryo, a doctor will implant up to four.) But the U.S. government has neglected to impose even the most basic medical regulations, in part because politically ART is impossible to touch. Who would possibly stand in the way of families having babies? Yet many procedures, most notably IVF, require producing excess embryos. And if it's unconscionable to create embryos for stem cell research, how can we countenance the thousands being created daily (most of which are ultimately discarded) for couples trying to have kids?

So far in this country no rules have been set. Literally, the only thing you can't do is use embryos created since 2001 for stem cell research in a lab that receives any federal funding. Other than that, anything goes. Women in their 60s have been assisted in having children. Semen has been extracted, without prior consent, from men who've died. In some states, embryos are treated as material possessions and deemed transferable as part of one's estate; in others, they're treated almost as children and cannot be harmed or destroyed, and, if abandoned, can be implanted by doctors in surrogates' wombs. Regularly the news is filled with stories: first surviving set of septuplets! Woman gives birth to two sets of identical twins! (Miracle, multiple ART births have become so common that just this spring a Missouri couple perpetrated the first sextuplet hoax, soliciting donations of cash, gift cards, a washer and dryer, and a van.) A new technology called PGD—preimplantation genetic diagnosis—allows doctors to test for genetic defects just three days after fertilization, when the conceptus, not yet technically an embryo, is still in a petri dish. And that's going to pose a whole new set of moral quandaries: Is it acceptable to screen against cystic fibrosis? What about mild disabilities, say, dyslexia? And what about sex? "To face this issue frontally and regulate," says Northeastern University legal scholar Wendy Parmet, "we first, as a society, need to come to terms and acknowledge the practice, and say, 'IVF and any of the ART procedures are okay except when . . . .' We haven't done that, nor are we aided by the fact that so much of the fertility industry takes place outside the centrifugal force of insurance." So, for now, the particularities around the right to give birth, like the particularities around the right to die, are contested and ill defined. "What we've got," says Parmet, "is a lot of talking and debate going on in professional societies, and not a lot of law."

The level of public debate about ART is so far behind the technology that we haven't even decided who should be deciding what's legal and just: the government, doctors, or patients themselves. Lawyers and bioethicists are fond of explaining that there are positive rights, known as entitlements, and negative rights, known as liberties. With regard to baby-making, a negative right is the right to do as you please, as long as it's consensual. No matter how poor an idea, no one will stop you from a drunken dalliance and parenting the child who may result. But there is no entitlement to have a baby. It goes without saying: The state will not furnish anybody a child. Nobody can demand a spouse for the purpose of creating a child, and, in this country at least, even if you do have a spouse, that spouse is not required by law to reproduce. All we seem to have agreed upon as a society is that reproducing is deeply meaningful and important, and that any attempts to keep people from doing so—i.e., forced sterilization—are abhorrent and illegal. (The 1942 case of *Skinner v. Oklahoma* struck down compulsory sterilization even for

In a Survey of Fertility Clinic Directors

59% agreed that everyone has the right to have a child.

44% believe that fertility doctors don't have the right to decide who is a fit parent.

48% said they were very or extremely likely to turn away a gay couple seeking a surrogate.

38% would turn away a couple on welfare who wanted to pay for ART with Social Security checks.

20% would turn away a single woman.

17% would turn away a lesbian couple.

13% would turn away a couple in which the woman had bipolar disorder.

9% would turn away a couple who wanted to replace a recently deceased child.

5% would turn away a biracial couple.

repeat sex offenders on the grounds that reproduction is "one of the basic civil rights of man.") Internationally, Article 16 of the United Nations Universal Declaration of Human Rights includes "the right to found a family." The International Covenant on Economic, Social, and Cultural Rights states that everybody has the right to enjoy the benefits of scientific progress. But legally this does not add up to a positive, enforceable right to access reproductive technologies. In the United States, there is not even a positive right to basic health care.

Which raises an interesting question: Should infertility be viewed as a medical problem? Says University of Wisconsin Law School bioethicist Alta Charo, "For many years infertility was not regarded as something sufficiently serious that it necessitated care. Treatment was discretionary, not necessary." RESOLVE and other infertility rights groups have worked hard to change this, as have ART clinics. Yet defining ART as a medical treatment is a bit forced, because "if you use the classic situation of a fertile woman with an infertile male spouse, she never had a fertility problem to begin with," notes Charo. A more logical line of reasoning might be to view her as having a social, not a medical, dilemma. She does not want to have sex outside her marriage—that's why she can't get pregnant. Should society step in to help her? Should this be covered by insurance?

To get around this dilemma, those in favor of greater access to ART like to position infertility as a disease of a couple—a rather unconventional diagnosis. But even if "an infertile couple" gets under the umbrella of medicine, there's no guarantee of particular services. "You have to start with the fact that in the United States of America, in terms of health care, with certain limited exceptions, you have a right to nothing," says Parmet. "If I want a hip replacement and I don't have the money"—be it through insurance or

otherwise—"I don't get a hip replacement." And, except for "certain no-no reasons," Parmet notes, all doctors, including fertility clinicians, are free to choose whom they want to treat. "Anybody can deny me care because my name is Wendy, but they can't deny me care because of my religion or my race."

In some states, like California, where Benitez was seeking care, doctors also cannot turn patients away due to sexual orientation, even if the doctor's objection stems from her own religious beliefs. (Perhaps because of this, when North Coast Women's Care challenged the initial ruling favoring Benitez, Dr. Brody claimed she refused to treat Benitez not because Benitez is a lesbian but because she's unmarried, as marital status is not a protected category. North Coast won this round of appeals.) Says Jennifer Pizer, senior counsel at Lambda Legal and Benitez's lawyer, "The courts say that the religious believer must pick a way to make a living that doesn't put them in conflict with society's rules." In other words, a fertility doctor can choose not to treat a patient for many reasons—the patient is not a good candidate for the procedure, the patient is a jerk, the doctor is too busy—but not because of the patient's race, religion, sexual orientation, or country of origin. And while a doctor can abstain from doing a particular procedure—say, in utero inseminations or IVF—across the board, such a doctor would presumably have a hard time practicing infertility medicine.

Some conservative legislators are trying to restrict access to fertility services for certain kinds of patients—most notably, single women and gays—and limit what can be done with embryos that result from IVF. Virginia tried to prohibit doctors and other health care professionals from helping single women get pregnant. (The law didn't pass.) Arizona has attempted to ban the sale of human eggs. (A bill is pending.) Louisiana has succeeded in making embryos "juridical persons," meaning they cannot be intentionally destroyed, and if they are abandoned, the clinician has discretion over what to do with them. Using ART regulation as a backdoor attack on abortion rights is a worrisome trend, says reproductive legal scholar Susan Crockin. "We're starting to hear a lot of talk about embryo adoptions even though very few are actually happening. This way, in the public's mind, you elevate embryos to fetuses, and fetuses to children, and then you can't do things with embryos."

After Benitez severed ties with the North Coast Women's Care Medical Group, she also switched jobs, because her old one required her to be in contact with North Coast and, she told me, she "couldn't handle seeing and hearing about things that they were doing for other couples that they wouldn't do for me." She fell into a depression, in part from worrying whether or not she and Clark should spend their limited earnings on ART.

Approximately 1 in 3 births that result from IVF involve "multiples," or more than one baby.

In the general population, only 3% of births involve multiples.

Babies born as twins are hospitalized twice as long as singletons, and over the first five years of life, their medical costs are three times as high.

Babies born as triplets have a significantly greater number of cognitive delays. The average cost of a triplet birth exceeds $500,000.

For women under 36, a single embryo transfer is just as likely to result in a live birth as is transferring multiple embryos.

Only 15 states mandate insurers or HMOs pay for any form of infertility treatment. Only 7 states insist insurers pay for at least one cycle of IVF. Of those, 2 states mandate the IVF benefit only if a spouse's sperm is used to fertilize his wife's egg.

Still, she did not give up on her dream of having a child. Benitez grew up in a family with 9 siblings, and never imagined not having kids. She got referred to another ART practice. Her treatments were no longer covered, but she and Clark decided to pay out of pocket for in utero insemination, twice. When Benitez still failed to get pregnant, they stepped up to pay for IVF. Luckily, Benitez conceived on her first IVF try. The couple's first child, Gabriel Benitez-Clark, is now age four.

For patients like Benitez, the best and worst thing about seeking fertility services in the United States is that ART is regulated, such as it is, by the free market, and while not every doctor will treat a nontraditional client, for the right price somebody probably will. That somebody, in fact, is frequently Geoffrey Sher, a man whose operation is so big and whose reputation is so well established he can afford not to manipulate his success rates. Sher's website, have-ababy.com, receives more than 1 million hits a month. His institute, composed of 10 franchises, offers a popular "outcome-based" fee structure, allowing any woman up to the age of 42 to pay a lump sum up front and receive a percentage back if she fails to have a baby—not just get pregnant, have a live baby—after three tries.

Sher is a wildly charismatic man, with a sturdy build, thinning dark hair, and a thick South African accent. The morning I met him, at his headquarters in Las Vegas, he was wearing jeans, sneakers, and a white lab coat and feeling full of his powers as a baby-maker. "Ten transfers today!" he announced, as he sat down in a windowless office with walls of white boards for a working lunch with his longtime business partner, Dr. Ghanima Maassarani. Sher believes every person who's medically fit has the right to access his services. In his 24 years of operation, he's turned down only a few patients for nonmedical reasons—one being a woman who wanted to harvest her eggs, fertilize them, freeze the embryos, have a sex change,

find a woman to marry, and then have his wife carry his babies. Sher came to his open-door philosophy in the early 1990s after a 51-year-old woman approached him with her 43-year-old husband. The woman wanted to get pregnant with a donated egg, and Sher told her she was too old. Maassarani retold the story: "She turned around and said, 'But who are you to judge? If my husband were 51 and I were 43, you would not have said that.' We learned a lesson: Don't make any judgments. As long as the woman is healthy, as long as she has medical clearance, as long as she can hold and carry on a pregnancy, why not?"

Other doctors take differing views. In 2005, *Fertility and Sterility* published a study concerning the screening practices in ART programs. Many clinics have been reluctant to discuss screening because, the authors wrote, "well-intended efforts to prevent the birth of a baby to a parent with a known history of violence against children could perhaps slide into discriminatory or eugenic practices." According to the study, 59 percent of ART program directors agreed that everyone has the right to have a child, yet only 44 percent agreed that fertility doctors don't have the right to decide who is a fit parent. Forty-eight percent of responding directors said they were very or extremely likely to turn away a gay couple seeking a surrogate, 38 percent said they would turn away a couple on welfare who wanted to pay for ART with Social Security checks, 20 percent said they would turn away a single woman, 17 percent would turn away a lesbian couple, 13 percent said they would turn away a couple in which the woman had bipolar disorder, 9 percent said they would turn away a couple who wanted to replace a recently deceased child, 5 percent said they would turn away a biracial couple. Are fertility clinic directors really the best people to decide who will be a good parent?

Given such a paternalistic stance, one might assume that fertility doctors would undertake only those procedures that ensure healthy outcomes, but many do not. In the early days of IVF, most doctors' approach to embryo implantation was, as Sher puts it, "Throw a bunch of spaghetti against the wall and see what sticks." In 1998, for instance, Merryl Fudel, a single, five-times-divorced, part-time airline reservations agent, 55 years old, sought and procured fertility services (IVF with donor eggs) and gave birth to quadruplets. This seems like a miracle, until you learn that the babies were born three months premature, one died eight days after birth, the others will likely have ongoing medical problems, and the hospital bill, largely footed by the state, topped $2 million in the babies' first four months.

In 2004, a review of scientific literature conducted by Johns Hopkins, the American Academy of Pediatrics, and the American Society for Reproductive Medicine found that the biggest risk of IVF is the one we're all aware of anecdotally: multiple births. More than 32 percent of IVF births involve "multiples," or more than one baby, compared to 3 percent in the general population. Nearly anything that can go wrong with a pregnancy goes wrong more often with "higher order births"—and the more babies a woman is carrying, the more frequently things go wrong. Babies born as twins are hospitalized twice as long as singletons, and over the first five years of life, their medical costs are three times as high. Babies born as triplets have a significantly greater number of cognitive delays. The average cost of a triplet birth exceeds $500,000.

Within academic medicine it is widely accepted that in most instances clinics should be practicing "single embryo transfer"—that is, placing only one embryo in a prospective mother's uterus instead of two, three, or more. Single embryo transfer is mandatory for most women in many European countries. The practice is voluntary and unpopular in the United States.

Why? Because by definition when a woman arrives in a fertility clinic, she very much wants to have a baby and has not had an easy time doing so. Since most families are paying for IVF out of pocket, if a woman wants more than one kid, there's a big economic incentive to go for two at once. ("They all want twins," says Rene Danford, patient coordinator for the Sher Institute. "Boy-girl twins. That's what they want. You're done!") And while multiple embryo transfer is no more likely to result in a baby for women under 36—it's just more likely to result in multiples—for older women it raises what can be pretty bleak odds, making the client happy and bolstering the clinic's success rates. The same is true of using donor eggs. In our pay-to-procreate system, the fertility doctor is also a businessman. Sher, arguably the best fertility businessman out there, speaks for many when he says, "My philosophy is it's not our job to tell people what to do. If someone says, 'I want four babies,' the answer is no. If someone says, 'I want three babies,' the answer is no. If someone says, 'I want two babies' and she has half a uterus because she was born that way, the answer is no. But if somebody says, 'I want to have twins' and she's healthy and I see no reason why she'll have a particularly complicated pregnancy, the answer is, 'Okay, I can do that.'"

To goose success rates, clinics encourage multiple embryo transfers and donor eggs, especially for older women. Among patients using their own eggs, the chances per IVF cycle of having a live birth are about:

37% for women age 34 and younger.

30% for women 35 to 37.

20% for women 38 to 40.

11% for women 41 to 42.

4% for women 43 and older.

But among women using donor eggs and fresh (non-frozen) embryos, the live birth rate is 49% whether the patient is 45 or only 32.

Were ART covered by insurance, insurers could pressure doctors into lowering the multiple birth rate, and everyone would save money—including insurers, because ART is relatively cheap compared with births of multiples. It would also help mitigate against the biggest injustice in the American ART system: the fact that if you are wealthy and infertile you are much more likely to have a baby (or two, or three) than if you are infertile and poor. But presently only 15 states mandate group insurers or HMOs pay for any form of ART; of those only 7 insist insurers pay for at least some IVF, and of those 2 mandate the IVF benefit only if a spouse's sperm is used to fertilize his wife's egg—no donated egg or sperm, lesbians or singles need not apply.

European governments have stepped in and regulated, to mixed results. In 2003, Italy enacted Europe's most restrictive policy, stipulating that only long-term heterosexual couples have a right to access IVF, no more than three eggs can be fertilized at any one time, and all fertilized eggs must be transferred to the uterus simultaneously. Italy has since seen pregnancy rates for women utilizing IVF drop from 38 to 30 percent. In 2004, England began limiting all doctors in all cases to implanting only two embryos. Zero women over 44 gave birth in England last year.

To skirt such rules, a Danish company plans to build a fertility ship, sailing in international waters, where people could sidestep their own country's regulations and pay for the services they want—be it transfer of multiple embryos or insemination with anonymous sperm. Fertility tourism already exists—middle-class Americans go to Israel, where services are cheaper; wealthy Europeans come here, where more treatment options are available.

None of this, however, answers the question: Is there, or should there be, a right to reproduce? Though perhaps thinking in terms of rights is not the best way to frame the problem. As Mary Warnock, former chair of the Committee of Enquiry Into Human Fertilization and Embryology in the United Kingdom, points out in her book *Making Babies: Is There a Right to Have Children?*, deep wishes easily slip into the language of rights, and patients who feel themselves to have rights over their doctors fundamentally change the doctor-patient relationship. Our system is already plenty skewed by the idea that if you throw enough money at your infertility problem, you will conceive and the problem will go away. "The patient becomes a client, the doctor obliged to provide what the patient wants. The doctor becomes more like, say, a hairdresser," Warnock writes. "People may well listen to the advice of their hairdressers, and will certainly rely on their hairdresser's skill, which they do not themselves possess. But in the last resort the hairdresser is the servant of the client."

Benitez's case is again on appeal and could reach the California State Supreme Court this fall. Lead counsel Pizer sees the case as seeking to establish a seemingly simple point: that the same framework used to protect people from discrimination in all public settings should also be used to protect people from discrimination in a fertility clinic. Yet at the heart of the case is a more emotional question: "Who is deemed acceptable to be a parent?" asks Pizer.

Benitez views her own case in less theoretical terms. "I want to make sure that these doctors can't do this to anybody else. It was horrible." She is not looking forward to taking the stand, nor to seeing Dr. Brody's face. But for now, at least, she has little time to worry. Ten months ago she gave birth to Shane and Sophia Benitez-Clark, a pair of twin girls conceived through IVF.

ELIZABETH WEIL is fascinated by the ways we build our families in the United States, and the general lack of public discussion surrounding them. A contributing writer for the *New York Times Magazine*, she is the author of *They All Laughed at Christopher Columbus*, which chronicles Gary Hudson's quest to build the first civilian spacecraft, and coauthor of *Crib Notes*, a cradle-side companion of facts and charts for new parents. Weil's work has appeared in *Time* and *Rolling Stone* and on National Public Radio's "This American Life." She lives in San Francisco.

The Sex Offender Next Door

Megan's Law was supposed to protect us from neighborhood predators. But in too many places, kids are still in danger.

AMY ENGELER

The sounds of children and splashing water caught Francine Johnson's attention on a weekday afternoon last May. Wondering if school had let out early, she looked out her window at her neighbor's above-ground pool and saw a half dozen young boys, each around eight years old, playing in the water. With them was Robert Forzano, the strapping blond automobile mechanic who lived next door to Johnson in suburban Rancho Cordova, California. She was puzzled, thinking it odd that Forzano, 42, who didn't socialize with other adults in their neighborhood, would be playing with children in the middle of a school day. "Whenever I saw him, he was standoffish with me. Kind of gruff, really," says Johnson. "So this was strange."

Johnson mentioned the pool party to her husband that night; and she kept up her vigil, watching boys come and go on several other afternoons. Both her backyard and Forzano's opened onto the busy White Rock Community Park, and the local elementary school was just across the street. In fact, the school's principal, Fay Kerekes, could nearly see Forzano's house from where she stood as kids poured into her school each morning. But there was one shocking fact that neither of these women knew: Forzano and his roommate, tow truck operator Brian McDaniel, 42, were both convicted child molesters.

Forzano had served four years in prison for molesting boys under age ten in Ventura County, California; after his parole, he moved in with McDaniel, who had a similar record of lewd acts with a child under age 14 (the men are thought to have met in prison). The two melted into this community outside Sacramento just as easily as they might have a decade earlier, before the passage of Megan's Law.

That landmark piece of legislation was named after seven-year-old Megan Kanka, murdered in 1994 by a convicted sex offender who lived across the street from the Kankas' New Jersey home. After Megan's death, her grief-stricken mother, Maureen, campaigned tirelessly for a law that would prevent other parents from having to endure a similar tragedy. In May 1996, President Clinton signed a law requiring all states to make information about pedophiles and rapists available to the public. But Congress gave the states a lot of leeway in how they

accomplished this goal. "Putting a law in place is one thing," Maureen Kanka says today. "Having law enforcement and the state work together to see that the registries are as up-to-date as possible and that they're being used effectively is another."

Had Forzano lived in Texas, Florida, or another state that is aggressive about implementing Megan's Law, the police might have been sent to the White Rock Elementary School to warn the principal that a convicted pedophile had moved in little more than a block away. Or flyers with his photo might have been handed out to neighbors by law-enforcement officials. But at the time, California's version of Megan's Law was among the most permissive in the country. Plus, California was doing a poor job of enforcing the requirements they did have: In 2003, 30 to 40 percent of the state's 100,000 convicted sex offenders were missing from the registry.

Luring the Children into a Trap

Forzano, at least, kept his appointments with the sheriff's office, spoke politely to detectives, and provided a correct address. But with the California state registry not yet online, his neighbors could have learned about Forzano's criminal history only by going to the police station, signing an application, and looking him up on a CD-ROM. Or, for $10, they could have called a 900 number to get information. Not surprisingly; says Laura Ahearn, executive director of the New York-based advocacy group Parents for Megan's Law, no neighbors made the call. "When Megan's Law was passed, there was so much hope that these laws would be strong," she says. "But some states have deluded the public into thinking they are being protected when they aren't."

Forzano and McDaniel kept their lawn trim and their driveway full of cars. Many mornings, Forzano would stand outside working under the hood of his old Mustang, greeting children who passed by on their way to school. Forzano's appearance caused no alarm—his tanned face and thick neck looked youthful and macho. To the eight-year-olds in the neighborhood, he was simply "Bob," or "my friend Bob." Forzano's young "friends"—almost a dozen boys between seven and 12 years old, mostly from low-income families newly arrived from Ukraine, according to the police—kept quiet as Forzano "groomed" them, as the long seduction of young victims is called. The friendly greetings over the hood of Forzano's Mustang turned into conversations in the park. Once Forzano was no longer a stranger, or someone to be feared, the boys came through the chain-link fence in his backyard and into the pool, police say, and then up the steps into his house. Forzano plied them with sodas and snacks and movies that weren't available at home and gave the older boys a refuge from school. "The parents didn't realize that their kids were skipping school," says Sgt. Micki Links, who is in charge of the sex offender registry for the Sacramento County Sheriff's Office. "The kids didn't want anyone to know, to stop a good thing. And when they said, 'We were at Bob's house,' the parents thought it was a little friend, not an adult."

Forzano kept his pool parties going for several weeks, police say, until Deputy Steve Wright, a resource officer with the Folsom-Rancho Cordova Unified School District, looked into curious absences by two boys from the nearby Mills Middle School. The boys wouldn't say where they had been, so the school asked for Wright to be put on the case. He got the boys to admit they'd been hanging out with an adult named Bob. Wright drove them past the house for confirmation, ran a check on the license plate of a car in the driveway, and learned of Forzano's status as a registered sex offender. Wright listened with concern as the boys talked about playing in Forzano's pool and in his house, sometimes with their seven- and eight-year-old brothers, students at White Rock Elementary School. One of those younger brothers, police learned, appeared to be Forzano's intended victim. Forzano showed the boy some child pornography, which is often the first step toward coercing sexual acts.

What the Search Warrant Revealed

At dawn on May 25, 2004, Principal Kerekes was awakened by a call from the sheriff's office. Now that someone was obviously in danger, California state law allowed police to warn the school about a sex offender. Principal Kerekes signed for the Megan's Law disclosure and received a rap sheet on Forzano. At the same time, the police, with a warrant, entered the men's neat, wood-shingled house and found a stash of child pornography on McDaniel's computer, a hidden video camera set up to capture children undressing and urinating, and a wealth of toys and games. "It was pretty scary," says Sergeant Links, "to see that these two grown men had more Walt Disney videos than most parents."

The next day, the police announced the arrest of Forzano on two felony charges of molesting or annoying a child under 14 (for improper touching in the pool) and on a misdemeanor—using a camcorder to film someone unknowingly for sexual gratification. They also arrested McDaniel for possessing child pornography.

By summer's end, only a brown spot on the ground hinted at the place where Forzano's pool had once stood. McDaniel tore it down after he bailed himself out of jail, while his housemate remained in custody awaiting prosecution. Later, McDaniel was convicted and sentenced to a 180-day work furlough program and three years' probation. In September, Governor Arnold Schwarzenegger signed a bill giving Californians Internet access to more of the state's sex offender registry. Meanwhile, a federal grand jury indicted Forzano for possessing, receiving, and distributing pornography of minors. (State charges are still pending.) The offense carries a maximum 60-year prison term. As of press time, he had not yet entered a plea. But if convicted, Forzano won't be around children for a very long time to come.

What Parents Need to Know about Megan's Law

Below, Karen Terry, Ph.D., editor of a Megan's Law sourcebook and an associate professor at John Jay College of Criminal Justice in New York City, answers questions on how to make Megan's Law better.

Q: What are the basic requirements of the law?
Anyone who commits any type of sexual offense (against a child or an adult) must register with the police as soon as he's released from prison. The offender has up to 30 days, depending on the state, to appear at the police station and give his address, a photo, and sometimes a DNA sample.

But states have a lot of leeway with public notification, the second part of the law. Most states rank sex offenders into three tiers: Level I is low risk (of reoffending), Level II is moderate risk, and Level III is high risk (known in some states as sexual predators). In almost every state, only information about Level III offenders is available to the public.

And each community can handle the notification differently. Some counties release names and photos only on the Web. Some have a book of names at the police station. In other areas, police will go door-to-door or hold a town meeting. Others will put up a poster at the post office. In some jurisdictions in Louisiana, the offender has to personally go door-to-door and tell neighbors that he is a sex offender.

Q: The law has been in place for almost ten years. How well is it working?
The law has been very helpful in investigations. When a crime occurs, the police look at the registries, match up the modus operandi, and they have a list of people to talk to. As for prevention of future crimes, supervision of convicted sex offenders—when the police can drop by an offender's house at any time to look for evidence of kids or any sign of relapse—may be effective. It's important for sex offenders to know that someone is watching them. Plus, these laws are popular because the public feels protected. But that may be a false sense of security; Megan's Law hasn't really been studied, and we can't prove that it deters future sexual assaults.

Q: What parts of the law need fixing?
The biggest issue is keeping the registries up-to-date. Some states, such as Florida, have been very good at this; others are having a hard time keeping up. Offenders move around quite a

bit. They may register with a false address, or they don't reregister when they move. Or they just take off immediately and never register. Most places don't have the resources to follow up. For instance, New York City has a monitoring unit with wonderful, hard-working, diligent officers. But seven officers are in charge of about 4,000 sex offenders.

Q: When the law was passed, some groups worried about vigilantism against sex offenders and privacy infringement. How has this played out?
The courts have pretty much decided that an offender's right to privacy is less important than public safety. The offender may be stigmatized or verbally abused, but that's not unconstitutional. But it does bring up another issue with Megan's Law: Generally, child molesters have poor self-esteem and don't relate well to adults, so their treatment involves learning to improve their social skills and form relationships with adults. But if they live in Texas, where one judge has made them put a sign in their yard that says "I am a sex offender" or a bumper sticker on their car, they are likely to be ostracized. They can't make friends or have appropriate sexual relationships, so it can start the cycle of offending again. Plus, if the notification process is too stigmatizing, offenders may not register, which is the part of the law that has been shown to be most helpful to law enforcement.

Q: What should parents do?
Look at the Internet registries. If a child molester lives down the street, show his picture to your child and say, "Take a good look at this person. This person has harmed children before. Stay away from him." But even if you don't find anyone on the registry in your area, it would be a mistake to say, "Phew! No sex offenders on my block. We're OK." Sex crimes are highly underreported. Sex offenders who are actually quite dangerous don't appear on those registries. Consider this: Nine times out of ten, the offender will be someone the child knows and not the stranger at the end of the block. So say to your child, "If anyone, including Uncle Joe or Aunt Sue, touches you in a way that's improper, you need to tell me."

Sexual Assault on Campus: What Colleges and Universities Are Doing about It

HEATHER M. KARJANE, PHD, BONNIE S. FISHER, PHD, AND FRANCIS T. CULLEN PHD

Campus crime in general and sexual assault in particular have been receiving more attention than in the past, and concern has been expressed at the highest levels of government. On the Federal level, Congress responded by enacting several laws requiring institutions of higher education to notify students about crime on campus, publicize their prevention and response policies, maintain open crime logs, and ensure sexual assault victims their basic rights.[1] The Clery Act, the most notable of these laws, mandates an annual security report from each Federally funded school (see "Recent Federal Laws on Campus Crime").

In 1999, Congress asked the National Institute of Justice to find out what policies and procedures schools use to prevent and respond to reports of sexual assault.[2] The resulting study revealed that schools are making strides in some areas but must continue efforts to increase student safety and accountability. After summarizing what is known about the nature and extent of sexual assault on campus, the researchers highlighted findings regarding response policies and procedures; reporting options; barriers and facilitators; reporter training and prevention programming; victim resources; and investigation, adjudication, and campus sanctions. The study's baseline information can be used to measure progress in how institutions of higher education respond to sexual assault.

The Scope of the Problem

Administrators want their campuses to be safe havens for students as they pursue their education and mature intellectually and socially. But institutions of higher education are by no means crime-free; women students face a high risk for sexual assault.

Just under 3 percent of all college women become victims of rape (either completed or attempted) in a given 9-month academic year. On first glance, the risk seems low, but the percentage translates into the disturbing figure of 35 such crimes for every 1,000 women students. For a campus with 10,000 women students, the number could reach 350. If the percentage is projected to a full calendar year, the proportion rises to nearly 5 percent of college women. When projected over a now-typical

Recent Federal Laws on Campus Crime

Starting in 1990, Congress acted to ensure that institutions of higher education have strategies to prevent and respond to sexual assault on campus and to provide students and their parents accurate information about campus crime. The major Federal laws pertaining to this study are:

Student Right-to-Know and Campus Security Act of 1990 (the "Clery Act"*) (20 U.S.C. § 1092). This law, Title II of Public Law 101–542, requires that schools annually disclose information about crime, including specific sexual crime categories, in and around campus.

Campus Sexual Assault Victims' Bill of Rights of 1992. This amendment to the 1990 act requires that schools develop prevention policies and provide certain assurances to victims. The law was amended again in 1998 to expand requirements, including the crime categories that must be reported.

*The act was renamed in 1998 the "Jeanne Clery Disclosure of Campus Security Policy and Campus Crime Statistics Act" in honor of a student who was sexually assaulted and murdered on her campus in 1986.

5-year college career, one in five young women experiences rape during college.[3]

Counter to widespread stranger-rape myths, in the vast majority of these crimes—between 80 and 90 percent—victim and assailant know each other.[4] In fact, the more intimate the relationship, the more likely it is for a rape to be completed rather than attempted.[5] Half of all student victims do not label the incident "rape."[6] This is particularly true when no weapon was used, no sign of physical injury is evident, and alcohol was involved—factors commonly associated with campus acquaintance rape.[7] Given the extent of non-stranger rape on campus, it is no surprise that the majority of victimized women do not define their experience as a rape.

These reasons help explain why campus sexual assault is not well reported. Less than 5 percent of completed and attempted rapes of college students are brought to the attention of campus authorities and/or law enforcement.[8] Failure to recognize and report the crime not only may result in underestimating the extent of the problem, but also may affect whether victims seek medical care and other professional help. Thus, a special concern of the study was what schools are doing to encourage victims to come forward.

Federal Law and the Schools' Response

Institutions of higher education vary widely in how well they comply with Clery Act mandates and respond to sexual victimization. Overall, a large proportion of the schools studied—close to 80 percent—submit the annual security report required by the Act to the U.S. Department of Education; more than two-thirds include their crime statistics in the report. Yet, according to a General Accounting Office study, schools find it difficult to consistently interpret and apply the Federal reporting requirements, such as deciding which incidents to cite in the annual report, classifying crimes, and the like.[9]

Definitions, even of such terms as "campus" and "student," are often a challenge and contribute to inconsistency in calculating the number of reported sexual assaults. Only 37 percent of the schools studied report their statistics in the required manner; for example, most schools failed to distinguish forcible and nonforcible sex offenses in their reports as required by the Clery Act.

The Issues and the Findings

Congress specified the issues to be investigated (see "Study Design"). Key areas of concern were whether schools have a written sexual assault response policy; whether and how they define sexual misconduct; who on campus is trained to respond to reports of sexual assault; how students can report sexual victimization; what resources are available to victims; and what investigation and adjudication procedures are followed once a report is made. Researchers also examined policies that encourage or discourage reporting and some promising practices (see "Promising Practices").

Definitions of Sexual Assault

Although the Clery Act instructs schools to use the FBI's Uniform Crime Report crime classification system as the basis for their annual statistics, schools may also define forms of "sexual misconduct" in their student code of conduct. Clear behavioral definitions—including definitions of consent and scenarios with nonstrangers—can help victims decide whether what happened to them should be reported to campus or law enforcement authorities. This strategy, used at schools with promising practices, directly challenges stranger-rape myths that disguise the problem and provide a false sense of safety.

Study Design[a]

In 1999, Congress mandated investigation of nine issues concerning how colleges and universities are responding to campus sexual assault. Most of these issues are discussed in this Research for Practice.[b]

To collect the mandated information, the researchers studied a random sample of schools in the United States and Puerto Rico that receive student financial aid from the Federal Government and therefore must comply with the Clery Act. Almost 2,500 schools were in the sample, including all Historically Black Colleges and Universities and all Tribal Colleges and Universities. Schools were classified using the U.S. Department of Education's classification system. Results were reported by school type. The policy analysis was derived from almost two-thirds of the dataset of results from 4-year and 2-year public institutions and 4-year private nonprofit schools.

The researchers used three methods to study how schools are complying:

- Content analysis of the written sexual assault policies of the schools.
- A survey of campus administrators that asked about the issues mandated for study.
- Using 29 criteria, onsite examination of 8 schools found to use promising practices in addressing sexual assault on campus.

The eight schools with promising practices were:

- Central Washington University, Ellensburg, Washington.
- Lafayette College, Easton, Pennsylvania.
- Lewis & Clark College, Portland, Oregon.
- Metropolitan Community College, Omaha, Nebraska.
- Oklahoma State University, Stillwater.
- University of California at Los Angeles.
- University of California at Santa Cruz.
- West Virginia State College, Institute, West Virginia.

Response rates varied by type of institution. Overall, 1,015 schools sent their policies, and 1,001 campus administrators participated in the survey.

Notes

a. A complete description of the study methodology is at Karjane, H.M., B.S. Fisher, and F.T. Cullen, *Campus Sexual Assault: How America's Institutions of Higher Education Respond,* final report to NIJ, Oct. 2002, NCJ 196676: chapter 2.

b. A list of the nine issues mandated for study can be found at ibid.: 12–13.

Congress asked about the prevalence and publication of school and State definitions of sexual assault. The researchers found:

- States have their own criminal codes; thus, definitions of acts that constitute sexual assault vary.
- Like State definitions, school definitions vary widely.
- A slight majority of the schools studied mentioned acquaintance rape in their sexual assault response policy.

Sexual Assault Response Policy

A formal policy that addresses sexual assault on campus is a statement of the school's commitment to recognizing and dealing with the problem. To meet the intent of the Federal laws, the policy should be widely and easily accessible to students.

Congress asked whether the schools have and disseminate a sexual assault response policy. The researchers found:

- Traditional 4-year public and private nonprofit schools—which educate the majority of students—are the most likely to have a written sexual assault response policy.
- About half the schools studied spell out specific policy goals; for example, not tolerating sexual offenses on campus or pursuing disciplinary action against perpetrators. This is more common in 4-year institutions and Historically Black Colleges and Universities (HBCUs).

Who Is Trained to Respond?

Students who are sexually assaulted are most likely to tell their friends first.[10] Research shows that social support from friends—and other "first responders"—can help the victim recognize what happened as a violation of the school's sexual misconduct policy and potentially a crime and encourage the victim to report it to the authorities.[11] For this reason it makes sense for schools to train students and staff in what to do if someone discloses that she or he has been sexually assaulted.

Congress wanted information about who is trained to respond to sexual assault and how much training is offered. The researchers found:

- Overall, only about 4 in 10 schools offer any sexual assault training. What training is available is usually for resident advisers and student security officers, not the general student population.
- Of the schools that provide training, about half train their faculty and staff in the school's response policies and procedures.
- Fewer than two in five schools train campus security personnel, even though formal complaints are likely to be reported to campus security. The majority of 4-year public institutions and HBCUs require this training.

How Do Students Report an Assault?

If students know what to do in the event of a sexual assault (for example, whom to notify) and what steps the school will take, they are more likely to feel reassured and report to authorities. The probability of reporting is also linked to concerns about confidentiality. Victims may be embarrassed or fear reprisal; and victims who may have been drinking before the assault might fear sanctions for violating campus policy on alcohol use. Confidential reporting can be essential in these instances. Some victims prefer anonymous reporting, which allows the crime to be "counted," while letting the victim decide whether to file an official report.

Congress asked what on- and off-campus reporting options are available to victims and what procedures the schools follow after an assault. The researchers found:

- Although 84 percent of the schools studied offer confidential reporting, only 46 percent offer anonymous reporting.
- Contact procedures are specified in the sexual assault response policies of almost three in four schools, with campus or local police the most frequently named contact.
- Even though almost half of schools with a contact procedure listed a phone number, less than half provide service after business hours.
- Information about filing criminal charges and campus reports is included in the policies of less than half the schools, although, following the pattern, the figures for 4-year institutions are higher.

Prevention Efforts and Resources for Victims

Services for victims are essential, but prevention is also key. Many 4-year colleges and universities offer a variety of educational programs geared to prevention, including rape awareness and self defense. Many schools also offer a combination of on- and off-campus services.

Congress asked what resources are available for victim safety, support, and health. The researchers found:

- About 6 in 10 schools offer safety-related educational programs. Of the programs offered by these schools, 6 in 10 address sexual assault.
- Of the schools that offer general educational programs, less than one-third include acquaintance rape prevention in the program. Even in 4-year public schools, less than half do so.
- Only about one-fourth of schools provide residence hall staff with safety training, have security staff on duty in the residences, or require overnight guests to register.
- For students who have been sexually assaulted, mental health crisis counseling is the most widely available service.

What Discourages Victims from Reporting?

The small proportion of sexual assault victims who report the offense to authorities attests to the existence of multiple reporting barriers.

When schools adopt sexual assault response policies, their goal is to protect victims and the general student population by holding the perpetrator accountable while also protecting the rights of the accused. But any policy that compromises or restricts the victim's ability to make informed choices about how to proceed may deter reporting. At the individual level, some victims do not initially recognize the assault as a crime, or they have concerns about their confidentiality. Others may not want to participate in adjudication because they want to avoid public disclosure; they are not certain they can prove a crime occurred or that the perpetrator will be punished. Nonstranger rapists are rarely convicted of their crimes.[12]

Congress asked what policies and practices may prevent reporting or obstruct justice. The researchers found:

- Campus policies on drug and alcohol use have been adopted at three-fourths of the schools studied. At more than half of these schools, administrators say these policies inhibit reporting.
- A majority of campus administrators believe that requiring victims to participate in adjudication discourages reporting; about one-third of schools still have such a policy.
- Campuses may unintentionally condone victim-blaming by overemphasizing the victim's responsibility to avoid sexual assault without balancing messages stressing the perpetrator's responsibility for committing a crime and strategies bystanders can use to intervene.
- A trauma response, which may involve high levels of psychological distress, some of it triggered by shame and self-blame, inhibits reporting.
- The desire to avoid the perceived—and real—stigma of having been victimized also inhibits reporting.

What Promotes Reporting?

Because barriers to reporting exist at many levels, a single policy or approach, such as allowing confidential reporting, is inadequate. The optimum approach to encourage reporting would be to combine a number of strategies, including making campus staff more responsive to reports of sexual assault and offering prevention education for the general student population as well as for specific groups.

Congress asked what policies aid in encouraging reporting. The researchers found:

- Services for victims, written law enforcement response protocols, coordination between campus and community, new student orientations, and campuswide publicity about past crimes are seen by administrators as facilitating reporting.
- Administrators at almost 90 percent of the schools studied believe that prevention programs targeting athletes and students in the Greek system encourage reporting. Only about one in five schools offers such programs, however, although over half of 4-year public schools have them.
- As noted earlier, most administrators believe that a policy allowing confidential and anonymous reporting encourages both victims and other students to report assaults.
- Most administrators consider sexual assault peer educators to be conducive to reporting, but only about one in five schools offers this type of program. Again, 4-year public institutions and HBCUs are more likely to have such programs.

Although campus administrators believe these policies encourage reporting, few have adopted them.

Investigating and Punishing Victimizers

In responding to and adjudicating reports of sexual assault, schools need to balance the victim's need for justice with the rights of the accused. Bringing victimizers to justice is made more complex by the dual jurisdiction of campus administration and law enforcement. Sexual assault may be a violation of the school's sexual misconduct policy, with the accused brought before a disciplinary board or other body to determine his or her *responsibility* in violating the student code of conduct, but it is also a crime and therefore within the jurisdiction of the criminal justice system to determine *guilt*.

Congress asked what procedures schools have adopted for investigating sexual assault and disciplining and punishing perpetrators. The researchers found:

- Most reports of sexual assault on campus are dealt with through binding administrative actions, such as no-contact orders.
- An information-gathering or investigative process is used at only one-fourth of schools overall, only one-fourth of 4-year private nonprofit schools, and less than half of 4-year public schools.
- Due process for the accused is guaranteed in fewer than 40 percent of schools that have disciplinary procedures.
- In about 80 percent of schools, the body that decides whether the student code of conduct has been violated is the disciplinary board. In just over half the schools, this body also decides what sanction will be imposed.
- The most common penalty is expulsion, imposed by 84 percent of the schools. Many schools suspend offenders or place them on probation. Offenders may also be censured, required to make restitution, or lose privileges.

Promising Practices

The researchers identified promising practices at eight schools (see "Study Design") in the areas of prevention, sexual assault policy, reporting, investigation, adjudication, and victim support services. Some examples are included here.[a]

Prevention

A campus sexual assault education program should include comprehensive education about rape myths, common circumstances under which the crime occurs, rapist characteristics, prevention strategies, rape trauma responses and the healing process, and campus policies and support services. To reach the entire student body, these messages should be disseminated in many forms, i.e., through student orientation, curriculum infusion, resource center trainings, campus events, and public information materials. For example, Lafayette College's sexual misconduct policy is communicated to students where they live as well as where they learn, in a kind of "road show." Much larger University of California, Santa Cruz (UCSC), conducts a weekly saturation campaign of flier dissemination all over campus.

Several schools have peer educators and advocates who present programs that feature scenarios followed by facilitated discussion. Some campuses gear prevention and intervention programs to all-male groups, such as male athletes, fraternity members, and male members of ROTC. These prevention programs stress male culpability for committing the vast majority of sex crimes, men's individual and collective responsibility for helping to prevent these crimes, and the attitudes men may hold that foster the crimes. For example, UCSC supports a "Mentors in Violence Prevention" program that emphasizes the bystander's role in violence prevention, in part by using a "playbook" of strategies men can use to interrupt their peers when they believe they may be edging toward criminal behavior.[b]

Sexual Assault Policy

A school's sexual assault policy should be a reader-friendly, easily accessible, and widely distributed statement of the school's definitions and expectations regarding sexual conduct. The policy should:

- Clearly define all forms of sexual misconduct, including operational and behavioral definitions of what acts constitute consent and what acts constitute a sexual assault.
- Discuss the prevalence of nonstranger sexual assault.
- Describe circumstances in which sexual assault most commonly occurs.
- Advise what to do if the student or someone she/he knows is sexually assaulted.
- List resources available on campus and in the local community.
- Identify a specific person or office to contact when a sexual assault occurs (preferably available 24/7) and when and where to file a complaint.
- Strongly encourage victims to report the incident to campus authorities and to the local criminal justice system.
- Provide for and list available reporting options, including a confidential option and preferably including an anonymous option.
- State the school's sanctions for violating the sexual misconduct policy.
- Provide an official statement prohibiting retaliation against individuals who report rape or sexual assault and specifying the school's disciplinary actions for retaliation attempts.
- Provide an official statement noting the separate actions available to the victim, i.e., reporting; investigating the report; informal administrative actions, such as issuing a no-contact order; formal adjudication on campus; and criminal prosecution.

Reporting

All eight schools allow anonymous, confidential, and third-party reporting. Highly recommended are reporting and response policies that allow the victim to participate in decisionmaking, to exert some control over the pace of the process, and to be in charge of making decisions as she/he moves through the campus adjudication and/or the local law enforcement system. Written response protocols ensure a coordinated, consistent, victim-centered response.[c]

For example, Oklahoma State University counsels student victims that reporting an incident, choosing to prosecute, adjudicating a complaint through the University, and filing a civil action are separate steps. Reporting the incident does not obligate the victim to prosecute, but does allow gathering of information. The student chooses whether to move to the next step in the process and is advised of the consequences of each action, what to expect, and how confidentiality will be maintained.

Investigation

Protocols to ensure confidentiality for the victim and the accused during the investigation are essential. Also important are protocols for shared collection and use of information to eliminate the need for the victim to retell the experience multiple times.

One of the most promising practices is providing victims access to a trained, certified Sexual Assault Nurse Examiner (SANE). SANE practitioners provide appropriate treatment and forensic examination. Their documentation of evidence can corroborate a victim's account.[d]

Adjudication

Many schools offer a range of adjudication options, from informal administrative actions that do not require a formal complaint to a formal adjudication board hearing. Proceedings should follow an established, documented, and consistent format that balances the rights of the complainant and the accused. Sexual misconduct adjudication boards are not criminal proceedings; their purpose is to establish

(Continued)

Promising Practices (continued)

whether the accused is responsible for violating the school's policy, not to determine the accused's guilt or innocence.[e]

Victim Support Services

The most promising practice in this area is the formation of partnerships between the school and the community to provide student victims access to a comprehensive, coordinated network of service providers—medical, psychological, advocacy, legal, and safety. More research is needed to help schools determine which practices are best for their campus and students.

Notes

a. A comprehensive review of promising practices is in Karjane, H., B. Fisher, and F.T. Cullen, *Campus Sexual Assault: How America's Institutions of Higher Education Respond,* final report to the National Institute of Justice, Oct. 2002, NCJ 196676.

b. See Katz, J., "Reconstructing Masculinity in the Locker Room: The Mentors in Violence Prevention Project," *Harvard Educational Review* 65(2)(1995): 163–174; also see Karjane et al., *Campus Sexual Assault:* 128.

c. See Karjane et al., *Campus Sexual Assault:* 133–134.

d. For more information about SANEs, see Littel, K., "Sexual Assault Nurse Examiner (SANE) Programs: Improving the Community Response to Sexual Assault Victims," *OVC Bulletin,* Washington, DC: U.S. Department of Justice, Office for Victims of Crime, 2001, available online at www.ojp.usdoj.gov/ovc/publications/bulletins/sane_4_2001/welcome.html. Also see Sommers, M.S., B.S. Fisher, and H.M. Karjane, "Using Colposcopy in the Rape Exam: Health Care, Forensic, and Criminal Justice Issues," *Journal of Forensic Nursing* 1(1)(2005): 28–34, 19.

e. For more about adjudication protocols and practices, see Karjane et al., *Campus Sexual Assault:* chapter 6 and 135–136.

- Only about half the schools keep the complainant apprised of the progress of the case; they are far more likely to notify the accused.
- Use of protocols for coordinating the responses of campus and local law enforcement agencies were found to be a promising practice, but only about one in four schools have them, most of these 4-year public institutions and HBCUs.

Do Schools Need to Do More?

The study confirmed that there is much confusion among schools about what the Clery Act requires. The fact that only 37 percent fully comply in reporting crime statistics indicates a need for guidance. The researchers recommend development of a policy that includes explicit and behavioral definitions of consent, sexual offenses, and other terminology and practices.

Many schools either do not have a sexual assault response policy or could not provide it for the study. The larger, 4-year institutions and HBCUs tend to have policies, often available on their Web sites, but these vary in clarity and thoroughness. This suggests a model policy could be useful to the schools as a template in developing their own.

More could be done to increase reporting. Practices that are perceived by college administrators to discourage or encourage reporting need to be examined empirically.

Because underreporting may be linked to the victim's inability to recognize sexual victimization as a violation of the school's student code of conduct and, further, as a crime, more research is needed into such issues as the perpetuation of stranger-rape myths, the relationship of the victim to the assailant, use of alcohol before the assault, and other contributory factors.

Notes

1. These laws affect all institutions of higher education that receive student financial aid from the Federal Government.

2. The study was mandated as part of the 1998 amendments to the Higher Education Act of 1965, Public Law 105–244.

3. Fisher et al., *The Sexual Victimization of College Women:* 10–11.

4. See ibid.: 17; also see Koss, M., C. Gidycz, and N. Wisniewski, "The Scope of Rape: Incidence and Prevalence of Sexual Aggression and Victimization in a National Sample of Higher Education Students," *Journal of Consulting and Clinical Psychology* 55(2)(1987): 162–170.

5. Fisher et al., "Extent and Nature of the Sexual Victimization of College Women": 89–90; 123–124.

6. Fisher, B.S., L.E. Daigle, F.T. Cullen, and M.G. Turner, "Acknowledging Sexual Victimization as Rape: Results From a National-Level Study," *Justice Quarterly* 20(3)(2000): 401–440. A study 13 years earlier reported that 3 in 4 women (73 percent) who had an experience that met Ohio penal code criteria for rape did not label the incident "rape." See Koss et al., "The Scope of Rape": 162–170.

7. See Bondurant, B., "University Women's Acknowledgment of Rape: Individual, Situational, and Social Factors," *Violence Against Women* 7(3)(2001): 294–314.

8. Fisher et al., *The Sexual Victimization of College Women:* 23.

9. *Campus Crime: Difficulties Meeting Federal Reporting Requirements,* Washington, DC: General Accounting Office, 1997.

10. Fisher, B.S., L.E. Daigle, F.T. Cullen, and M.G. Turner, "Reporting Sexual Victimization to the Police and Others: Results from a National-level Study of College Women," *Criminal Justice and Behavior: An International Journal* 30(1)(2003): 6–38.

11. Kahn, A., and V. Andreoli Mathie, "Understanding the Unacknowledged Rape Victim," in *Sexuality, Society and Feminism,* ed. C. Travis and J. White, Washington, DC: American Psychological Association, 2000: 337–403; Neville, H., and A. Pugh, "General and Culture-Specific Factors Influencing African American Women's Reporting Patterns and Perceived Social Support Following Sexual Assault," *Violence Against Women* 3(4)(1997): 361–381.

12. See Spohn, C., and D. Holleran, "Prosecuting Sexual Assault: A Comparison of Charging Decisions in Sexual Assault Cases Involving Strangers, Acquaintances, and Intimate Partners," *Justice Quarterly* 18(3)(2001): 651–688.

HEATHER M. KARJANE, PhD, is coordinator for gender issues at the Commonwealth of Massachusetts Administrative Office of the Trial Court. **BONNIE S. FISHER,** PhD and **FRANCIS T. CULLEN,** PhD, are faculty in the Division of Criminal Justice at the University of Cincinnati. The Police Executive Research Forum conducted some of the field research.

Human Rights, Sex Trafficking, and Prostitution

ALICE LEUCHTAG

Despite laws against slavery in practically every country, an estimated twenty-seven million people live as slaves. Kevin Bales, in his book *Disposable People: New Slavery in the Global Economy* (University of California Press, Berkeley, 1999), describes those who endure modern forms of slavery. These include indentured servants, persons held in hereditary bondage, child slaves who pick plantation crops, child soldiers, and adults and children trafficked and sold into sex slavery.

A Life Narrative

Of all forms of slavery, sex slavery is one of the most exploitative and lucrative with some 200,000 sex slaves worldwide bringing their slaveholders an annual profit of $10.5 billion. Although the great preponderance of sex slaves are women and girls, a smaller but significant number of males—both adult and children—are enslaved for homosexual prostitution.

The life narrative of a Thai girl named Siri, as told to Bales, illustrates how sex slavery happens to vulnerable girls and women. Siri is born in northeastern Thailand to a poor family that farms a small plot of land, barely eking out a living. Economic policies of structural adjustment pursued by the Thai government under the aegis of the World Bank and the International Monetary Fund have taken former government subsidies away from rice farmers, leaving them to compete against imported, subsidized rice that keeps the market price artificially depressed.

Siri attends four years of school, then is kept at home to help care for her three younger siblings. When Siri is fourteen, a well-dressed woman visits her village. She offers to find Siri a "good job," advancing her parents $2,000 against future earnings. This represents at least a year's income for the family. In a town in another province the woman, a trafficker, "sells" Siri to a brothel for $4,000. Owned by an "investment club" whose members are business and professional men—government bureaucrats and local politicians—the brothel is extremely profitable. In a typical thirty-day period it nets its investors $88,000.

To maintain the appearance that their hands are clean, members of the club's board of directors leave the management of the brothel to a pimp and a bookkeeper. Siri is initiated into prostitution by the pimp who rapes her. After being abused by her first "customer," Siri escapes, but a policeman—who gets a percentage of the brothel profits—brings her back, whereupon the pimp beats her up. As further punishment, her "debt" is doubled from $4,000 to $8,000. She must now repay this, along with her monthly rent and food, all from her earnings of $4 per customer. She will have to have sex with three hundred men a month just to pay her rent. Realizing she will never be able to get out of debt, Siri tries to build a relationship with the pimp simply in order to survive.

The pimp uses culture and religion to reinforce his control over Siri. He tells her she must have committed terrible sins in a past life to have been born a female; she must have accumulated a karmic debt to deserve the enslavement and abuse to which she must reconcile herself. Gradually Siri begins to see herself from the point of view of the slaveholder—as someone unworthy and deserving of punishment. By age fifteen she no longer protests or runs away. Her physical enslavement has become psychological as well, a common occurrence in chronic abuse.

Siri is administered regular injections of the contraceptive drug Depo-Provera for which she is charged. As the same needle is used for all the girls, there is a high risk of HIV and other sexual diseases from the injections. Siri knows that a serious illness threatens her and she prays to Buddha at the little shrine in her room, hoping to earn merit so he will protect her from dreaded disease. Once a month she and the others, at their own expense, are tested for HIV. So far Siri's tests have been negative. When Siri tries to get the male customers to wear condoms—distributed free to brothels by the Thai Ministry of Health—some resist wearing them and she can't make them do so.

As one of an estimated 35,000 women working as brothel slaves in Thailand—a country where 500,000 to one million prostituted women and girls work in conditions of degradation and exploitation short of brothel slavery—Siri faces at least a 40 percent chance of contracting the HIV virus. If she is lucky, she can look forward to live more years before she becomes too ill to work and is pushed out into the street.

Thailand's Sex Tourism

Though the Thai government denies it, the World Health Organization finds that HIV is epidemic in Thailand, with the largest segment of new cases among wives and girlfriends of men who buy prostitute sex. Viewing its women as a cash crop to be exploited, and depending on sex tourism for foreign exchange dollars to help pay interest on the foreign debt, the Thai government can't acknowledge the epidemic without contradicting the continued promotion of sex tourism and prostitution.

By encouraging investment in the sex industry, sex tourism creates a business climate conducive to the trafficking and enslavement of vulnerable girls such as Siri. In 1996 nearly five million sex tourists from the United States, Western Europe, Australia, and Japan visited Thailand. These transactions brought in about $26.2 billion—thirteen times more than Thailand earned by building and exporting computers.

In her 1999 report *Pimps and Predators on the Internet: Globalizing the Sexual Exploitation of Women and Children,* published by the Coalition Against Trafficking in Women (CATW), Donna Hughes quotes from postings on an Internet site where sex tourists share experiences and advise one another. The following is one man's description of having sex with a fourteen-year-old prostituted girl in Bangkok:

> "Even though I've had a lot of better massages . . . after fifteen minutes, I was much more relaxed. . . . Then I asked for a condom and I fucked her for another thirty minutes. Her face looked like she was feeling a lot of pain. . . . She blocked my way when I wanted to leave the room and she asked for a tip. I gave her 600 bath. Altogether, not a good experience."

Hughes says, "To the men who buy sex, a 'bad experience' evidently means not getting their money's worth, or that the prostituted woman or girl didn't keep up the act of enjoying what she had to do . . . one glimpses the humiliation and physical pain most girls and women in prostitution endure."

Nor are the men oblivious to the existence of sexual slavery. One customer states, "Girls in Bangkok virtually get sold by their families into the industry; they work against their will." His knowledge of their sexual slavery and lack of sensitivity thereof is evident in that he then names the hotels in which girls are kept and describes how much they cost!

As Hughes observes, sex tourists apparently feel they have a right to prostitute sex, perceiving prostitution only from a self-interested perspective in which they commodify and objectify women of other cultures, nationalities, and ethnic groups. Their awareness of racism, colonialism, global economic inequalities, and sexism seems limited to the way these realities benefit them as sex consumers.

Sex Traffickers Cast Their Nets

According to the *Guide to the New UN Trafficking Protocol* by Janice Raymond, published by the CATW in 2001, the United Nations estimates that sex trafficking in human beings is a $5 billion to $7 billion operation annually. Four million persons are moved illegally from one country to another and within countries each year, a large proportion of them women and girls being trafficked into prostitution. The United Nations International Children's Emergency Fund (UNICEF) estimates that some 30 percent of women being trafficked are minors, many under age thirteen. The International Organization on Migration estimates that some 500,000 women per year are trafficked into Western Europe from poorer regions of the world. According to *Sex Trafficking of Women in the United States: International and Domestic Trends,* also published by the CATW in 2001, some 50,000 women and children are trafficked into the United States each year, mainly from Asia and Latin America.

Because prostitution as a system of organized sexual exploitation depends on a continuous supply of new "recruits," trafficking is essential to its continued existence. When the pool of available women and girls dries up, new women must be procured. Traffickers cast their nets ever wide and become ever more sophisticated. The Italian Camorra, Chinese Triads, Russian Mafia, and Japanese Yakuza are powerful criminal syndicates consisting of traffickers, pimps, brothel keepers, forced labor lords, and gangs which operate globally.

After the breakdown of the Soviet Union, an estimated five thousand criminal groups formed the Russian Mafia, which operates in thirty countries. The Russian Mafia traffics women from African countries, the Ukraine, the Russian Federation, and Eastern Europe into Western Europe, the United States, and Israel. The Triads traffick women from China, Korea, Thailand, and other Southeast Asian countries into the United States and Europe. The Camorra traffics women from Latin America into Europe. The Yakuza traffics women from the Philipines, Thailand, Burma, Cambodia, Korea, Nepal, and Laos into Japan.

A Global Problem Meets a Global Response

Despite these appalling facts, until recently no generally agreed upon definition of trafficking in human beings was written into international law. In Vienna, Austria, during 1999 and 2000, 120 countries participated in debates over a definition of trafficking. A few nongovernmental organizations (NGOs) and a minority of governments—including Australia, Canada, Denmark, Germany, Ireland, Japan, the Netherlands, Spain, Switzerland, Thailand, and the United Kingdom—wanted to separate issues of trafficking from issues of prostitution. They argued that persons being trafficked should be divided into those who are forced and those who give their consent, with the burden of proof being placed on persons being trafficked. They also urged that the less explicit means of control over trafficked persons—such as abuse of a victim's vulnerability—not be included in the definition of trafficking and that the word *exploitation* not be used. Generally supporters of this position were wealthier countries where large numbers of women were being trafficked and countries in which prostitution was legalized or sex tourism encouraged.

> **People being trafficked shouldn't be divided into those who are forced and those who give their consent because trafficked persons are in no position to give meaningful consent.**

The CATW—140 other NGOs that make up the International Human Rights Network plus many governments (including those of Algeria, Bangladesh, Belgium, China, Columbia, Cuba, Egypt, Finland, France, India, Mexico, Norway, Pakistan, the Philippines, Sweden, Syria, Venezuela, and Vietnam)—maintains that trafficking can't be separated from prostitution. Persons being trafficked shouldn't be divided into those who are forced and those who give their consent because trafficked persons are in no position to give meaningful consent. The subtler methods used by traffickers, such as abuse of a victim's vulnerability, should be included in the definition of trafficking and the word *exploitation* be an essential part of the definition. Generally supporters of this majority view were poorer countries from which large numbers of women were being trafficked or countries in which strong feminist, anti-colonialist, or socialist influences existed. The United States, though initially critical of the majority position, agreed to support a definition of trafficking that would be agreed upon by consensus.

The struggle—led by the CATW to create a definition of trafficking that would penalize traffickers while ensuring that all victims of trafficking would be protected—succeeded when a compromise proposal by Sweden was agreed to. A strongly worded and inclusive *UN Protocol to Prevent, Suppress, and Punish Trafficking in Persons*—especially women and children—was drafted by an ad hoc committee of the UN as a supplement to the Convention Against Transnational Organized Crime. The UN protocol specifically addresses the trade in human beings for purposes of prostitution and other forms of sexual exploitation, forced labor or services, slavery or practices similar to slavery, servitude, and the removal of organs. The protocol defines trafficking as:

> The recruitment, transportation, transfer, harboring or receipt of persons, by means of the threat or use of force or other forms of coercion, of abduction, of fraud, of deception, of the abuse of power or of a position of vulnerability or of the giving or receiving of payments or benefits to achieve the consent of a person having control over another person, for the purpose of exploitation.

While recognizing that the largest amount of trafficking involves women and children, the wording of the UN protocol clearly is gender and age neutral, inclusive of trafficking in both males and females, adults and children.

In 2000 the UN General Assembly adopted this convention and its supplementary protocol; 121 countries signed the convention and eighty countries signed the protocol. For the convention and protocol to become international law, forty countries must ratify them.

Highlights
Some highlights of the new convention and protocol are:

For the first time there is an accepted international definition of trafficking and an agreed-upon set of prosecution, protection, and prevention mechanisms on which countries can base their national legislation.

- The various criminal means by which trafficking takes place, including indirect and subtle forms of coercion, are covered.
- Trafficked persons, especially women in prostitution and child laborers, are no longer viewed as illegal migrants but as victims of a crime.

> **For the first time there is an accepted international definition of trafficking and an agreed-upon set of prosecution, protection, and prevention mechanisms on which countries can base their national legislation.**

- The convention doesn't limit its scope to criminal syndicates but defines an organized criminal group as "any structured group of three or more persons which engages in criminal activities such as trafficking and pimping."
- All victims of trafficking in persons are protected, not just those who can prove that force was used against them.
- The consent of a victim of trafficking is meaningless and irrelevant.
- Victims of trafficking won't have to bear the burden of proof.
- Trafficking and sexual exploitation are intrinsically connected and not to be separated.
- Because women trafficked domestically into local sex industries suffer harmful effects similar to those experienced by women trafficked transnationally, these women also come under the protections of the protocol.
- The key element in trafficking is the exploitative purpose rather than the movement across a border.

The protocol is the first UN instrument to address the demand for prostitution sex, a demand that results in the human rights abuses of women and children being trafficked. The protocol recognizes an urgent need for governments to put the buyers of prostitution sex on their policy and legislative agendas, and it calls upon countries to take or strengthen legislative or other measures to discourage demand, which fosters all the forms of sexual exploitation of women and children.

As Raymond says in the *Guide to the New UN Trafficking Protocol:*

"The least discussed part of the prostitution and trafficking chain has been the men who buy women for sexual exploitation in prostitution. . . . If we are to find a permanent path to ending these human rights abuses, then we cannot just shrug our shoulders and say, "men are like this," or "boys will be boys," or "prostitution has always been around." Or tell women and girls in prostitution that they must continue to do what they do because prostitution is inevitable. Rather, our responsibility is to make men change their behavior, by all means available— educational, cultural and legal."

Two U.S. feminist, human rights organizations—Captive Daughters and Equality Now—have been working toward that goal. Surita Sandosham of Equality Now says that when her organization asked women's groups in Thailand and the Philippines how it could assist them, the answer came back, "Do something about the demand." Since then the two organizations have legally challenged sex tours originating in the United States and have succeeded in closing down at least one operation.

Refugees, Not Illegal Aliens

In October 2000 the U.S. Congress passed a bill, the Victims of Trafficking and Violence Protection Act of 2000, introduced by New Jersey republican representative Chris Smith. Under this law penalties for traffickers are raised and protections for victims increased. Reasoning that desperate women are unable to give meaningful consent to their own sexual exploitation, the law adopts a broad definition of sex trafficking so as not to exclude so-called consensual prostitution or trafficking that occurs solely within the United States. In these respects the new federal law conforms to the UN protocol.

Two features of the law are particularly noteworthy:

- In order to pressure other countries to end sex trafficking, the U.S. State Department is to make a yearly assessment of other countries' anti-trafficking efforts and to rank them according to how well they discourage trafficking. After two years of failing to meet even minimal standards, countries are subject to sanctions, although not sanctions on humanitarian aid. "Tier 3" countries—those failing to meet even minimal standards—include Greece, Indonesia, Israel, Pakistan, Russia, Saudi Arabia, South Korea, and Thailand.
- Among persons being trafficked into the United States, special T-visas will be provided to those who meet the criteria for having suffered the most serious trafficking abuses. These visas will protect them from deportation so they can testify against their traffickers. T-non immigrant status allows eligible aliens to remain in the United States temporarily and grants specific non-immigrant benefits. Those acquiring T-1 non-immigrant status will be able to remain for a period of three years

and will be eligible to receive certain kinds of public assistance—to the same extent as refugees. They will also be issued employment authorization to "assist them in finding safe, legal employment while they attempt to retake control of their lives."

A Debate Rages

A worldwide debate rages about legalization of prostitution fueled by a 1998 International Labor Organization (ILO) report entitled *The Sex Sector: The Economic and Social Bases of Prostitution in Southeast Asia.* The report follows years of lobbying by the sex industry for recognition of prostitution as "sex work." Citing the sex industry's unrecognized contribution to the gross domestic product of four countries in Southeast Asia, the ILO urges governments to officially recognize the "sex sector" and "extend taxation nets to cover many of the lucrative activities connected with it." Though the ILO report says it stops short of calling for legalization of prostitution, official recognition of the sex industry would be impossible without it.

Raymond points out that the ILO's push to redefine prostitution as sex work ignores legislation demonstrating that countries can reduce organized sexual exploitation rather than capitulate to it. For example, Sweden prohibits the purchase of sexual services with punishments of still fines or imprisonment, thus declaring that prostitution isn't a desirable economic and labor sector. The government also helps women getting out of prostitution to rebuild their lives. Venezuela's Ministry of Labor has ruled that prostitution can't be considered work because it lacks the basic elements of dignity and social justice. The Socialist Republic of Vietnam punishes pimps, traffickers, brothel owners, and buyers—sometimes publishing buyer's names in the mass media. For women in prostitution, the government finances medical, educational, and economic rehabilitation.

Instead of transforming the male buyer into a legitmate customer, the ILO should give thought to innovative programs that make the buyer accountable for his sexual exploitation.

Raymond suggests that instead of transforming the male buyer into a legitimate customer, the ILO should give thought to innovative programs that make the buyer accountable for his sexual exploitation. She cites the Sage Project, Inc. (SAGE) program in San Francisco, California, which educates men arrested for soliciting women in prostitution about the risks and impacts of their behavior.

Legalization advocates argue that the violence, exploitation, and health effects suffered by women in prostitution aren't inherent to prostitution but simply result from the random behaviors of bad pimps or buyers, and that if prostitution were regulated by the state these harms would diminish. But examples show these arguments to be false.

Prostituted women are even more marginalized and tightly locked into the system of organized sexual exploitation while the state, now an official party to the exploitation, has become the biggest pimp of all.

In the pamphlet entitled *Legalizing Prostitution Is Not the Answer: The Example of Victoria, Australia,* published by the CATW in 2001, Mary Sullivan and Sheila Jeffreys describe the way legalization in Australia has perpetuated and strengthened the culture of violence and exploitation inherent in prostitution. Under legalization, legal and illegal brothels have proliferated, and trafficking in women has accelerated to meet the increased demand. Pimps, having even more power, continue threatening and brutalizing the women they control. Buyers continue to abuse women, refuse to wear condoms, and spread the HIV virus—and other sexually transmitted diseases—to their wives and girlfriends. Stigmatized by identity cards and medial inspections, prostituted women are even more marginalized and tightly locked into the system of organized sexual exploitation while the state, now an official party to the exploitation, has become the biggest pimp of all.

The government of the Netherlands has legalized prostitution, doesn't enforce laws against pimping, and virtually lives off taxes from the earnings of prostituted women. In the book *Making the Harm Visible* (published by the CATW in 1999), Marie-Victoire Louis describes the effects on prostituted women of municipal regulation of brothels in Amsterdam and other Dutch cities. Her article entitled "Legalizing Pimping, Dutch Style" explains the way immigration policies in the Netherlands are shaped to fit the needs of the prostitution industry so that traffickers are seldom prosecuted and a continuous supply of women is guaranteed. In Amsterdam's 250 officially listed brothels, 80 percent of the prostitutes have been trafficked in from other countries and 70 percent possess no legal papers. Without money, papers, or contact with the outside world, these immigrant women live in terror instead of being protected by the regulations governing brothels, prostituted women are frequently beaten up and raped by pimps. These "prostitution managers" have practically been given a free hand by the state and by buyers who, as "consumers of prostitution," feel themselves entitled to abuse the women they buy. Sadly and ironically the "Amsterdam model" of legalization and regulation is touted by the Netherlands and Germany as "self-determination and empowerment for women." In reality it simply legitimizes the "right" to buy, sexually use, and profit from the sexual exploitation of someone else's body.

A Human Rights Approach

As part of a system of organized sexual exploitation, prostitution can be visualized along a continuum of abuse with brothel slavery at the furthest extreme. All along the continuum, fine lines divide the degrees of harm done to those caught up in the system. At the core lies a great social injustice no cosmetic reforms can right: the setting aside of a segment of people whose bodies can be purchased for sexual use by others. When this basic injustice is legitimized and regulated by the state and when the state profits from it, that injustice is compounded.

In her book *The Prostitution of Sexuality* (New York University Press, 1995), Kathleen Barry details a feminist human rights approach to prostitution that points the way to the future. Ethically it recognizes prostitution, sex trafficking, and the globalized industrialization of sex as massive violations of women's human rights. Sociologically it considers how and to what extent prostitution promotes sex discrimination against individual women, against different racial categories of women, and against women as a group. Politically it calls for decriminalizing prostitutes while penalizing pimps, traffickers, brothel owners, and buyers.

Understanding that human rights and restorative justice go hand in hand, the feminist human rights approach to prostitution addresses the harm and the need to repair the damage. As Barry says:

"Legal proposals to criminalize customers, based on the recognition that prostitution violates and harms women, must . . . include social-service, health and counseling and job retraining programs. Where states would be closing down brothels if customers were criminalized, the economic resources poured into the former prostitution areas could be turned toward producing gainful employment for women."

With the help of women's projects in many countries—such as Buklod in the Philippines and the Council for Prostitution Alternatives in the United States—some women have begun to confront their condition by leaving prostitution, speaking out against it, revealing their experiences, and helping other women leave the sex industry.

Ending the sexual exploitation of trafficking and prostitution will mean the beginning of a new chapter in building, a humanist future—a more peaceful and just future in which men and women can join together in love and respect, recognizing one another's essential dignity and humanity. Humanity's sexuality then will no longer be hijacked and distorted.

Freelance writer **ALICE LEUCHTAG** has worked as a social worker, counselor, college instructor, and researcher. Active in the civil rights, peace, socialist, feminist, and humanist movements, she has helped organize women in Houston to oppose sex trafficking.

Test-Your-Knowledge Form

We encourage you to photocopy and use this page as a tool to assess how the articles in *Annual Editions* expand on the information in your textbook. By reflecting on the articles you will gain enhanced text information. You can also access this useful form on a product's book support Web site at *http://www.mhcls.com*.

NAME: DATE:

_____

TITLE AND NUMBER OF ARTICLE:

_____

BRIEFLY STATE THE MAIN IDEA OF THIS ARTICLE:

_____

LIST THREE IMPORTANT FACTS THAT THE AUTHOR USES TO SUPPORT THE MAIN IDEA:

_____

WHAT INFORMATION OR IDEAS DISCUSSED IN THIS ARTICLE ARE ALSO DISCUSSED IN YOUR TEXTBOOK OR OTHER READINGS THAT YOU HAVE DONE? LIST THE TEXTBOOK CHAPTERS AND PAGE NUMBERS:

_____

LIST ANY EXAMPLES OF BIAS OR FAULTY REASONING THAT YOU FOUND IN THE ARTICLE:

_____

LIST ANY NEW TERMS/CONCEPTS THAT WERE DISCUSSED IN THE ARTICLE, AND WRITE A SHORT DEFINITION:

We Want Your Advice

ANNUAL EDITIONS revisions depend on two major opinion sources: one is our Advisory Board, listed in the front of this volume, which works with us in scanning the thousands of articles published in the public press each year; the other is you—the person actually using the book. Please help us and the users of the next edition by completing the prepaid article rating form on this page and returning it to us. Thank you for your help!

ANNUAL EDITIONS: Human Sexualities 31/e

ARTICLE RATING FORM

Here is an opportunity for you to have direct input into the next revision of this volume.
We would like you to rate each of the articles listed below, using the following scale:

1. **Excellent: should definitely be retained**
2. **Above average: should probably be retained**
3. **Below average: should probably be deleted**
4. **Poor: should definitely be deleted**

Your ratings will play a vital part in the next revision.
Please mail this prepaid form to us as soon as possible.
Thanks for your help!

RATING	ARTICLE	RATING	ARTICLE
	1. Vox Populi: Sex, Lies, and Blood Sport		25. Behind the Cloak of Polygamy
	2. The Baby Deficit		26. Love at the Margins: Extreme Relationships Demand Extreme Commitment
	3. Three 'Rules' That Don't Apply		27. My Cheatin' Heart
	4. Everyone's Queer		28. A Case for Angry Men and Happy Women
	5. A Mind Dismembered: In Search of the Magical Penis Thieves		29. Learning and Gender
	6. Afterbirths in the Afterlife: Cultural Meaning of Placental Disposal in a Hmong American Community		30. Goodbye to Girlhood
	7. Gender Is Powerful: The Long Reach of Feminism		31. (Rethinking) Gender
	8. How AIDS Changed America		32. Finding the Switch
	9. Starting the Good Life in the Womb		33. Children of Lesbian and Gay Parents
	10. Success at Last		34. Broadcast News: The Insider Is Out
	11. A Man's Shelf Life		35. Sex, Health & Happiness
	12. The Orgasmic Mind		36. Fighting the Cancer a Mammo Can't Catch
	13. Women's Sexual Desire: A Feminist Critique		37. When Sex Hurts
	14. How to Talk about Sex		38. Popping the *Other* Question
	15. The Birds and the Bees and Curious Kids		39. Sex, Drugs, Prisons, and HIV
	16. What to Tell the Kids about Sex		40. HIV Plan B
	17. Teenage Fatherhood and Involvement in Delinquent Behavior		41. HIV Apathy
	18. Torn between Two *Mothers*		42. Flower Grandma's Secret
	19. Staying up Late with Sue		43. You Can't Do That on Television
	20. Women's Sexuality as They Age: The More Things Change, the More They Stay the Same		44. Sex, Politics, and Morality at the FDA: Reflections on the Plan B Decision
	21. Free as a Bird and Loving It		45. Guess Who's Watching Porn
	22. Happily Never Married		46. Breeder Reaction
	23. This Thing Called Love		47. The Sex Offender Next Door
	24. Pillow Talk		48. Sexual Assault on Campus: What Colleges and Universities Are Doing about It
			49. Human Rights, Sex Trafficking, and Prostitution

BUSINESS REPLY MAIL
FIRST CLASS MAIL PERMIT NO. 551 DUBUQUE IA

POSTAGE WILL BE PAID BY ADDRESSEE

McGraw-Hill Contemporary Learning Series
501 BELL STREET
DUBUQUE, IA 52001

NO POSTAGE
NECESSARY
IF MAILED
IN THE
UNITED STATES

ABOUT YOU

Name

Date

Are you a teacher? ☐ A student? ☐
Your school's name

Department

Address   City   State   Zip

School telephone #

YOUR COMMENTS ARE IMPORTANT TO US!

Please fill in the following information:
For which course did you use this book?

Did you use a text with this ANNUAL EDITION? ☐ yes ☐ no
What was the title of the text?

What are your general reactions to the Annual Editions concept?

Have you read any pertinent articles recently that you think should be included in the next edition? Explain.

Are there any articles that you feel should be replaced in the next edition? Why?

Are there any World Wide Web sites that you feel should be included in the next edition? Please annotate.

May we contact you for editorial input? ☐ yes ☐ no
May we quote your comments? ☐ yes ☐ no